MA[...]

Date

1 - 1st Su[...]
8 - 2nd Sunday of Advent...... 116
15 - 3rd Sunday of Advent 121
22 - 4th Sunday of Advent 125
25 - Nativity of the Lord ... 130-143
29 - Holy Family 144

2025

JANUARY
1 - Mary, Holy Mother of God . 152
5 - The Epiphany of the Lord . 157
12 - The Baptism of the Lord .. 165
19 - 2nd Sun. in Ord. Time...... 173
26 - 3rd Sun. in Ord. Time....... 178

FEBRUARY
2 - Presentation of the Lord .. 184
9 - 5th Sun. in Ord. Time....... 193
16 - 6th Sun. in Ord. Time....... 199
23 - 7th Sun. in Ord. Time....... 204

MARCH
2 - 8th Sun. in Ord. Time....... 210
9 - 1st Sunday of Lent.......... 215
16 - 2nd Sunday of Lent.......... 221
23 - 3rd Sunday of Lent.......... 227
30 - 4th Sunday of Lent 240

APRIL
6 - 5th Sunday of Lent.......... 253
13 - Palm Sunday.................... 265
17 - Holy Thursday 287
—Evening Mass............. 294
18 - Good Friday.................... 308
19 - Easter Vigil 335
20 - Easter Sunday.................. 383
27 - 2nd Sunday of Easter 391

5th Sunday of Easter...... 408
25 - 6th Sunday of Easter....... 412
29 - Ascension of the Lord 417

JUNE
1 - 7th Sunday of Easter....... 425
8 - Pentecost Sunday 429
15 - Most Holy Trinity 451
22 - Body and Blood of Christ. 456
29 - Sts. Peter and Paul.......... 463

JULY
6 - 14th Sun. in Ord. Time..... 473
13 - 15th Sun. in Ord. Time..... 478
20 - 16th Sun. in Ord. Time..... 484
27 - 17th Sun. in Ord. Time..... 489

AUGUST
3 - 18th Sun. in Ord. Time..... 494
10 - 19th Sun. in Ord. Time..... 499
15 - Assumption...................... 505
17 - 20th Sun. in Ord. Time..... 515
24 - 21st Sun. in Ord. Time..... 520
31 - 22nd Sun. in Ord. Time... 524

SEPTEMBER
7 - 23rd Sun. in Ord. Time..... 529
14 - Exaltation of Holy Cross... 534
21 - 25th Sun. in Ord. Time..... 539
28 - 26th Sun. in Ord. Time..... 545

OCTOBER
5 - 27th Sun. in Ord. Time..... 550
12 - 28th Sun. in Ord. Time..... 554
19 - 29th Sun. in Ord. Time..... 559
26 - 30th Sun. in Ord. Time..... 564

NOVEMBER
1 - All Saints 568
2 - All Souls.......................... 574
9 - Ded. of Lateran Basilica.. 589
16 - 33rd Sun. in Ord. Time..... 595
23 - Our Lord Jesus Christ,
King of the Universe......... 600

The Value of a Missal

"*Hand Missals which are drawn up according to the requirements of the modern liturgical renewal and which contain not only the Ordinary of the Mass but a version of all the liturgical texts approved by the competent authority are still necessary for the more perfect understanding of the total mystery of salvation celebrated during the liturgical year, for drawing meditation and fervor from the inexhaustible riches of the liturgical texts, and for facilitating actual participation.*

"*This demands not only that the Word of God be proclaimed within the gathered community and attentively listened to by it, but also that the holy people respond to the Word of God which they have received and celebrate the Sacred (Mysteries) by singing or reciting the parts of the Ordinary and Proper [of the Mass], hymns and Psalms.*

"*[Missals are] especially necessary for . . . those who participate in daily Mass, or who desire to live and pray every day in the spirit of the liturgy; those who because of sickness or inconvenience or other similar reasons cannot assemble with their own liturgical community, so that they may be joined to their prayer more truly and intimately; children who are to be initiated progressively into the mystery of the liturgy.*"

Postconciliar Commission for the Implementation
of the Constitution on the Sacred Liturgy

This Missal belongs to

....

Year C
For 2024-2025

New *Saint Joseph*
SUNDAY MISSAL
PRAYERBOOK AND HYMNAL

This Missal has been especially designed to help you participate at Mass . . . in the fullest and most active way possible.

How easy it is to use this Missal

- Refer to the Calendar inside the front cover for the page of the Sunday or Holyday Mass (the "Proper").

- This arrow (↓) means continue to read. This arrow (→) indicates a reference back to the Order of Mass ("Ordinary") or to another part of the "Proper."

- Boldface type always indicates the people's parts that are to be recited aloud.

ORDER
OF MASS
(Ordinary)
pp. 10-77

MASS TEXT
for each
Sunday/
Holyday of
Obligation
pp. 111-605

POPULAR
HYMNS
pp. 606-645

TREASURY OF
PRAYERS
pp. 646-663

MAJOR
PRACTICES
pp. 664-672

"Take this, all of you, and eat of it, for this is my Body, which will be given up for you."

New . . . St. Joseph

SUNDAY MISSAL

PRAYERBOOK AND HYMNAL

For 2024-2025

THE COMPLETE MASSES FOR SUNDAYS, HOLYDAYS, and the SACRED PASCHAL TRIDUUM

With the People's Parts of Holy Mass
Printed in Boldface Type
and Arranged for Parish Participation

IN ACCORD WITH THE THIRD TYPICAL EDITION
OF THE ROMAN MISSAL

WITH THE "NEW AMERICAN BIBLE" TEXT
FROM THE REVISED SUNDAY LECTIONARY,
SHORT HELPFUL NOTES AND EXPLANATIONS,
AND A TREASURY OF POPULAR PRAYERS

Dedicated to St. Joseph
Patron of the Universal Church

CATHOLIC BOOK PUBLISHING CORP.
New Jersey

NIHIL OBSTAT: Rev. Pawel Tomczyk, Ph.D.
Censor Librorum

IMPRIMATUR: ✠ Kevin J. Sweeney, D.D.
Bishop of Paterson

April 12, 2024

Published with the approval of the
Committee on Divine Worship,
United States Conference of Catholic Bishops

The St. Joseph Missals have been diligently prepared with the invaluable assistance of a special Board of Editors, including specialists in Liturgy and Sacred Scripture, Catechetics, Sacred Music and Art.

In this Sunday Missal Edition the musical notations for responsorial antiphons are by Rev. John Selner, S.S.

(T-2025)
ISBN 978-1-958237-46-5
© 2024 by *Catholic Book Publishing Corp.*, N.J.
catholicbookpublishing.com
Printed in the USA   24 SH 1

PREFACE

IN the words of the Second Vatican Council in the *Constitution on the Liturgy*, the *Mass* "is an action of Christ the priest and of his body which is the Church; it is a sacred action surpassing all others; no other action of the Church can equal its efficacy by the same title and to the same degree" (art. 7). Hence the Mass is a sacred sign, something visible which brings the invisible reality of Christ to us in the worship of the Father.

The Mass is the re-presentation of the Paschal Mystery, which delivers us from sin, death, and the devil and whereby we merit to receive a share in the eternal life of the Resurrected Christ.

"At the Last Supper, on the night when he was betrayed, our Savior instituted the Eucharistic sacrifice of his body and blood. He did this in order to perpetuate the sacrifice of the Cross throughout the centuries until he should come again, and so to entrust to his beloved spouse, the Church, a memorial of his death and resurrection: a sacrament of love, a sign of unity, a bond of charity, a Paschal banquet in which Christ is eaten, the mind is filled with grace, and a pledge of future glory is given to us.

"The Church, therefore, earnestly desires that Christ's faithful, when present at this mystery of faith, should not be there as strangers or silent spectators; on the contrary, through a good understanding of the rites and prayers they should take part in the sacred action conscious of what they are doing, with devotion and full

7

collaboration. They should be instructed by God's word and be nourished at the table of the Lord's body; they should give thanks to God; by offering the immaculate Victim, not only through the hands of the priests but also with him, they should learn also to offer themselves; through Christ the Mediator, they should be drawn day by day into ever more perfect union with God and with each other, so that . . . God may be all in all" (art. 47-48).

Accordingly, this new Sunday Missal has been edited, in conformity with the latest findings of modern liturgists, especially to enable the people to attain the most active participation.

To insure that "each . . . lay person who has an office to perform [will] do all of, but only, those parts which pertain to his office" (art. 28), a simple method of instant identification of the various parts of the Mass, has been designed, using different typefaces:

(1) **boldface type**—clearly identifies all people's parts for each Mass.

(2) lightface type—indicates the Priest's, Deacon's, or reader's parts.

In order to enable the faithful to prepare for each Mass AT HOME and so participate more actively AT MASS, the editors have added short helpful explanations of the new scripture readings, geared to the spiritual needs of daily life. A large selection of hymns for congregational singing has been included as well as a treasury of private prayers.

We trust that all these special features will help Catholics who use this new St. Joseph Missal to be led— in keeping with the desire of the Church—"to that full, conscious, and active participation in liturgical celebrations which is demanded by the very nature of the liturgy. Such participation by the Christian people as a chosen race, a royal priesthood, a holy nation, a redeemed people (1 Pt 2:9; cf. 2:4-5), is their right and duty by reason of their baptism" (art. 14).

THE ORDER OF MASS TITLES

THE INTRODUCTORY RITES

1. Entrance Chant
2. Greeting
3. Rite for the Blessing and Sprinkling of Water
4. Penitential Act
5. Kyrie
6. Gloria
7. Collect **(Proper)**

THE LITURGY OF THE WORD

8. First Reading **(Proper)**
9. Responsorial Psalm **(Proper)**
10. Second Reading **(Proper)**
11. Gospel Acclamation **(Proper)**
12. Gospel Dialogue
13. Gospel Reading **(Proper)**
14. Homily
15. Profession of Faith **(Creed)**
16. Universal Prayer

THE LITURGY OF THE EUCHARIST

17. Presentation and Preparation of the Gifts
18. Invitation to Prayer
19. Prayer over the Offerings **(Proper)**
20. Eucharistic Prayer
21. Preface Dialogue
22. Preface
23. Preface Acclamation
    Eucharistic Prayer
    1, 2, 3, 4
    Reconciliation 1, 2
    Various Needs 1, 2, 3, 4

THE COMMUNION RITE

24. The Lord's Prayer
25. Sign of Peace
26. Lamb of God
27. Invitation to Communion
28. Communion
29. Prayer after Communion **(Proper)**

THE CONCLUDING RITES

30. Solemn Blessing
31. Final Blessing
32. Dismissal

THE ORDER OF MASS

Options are indicated by A, B, C, D in the margin.

THE INTRODUCTORY RITES

Acts of prayer and penitence prepare us to meet Christ as he comes in Word and Sacrament. We gather as a worshiping community to celebrate our unity with him and with one another in faith.

1 ENTRANCE CHANT   STAND

If it is not sung, it is recited by all or some of the people.

Joined together as Christ's people, we open the celebration by raising our voices in praise of God who is present among us. This song should deepen our unity as it introduces the Mass we celebrate today.

→ Turn to Today's Mass

2 GREETING (3 forms)

When the Priest comes to the altar, he makes the customary reverence with the ministers and kisses the altar. Then, with the ministers, he goes to his chair. After the Entrance Chant, all make the Sign of the Cross:

Priest: In the name of the Father, and of the Son, and of the Holy Spirit.

PEOPLE: **Amen.**

The Priest welcomes us in the name of the Lord. We show our union with God, our neighbor, and the Priest by a united response to his greeting.

A ————————————————————————

Priest: The grace of our Lord Jesus Christ,
and the love of God,
and the communion of the Holy Spirit
be with you all.

PEOPLE: **And with your spirit.**

B ———————— OR ————————

Priest: Grace to you and peace from God our Father
and the Lord Jesus Christ.

PEOPLE: **And with your spirit.**

C ———————— OR ————————

Priest: The Lord be with you.

PEOPLE: **And with your spirit.**

[Bishop: Peace be with you.

PEOPLE: **And with your spirit.**]

3 RITE FOR the BLESSING and SPRINKLING OF WATER

From time to time on Sundays, especially in Easter Time, instead of the customary Penitential Act, the Blessing and Sprinkling of Water may take place (see pp. 78-81) as a reminder of Baptism.

4 PENITENTIAL ACT (3 forms)

(Omitted when the Rite for the Blessing and Sprinkling of Water [see pp. 78-81] has taken place or some part of the liturgy of the hours has preceded.)

Before we hear God's word, we acknowledge our sins humbly, ask for mercy, and accept his pardon.

Invitation to repent:

After the introduction to the day's Mass, the Priest invites the people to recall their sins and to repent of them in silence:

Priest: Brethren (brothers and sisters), let us acknowledge our sins,
and so prepare ourselves to celebrate the sacred mysteries.

Then, after a brief silence, one of the following forms is used.

A

Priest and **PEOPLE:**

**I confess to almighty God
and to you, my brothers and sisters,
that I have greatly sinned,
in my thoughts and in my words,
in what I have done and in what I have
failed to do,**

They strike their breast:

**through my fault, through my fault,
through my most grievous fault;**

Then they continue:

**therefore I ask blessed Mary ever-Virgin,
all the Angels and Saints,
and you, my brothers and sisters,
to pray for me to the Lord our God.**

B ──────── **OR** ────────

Priest: Have mercy on us, O Lord.

PEOPLE: For we have sinned against you.

Priest: Show us, O Lord, your mercy.

PEOPLE: And grant us your salvation.

C ──────── **OR** ────────

Priest, or a Deacon or another minister:

> You were sent to heal the contrite of heart:
> Lord, have mercy.

PEOPLE: Lord, have mercy.

Priest or other minister:

> You came to call sinners:
> Christ, have mercy.

PEOPLE: Christ, have mercy.

Priest or other minister:

> You are seated at the right hand of the Father to intercede for us:
> Lord, have mercy.

PEOPLE: Lord, have mercy.

───────

Absolution:

At the end of any of the forms of the Penitential Act:

Priest: May almighty God have mercy on us,
forgive us our sins,
and bring us to everlasting life.

PEOPLE: Amen.

5 KYRIE

Unless included in the Penitential Act, the Kyrie is sung or said by all, with alternating parts for the choir or cantor and for the people:

℣. Lord, have mercy.

℟. **Lord, have mercy.**

℣. Christ, have mercy.

℟. **Christ, have mercy.**

℣. Lord, have mercy.

℟. **Lord, have mercy.**

6 GLORIA

As the Church assembled in the Spirit we praise and pray to the Father and the Lamb.

When the Gloria is sung or said, the Priest or the cantors or everyone together may begin it:

**Glory to God in the highest,
and on earth peace to people of good will.**

**We praise you,
we bless you,
we adore you,
we glorify you,
we give you thanks for your great glory,
Lord God, heavenly King,
O God, almighty Father.**

**Lord Jesus Christ, Only Begotten Son,
Lord God, Lamb of God, Son of the Father,
you take away the sins of the world,
    have mercy on us;**

you take away the sins of the world,
    receive our prayer;
you are seated at the right hand of the Father,
    have mercy on us.

For you alone are the Holy One,
you alone are the Lord,
you alone are the Most High,
Jesus Christ,
with the Holy Spirit,
in the glory of God the Father.
Amen.

7 COLLECT

The Priest invites us to pray silently for a moment and then, in our name, expresses the theme of the day's celebration and petitions God the Father through the mediation of Christ in the Holy Spirit.

Priest: Let us pray.

→ **Turn to Today's Mass**

Priest and people pray silently for a while. Then the Priest says the Collect prayer, at the end of which the people acclaim:

PEOPLE: Amen.

THE LITURGY OF THE WORD

The proclamation of God's Word is always centered on Christ, present through his Word. Old Testament writings prepare for him; New Testament books speak of him directly. All of scripture calls us to believe once more and to follow. After the reading we reflect on God's words and respond to them.

As in Today's Mass　　　SIT

8 FIRST READING

At the end of the reading: Reader: The word of the Lord.

PEOPLE: Thanks be to God.

9 RESPONSORIAL PSALM

The people repeat the response sung by the cantor the first time and then after each verse.

10 SECOND READING

At the end of the reading: Reader: The word of the Lord.

PEOPLE: Thanks be to God.

11 GOSPEL ACCLAMATION　　STAND

Jesus will speak to us in the Gospel. We rise now out of respect and prepare for his message with the Alleluia.

The people repeat the Alleluia after the cantor's Alleluia and then after the verse. During Lent one of the following invocations is used as a response instead of the Alleluia:

(a) **Glory and praise to you, Lord Jesus Christ!**
(b) **Glory to you, Lord Jesus Christ, Wisdom of God the Father!**
(c) **Glory to you, Word of God, Lord Jesus Christ!**
(d) **Glory to you, Lord Jesus Christ, Son of the Living God!**

(e) **Praise and honor to you, Lord Jesus Christ!**
(f) **Praise to you, Lord Jesus Christ, King of endless glory!**
(g) **Marvelous and great are your works, O Lord!**
(h) **Salvation, glory, and power to the Lord Jesus Christ!**

12 GOSPEL DIALOGUE

Before proclaiming the Gospel, the Deacon asks the Priest: Your blessing, Father. *The Priest says:*

May the Lord be in your heart and on your lips,
that you may proclaim his Gospel worthily and well,
in the name of the Father, and of the Son, ✠ and of
the Holy Spirit. *The Deacon answers:* Amen.

If there is no Deacon, the Priest says inaudibly:

Cleanse my heart and my lips, almighty God,
that I may worthily proclaim your holy Gospel.

13 GOSPEL READING

Deacon (or Priest):
        The Lord be with you.

PEOPLE: And with your spirit.

Deacon (or Priest):

✠ A reading from the holy Gospel according to N.

PEOPLE: Glory to you, O Lord.

At the end:

Deacon (or Priest):
        The Gospel of the Lord.

PEOPLE: Praise to you, Lord Jesus Christ.

Then the Deacon (or Priest) kisses the book, saying inaudibly: Through the words of the Gospel may our sins be wiped away.

14 HOMILY   SIT

God's word is spoken again in the Homily. The Holy Spirit speaking through the lips of the preacher explains and applies today's biblical readings to the needs of this particular congregation. He calls us to respond to Christ through the life we lead.

15 PROFESSION OF FAITH (CREED) `STAND`

As a people we express our acceptance of God's message in the Scriptures and Homily. We summarize our faith by proclaiming a creed handed down from the early Church.

All say the Profession of Faith on Sundays.

———————— THE NICENE CREED ————————

I believe in one God,
the Father almighty,
maker of heaven and earth,
of all things visible and invisible.

I believe in one Lord Jesus Christ,
the Only Begotten Son of God,
born of the Father before all ages.
God from God, Light from Light,
true God from true God,
begotten, not made, consubstantial with the Father;
through him all things were made.
For us men and for our salvation
he came down from heaven,
and by the Holy Spirit was incarnate of the Virgin
   Mary, } *bow*
and became man.

For our sake he was crucified under Pontius Pilate,
he suffered death and was buried,
and rose again on the third day
in accordance with the Scriptures.
He ascended into heaven
and is seated at the right hand of the Father.
He will come again in glory
to judge the living and the dead
and his kingdom will have no end.

I believe in the Holy Spirit, the Lord, the giver of life,
who proceeds from the Father and the Son,
who with the Father and the Son is adored and
   glorified,
who has spoken through the prophets.

I believe in one, holy, catholic and apostolic Church.
I confess one Baptism for the forgiveness of sins
and I look forward to the resurrection of the dead
and the life of the world to come. Amen.

OR ──────── APOSTLES' CREED ────────

*Especially during Lent and Easter Time, the Apostles'
Creed may be said after the Homily.*

I believe in God,
the Father almighty,
Creator of heaven and earth,
and in Jesus Christ, his only Son, our Lord,
who was conceived by the Holy Spirit, } *bow*
born of the Virgin Mary,
suffered under Pontius Pilate,
was crucified, died and was buried;
he descended into hell;
on the third day he rose again from the dead;
he ascended into heaven,
and is seated at the right hand of God the Father
    almighty;
from there he will come to judge the living and the dead.

I believe in the Holy Spirit,
the holy catholic Church,
the communion of saints,
the forgiveness of sins,
the resurrection of the body,
and life everlasting. Amen.

16 UNIVERSAL PRAYER   (Prayer of the Faithful)

As a priestly people we unite with one another to pray for today's
needs in the Church and the world.

*After the Priest gives the introduction the Deacon or other
minister sings or says the invocations.*

PEOPLE: Lord, hear our prayer.
(or other response, according to local custom)
At the end the Priest says the concluding prayer:
PEOPLE: Amen.

THE LITURGY OF THE EUCHARIST

17 PRESENTATION AND PREPARATION `SIT`
OF THE GIFTS

While the people's gifts are brought forward to the Priest and are placed on the altar, the Offertory Chant is sung.

Before placing the bread on the altar, the Priest says inaudibly:

Blessed are you, Lord God of all creation,
for through your goodness we have received
the bread we offer you:
fruit of the earth and work of human hands,
it will become for us the bread of life.

If there is no singing, the Priest may say this prayer aloud, and the people may respond:

PEOPLE: Blessed be God for ever.

When he pours wine and a little water into the chalice, the Deacon (or the Priest) says inaudibly:

By the mystery of this water and wine
may we come to share in the divinity of Christ
who humbled himself to share in our humanity.

Before placing the chalice on the altar, he says:

Blessed are you, Lord God of all creation,
for through your goodness we have received
the wine we offer you:
fruit of the vine and work of human hands,
it will become our spiritual drink.

If there is no singing, the Priest may say this prayer aloud, and the people may respond:

PEOPLE: **Blessed be God for ever.**

The Priest says inaudibly:

With humble spirit and contrite heart
may we be accepted by you, O Lord,
and may our sacrifice in your sight this day
be pleasing to you, Lord God.

Then he washes his hands, saying:

Wash me, O Lord, from my iniquity
and cleanse me from my sin.

18 INVITATION TO PRAYER

Priest: Pray, brethren (brothers and sisters),
         that my sacrifice and yours
         may be acceptable to God,
         the almighty Father.   `STAND`

PEOPLE:

**May the Lord accept the sacrifice at your hands
for the praise and glory of his name,
for our good
and the good of all his holy Church.**

19 PRAYER OVER THE OFFERINGS

*The Priest, speaking in our name, asks the Father to
bless and accept these gifts.*

→ `Turn to Today's Mass`

At the end, **PEOPLE:** **Amen.**

20 EUCHARISTIC PRAYER

We begin the eucharistic service of praise and thanksgiving, the center of the entire celebration, the central prayer of worship. We lift our hearts to God, and offer praise and thanks as the Priest addresses this prayer to the Father through Jesus Christ. Together we join Christ in his sacrifice, celebrating his memorial in the holy meal and acknowledging with him the wonderful works of God in our lives.

21 PREFACE DIALOGUE

Priest: The Lord be with you.
PEOPLE: **And with your spirit.**

Priest: Lift up your hearts.
PEOPLE: **We lift them up to the Lord.**

Priest: Let us give thanks to the Lord our God.
PEOPLE: **It is right and just.**

22 PREFACE

As indicated in the individual Masses of this Missal, the Priest may say one of the following Prefaces (listed in numerical order).

No.		Page	No.		Page
P 1:	Advent I	82	**P 15:** 4th Sun. of Lent		251
P 2:	Advent II	82	**P 16:** 5th Sun. of Lent		263
P 3:	Nativity of the Lord I	83	**P 19:** Palm Sunday of the		
P 4:	Nativity of the Lord II	83		Passion of the Lord	285
P 5:	Nativity of the Lord III	84	**P 20:** Holy Thursday		293
P 6:	Epiphany of Lord	161	**P 21:** Easter I		85
P 7:	Baptism of the Lord	170	**P 22:** Easter II		86
P 8:	Lent I	84	**P 23:** Easter III		86
P 9:	Lent II	85	**P 24:** Easter IV		86
P 12:	1st Sun. of Lent	219	**P 25:** Easter V		87
P 13:	2nd Sun. of Lent	225	**P 26:** Ascension I		87
P 14:	3rd Sun. of Lent	238			

22

No.	Page	No.	Page
P 27: Ascension II	88	**P 48:** Holy Eucharist II	92
P 28: Pentecost Sunday	449	**P 49:** Presentation of Lord	192
P 29: Ordinary Sunday I	88	**P 51:** Jesus Christ, King	
P 30: Ordinary Sunday II	89	of the Universe	604
P 31: Ordinary Sunday III	89	**P 53:** Ded. of Church II	593
P 32: Ordinary Sunday IV	90	**P 56:** Blessed Virgin I	155
P 33: Ordinary Sunday V	90	**P 59:** Assumption	513
P 34: Ordinary Sunday VI	91	**P 63:** Apostles I	471
P 35: Ordinary Sunday VII	91	**P 71:** All Saints	572
P 36: Ordinary Sunday VIII	91	**P 77:** For the Dead I	93
P 43: Most Holy Trinity	455	**P 78:** For the Dead II	94
P 46: Exaltation of Holy		**P 79:** For the Dead III	94
Cross	538	**P 80:** For the Dead IV	94
P 47: Holy Eucharist I	92	**P 81:** For the Dead V	95

23 PREFACE ACCLAMATION

Priest and **PEOPLE:**

Holy, Holy, Holy Lord God of hosts.
Heaven and earth are full of your glory.
Hosanna in the highest.
Blessed is he who comes in the name of the Lord.
Hosanna in the highest. `KNEEL`

Then the Priest continues with one of the following Eucharistic Prayers.

EUCHARISTIC PRAYER .... Choice of ten

1	To you, therefore, most merciful Father ..	p. 24
2	You are indeed Holy, O Lord, the fount ...	p. 31
3	You are indeed Holy, O Lord, and all	p. 34
4	We give you praise, Father most holy	p. 39
R1	You are indeed Holy, O Lord, and from ...	p. 44
R2	You, therefore, almighty Father	p. 49
V1	You are indeed Holy and to be glorified ..	p. 53
V2	You are indeed Holy and to be glorified ..	p. 58
V3	You are indeed Holy and to be glorified ..	p. 63
V4	You are indeed Holy and to be glorified ..	p. 68

EUCHARISTIC PRAYER No. 1

The Roman Canon

(This Eucharistic Prayer is especially suitable for Sundays and Masses with proper Communicantes *and* Hanc igitur.*)*

[The words within parentheses may be omitted.]

To you, therefore, most merciful Father,
we make humble prayer and petition
through Jesus Christ, your Son, our Lord:
that you accept
and bless ✠ these gifts, these offerings,
these holy and unblemished sacrifices,
which we offer you firstly
for your holy catholic Church.
Be pleased to grant her peace,
to guard, unite and govern her
throughout the whole world,
together with your servant N. our Pope,
and N. our Bishop,
and all those who, holding to the truth,
hand on the catholic and apostolic faith.

Remember, Lord, your servants N. and N.
and all gathered here,
whose faith and devotion are known to you.
For them, we offer you this sacrifice of praise
or they offer it for themselves
and all who are dear to them:
for the redemption of their souls,
in hope of health and well-being,
and paying their homage to you,
the eternal God, living and true.

In communion with those whose memory we 1
    venerate,
especially the glorious ever-Virgin Mary,
Mother of our God and Lord, Jesus Christ,
† and blessed Joseph, her Spouse,
your blessed Apostles and Martyrs
Peter and Paul, Andrew,
(James, John,
Thomas, James, Philip,
Bartholomew, Matthew,
Simon and Jude;
Linus, Cletus, Clement, Sixtus,
Cornelius, Cyprian,
Lawrence, Chrysogonus,
John and Paul,
Cosmas and Damian)
and all your Saints;
we ask that through their merits and prayers,
in all things we may be defended
by your protecting help.
(Through Christ our Lord. Amen.)

Therefore, Lord, we pray:*
graciously accept this oblation of our service,
that of your whole family;
order our days in your peace,
and command that we be delivered from eternal
    damnation
and counted among the flock of those you have
    chosen.
(Through Christ our Lord. Amen.)

Be pleased, O God, we pray,
to bless, acknowledge,
and approve this offering in every respect;

† * *See p. 95 for proper* Communicantes *and* Hanc igitur.

1 make it spiritual and acceptable,
so that it may become for us
the Body and Blood of your most beloved Son,
our Lord Jesus Christ.

On the day before he was to suffer,
he took bread in his holy and venerable hands,
and with eyes raised to heaven
to you, O God, his almighty Father,
giving you thanks, he said the blessing,
broke the bread
and gave it to his disciples, saying:

Take this, all of you, and eat of it,
for this is my Body,
which will be given up for you.

In a similar way when supper was ended,
he took this precious chalice
in his holy and venerable hands,
and once more giving you thanks, he said the
    blessing
and gave the chalice to his disciples, saying:

Take this, all of you, and drink from it,
for this is the chalice of my Blood,
the Blood of the new and eternal covenant,
which will be poured out for you and for many
for the forgiveness of sins.

Do this in memory of me.

Priest: The mystery of faith. *(Memorial Acclamation)*
PEOPLE:

A We proclaim your Death, O Lord,
    and profess your Resurrection
    until you come again.

B When we eat this Bread and drink this Cup,
we proclaim your Death, O Lord,
until you come again.

C Save us, Savior of the world,
for by your Cross and Resurrection
you have set us free.

Therefore, O Lord,
as we celebrate the memorial of the blessed Passion,
the Resurrection from the dead,
and the glorious Ascension into heaven
of Christ, your Son, our Lord,
we, your servants and your holy people,
offer to your glorious majesty
from the gifts that you have given us,
this pure victim,
this holy victim,
this spotless victim,
the holy Bread of eternal life
and the Chalice of everlasting salvation.

Be pleased to look upon these offerings
with a serene and kindly countenance,
and to accept them,
as once you were pleased to accept
the gifts of your servant Abel the just,
the sacrifice of Abraham, our father in faith,
and the offering of your high priest Melchizedek,
a holy sacrifice, a spotless victim.

In humble prayer we ask you, almighty God:
command that these gifts be borne
by the hands of your holy Angel
to your altar on high

1 in the sight of your divine majesty,
so that all of us, who through this participation at
  the altar
receive the most holy Body and Blood of your Son,
may be filled with every grace and heavenly
  blessing.
(Through Christ our Lord. Amen.)

Remember also, Lord, your servants N. and N.,
who have gone before us with the sign of faith
and rest in the sleep of peace.
Grant them, O Lord, we pray,
and all who sleep in Christ,
a place of refreshment, light and peace.
(Through Christ our Lord. Amen.)

To us, also, your servants, who, though sinners,
hope in your abundant mercies,
graciously grant some share
and fellowship with your holy Apostles and
  Martyrs:
with John the Baptist, Stephen,
Matthias, Barnabas,
(Ignatius, Alexander,
Marcellinus, Peter,
Felicity, Perpetua,
Agatha, Lucy,
Agnes, Cecilia, Anastasia)
and all your Saints;
admit us, we beseech you,
into their company,
not weighing our merits,
but granting us your pardon,
through Christ our Lord.

1

Through whom
you continue to make all these good things,
O Lord;
you sanctify them, fill them with life,
bless them, and bestow them upon us.

(Concluding Doxology)

Through him, and with him, and in him,
O God, almighty Father,
in the unity of the Holy Spirit,
all glory and honor is yours,
for ever and ever.

The people acclaim: **Amen.**

Continue with the Mass, as on p. 72.

(This Eucharistic Prayer is particularly suitable on Weekdays or for special circumstances.)

`STAND`

℣. The Lord be with you.
℟. **And with your spirit.**

℣. Lift up your hearts.
℟. **We lift them up to the Lord.**

℣. Let us give thanks to the Lord our God.
℟. **It is right and just.**

It is truly right and just, our duty and our salvation,
always and everywhere to give you thanks, Father
    most holy,
through your beloved Son, Jesus Christ,
your Word through whom you made all things,
whom you sent as our Savior and Redeemer,
incarnate by the Holy Spirit and born of the Virgin.

Fulfilling your will
    and gaining for you a holy people,
he stretched out his hands
    as he endured his Passion,
so as to break the bonds of death
    and manifest the resurrection.

And so, with the Angels and all the Saints
we declare your glory,
as with one voice we acclaim:

2

Holy, Holy, Holy Lord God of hosts.
Heaven and earth are full of your glory.
Hosanna in the highest.
Blessed is he who comes in the name of the Lord.
Hosanna in the highest.

KNEEL

You are indeed Holy, O Lord,
the fount of all holiness.

Make holy, therefore, these gifts, we pray,
by sending down your Spirit upon them like the
    dewfall,
so that they may become for us
the Body and ✠ Blood of our Lord Jesus Christ.

At the time he was betrayed
and entered willingly into his Passion,
he took bread and, giving thanks, broke it,
and gave it to his disciples, saying:

Take this, all of you, and eat of it,
for this is my Body,
which will be given up for you.

In a similar way, when supper was ended,
he took the chalice
and, once more giving thanks,
he gave it to his disciples, saying:

Take this, all of you, and drink from it,
for this is the chalice of my Blood,
the Blood of the new and eternal covenant,
which will be poured out for you and for many
for the forgiveness of sins.
Do this in memory of me.

2 Priest: The mystery of faith. *(Memorial Acclamation)*

PEOPLE:

A   We proclaim your Death, O Lord,
and profess your Resurrection
until you come again.

B   When we eat this Bread and drink this Cup,
we proclaim your Death, O Lord,
until you come again.

C   Save us, Savior of the world,
for by your Cross and Resurrection
you have set us free.

Therefore, as we celebrate
the memorial of his Death and Resurrection,
we offer you, Lord,
the Bread of life and the Chalice of salvation,
giving thanks that you have held us worthy
to be in your presence and minister to you.

Humbly we pray
that, partaking of the Body and Blood of Christ,
we may be gathered into one by the Holy Spirit.

Remember, Lord, your Church,
spread throughout the world,
and bring her to the fullness of charity,
together with *N.* our Pope and *N.* our Bishop
and all the clergy.

In Masses for the Dead, the following may be added:

Remember your servant *N.*,
whom you have called (today)
from this world to yourself.

2

Grant that he (she) who was united with your Son in a
    death like his,
may also be one with him in his Resurrection.

Remember also our brothers and sisters
who have fallen asleep in the hope of the
    resurrection,
and all who have died in your mercy:
welcome them into the light of your face.
Have mercy on us all, we pray,
that with the Blessed Virgin Mary, Mother of
    God,
with blessed Joseph, her Spouse,
with the blessed Apostles,
and all the Saints who have pleased you
    throughout the ages,
we may merit to be coheirs to eternal life,
and may praise and glorify you
through your Son, Jesus Christ.

(Concluding Doxology)

Through him, and with him, and in him,
O God, almighty Father,
in the unity of the Holy Spirit,
all glory and honor is yours,
for ever and ever.

The people acclaim: **Amen.**

Continue with the Mass, as on p. 72.

(This Eucharistic Prayer may be used with any Preface and preferably on Sundays and feast days.)

KNEEL

You are indeed Holy, O Lord,
and all you have created
rightly gives you praise,
for through your Son our Lord Jesus Christ,
by the power and working of the Holy Spirit,
you give life to all things and make them holy,
and you never cease to gather a people to yourself,
so that from the rising of the sun to its setting
a pure sacrifice may be offered to your name.

Therefore, O Lord, we humbly implore you:
by the same Spirit graciously make holy
these gifts we have brought to you for
    consecration,
that they may become the Body and ✛ Blood
of your Son our Lord Jesus Christ,
at whose command we celebrate these mysteries.

For on the night he was betrayed
he himself took bread,
and, giving you thanks, he said the blessing,
broke the bread and gave it to his disciples,
    saying:

Take this, all of you, and eat of it,
for this is my Body,
which will be given up for you.

In a similar way, when supper was ended,
he took the chalice,

3

and, giving you thanks, he said the blessing,
and gave the chalice to his disciples, saying:

Take this, all of you, and drink from it,
for this is the chalice of my Blood,
the Blood of the new and eternal covenant,
which will be poured out for you and for many
for the forgiveness of sins.

Do this in memory of me.

Priest: The mystery of faith. *(Memorial Acclamation)*

PEOPLE:

A We proclaim your Death, O Lord,
    and profess your Resurrection
    until you come again.

B When we eat this Bread and drink this Cup,
    we proclaim your Death, O Lord,
    until you come again.

C Save us, Savior of the world,
    for by your Cross and Resurrection
    you have set us free.

Therefore, O Lord, as we celebrate the memorial
of the saving Passion of your Son,
his wondrous Resurrection
and Ascension into heaven,
and as we look forward to his second coming,
we offer you in thanksgiving
this holy and living sacrifice.

Look, we pray, upon the oblation of your Church
and, recognizing the sacrificial Victim by whose
    death
you willed to reconcile us to yourself,

3 grant that we, who are nourished
by the Body and Blood of your Son
and filled with his Holy Spirit,
may become one body, one spirit in Christ.

May he make of us
an eternal offering to you,
so that we may obtain an inheritance with your elect,
especially with the most Blessed Virgin Mary,
    Mother of God,
with blessed Joseph, her Spouse,
with your blessed Apostles and glorious Martyrs
(with Saint N.: the Saint of the day or Patron Saint)
and with all the Saints,
on whose constant intercession in your presence
we rely for unfailing help.

May this Sacrifice of our reconciliation,
we pray, O Lord,
advance the peace and salvation of all the world.
Be pleased to confirm in faith and charity
your pilgrim Church on earth,
with your servant N. our Pope and N. our Bishop,
the Order of Bishops, all the clergy,
and the entire people you have gained for your
    own.

Listen graciously to the prayers of this family,
whom you have summoned before you:
in your compassion, O merciful Father,
gather to yourself all your children
scattered throughout the world.

† To our departed brothers and sisters
and to all who were pleasing to you
at their passing from this life,
give kind admittance to your kingdom.

3

There we hope to enjoy for ever the fullness of
  your glory
through Christ our Lord,
through whom you bestow on the world all that
  is good. †

(Concluding Doxology)

Through him, and with him, and in him,
O God, almighty Father,
in the unity of the Holy Spirit,
all glory and honor is yours,
for ever and ever.

The people acclaim: **Amen.**

Continue with the Mass, as on p. 72.

---

† *In Masses for the Dead the following may be said:*
†Remember your servant *N.*
whom you have called (today)
from this world to yourself.
Grant that he (she) who was united with your Son in a
  death like his,
may also be one with him in his Resurrection,
when from the earth
he will raise up in the flesh those who have died,
and transform our lowly body
after the pattern of his own glorious body.
To our departed brothers and sisters, too,
and to all who were pleasing to you
at their passing from this life,
give kind admittance to your kingdom.
There we hope to enjoy for ever the fullness of your glory,
when you will wipe away every tear from our eyes.
For seeing you, our God, as you are,
we shall be like you for all the ages
and praise you without end,
through Christ our Lord,
through whom you bestow on the world all that is good. †

℣. The Lord be with you. **STAND**
℟. **And with your spirit.**

℣. Lift up your hearts.
℟. **We lift them up to the Lord.**

℣. Let us give thanks to the Lord our God.
℟. **It is right and just.**

It is truly right to give you thanks,
truly just to give you glory, Father most holy,
for you are the one God living and true,
existing before all ages and abiding for all eternity,
dwelling in unapproachable light;
yet you, who alone are good, the source of life,
have made all that is,
so that you might fill your creatures with blessings
and bring joy to many of them by the glory of your
    light.

And so, in your presence are countless hosts of
    Angels,
who serve you day and night
and, gazing upon the glory of your face,
glorify you without ceasing.

With them we, too, confess your name in exultation,
giving voice to every creature under heaven,
as we acclaim:

Holy, Holy, Holy Lord God of hosts.
Heaven and earth are full of your glory.
Hosanna in the highest.

Blessed is he who comes in the name of the Lord.
Hosanna in the highest.

4

`KNEEL`

We give you praise, Father most holy,
for you are great
and you have fashioned all your works
in wisdom and in love.
You formed man in your own image
and entrusted the whole world to his care,
so that in serving you alone, the Creator,
he might have dominion over all creatures.
And when through disobedience he had lost your
   friendship,
you did not abandon him to the domain of death.
For you came in mercy to the aid of all,
so that those who seek might find you.
Time and again you offered them covenants
and through the prophets
taught them to look forward to salvation.

And you so loved the world, Father most holy,
that in the fullness of time
you sent your Only Begotten Son to be our Savior.
Made incarnate by the Holy Spirit
and born of the Virgin Mary,
he shared our human nature
in all things but sin.
To the poor he proclaimed the good news of
   salvation,
to prisoners, freedom,
and to the sorrowful of heart, joy.
To accomplish your plan,
he gave himself up to death,
and, rising from the dead,
he destroyed death and restored life.

4 And that we might live no longer for ourselves
but for him who died and rose again for us,
he sent the Holy Spirit from you, Father,
as the first fruits for those who believe,
so that, bringing to perfection his work in the world,
he might sanctify creation to the full.

Therefore, O Lord, we pray:
may this same Holy Spirit
graciously sanctify these offerings,
that they may become
the Body and ✠ Blood of our Lord Jesus Christ
for the celebration of this great mystery,
which he himself left us
as an eternal covenant.

For when the hour had come
for him to be glorified by you, Father most holy,
having loved his own who were in the world,
he loved them to the end:
and while they were at supper,
he took bread, blessed and broke it,
and gave it to his disciples, saying:

Take this, all of you, and eat of it,
for this is my Body,
which will be given up for you.

In a similar way,
taking the chalice filled with the fruit of the vine,
he gave thanks,
and gave the chalice to his disciples, saying:

Take this, all of you, and drink from it,
for this is the chalice of my Blood,
the Blood of the new and eternal covenant,

4

*which will be poured out for you and for many
for the forgiveness of sins.*

Do this in memory of me.

Priest: The mystery of faith. *(Memorial Acclamation)*

PEOPLE:

A We proclaim your Death, O Lord,
and profess your Resurrection
until you come again.

B When we eat this Bread and drink this Cup,
we proclaim your Death, O Lord,
until you come again.

C Save us, Savior of the world,
for by your Cross and Resurrection
you have set us free.

Therefore, O Lord,
as we now celebrate the memorial of our
    redemption,
we remember Christ's Death
and his descent to the realm of the dead,
we proclaim his Resurrection
and his Ascension to your right hand,
and, as we await his coming in glory,
we offer you his Body and Blood,
the sacrifice acceptable to you
which brings salvation to the whole world.

Look, O Lord, upon the Sacrifice
which you yourself have provided for your Church,
and grant in your loving kindness
to all who partake of this one Bread and one
    Chalice
that, gathered into one body by the Holy Spirit,

4 they may truly become a living sacrifice in Christ
to the praise of your glory.

Therefore, Lord, remember now
all for whom we offer this sacrifice:
especially your servant N. our Pope,
N. our Bishop, and the whole Order of Bishops,
all the clergy,
those who take part in this offering,
those gathered here before you,
your entire people,
and all who seek you with a sincere heart.

Remember also
those who have died in the peace of your Christ
and all the dead,
whose faith you alone have known.

To all of us, your children,
grant, O merciful Father,
that we may enter into a heavenly inheritance
with the Blessed Virgin Mary, Mother of God,
with blessed Joseph, her Spouse,
and with your Apostles and Saints in your kingdom.
There, with the whole of creation,
freed from the corruption of sin and death,
may we glorify you through Christ our Lord,
through whom you bestow on the world all that
is good.

(Concluding Doxology)

Through him, and with him, and in him,
O God, almighty Father,
in the unity of the Holy Spirit,
all glory and honor is yours,
for ever and ever.

The people acclaim: **Amen.**

Continue with the Mass, as on p. 72.

EUCHARISTIC PRAYER FOR RECONCILIATION I

STAND

℣.   The Lord be with you.

℟.   **And with your spirit.**

℣.   Lift up your hearts.

℟.   **We lift them up to the Lord.**

℣.   Let us give thanks to the Lord our God.

℟.   **It is right and just.**

It is truly right and just
that we should always give you thanks,
Lord, holy Father, almighty and eternal God.

For you do not cease to spur us on
to possess a more abundant life
and, being rich in mercy,
you constantly offer pardon
and call on sinners
to trust in your forgiveness alone.

Never did you turn away from us,
and, though time and again we have broken your
   covenant,
you have bound the human family to yourself
through Jesus your Son, our Redeemer,
with a new bond of love so tight
that it can never be undone.

Even now you set before your people
a time of grace and reconciliation,
and, as they turn back to you in spirit,
you grant them hope in Christ Jesus
and a desire to be of service to all,

R1

while they entrust themselves
more fully to the Holy Spirit.

And so, filled with wonder,
we extol the power of your love,
and, proclaiming our joy
at the salvation that comes from you,
we join in the heavenly hymn of countless hosts,
as without end we acclaim:

Holy, Holy, Holy Lord God of hosts.
Heaven and earth are full of your glory.
Hosanna in the highest.
Blessed is he who comes in the name of the Lord.
Hosanna in the highest.

KNEEL

You are indeed Holy, O Lord,
and from the world's beginning
are ceaselessly at work,
so that the human race may become holy,
just as you yourself are holy.

Look, we pray, upon your people's offerings
and pour out on them the power of your Spirit,
that they may become the Body and ✚ Blood
of your beloved Son, Jesus Christ,
in whom we, too, are your sons and daughters.

Indeed, though we once were lost
and could not approach you,
you loved us with the greatest love:
for your Son, who alone is just,
handed himself over to death,

**R
1**

and did not disdain to be nailed for our sake
to the wood of the Cross.

But before his arms were outstretched between
    heaven and earth,
to become the lasting sign of your covenant,
he desired to celebrate the Passover with his
    disciples.

As he ate with them,
he took bread
and, giving you thanks, he said the blessing,
broke the bread and gave it to them, saying:

Take this, all of you, and eat of it,
for this is my Body,
which will be given up for you.

In a similar way, when supper was ended,
knowing that he was about to reconcile all things
    in himself
through his Blood to be shed on the Cross,
he took the chalice, filled with the fruit of the
    vine,
and once more giving you thanks,
handed the chalice to his disciples, saying:

Take this, all of you, and drink from it,
for this is the chalice of my Blood,
the Blood of the new and eternal covenant,
which will be poured out for you and for many
for the forgiveness of sins.
Do this in memory of me.

R 1

Priest: The mystery of faith. *(Memorial Acclamation)*
PEOPLE:

A We proclaim your Death, O Lord,
and profess your Resurrection
until you come again.

B When we eat this Bread and drink this Cup,
we proclaim your Death, O Lord,
until you come again.

C Save us, Savior of the world,
for by your Cross and Resurrection
you have set us free.

Therefore, as we celebrate
the memorial of your Son Jesus Christ,
who is our Passover and our surest peace,
we celebrate his Death and Resurrection from the
      dead,
and looking forward to his blessed Coming,
we offer you, who are our faithful and merciful
      God,
this sacrificial Victim
who reconciles to you the human race.

Look kindly, most compassionate Father,
on those you unite to yourself
by the Sacrifice of your Son,
and grant that, by the power of the Holy Spirit,
as they partake of this one Bread and one
      Chalice,
they may be gathered into one Body in Christ,
who heals every division.

R 1

Be pleased to keep us always
in communion of mind and heart,
together with *N.* our Pope and *N.* our Bishop.
Help us to work together
for the coming of your Kingdom,
until the hour when we stand before you,
Saints among the Saints in the halls of heaven,
with the Blessed Virgin Mary, Mother of God,
the blessed Apostles and all the Saints,
and with our deceased brothers and sisters,
whom we humbly commend to your mercy.

Then, freed at last from the wound of corruption
and made fully into a new creation,
we shall sing to you with gladness
the thanksgiving of Christ,
who lives for all eternity.

(Concluding Doxology)

Through him, and with him, and in him,
O God, almighty Father,
in the unity of the Holy Spirit,
all glory and honor is yours,
for ever and ever.

The people acclaim: **Amen.**

Continue with the Mass, as on p. 72.

R 2

EUCHARISTIC PRAYER FOR
RECONCILIATION II

STAND

℣. The Lord be with you.
℟. **And with your spirit.**

℣. Lift up your hearts.
℟. **We lift them up to the Lord.**

℣. Let us give thanks to the Lord our God.
℟. **It is right and just.**

It is truly right and just
that we should give you thanks and praise,
O God, almighty Father,
for all you do in this world,
through our Lord Jesus Christ.

For though the human race
is divided by dissension and discord,
yet we know that by testing us
you change our hearts
to prepare them for reconciliation.

Even more, by your Spirit you move human hearts
that enemies may speak to each other again,
adversaries join hands,
and peoples seek to meet together.

By the working of your power
it comes about, O Lord,
that hatred is overcome by love,
revenge gives way to forgiveness,
and discord is changed to mutual respect.

Therefore, as we give you ceaseless thanks
with the choirs of heaven,

R 2

we cry out to your majesty on earth,
and without end we acclaim:

Holy, Holy, Holy Lord God of hosts.
Heaven and earth are full of your glory.
Hosanna in the highest.
Blessed is he who comes in the name of the Lord.
Hosanna in the highest.

You, therefore, almighty Father,   `KNEEL`
we bless through Jesus Christ your Son,
who comes in your name.
He himself is the Word that brings salvation,
the hand you extend to sinners,
the way by which your peace is offered to us.
When we ourselves had turned away from you
on account of our sins,
you brought us back to be reconciled, O Lord,
so that, converted at last to you,
we might love one another
through your Son,
whom for our sake you handed over to death.

And now, celebrating the reconciliation
Christ has brought us,
we entreat you:
sanctify these gifts by the outpouring of your Spirit,
that they may become the Body and ✟ Blood of
    your Son,
whose command we fulfill
when we celebrate these mysteries.

For when about to give his life to set us free,
as he reclined at supper,
he himself took bread into his hands,

R 2

and, giving you thanks, he said the blessing,
broke the bread and gave it to his disciples, saying:

Take this, all of you, and eat of it,
for this is my Body,
which will be given up for you.

In a similar way, on that same evening,
he took the chalice of blessing in his hands,
confessing your mercy,
and gave the chalice to his disciples, saying:

Take this, all of you, and drink from it,
for this is the chalice of my Blood,
the Blood of the new and eternal covenant,
which will be poured out for you and for many
for the forgiveness of sins.

Do this in memory of me.

Priest: The mystery of faith. *(Memorial Acclamation)*

PEOPLE:

A We proclaim your Death, O Lord,
and profess your Resurrection
until you come again.

B When we eat this Bread and drink this Cup,
we proclaim your Death, O Lord,
until you come again.

C Save us, Savior of the world,
for by your Cross and Resurrection
you have set us free.

Celebrating, therefore, the memorial
of the Death and Resurrection of your Son,
who left us this pledge of his love,
we offer you what you have bestowed on us,
the Sacrifice of perfect reconciliation.

R 2

Holy Father, we humbly beseech you
to accept us also, together with your Son,
and in this saving banquet
graciously to endow us with his very Spirit,
who takes away everything
that estranges us from one another.

May he make your Church a sign of unity
and an instrument of your peace among all people
and may he keep us in communion
with N. our Pope and N. our Bishop
and all the Bishops
and your entire people.

Just as you have gathered us now at the table of
     your Son,
so also bring us together,
with the glorious Virgin Mary, Mother of God,
with your blessed Apostles and all the Saints,
with our brothers and sisters
and those of every race and tongue
who have died in your friendship.
Bring us to share with them the unending banquet
     of unity
in a new heaven and a new earth,
where the fullness of your peace will shine forth
in Christ Jesus our Lord.

(Concluding Doxology)

Through him, and with him, and in him,
O God, almighty Father,
in the unity of the Holy Spirit,
all glory and honor is yours,
for ever and ever.

The people acclaim: **Amen.**

Continue with the Mass, as on p. 72.

V EUCHARISTIC PRAYER FOR USE IN
1 MASSES FOR VARIOUS NEEDS I

℣. The Lord be with you.

℟. **And with your spirit.**

℣. Lift up your hearts.

℟. **We lift them up to the Lord.**

℣. Let us give thanks to the Lord our God.

℟. **It is right and just.**

It is truly right and just to give you thanks
and raise to you a hymn of glory and praise,
O Lord, Father of infinite goodness.

For by the word of your Son's Gospel
you have brought together one Church
from every people, tongue, and nation,
and, having filled her with life by the power of
    your Spirit,
you never cease through her
to gather the whole human race into one.

Manifesting the covenant of your love,
she dispenses without ceasing
the blessed hope of your Kingdom
and shines bright as the sign of your faithfulness,
which in Christ Jesus our Lord
you promised would last for eternity.

And so, with all the Powers of heaven,
we worship you constantly on earth,
while, with all the Church,
as one voice we acclaim:

V
1

Holy, Holy, Holy Lord God of hosts.
Heaven and earth are full of your glory.
Hosanna in the highest.
Blessed is he who comes in the name of the Lord.
Hosanna in the highest.

`KNEEL`

You are indeed Holy and to be glorified, O God,
who love the human race
and who always walk with us on the journey of life.
Blessed indeed is your Son,
present in our midst
when we are gathered by his love
and when, as once for the disciples, so now for us,
he opens the Scriptures and breaks the bread.

Therefore, Father most merciful,
we ask that you send forth your Holy Spirit
to sanctify these gifts of bread and wine,
that they may become for us
the Body and ✠ Blood
of our Lord Jesus Christ.

On the day before he was to suffer,
on the night of the Last Supper,
he took bread and said the blessing,
broke the bread and gave it to his disciples, saying:

Take this, all of you, and eat of it,
for this is my Body,
which will be given up for you.

In a similar way, when supper was ended,
he took the chalice, gave you thanks
and gave the chalice to his disciples, saying:

**V
1**

Take this, all of you, and drink from it,
for this is the chalice of my Blood,
the Blood of the new and eternal covenant,
which will be poured out for you and for many
for the forgiveness of sins.

Do this in memory of me.

Priest: The mystery of faith. *(Memorial Acclamation)*

PEOPLE:

A We proclaim your Death, O Lord,
and profess your Resurrection
until you come again.

B When we eat this Bread and drink this Cup,
we proclaim your Death, O Lord,
until you come again.

C Save us, Savior of the world,
for by your Cross and Resurrection
you have set us free.

Therefore, holy Father,
as we celebrate the memorial of Christ your Son,
    our Savior,
whom you led through his Passion and Death on
    the Cross
to the glory of the Resurrection,
and whom you have seated at your right hand,
we proclaim the work of your love until he comes
    again
and we offer you the Bread of life
and the Chalice of blessing.

Look with favor on the oblation of your Church,
in which we show forth

the paschal Sacrifice of Christ that has been handed on to us,
and grant that, by the power of the Spirit of your love,
we may be counted now and until the day of eternity
among the members of your Son,
in whose Body and Blood we have communion.

Lord, renew your Church (which is in N.)
by the light of the Gospel.
Strengthen the bond of unity
between the faithful and the pastors of your people,
together with N. our Pope, N. our Bishop,
and the whole Order of Bishops,
that in a world torn by strife
your people may shine forth
as a prophetic sign of unity and concord.

Remember our brothers and sisters (N. and N.),
who have fallen asleep in the peace of your Christ,
and all the dead, whose faith you alone have known.
Admit them to rejoice in the light of your face,
and in the resurrection give them the fullness of life.

Grant also to us,
when our earthly pilgrimage is done,
that we may come to an eternal dwelling place
and live with you for ever;
there, in communion with the Blessed Virgin Mary, Mother of God,
with the Apostles and Martyrs,

V 1

V1

(with Saint *N.*: the Saint of the day or Patron)
and with all the Saints,
we shall praise and exalt you
through Jesus Christ, your Son.

(Concluding Doxology)

Through him, and with him, and in him,
O God, almighty Father,
in the unity of the Holy Spirit,
all glory and honor is yours,
for ever and ever.

The people acclaim: **Amen.**

Continue with the Mass, as on p. 72.

EUCHARISTIC PRAYER FOR USE IN MASSES FOR VARIOUS NEEDS II

STAND

℣. The Lord be with you.
℟. **And with your spirit.**

℣. Lift up your hearts.
℟. **We lift them up to the Lord.**

℣. Let us give thanks to the Lord our God.
℟. **It is right and just.**

It is truly right and just, our duty and our salvation,
always and everywhere to give you thanks,
Lord, holy Father,
creator of the world and source of all life.

For you never forsake the works of your wisdom,
but by your providence are even now at work in our midst.
With mighty hand and outstretched arm
you led your people Israel through the desert.
Now, as your Church makes her pilgrim journey in the world,
you always accompany her
by the power of the Holy Spirit
and lead her along the paths of time
to the eternal joy of your Kingdom,
through Christ our Lord.

And so, with the Angels and Saints,
we, too, sing the hymn of your glory,
as without end we acclaim:

57

V 2 **Holy, Holy, Holy Lord God of hosts.**
Heaven and earth are full of your glory.
Hosanna in the highest.
Blessed is he who comes in the name of the Lord.
Hosanna in the highest.

KNEEL

You are indeed Holy and to be glorified, O God,
who love the human race
and who always walk with us on the journey of life.
Blessed indeed is your Son,
present in our midst
when we are gathered by his love,
and when, as once for the disciples, so now for us,
he opens the Scriptures and breaks the bread.

Therefore, Father most merciful,
we ask that you send forth your Holy Spirit
to sanctify these gifts of bread and wine,
that they may become for us
the Body and ✝ Blood
of our Lord Jesus Christ.

On the day before he was to suffer,
on the night of the Last Supper,
he took bread and said the blessing,
broke the bread and gave it to his disciples, saying:

Take this, all of you, and eat of it,
for this is my Body,
which will be given up for you.

In a similar way, when supper was ended,
he took the chalice, gave you thanks
and gave the chalice to his disciples, saying:

V2

Take this, all of you, and drink from it,
for this is the chalice of my Blood,
the Blood of the new and eternal covenant,
which will be poured out for you and for many
for the forgiveness of sins.

Do this in memory of me.

Priest: The mystery of faith. *(Memorial Acclamation)*

PEOPLE:

A We proclaim your Death, O Lord,
and profess your Resurrection
until you come again.

B When we eat this Bread and drink this Cup,
we proclaim your Death, O Lord,
until you come again.

C Save us, Savior of the world,
for by your Cross and Resurrection
you have set us free.

Therefore, holy Father,
as we celebrate the memorial of Christ your Son,
    our Savior,
whom you led through his Passion and Death on
    the Cross
to the glory of the Resurrection,
and whom you have seated at your right hand,
we proclaim the work of your love until he comes
    again
and we offer you the Bread of life
and the Chalice of blessing.

Look with favor on the oblation of your Church,
in which we show forth

V 2

the paschal Sacrifice of Christ that has been
handed on to us,
and grant that, by the power of the Spirit of your
love,
we may be counted now and until the day of
eternity
among the members of your Son,
in whose Body and Blood we have communion.

And so, having called us to your table, Lord,
confirm us in unity,
so that, together with N. our Pope and N. our
Bishop,
with all Bishops, Priests and Deacons,
and your entire people,
as we walk your ways with faith and hope,
we may strive to bring joy and trust into the world.

Remember our brothers and sisters (N. and N.),
who have fallen asleep in the peace of your Christ,
and all the dead, whose faith you alone have
known.
Admit them to rejoice in the light of your face,
and in the resurrection give them the fullness of
life.

Grant also to us,
when our earthly pilgrimage is done,
that we may come to an eternal dwelling place
and live with you for ever;
there, in communion with the Blessed Virgin Mary,
Mother of God,
with the Apostles and Martyrs,
(with Saint N.: the Saint of the day or Patron)

V 2

and with all the Saints,
we shall praise and exalt you
through Jesus Christ, your Son.

(Concluding Doxology)

Through him, and with him, and in him,
O God, almighty Father,
in the unity of the Holy Spirit,
all glory and honor is yours,
for ever and ever.

The people acclaim: **Amen.**

Continue with the Mass, as on p. 72.

V 3 EUCHARISTIC PRAYER FOR USE IN MASSES FOR VARIOUS NEEDS III

℣. The Lord be with you.
℟. **And with your spirit.**

℣. Lift up your hearts.
℟. **We lift them up to the Lord.**

℣. Let us give thanks to the Lord our God.
℟. **It is right and just.**

It is truly right and just, our duty and our
   salvation,
always and everywhere to give you thanks,
holy Father, Lord of heaven and earth,
through Christ our Lord.

For by your Word you created the world
and you govern all things in harmony.
You gave us the same Word made flesh as Mediator,
and he has spoken your words to us
and called us to follow him.
He is the way that leads us to you,
the truth that sets us free,
the life that fills us with gladness.

Through your Son
you gather men and women,
whom you made for the glory of your name,
into one family,
redeemed by the Blood of his Cross
and signed with the seal of the Spirit.

Therefore, now and for ages unending,
with all the Angels,

we proclaim your glory,
as in joyful celebration we acclaim:

Holy, Holy, Holy Lord God of hosts.
Heaven and earth are full of your glory.
Hosanna in the highest.
Blessed is he who comes in the name of the Lord.
Hosanna in the highest.

`KNEEL`

You are indeed Holy and to be glorified, O God,
who love the human race
and who always walk with us on the journey of life.
Blessed indeed is your Son,
present in our midst
when we are gathered by his love
and when, as once for the disciples, so now for us,
he opens the Scriptures and breaks the bread.

Therefore, Father most merciful,
we ask that you send forth your Holy Spirit
to sanctify these gifts of bread and wine,
that they may become for us
the Body and ✠ Blood
of our Lord Jesus Christ.

On the day before he was to suffer,
on the night of the Last Supper,
he took bread and said the blessing,
broke the bread and gave it to his disciples, saying:

Take this, all of you, and eat of it,
for this is my Body,
which will be given up for you.

**V
3**

In a similar way, when supper was ended,
he took the chalice, gave you thanks
and gave the chalice to his disciples, saying:

Take this, all of you, and drink from it,
for this is the chalice of my Blood,
the Blood of the new and eternal covenant,
which will be poured out for you and for many
for the forgiveness of sins.

Do this in memory of me.

Priest: The mystery of faith. *(Memorial Acclamation)*

PEOPLE:

A **We proclaim your Death, O Lord,**
    and profess your Resurrection
    until you come again.

B **When we eat this Bread and drink this Cup,**
    we proclaim your Death, O Lord,
    until you come again.

C **Save us, Savior of the world,**
    for by your Cross and Resurrection
    you have set us free.

Therefore, holy Father,
as we celebrate the memorial of Christ your Son,
    our Savior,
whom you led through his Passion and Death on
    the Cross
to the glory of the Resurrection,
and whom you have seated at your right hand,
we proclaim the work of your love until he comes
    again
and we offer you the Bread of life
and the Chalice of blessing.

V 3

Look with favor on the oblation of your Church,
in which we show forth
the paschal Sacrifice of Christ that has been
    handed on to us,
and grant that, by the power of the Spirit of your
    love,
we may be counted now and until the day of
    eternity
among the members of your Son,
in whose Body and Blood we have communion.

By our partaking of this mystery, almighty Father,
give us life through your Spirit,
grant that we may be conformed to the image of
    your Son,
and confirm us in the bond of communion,
together with N. our Pope and N. our Bishop,
with all other Bishops,
with Priests and Deacons,
and with your entire people.

Grant that all the faithful of the Church,
looking into the signs of the times by the light of
    faith,
may constantly devote themselves
to the service of the Gospel.

Keep us attentive to the needs of all
that, sharing their grief and pain,
their joy and hope,
we may faithfully bring them the good news of
    salvation
and go forward with them
along the way of your Kingdom.

**V
3**

Remember our brothers and sisters (*N.* and *N.*),
who have fallen asleep in the peace of your Christ,
and all the dead, whose faith you alone have known.
Admit them to rejoice in the light of your face,
and in the resurrection give them the fullness of life.

Grant also to us,
when our earthly pilgrimage is done,
that we may come to an eternal dwelling place
and live with you for ever;
there, in communion with the Blessed Virgin Mary,
    Mother of God,
with the Apostles and Martyrs,
(with Saint *N.*: the Saint of the day or Patron)
and with all the Saints,
we shall praise and exalt you
through Jesus Christ, your Son.

(Concluding Doxology)

Through him, and with him, and in him,
O God, almighty Father,
in the unity of the Holy Spirit,
all glory and honor is yours,
for ever and ever.

The people acclaim: **Amen.**

Continue with the Mass, as on p. 72.

EUCHARISTIC PRAYER FOR USE IN MASSES FOR VARIOUS NEEDS IV

V 4

STAND

℣. The Lord be with you.
℟. **And with your spirit.**

℣. Lift up your hearts.
℟. **We lift them up to the Lord.**

℣. Let us give thanks to the Lord our God.
℟. **It is right and just.**

It is truly right and just, our duty and our salvation,
always and everywhere to give you thanks,
Father of mercies and faithful God.

For you have given us Jesus Christ, your Son,
as our Lord and Redeemer.

He always showed compassion
for children and for the poor,
for the sick and for sinners,
and he became a neighbor
to the oppressed and the afflicted.

By word and deed he announced to the world
that you are our Father
and that you care for all your sons and daughters.

And so, with all the Angels and Saints,
we exalt and bless your name
and sing the hymn of your glory,
as without end we acclaim:

67

**V
4**

**Holy, Holy, Holy Lord God of hosts.
Heaven and earth are full of your glory.
Hosanna in the highest.
Blessed is he who comes in the name of the Lord.
Hosanna in the highest.**

`KNEEL`

You are indeed Holy and to be glorified, O God,
who love the human race
and who always walk with us on the journey of life.
Blessed indeed is your Son,
present in our midst
when we are gathered by his love
and when, as once for the disciples, so now for us,
he opens the Scriptures and breaks the bread.

Therefore, Father most merciful,
we ask that you send forth your Holy Spirit
to sanctify these gifts of bread and wine,
that they may become for us
the Body and ✠ Blood
of our Lord Jesus Christ.

On the day before he was to suffer,
on the night of the Last Supper,
he took bread and said the blessing,
broke the bread and gave it to his disciples, saying:

*Take this, all of you, and eat of it,
for this is my Body,
which will be given up for you.*

In a similar way, when supper was ended,
he took the chalice, gave you thanks
and gave the chalice to his disciples, saying:

V
4

Take this, all of you, and drink from it,
for this is the chalice of my Blood,
the Blood of the new and eternal covenant,
which will be poured out for you and for many
for the forgiveness of sins.

Do this in memory of me.

Priest: The mystery of faith. *(Memorial Acclamation)*

PEOPLE:

A We proclaim your Death, O Lord,
    and profess your Resurrection
    until you come again.

B When we eat this Bread and drink this Cup,
    we proclaim your Death, O Lord,
    until you come again.

C Save us, Savior of the world,
    for by your Cross and Resurrection
    you have set us free.

Therefore, holy Father,
as we celebrate the memorial of Christ your Son,
    our Savior,
whom you led through his Passion and Death on
    the Cross
to the glory of the Resurrection,
and whom you have seated at your right hand,
we proclaim the work of your love until he comes
    again
and we offer you the Bread of life
and the Chalice of blessing.

Look with favor on the oblation of your Church,
in which we show forth

V 4 the paschal Sacrifice of Christ that has been
handed on to us,
and grant that, by the power of the Spirit of your
love,
we may be counted now and until the day of
eternity
among the members of your Son,
in whose Body and Blood we have communion.

Bring your Church, O Lord,
to perfect faith and charity,
together with *N.* our Pope and *N.* our Bishop,
with all Bishops, Priests and Deacons,
and the entire people you have made your own.

Open our eyes
to the needs of our brothers and sisters;
inspire in us words and actions
to comfort those who labor and are burdened.
Make us serve them truly,
after the example of Christ and at his command.
And may your Church stand as a living witness
to truth and freedom,
to peace and justice,
that all people may be raised up to a new hope.

Remember our brothers and sisters (*N.* and *N.*),
who have fallen asleep in the peace of your Christ,
and all the dead, whose faith you alone have
known.
Admit them to rejoice in the light of your face,
and in the resurrection give them the fullness of
life.

V 4

Grant also to us,
when our earthly pilgrimage is done,
that we may come to an eternal dwelling place
and live with you for ever;
there, in communion with the Blessed Virgin Mary,
　Mother of God,
with the Apostles and Martyrs,
(with Saint *N.:* the Saint of the day or Patron)
and with all the Saints,
we shall praise and exalt you
through Jesus Christ, your Son.

(Concluding Doxology)

Through him, and with him, and in him,
O God, almighty Father,
in the unity of the Holy Spirit,
all glory and honor is yours,
for ever and ever.

The people acclaim: **Amen.**

Continue with the Mass, as on p. 72.

THE COMMUNION RITE

To prepare for the paschal meal, to welcome the Lord, we pray for forgiveness and exchange a sign of peace. Before eating Christ's Body and drinking his Blood, we must be one with him and with all our brothers and sisters in the Church.

24 THE LORD'S PRAYER `STAND`

Priest:　At the Savior's command
　　　　　and formed by divine teaching,
　　　　　we dare to say:

Priest and **PEOPLE:**

**Our Father, who art in heaven,
hallowed be thy name;
thy kingdom come,
thy will be done
on earth as it is in heaven.
Give us this day our daily bread,
and forgive us our trespasses,
as we forgive those who trespass against us;
and lead us not into temptation,
but deliver us from evil.**

Priest:　Deliver us, Lord, we pray, from every evil,
　　　　　graciously grant us peace in our days,
　　　　　that, by the help of your mercy,
　　　　　we may be always free from sin
　　　　　and safe from all distress,
　　　　　as we await the blessed hope
　　　　　and the coming of our Savior, Jesus Christ.

**PEOPLE: For the kingdom,
            the power and the glory are yours
            now and for ever.**

25 SIGN OF PEACE

The Church is a community of Christians joined by the Spirit in love. It needs to express, deepen, and restore its peaceful unity before eating the one Body of the Lord and drinking from the one cup of salvation. We do this by a sign of peace.

The Priest says the prayer for peace:

Lord Jesus Christ,
who said to your Apostles:
Peace I leave you, my peace I give you,
look not on our sins,
but on the faith of your Church,
and graciously grant her peace and unity
in accordance with your will.
Who live and reign for ever and ever.

PEOPLE: Amen.

Priest: The peace of the Lord be with you always.

PEOPLE: And with your spirit.

Deacon (or Priest):
  Let us offer each other the sign of peace.

The people exchange a sign of peace, communion and charity, according to local customs.

26 LAMB OF GOD

Christians are gathered for the "breaking of the bread," another name for the Mass. In Communion, though many we are made one body in the one bread, which is Christ.

The Priest breaks the host over the paten and places a small piece in the chalice, saying quietly:

May this mingling of the Body and Blood
of our Lord Jesus Christ
bring eternal life to us who receive it.

Meanwhile the following is sung or said:

PEOPLE:

> **Lamb of God, you take away the sins of the**
> **world,**
>> **have mercy on us.**
> **Lamb of God, you take away the sins of the**
> **world,**
>> **have mercy on us.**
> **Lamb of God, you take away the sins of the**
> **world,**
>> **grant us peace.**

The invocation may even be repeated several times if the breaking of the bread is prolonged. Only the final time, however, is grant us peace *said.*

KNEEL

We pray in silence and then voice words of humility and hope
as our final preparation before meeting Christ in the Eucharist.

Before Communion, the Priest says quietly one of the following prayers:

Lord Jesus Christ, Son of the living God,
who, by the will of the Father
and the work of the Holy Spirit,
through your Death gave life to the world,
free me by this, your most holy Body and Blood,
from all my sins and from every evil;
keep me always faithful to your commandments,
and never let me be parted from you.

———————— **OR** ————————

May the receiving of your Body and Blood,
Lord Jesus Christ,
not bring me to judgment and condemnation,
but through your loving mercy
be for me protection in mind and body
and a healing remedy.

27 INVITATION TO COMMUNION*

The Priest genuflects, takes the host and, holding it slightly raised above the paten or above the chalice, while facing the people, says aloud:

Priest: Behold the Lamb of God,
behold him who takes away the sins of the world.
Blessed are those called to the supper of the Lamb.

Priest and **PEOPLE** (once only):

**Lord, I am not worthy
that you should enter under my roof,
but only say the word
and my soul shall be healed.**

Before reverently consuming the Body of Christ, the Priest says quietly:

May the Body of Christ
keep me safe for eternal life.

Then, before reverently consuming the Blood of Christ, he takes the chalice and says quietly:

May the Blood of Christ
keep me safe for eternal life.

* *See Guidelines on pp. 664-665.*

28 COMMUNION

He then gives Communion to the people.

Priest: The Body of Christ. Communicant: **Amen.**
Priest: The Blood of Christ. Communicant: **Amen.**

The Communion Psalm or other appropriate chant is sung while Communion is given to the faithful. If there is no singing, the Communion Antiphon is said.

→ **Turn to Today's Mass**

The vessels are purified by the Priest or Deacon or acolyte. Meanwhile he says quietly:

What has passed our lips as food, O Lord,
may we possess in purity of heart,
that what has been given to us in time
may be our healing for eternity.

After Communion there may be a period of sacred silence, or a canticle of praise or a hymn may be sung.

29 PRAYER AFTER COMMUNION   STAND

The Priest prays in our name that we may live the life of faith since we have been strengthened by Christ himself. Our *Amen* makes his prayer our own.

Priest: Let us pray.

Priest and people may pray silently for a while unless silence has just been observed. Then the Priest says the Prayer after Communion.

→ **Turn to Today's Mass**

At the end, **PEOPLE: Amen.**

THE CONCLUDING RITES

We have heard God's Word and eaten the Body of Christ. Now it is time for us to leave, to do good works, to praise and bless the Lord in our daily lives.

30 SOLEMN BLESSING `STAND`

After any brief announcements, the Blessing and Dismissal follow:

Priest: The Lord be with you.

PEOPLE: And with your spirit.

31 FINAL BLESSING

Priest: May almighty God bless you,
the Father, and the Son, ✝ and the Holy Spirit.

PEOPLE: Amen.

On certain days or occasions, this formula of blessing is preceded, in accordance with the rubrics, by another more solemn formula of blessing (pp. 97-105) or by a prayer over the people (pp. 105-110).

32 DISMISSAL

Deacon (or Priest):

A Go forth, the Mass is ended.

B Go and announce the Gospel of the Lord.

C Go in peace, glorifying the Lord by your life.

D Go in peace.

PEOPLE: Thanks be to God.

If any liturgical service follows immediately, the rites of dismissal are omitted.

RITE FOR THE BLESSING
AND SPRINKLING OF WATER

If this rite is celebrated during Mass, it takes the place of the usual Penitential Act at the beginning of Mass.

After the greeting, the Priest stands at his chair and faces the people. With a vessel containing the water to be blessed before him, he calls upon the people to pray in these or similar words:

Dear brethren (brothers and sisters),
let us humbly beseech the Lord our God
to bless this water he has created,
which will be sprinkled on us
as a memorial of our Baptism.
May he help us by his grace
to remain faithful to the Spirit we have received.

And after a brief pause for silence, he continues with hands joined:

Almighty ever-living God,
who willed that through water,
the fountain of life and the source of purification,
even souls should be cleansed
and receive the gift of eternal life;
be pleased, we pray, to ✢ bless this water,
by which we seek protection on this your day, O Lord.
Renew the living spring of your grace within us
and grant that by this water we may be defended
from all ills of spirit and body,
and so approach you with hearts made clean
and worthily receive your salvation.
Through Christ our Lord. ℟. **Amen.**

Or:

Almighty Lord and God,
who are the source and origin of all life,

whether of body or soul,
we ask you to ✝ bless this water,
which we use in confidence
to implore forgiveness for our sins
and to obtain the protection of your grace
against all illness and every snare of the enemy.
Grant, O Lord, in your mercy,
that living waters may always spring up for our
    salvation,
and so may we approach you with a pure heart
and avoid all danger to body and soul.
Through Christ our Lord. ℟. **Amen.**

Or (during Easter Time):

Lord our God,
in your mercy be present to your people's prayers,
and, for us who recall the wondrous work of our creation
and the still greater work of our redemption,
graciously ✝ bless this water.
For you created water to make the fields fruitful
and to refresh and cleanse our bodies.
You also made water the instrument of your mercy:
for through water you freed your people from slavery
and quenched their thirst in the desert;
through water the Prophets proclaimed the new
    covenant
you were to enter upon with the human race;
and last of all,
through water, which Christ made holy in the Jordan,
you have renewed our corrupted nature
in the bath of regeneration.
Therefore, may this water be for us
a memorial of the Baptism we have received,
and grant that we may share
in the gladness of our brothers and sisters
who at Easter have received their Baptism.
Through Christ our Lord. ℟. **Amen.**

Where the circumstances of the place or the custom of the people suggest that the mixing of salt be preserved in the blessing of water, the Priest may bless salt, saying:

We humbly ask you, almighty God:
be pleased in your faithful love to bless ✠ this salt
you have created,
for it was you who commanded the prophet Elisha
to cast salt into water,
that impure water might be purified.
Grant, O Lord, we pray,
that, wherever this mixture of salt and water is sprinkled,
every attack of the enemy may be repulsed
and your Holy Spirit may be present
to keep us safe at all times.
Through Christ our Lord. ℟. **Amen.**

Then he pours the salt into the water, without saying anything.

Afterward, taking the aspergillum, the Priest sprinkles himself and the ministers, then the clergy and people, moving through the church, if appropriate.

Meanwhile, one of the following chants, or another appropriate chant is sung.

Outside Easter Time

ANTIPHON 1 Ps 51 (50):9

Sprinkle me with hyssop, O Lord, and I shall be cleansed; wash me and I shall be whiter than snow.

ANTIPHON 2 Ez 36:25-26

I will pour clean water upon you, and you will be made clean of all your impurities, and I shall give you a new spirit, says the Lord.

HYMN Cf. 1 Pt 1:3-5

Blessed be the God and Father of our Lord Jesus Christ, who in his great mercy has given us new birth into a living hope through the Resurrection of Jesus Christ from

the dead, into an inheritance that will not perish, preserved for us in heaven for the salvation to be revealed in the last time!

During Easter Time

ANTIPHON 1 Cf. Ez 47:1-2, 9

I saw water flowing from the Temple, from its right-hand side, alleluia: and all to whom this water came were saved and shall say: Alleluia, alleluia.

ANTIPHON 2 Cf. Zeph 3:8; Ez 36:25

On the day of my resurrection, says the Lord, alleluia, I will gather the nations and assemble the kingdoms and I will pour clean water upon you, alleluia.

ANTIPHON 3 Cf. Dn 3:77, 79

You springs and all that moves in the waters, sing a hymn to God, alleluia.

ANTIPHON 4 1 Pt 2:9

O chosen race, royal priesthood, holy nation, proclaim the mighty works of him who called you out of darkness into his wonderful light, alleluia.

ANTIPHON 5

From your side, O Christ, bursts forth a spring of water, by which the squalor of the world is washed away and life is made new again, alleluia.

When he returns to his chair and the singing is over, the Priest stands facing the people and, with hands joined, says:

May almighty God cleanse us of our sins,
and through the celebration of this Eucharist
make us worthy to share at the table of his Kingdom.
℟. **Amen**.

Then, when it is prescribed, the hymn Gloria in excelsis *(*Glory to God in the highest*) is sung or said.*

PREFACES

PREFACE I OF ADVENT (P 1)

The two comings of Christ

(From the First Sunday of Advent to December 16)

It is truly right and just, our duty and our salvation,
always and everywhere to give you thanks,
Lord, holy Father, almighty and eternal God,
through Christ our Lord.

For he assumed at his first coming
the lowliness of human flesh,
and so fulfilled the design you formed long ago,
and opened for us the way to eternal salvation,
that, when he comes again in glory and majesty
and all is at last made manifest,
we who watch for that day
may inherit the great promise
in which now we dare to hope.

And so, with Angels and Archangels,
with Thrones and Dominions,
and with all the hosts and Powers of heaven,
we sing the hymn of your glory,
as without end we acclaim:
→ No. 23, p. 23

PREFACE II OF ADVENT (P 2)

The twofold expectation of Christ

(From December 17 to December 24)

It is truly right and just, our duty and our salvation,
always and everywhere to give you thanks,
Lord, holy Father, almighty and eternal God,
through Christ our Lord.

For all the oracles of the prophets foretold him,
the Virgin Mother longed for him
with love beyond all telling,

John the Baptist sang of his coming
and proclaimed his presence when he came.

It is by his gift that already we rejoice
at the mystery of his Nativity,
so that he may find us watchful in prayer
and exultant in his praise.

And so, with Angels and Archangels,
with Thrones and Dominions,
and with all the hosts and Powers of heaven,
we sing the hymn of your glory,
as without end we acclaim: ➟ No. 23, p. 23

PREFACE I OF THE NATIVITY OF THE LORD (P 3)
Christt the Light
(For the Nativity of the Lord, its Octave Day and within the Octave)

It is truly right and just, our duty and our salvation,
always and everywhere to give you thanks,
Lord, holy Father, almighty and eternal God.

For in the mystery of the Word made flesh
a new light of your glory has shone upon the eyes of our
    mind,
so that, as we recognize in him God made visible,
we may be caught up through him in love of things invisible.

And so, with Angels and Archangels,
with Thrones and Dominions,
and with all the hosts and Powers of heaven,
we sing the hymn of your glory,
as without end we acclaim: ➟ No. 23, p. 23

PREFACE II OF THE NATIVITY OF THE LORD (P 4)
The restoration of all things in the Incarnation
(For the Nativity of the Lord, its Octave Day and within the Octave)

It is truly right and just, our duty and our salvation,
always and everywhere to give you thanks,
Lord, holy Father, almighty and eternal God,
through Christ our Lord.

For on the feast of this awe-filled mystery,
though invisible in his own divine nature,

he has appeared visibly in ours;
and begotten before all ages,
he has begun to exist in time;
so that, raising up in himself all that was cast down,
he might restore unity to all creation
and call straying humanity back to the heavenly Kingdom.

And so, with all the Angels, we praise you,
as in joyful celebration we acclaim: ➙ No. 23, p. 23

PREFACE III OF THE NATIVITY OF THE LORD (P 5)

The exchange in the Incarnation of the Word

(For the Nativity of the Lord, its Octave Day and within the Octave)

It is truly right and just, our duty and our salvation,
always and everywhere to give you thanks,
Lord, holy Father, almighty and eternal God,
through Christ our Lord.

For through him the holy exchange that restores our life
has shone forth today in splendor:
when our frailty is assumed by your Word
not only does human mortality receive unending honor
but by this wondrous union we, too, are made eternal.

And so, in company with the choirs of Angels,
we praise you, and with joy we proclaim: ➙ No. 23, p. 23

PREFACE I OF LENT (P 8)

The spiritual meaning of Lent

It is truly right and just, our duty and our salvation,
always and everywhere to give you thanks,
Lord, holy Father, almighty and eternal God,
through Christ our Lord.

For by your gracious gift each year
your faithful await the sacred paschal feasts
with the joy of minds made pure,
so that, more eagerly intent on prayer
and on the works of charity,
and participating in the mysteries
by which they have been reborn,

they may be led to the fullness of grace
that you bestow on your sons and daughters.

And so, with Angels and Archangels,
with Thrones and Dominions,
and with all the hosts and Powers of heaven,
we sing the hymn of your glory,
as without end we acclaim: ➜ No. 23, p. 23

PREFACE II OF LENT (P 9)
Spiritual penance

It is truly right and just, our duty and our salvation,
always and everywhere to give you thanks,
Lord, holy Father, almighty and eternal God.

For you have given your children a sacred time
for the renewing and purifying of their hearts,
that, freed from disordered affections,
they may so deal with the things of this passing world
as to hold rather to the things that eternally endure.

And so, with all the Angels and Saints,
we praise you, as without end we acclaim: ➜ No. 23, p. 23

PREFACE I OF EASTER I (P 21)
The Paschal Mystery

(At the Easter Vigil, is said "on this night"; on Easter Sunday and throughout the Octave of Easter, is said "on this day"; on other days of Easter Time, is said "in this time.")

It is truly right and just, our duty and our salvation,
at all times to acclaim you, O Lord,
but (on this night / on this day / in this time) above all
to laud you yet more gloriously,
when Christ our Passover has been sacrificed.

For he is the true Lamb
who has taken away the sins of the world;
by dying he has destroyed our death,
and by rising, restored our life.

Therefore, overcome with paschal joy,
every land, every people exults in your praise
and even the heavenly Powers, with the angelic hosts,
sing together the unending hymn of your glory,
as they acclaim: ➜ No. 23, p. 23

PREFACE II OF EASTER (P 22)
New life in Christ

It is truly right and just, our duty and our salvation,
at all times to acclaim you, O Lord,
but in this time above all to laud you yet more gloriously,
when Christ our Passover has been sacrificed.

Through him the children of light rise to eternal life
and the halls of the heavenly Kingdom
are thrown open to the faithful;
for his Death is our ransom from death,
and in his rising the life of all has risen.

Therefore, overcome with paschal joy,
every land, every people exults in your praise
and even the heavenly Powers, with the angelic hosts,
sing together the unending hymn of your glory,
as they acclaim: ➜ No. 23, p. 23

PREFACE III OF EASTER (P 23)
Christ living and always interceding for us

It is truly right and just, our duty and our salvation,
at all times to acclaim you, O Lord,
but in this time above all to laud you yet more gloriously,
when Christ our Passover has been sacrificed.

He never ceases to offer himself for us
but defends us and ever pleads our cause before you:
he is the sacrificial Victim who dies no more,
the Lamb, once slain, who lives for ever.

Therefore, overcome with paschal joy,
every land, every people exults in your praise
and even the heavenly Powers, with the angelic hosts,
sing together the unending hymn of your glory,
as they acclaim: ➜ No. 23, p. 23

PREFACE IV OF EASTER (P 24)
The restoration of the universe through the Paschal Mystery

It is truly right and just, our duty and our salvation,
at all times to acclaim you, O Lord,

but in this time above all to laud you yet more gloriously,
when Christ our Passover has been sacrificed.

For, with the old order destroyed,
a universe cast down is renewed,
and integrity of life is restored to us in Christ.

Therefore, overcome with paschal joy,
every land, every people exults in your praise
and even the heavenly Powers, with the angelic hosts,
sing together the unending hymn of your glory,
as they acclaim: → No. 23, p. 23

PREFACE V OF EASTER (P 25)
Christ, Priest and Victim

It is truly right and just, our duty and our salvation,
at all times to acclaim you, O Lord,
but in this time above all to laud you yet more gloriously,
when Christ our Passover has been sacrificed.

By the oblation of his Body,
he brought the sacrifices of old to fulfillment
in the reality of the Cross
and, by commending himself to you for our salvation,
showed himself the Priest, the Altar, and the Lamb of
    sacrifice.

Therefore, overcome with paschal joy,
every land, every people exults in your praise
and even the heavenly Powers, with the angelic hosts,
sing together the unending hymn of your glory,
as they acclaim: → No. 23, p. 23

PREFACE I OF THE ASCENSION OF THE LORD (P 26)
The mystery of the Ascension
(Ascension to the Saturday before Pentecost inclusive)

It is truly right and just, our duty and our salvation,
always and everywhere to give you thanks,
Lord, holy Father, almighty and eternal God.

For the Lord Jesus, the King of glory,
conqueror of sin and death,

ascended (today) to the highest heavens,
as the Angels gazed in wonder.

Mediator between God and man,
judge of the world and Lord of hosts,
he ascended, not to distance himself from our lowly state
but that we, his members, might be confident of following
where he, our Head and Founder, has gone before.

Therefore, overcome with paschal joy,
every land, every people exults in your praise
and even the heavenly Powers, with the angelic hosts,
sing together the unending hymn of your glory,
as they acclaim: ➜ No. 23, p. 23

PREFACE II OF THE ASCENSION OF THE LORD (P 27)

The mystery of the Ascension
(Ascension to the Saturday before Pentecost inclusive)

It is truly right and just, our duty and our salvation,
always and everywhere to give you thanks,
Lord, holy Father, almighty and eternal God,
through Christ our Lord.

For after his Resurrection
he plainly appeared to all his disciples
and was taken up to heaven in their sight,
that he might make us sharers in his divinity.

Therefore, overcome with paschal joy,
every land, every people exults in your praise
and even the heavenly Powers, with the angelic hosts,
sing together the unending hymn of your glory,
as they acclaim: ➜ No. 23, p. 23

PREFACE I OF THE SUNDAYS IN ORDINARY TIME (P 29)

The Paschal Mystery and the People of God

It is truly right and just, our duty and our salvation,
always and everywhere to give you thanks,
Lord, holy Father, almighty and eternal God,
through Christ our Lord.

For through his Paschal Mystery,
he accomplished the marvelous deed,

by which he has freed us from the yoke of sin and death,
summoning us to the glory of being now called
a chosen race, a royal priesthood,
a holy nation, a people for your own possession,
to proclaim everywhere your mighty works,
for you have called us out of darkness
into your own wonderful light.

And so, with Angels and Archangels,
with Thrones and Dominions,
and with all the hosts and Powers of heaven,
we sing the hymn of your glory,
as without end we acclaim: → No. 23, p. 23

PREFACE II OF THE SUNDAYS IN ORDINARY TIME (P 30)

The mystery of salvation

It is truly right and just, our duty and our salvation,
always and everywhere to give you thanks,
Lord, holy Father, almighty and eternal God,
through Christ our Lord.

For out of compassion for the waywardness that is ours,
he humbled himself and was born of the Virgin;
by the passion of the Cross he freed us from unending death,
and by rising from the dead he gave us life eternal.

And so, with Angels and Archangels,
with Thrones and Dominions,
and with all the hosts and Powers of heaven,
we sing the hymn of your glory,
as without end we acclaim: → No. 23, p. 23

PREFACE III OF THE SUNDAYS IN ORDINARY TIME (P 31)

The salvation of man by a man

It is truly right and just, our duty and our salvation,
always and everywhere to give you thanks,
Lord, holy Father, almighty and eternal God.

For we know it belongs to your boundless glory,
that you came to the aid of mortal beings with your divinity
and even fashioned for us a remedy out of mortality itself,
that the cause of our downfall

might become the means of our salvation,
through Christ our Lord.

Through him the host of Angels adores your majesty
and rejoices in your presence for ever.
May our voices, we pray, join with theirs
in one chorus of exultant praise, as we acclaim:
→ No. 23, p. 23

PREFACE IV OF THE SUNDAYS IN ORDINARY TIME (P 32)
The history of salvation

It is truly right and just, our duty and our salvation,
always and everywhere to give you thanks,
Lord, holy Father, almighty and eternal God,
through Christ our Lord.

For by his birth he brought renewal
to humanity's fallen state,
and by his suffering, canceled out our sins;
by his rising from the dead
he has opened the way to eternal life,
and by ascending to you, O Father,
he has unlocked the gates of heaven.

And so, with the company of Angels and Saints,
we sing the hymn of your praise,
as without end we acclaim:
→ No. 23, p. 23

PREFACE V OF THE SUNDAYS IN ORDINARY TIME (P 33)
Creation

It is truly right and just, our duty and our salvation,
always and everywhere to give you thanks,
Lord, holy Father, almighty and eternal God.

For you laid the foundations of the world
and have arranged the changing of times and seasons;
you formed man in your own image
and set humanity over the whole world in all its wonder,
to rule in your name over all you have made
and for ever praise you in your mighty works,
through Christ our Lord.

And so, with all the Angels, we praise you,
as in joyful celebration we acclaim: ➙ No. 23, p. 23

PREFACE VI OF THE SUNDAYS IN ORDINARY TIME (P 34)

The pledge of the eternal Passover

It is truly right and just, our duty and our salvation,
always and everywhere to give you thanks,
Lord, holy Father, almighty and eternal God.

For in you we live and move and have our being,
and while in this body
we not only experience the daily effects of your care,
but even now possess the pledge of life eternal.

For, having received the first fruits of the Spirit,
through whom you raised up Jesus from the dead,
we hope for an everlasting share in the Paschal Mystery.

And so, with all the Angels, we praise you,
as in joyful celebration we acclaim: ➙ No. 23, p. 23

PREFACE VII OF THE SUNDAYS IN ORDINARY TIME (P 35)

Salvation through the obedience of Christ

It is truly right and just, our duty and our salvation,
always and everywhere to give you thanks,
Lord, holy Father, almighty and eternal God.

For you so loved the world
that in your mercy you sent us the Redeemer,
to live like us in all things but sin,
so that you might love in us what you loved in your Son,
by whose obedience we have been restored to those gifts
   of yours
that, by sinning, we had lost in disobedience.

And so, Lord, with all the Angels and Saints,
we, too, give you thanks, as in exultation we acclaim:
➙ No. 23, p. 23

PREFACE VIII OF THE SUNDAYS IN ORDINARY TIME (P 36)

The Church united by the unity of the Trinity

It is truly right and just, our duty and our salvation,
always and everywhere to give you thanks,
Lord, holy Father, almighty and eternal God.

For, when your children were scattered afar by sin,
through the Blood of your Son and the power of the Spirit,
you gathered them again to yourself,
that a people, formed as one by the unity of the Trinity,
made the body of Christ and the temple of the Holy Spirit,
might, to the praise of your manifold wisdom,
be manifest as the Church.

And so, in company with the choirs of Angels,
we praise you, and with joy we proclaim: → No. 23, p. 23

PREFACE I OF THE MOST HOLY EUCHARIST (P 47)
The Sacrifice and the Sacrament of Christ

It is truly right and just, our duty and our salvation,
always and everywhere to give you thanks,
Lord, holy Father, almighty and eternal God,
through Christ our Lord.

For he is the true and eternal Priest,
who instituted the pattern of an everlasting sacrifice
and was the first to offer himself as the saving Victim,
commanding us to make this offering as his memorial.
As we eat his flesh that was sacrificed for us,
we are made strong,
and, as we drink his Blood that was poured out for us,
we are washed clean.

And so, with Angels and Archangels,
with Thrones and Dominions,
and with all the hosts and Powers of heaven,
we sing the hymn of your glory,
as without end we acclaim: → No. 23, p. 23

PREFACE II OF THE MOST HOLY EUCHARIST (P 48)
The fruits of the Most Holy Eucharist

It is truly right and just, our duty and our salvation,
always and everywhere to give you thanks,
Lord, holy Father, almighty and eternal God,
through Christ our Lord.

For at the Last Supper with his Apostles,
establishing for the ages to come the saving memorial of
the Cross,
he offered himself to you as the unblemished Lamb,
the acceptable gift of perfect praise.

Nourishing your faithful by this sacred mystery,
you make them holy, so that the human race,
bounded by one world,
may be enlightened by one faith
and united by one bond of charity.

And so, we approach the table of this wondrous Sacrament,
so that, bathed in the sweetness of your grace,
we may pass over to the heavenly realities here foreshadowed.

Therefore, all creatures of heaven and earth
sing a new song in adoration,
and we, with all the host of Angels,
cry out, and without end we acclaim: → No. 23, p. 23

PREFACE I FOR THE DEAD (P 77)
The hope of resurrection in Christ

It is truly right and just, our duty and our salvation,
always and everywhere to give you thanks,
Lord, holy Father, almighty and eternal God,
through Christ our Lord.

In him the hope of blessed resurrection has dawned,
that those saddened by the certainty of dying
might be consoled by the promise of immortality to come.
Indeed for your faithful, Lord,
life is changed not ended,
and, when this earthly dwelling turns to dust,
an eternal dwelling is made ready for them in heaven.

And so, with Angels and Archangels,
with Thrones and Dominions,
and with all the hosts and Powers of heaven,
we sing the hymn of your glory,
as without end we acclaim: → No. 23, p. 23

PREFACE II FOR THE DEAD (P 78)
Christ died so that we might live

It is truly right and just, our duty and our salvation,
always and everywhere to give you thanks,
Lord, holy Father, almighty and eternal God,
through Christ our Lord.

For as one alone he accepted death,
so that we might all escape from dying;
as one man he chose to die,
so that in your sight we all might live for ever.

And so, in company with the choirs of Angels,
we praise you, and with joy we proclaim: → No. 23, p. 23

PREFACE III FOR THE DEAD (P 79)
Christ, the salvation and the life

It is truly right and just, our duty and our salvation,
always and everywhere to give you thanks,
Lord, holy Father, almighty and eternal God,
through Christ our Lord.

For he is the salvation of the world,
the life of the human race,
the resurrection of the dead.

Through him the host of Angels adores your majesty
and rejoices in your presence for ever.
May our voices, we pray, join with theirs
in one chorus of exultant praise, as we acclaim:
→ No. 23, p. 23

PREFACE IV FOR THE DEAD (P 80)
From earthly life to heavenly glory

It is truly right and just, our duty and our salvation,
always and everywhere to give you thanks,
Lord, holy Father, almighty and eternal God.

For it is at your summons that we come to birth,
by your will that we are governed,
and at your command that we return,
on account of sin,
to that earth from which we came.

And when you give the sign,
we who have been redeemed by the Death of your Son,
shall be raised up to the glory of his Resurrection.

And so, with the company of Angels and Saints,
we sing the hymn of your praise,
as without end we acclaim: ➙ No. 23, p. 23

PREFACE V FOR THE DEAD (P 81)
Our resurrection through the victory of Christ

It is truly right and just, our duty and our salvation,
always and everywhere to give you thanks,
Lord, holy Father, almighty and eternal God.

For even though by our own fault we perish,
yet by your compassion and your grace,
when seized by death according to our sins,
we are redeemed through Christ's great victory,
and with him called back into life.

And so, with the Powers of heaven,
we worship you constantly on earth,
and before your majesty
without end we acclaim: ➙ No. 23, p. 23

PROPER COMMUNICANTES AND HANC IGITUR

FOR EUCHARISTIC PRAYER I (THE ROMAN CANON)

Communicantes for the Nativity of the Lord and throughout the Octave

Celebrating the most sacred night (day)
on which blessed Mary the immaculate Virgin
brought forth the Savior for this world,
and in communion with those whose memory we venerate,
especially the glorious ever-Virgin Mary,
Mother of our God and Lord, Jesus Christ,† etc., p. 25.

Communicantes for the Epiphany of the Lord

Celebrating the most sacred day
on which your Only Begotten Son,
eternal with you in your glory,
appeared in a human body, truly sharing our flesh,

and in communion with those whose memory we venerate,
especially the glorious ever-Virgin Mary,
Mother of our God and Lord, Jesus Christ,† etc., p. 25.

Communicantes for Easter

Celebrating the most sacred night (day)
of the Resurrection of our Lord Jesus Christ in the flesh,
and in communion with those whose memory we venerate,
especially the glorious ever-Virgin Mary,
Mother of our God and Lord, Jesus Christ,† etc., p. 25.

Hanc Igitur for the Easter Vigil
until the Second Sunday of Easter

Therefore, Lord, we pray:
graciously accept this oblation of our service,
that of your whole family,
which we make to you
also for those to whom you have been pleased to give
the new birth of water and the Holy Spirit,
granting them forgiveness of all their sins;
order our days in your peace,
and command that we be delivered from eternal damnation
and counted among the flock of those you have chosen.
(Through Christ our Lord. Amen.)   ➔ *Canon*, p. 25.

Communicantes for the Ascension of the Lord

Celebrating the most sacred day
on which your Only Begotten Son, our Lord,
placed at the right hand of your glory
our weak human nature,
which he had united to himself,
and in communion with those whose memory we venerate,
especially the glorious ever-Virgin Mary,
Mother of our God and Lord, Jesus Christ,† etc., p. 25.

Communicantes for Pentecost Sunday

Celebrating the most sacred day of Pentecost,
on which the Holy Spirit
appeared to the Apostles in tongues of fire,
and in communion with those whose memory we venerate,
especially the glorious ever-Virgin Mary,
Mother of our God and Lord, Jesus Christ,† etc., p. 25.

BLESSINGS AT THE END OF MASS AND PRAYERS OVER THE PEOPLE

SOLEMN BLESSINGS

The following blessings may be used, at the discretion of the Priest, at the end of the celebration of Mass, or of a Liturgy of the Word, or of the Office, or of the Sacraments.

The Deacon or, in his absence, the Priest himself, says the invitation: Bow down for the blessing. *Then the Priest, with hands extended over the people, says the blessing, with all responding:* **Amen**.

I. For Celebrations in the Different Liturgical Times

1. ADVENT

May the almighty and merciful God,
by whose grace you have placed your faith
in the First Coming of his Only Begotten Son
and yearn for his coming again,
sanctify you by the radiance of Christ's Advent
and enrich you with his blessing. ℟. **Amen.**

As you run the race of this present life,
may he make you firm in faith,
joyful in hope and active in charity. ℟. **Amen.**

So that, rejoicing now with devotion
at the Redeemer's coming in the flesh,
you may be endowed with the rich reward of eternal life
when he comes again in majesty. ℟. **Amen.**

And may the blessing of almighty God,
the Father, and the Son, ✠ and the Holy Spirit,
come down on you and remain with you for ever. ℟. **Amen.**

2. THE NATIVITY OF THE LORD

May the God of infinite goodness,
who by the Incarnation of his Son has driven darkness from the world
and by that glorious Birth has illumined this most holy night (day),
drive far from you the darkness of vice
and illumine your hearts with the light of virtue. ℟. **Amen.**

97

May God, who willed that the great joy
of his Son's saving Birth
be announced to shepherds by the Angel,
fill your minds with the gladness he gives
and make you heralds of his Gospel. ℟. **Amen.**

And may God, who by the Incarnation
brought together the earthly and heavenly realm,
fill you with the gift of his peace and favor
and make you sharers with the Church in heaven. ℟. **Amen.**

And may the blessing of almighty God,
the Father, and the Son, ✛ and the Holy Spirit,
come down on you and remain with you for ever. ℟. **Amen.**

3. THE BEGINNING OF THE YEAR

May God, the source and origin of all blessing,
grant you grace,
pour out his blessing in abundance,
and keep you safe from harm throughout the year. ℟. **Amen.**

May he give you integrity in the faith,
endurance in hope,
and perseverance in charity
with holy patience to the end. ℟. **Amen.**

May he order your days and your deeds in his peace,
grant your prayers in this and in every place,
and lead you happily to eternal life. ℟. **Amen.**

And may the blessing of almighty God,
the Father, and the Son, ✛ and the Holy Spirit,
come down on you and remain with you for ever. ℟. **Amen.**

4. THE EPIPHANY OF THE LORD

May God, who has called you
out of darkness into his wonderful light,
pour out in kindness his blessing upon you
and make your hearts firm
in faith, hope and charity. ℟. **Amen.**

And since in all confidence you follow Christ,
who today appeared in the world
as a light shining in darkness,

may God make you, too,
a light for your brothers and sisters. ℞. **Amen.**

And so when your pilgrimage is ended,
may you come to him
whom the Magi sought as they followed the star
and whom they found with great joy, the Light from Light,
who is Christ the Lord. ℞. **Amen.**

And may the blessing of almighty God,
the Father, and the Son, ✠ and the Holy Spirit,
come down on you and remain with you for ever. ℞. **Amen.**

5. THE PASSION OF THE LORD

May God, the Father of mercies,
who has given you an example of love
in the Passion of his Only Begotten Son,
grant that, by serving God and your neighbor,
you may lay hold of the wondrous gift of his blessing.
  ℞. **Amen.**

So that you may receive the reward of everlasting life from
  him,
through whose earthly Death
you believe that you escape eternal death. ℞. **Amen.**

And by following the example of his self-abasement,
may you possess a share in his Resurrection. ℞. **Amen.**

And may the blessing of almighty God,
the Father, and the Son, ✠ and the Holy Spirit,
come down on you and remain with you for ever. ℞. **Amen.**

6. EASTER TIME

May God, who by the Resurrection of his Only Begotten Son
was pleased to confer on you
the gift of redemption and of adoption,
give you gladness by his blessing. ℞. **Amen.**

May he, by whose redeeming work
you have received the gift of everlasting freedom,
make you heirs to an eternal inheritance. ℞. **Amen.**

And may you, who have already risen with Christ
in Baptism through faith,

by living in a right manner on this earth,
be united with him in the homeland of heaven. ℟. **Amen.**

And may the blessing of almighty God,
the Father, and the Son, ✚ and the Holy Spirit,
come down on you and remain with you for ever. ℟. **Amen.**

7. THE ASCENSION OF THE LORD

May almighty God bless you,
for on this very day his Only Begotten Son
pierced the heights of heaven
and unlocked for you the way
to ascend to where he is. ℟. **Amen.**

May he grant that,
as Christ after his Resurrection
was seen plainly by his disciples,
so when he comes as Judge
he may show himself merciful to you for all eternity.
℟. **Amen.**

And may you, who believe he is seated
with the Father in his majesty,
know with joy the fulfillment of his promise
to stay with you until the end of time. ℟. **Amen.**

And may the blessing of almighty God,
the Father, and the Son, ✚ and the Holy Spirit,
come down on you and remain with you for ever. ℟. **Amen.**

8. THE HOLY SPIRIT

May God, the Father of lights,
who was pleased to enlighten the disciples' minds
by the outpouring of the Spirit, the Paraclete,
grant you gladness by his blessing
and make you always abound with the gifts of the same
Spirit. ℟. **Amen.**

May the wondrous flame that appeared above the disciples,
powerfully cleanse your hearts from every evil
and pervade them with its purifying light. ℟. **Amen.**

And may God, who has been pleased to unite many
tongues

in the profession of one faith,
give you perseverance in that same faith
and, by believing, may you journey from hope to clear
    vision. ℟. **Amen.**

And may the blessing of almighty God,
the Father, and the Son, ✠ and the Holy Spirit,
come down on you and remain with you for ever. ℟. **Amen.**

9. ORDINARY TIME I

May the Lord bless you and keep you. ℟. **Amen.**

May he let his face shine upon you
and show you his mercy. ℟. **Amen.**

May he turn his countenance towards you
and give you his peace. ℟. **Amen.**

And may the blessing of almighty God,
the Father, and the Son, ✠ and the Holy Spirit,
come down on you and remain with you for ever. ℟. **Amen.**

10. ORDINARY TIME II

May the peace of God,
which surpasses all understanding,
keep your hearts and minds
in the knowledge and love of God,
and of his Son, our Lord Jesus Christ. ℟. **Amen.**

And may the blessing of almighty God,
the Father, and the Son, ✠ and the Holy Spirit,
come down on you and remain with you for ever. ℟. **Amen.**

11. ORDINARY TIME III

May almighty God bless you in his kindness
and pour out saving wisdom upon you. ℟. **Amen.**

May he nourish you always with the teachings of the faith
and make you persevere in holy deeds. ℟. **Amen.**

May he turn your steps towards himself
and show you the path of charity and peace. ℟. **Amen.**

And may the blessing of almighty God,
the Father, and the Son, ✚ and the Holy Spirit,
come down on you and remain with you for ever. ℟. **Amen.**

12. ORDINARY TIME IV

May the God of all consolation order your days in his peace
and grant you the gifts of his blessing. ℟. **Amen.**

May he free you always from every distress
and confirm your hearts in his love. ℟. **Amen.**

So that on this life's journey
you may be effective in good works,
rich in the gifts of hope, faith and charity,
and may come happily to eternal life. ℟. **Amen.**

And may the blessing of almighty God,
the Father, and the Son, ✚ and the Holy Spirit,
come down on you and remain with you for ever. ℟. **Amen.**

13. ORDINARY TIME V

May almighty God always keep every adversity far from you
and in his kindness pour out upon you the gifts of his
      blessing. ℟. **Amen.**

May God keep your hearts attentive to his words,
that they may be filled with everlasting gladness. ℟. **Amen.**

And so, may you always understand what is good and right,
and be found ever hastening along
in the path of God's commands,
made coheirs with the citizens of heaven. ℟. **Amen.**

And may the blessing of almighty God,
the Father, and the Son, ✚ and the Holy Spirit,
come down on you and remain with you for ever. ℟. **Amen.**

14. ORDINARY TIME VI

May God bless you with every heavenly blessing,
make you always holy and pure in his sight,
pour out in abundance upon you the riches of his glory,
and teach you with the words of truth;
may he instruct you in the Gospel of salvation,
and ever endow you with fraternal charity.
Through Christ our Lord. ℟. **Amen.**

And may the blessing of almighty God,
the Father, and the Son, ✠ and the Holy Spirit,
come down on you and remain with you for ever. ℟. **Amen.**

II. For Celebrations of the Saints

15. THE BLESSED VIRGIN MARY

May God, who through the childbearing of the Blessed
    Virgin Mary
willed in his great kindness to redeem the human race,
be pleased to enrich you with his blessing. ℟. **Amen.**

May you know always and everywhere the protection of
    her,
through whom you have been found worthy to receive the
    author of life. ℟. **Amen.**

May you, who have devoutly gathered on this day,
carry away with you the gifts of spiritual joys and heavenly
    rewards. ℟. **Amen.**

And may the blessing of almighty God,
the Father, and the Son, ✠ and the Holy Spirit,
come down on you and remain with you for ever. ℟. **Amen.**

16. SAINTS PETER AND PAUL, APOSTLES

May almighty God bless you,
for he has made you steadfast in Saint Peter's saving
    confession
and through it has set you on the solid rock of the Church's
    faith. ℟. **Amen.**

And having instructed you
by the tireless preaching of Saint Paul,
may God teach you constantly by his example
to win brothers and sisters for Christ. ℟. **Amen.**

So that by the keys of St. Peter and the words of St. Paul,
and by the support of their intercession,
God may bring us happily to that homeland
that Peter attained on a cross
and Paul by the blade of a sword. ℟. **Amen.**

And may the blessing of almighty God,
the Father, and the Son, ✛ and the Holy Spirit,
come down on you and remain with you for ever. ℟. **Amen.**

17. THE APOSTLES

May God, who has granted you
to stand firm on apostolic foundations,
graciously bless you through the glorious merits
of the holy Apostles *N.* and *N.* (the holy Apostle *N.*). ℟.
   Amen.

And may he, who endowed you
with the teaching and example of the Apostles,
make you, under their protection,
witnesses to the truth before all. ℟. **Amen.**

So that through the intercession of the Apostles,
you may inherit the eternal homeland,
for by their teaching you possess firmness of faith. ℟. **Amen.**

And may the blessing of almighty God,
the Father, and the Son, ✛ and the Holy Spirit,
come down on you and remain with you for ever. ℟. **Amen.**

18. ALL SAINTS

May God, the glory and joy of the Saints,
who has caused you to be strengthened
by means of their outstanding prayers,
bless you with unending blessings. ℟. **Amen.**

Freed through their intercession from present ills
and formed by the example of their holy way of life,
may you be ever devoted
to serving God and your neighbor. ℟. **Amen.**

So that, together with all,
you may possess the joys of the homeland,
where Holy Church rejoices
that her children are admitted in perpetual peace
to the company of the citizens of heaven. ℟. **Amen.**

And may the blessing of almighty God,
the Father, and the Son, ✛ and the Holy Spirit,
come down on you and remain with you for ever. ℟. **Amen.**

III. Other Blessings

19. FOR THE DEDICATION OF A CHURCH

May God, the Lord of heaven and earth,
who has gathered you today for the dedication of this
    church,
make you abound in heavenly blessings. ℟. **Amen.**

And may he, who has willed that all his scattered children
should be gathered together in his Son,
grant that you may become his temple
and the dwelling place of the Holy Spirit. ℟. **Amen.**

And so, when you are thoroughly cleansed,
may God dwell within you
and grant you to possess with all the Saints
the inheritance of eternal happiness. ℟. **Amen.**

And may the blessing of almighty God,
the Father, ✝ and the Son, ✝ and the Holy ✝ Spirit,
come down on you and remain with you for ever. ℟. **Amen.**

20. IN CELEBRATIONS FOR THE DEAD

May the God of all consolation bless you,
for in his unfathomable goodness he created the human
    race,
and in the Resurrection of his Only Begotten Son
he has given believers the hope of rising again. ℟. **Amen.**

To us who are alive, may God grant pardon for our sins,
and to all the dead, a place of light and peace. ℟. **Amen.**

So may we all live happily for ever with Christ,
whom we believe truly rose from the dead. ℟. **Amen.**

And may the blessing of almighty God,
the Father, and the Son, ✝ and the Holy Spirit,
come down on you and remain with you for ever. ℟. **Amen.**

PRAYERS OVER THE PEOPLE

*The following prayers may be used, at the discretion
of the Priest, at the end of the celebration of Mass,
or of a Liturgy of the Word, or of the Office, or of the
Sacraments.*

The Deacon or, in his absence, the Priest himself, says the invitation: Bow down for the blessing. *Then the Priest, with hands outstretched over the people, says the prayer, with all responding:* **Amen**.

After the prayer, the Priest always adds: And may the blessing of almighty God, the Father, and the Son, ✠ and the Holy Spirit, come down on you and remain with you for ever. ℟. **Amen.**

1. Be gracious to your people, O Lord,
   and do not withhold consolation on earth
   from those you call to strive for heaven.
   Through Christ our Lord.

2. Grant, O Lord, we pray,
   that the Christian people
   may understand the truths they profess
   and love the heavenly liturgy
   in which they participate.
   Through Christ our Lord.

3. May your people receive your holy blessing,
   O Lord, we pray,
   and, by that gift,
   spurn all that would harm them
   and obtain what they desire.
   Through Christ our Lord.

4. Turn your people to you with all their heart,
   O Lord, we pray,
   for you protect even those who go astray,
   but when they serve you with undivided heart,
   you sustain them with still greater care.
   Through Christ our Lord.

5. Graciously enlighten your family, O Lord, we pray,
   that by holding fast to what is pleasing to you,
   they may be worthy to accomplish all that is good.
   Through Christ our Lord.

6. Bestow pardon and peace, O Lord, we pray,
   upon your faithful,
   that they may be cleansed from every offense

and serve you with untroubled hearts.
Through Christ our Lord.

7. May your heavenly favor, O Lord, we pray,
increase in number the people subject to you
and make them always obedient to your commands.
Through Christ our Lord.

8. Be propitious to your people, O God,
that, freed from every evil,
they may serve you with all their heart
and ever stand firm under your protection.
Through Christ our Lord.

9. May your family always rejoice together, O God,
over the mysteries of redemption they have celebrated,
and grant its members the perseverance
to attain the effects that flow from them.
Through Christ our Lord.

10. Lord God, from the abundance of your mercies
provide for your servants and ensure their safety,
so that, strengthened by your blessings,
they may at all times abound in thanksgiving
and bless you with unending exultation.
Through Christ our Lord.

11. Keep your family, we pray, O Lord,
in your constant care,
so that, under your protection,
they may be free from all troubles
and by good works show dedication to your name.
Through Christ our Lord.

12. Purify your faithful, both in body and in mind,
O Lord, we pray,
so that, feeling the compunction you inspire,
they may be able to avoid harmful pleasures
and ever feed upon your delights.
Through Christ our Lord.

13. May the effects of your sacred blessing, O Lord,
make themselves felt among your faithful,

to prepare with spiritual sustenance the minds of all,
that they may be strengthened by the power of your
   love
to carry out works of charity.
Through Christ our Lord.

14. The hearts of your faithful submitted to your name,
    entreat your help, O Lord,
    and since without you they can do nothing that is just,
    grant by your abundant mercy
    that they may both know what is right
    and receive all that they need for their good.
    Through Christ our Lord.

15. Hasten to the aid of your faithful people
    who call upon you, O Lord, we pray,
    and graciously give strength in their human weakness,
    so that, being dedicated to you in complete sincerity,
    they may find gladness in your remedies
    both now and in the life to come.
    Through Christ our Lord.

16. Look with favor on your family, O Lord,
    and bestow your endless mercy on those who seek it:
    and just as without your mercy,
    they can do nothing truly worthy of you,
    so through it,
    may they merit to obey your saving commands.
    Through Christ our Lord.

17. Bestow increase of heavenly grace
    on your faithful, O Lord;
    may they praise you with their lips,
    with their souls, with their lives;
    and since it is by your gift that we exist,
    may our whole lives be yours.
    Through Christ our Lord.

18. Direct your people, O Lord, we pray,
    with heavenly instruction,
    that by avoiding every evil
    and pursuing all that is good,
    they may earn not your anger

but your unending mercy.
Through Christ our Lord.

19. Be near to those who call on you, O Lord,
and graciously grant your protection
to all who place their hope in your mercy,
that they may remain faithful in holiness of life
and, having enough for their needs in this world,
they may be made full heirs of your promise for eternity.
Through Christ our Lord.

20. Bestow the grace of your kindness
upon your supplicant people, O Lord,
that, formed by you, their creator,
and restored by you, their sustainer,
through your constant action they may be saved.
Through Christ our Lord.

21. May your faithful people, O Lord, we pray,
always respond to the promptings of your love
and, moved by wholesome compunction,
may they do gladly what you command,
so as to receive the things you promise.
Through Christ our Lord.

22. May the weakness of your devoted people
stir your compassion, O Lord, we pray,
and let their faithful pleading win your mercy,
that what they do not presume upon by their merits
they may receive by your generous pardon.
Through Christ our Lord.

23. In defense of your children, O Lord, we pray,
stretch forth the right hand of your majesty,
so that, obeying your fatherly will,
they may have the unfailing protection
of your fatherly care.
Through Christ our Lord.

24. Look, O Lord, on the prayers of your family,
and grant them the assistance they humbly implore,
so that, strengthened by the help they need,
they may persevere in confessing your name.
Through Christ our Lord.

25. Keep your family safe, O Lord, we pray,
    and grant them the abundance of your mercies,
    that they may find growth
    through the teachings and the gifts of heaven.
    Through Christ our Lord.

26. May your faithful people rejoice, we pray, O Lord,
    to be upheld by your right hand,
    and, progressing in the Christian life,
    may they delight in good things
    both now and in the time to come.
    Through Christ our Lord.

ON FEASTS OF SAINTS

27. May the Christian people exult, O Lord,
    at the glorification of the illustrious members of your
        Son's Body,
    and may they gain a share in the eternal lot
    of the Saints on whose feast day
    they reaffirm their devotion to you,
    rejoicing with them for ever in your glory.
    Through Christ our Lord.

28. Turn the hearts of your people
    always to you, O Lord, we pray,
    and, as you give them the help of such great patrons as
        these,
    grant also the unfailing help of your protection.
    Through Christ our Lord.

"Pray that you have the strength to escape . . . and to stand before the Son of Man."

DECEMBER 1, 2024

1st SUNDAY OF ADVENT

ENTRANCE ANT. Cf. Ps 25 (24):1-3   [Hope]
To you, I lift up my soul, O my God. In you, I have trusted; let me not be put to shame. Nor let my enemies exult over me; and let none who hope in you be put to shame. ➜ No. 2, p. 10 (Omit Gloria)

COLLECT   [Meeting Christ]
Grant your faithful, we pray, almighty God,
the resolve to run forth to meet your Christ
with righteous deeds at his coming,
so that, gathered at his right hand,
they may be worthy to possess the heavenly Kingdom.
Through our Lord Jesus Christ, your Son,
who lives and reigns with you in the unity of the Holy
   Spirit,
God, for ever and ever. ℟. **Amen.** ↓

FIRST READING Jer 33:14-16   [The Lord's Messiah]

Jeremiah reveals the promise of the Lord made to the House of Israel. A shoot from David shall do what is right and just. Judah and Jerusalem shall be safe.

A reading from the Book of the Prophet Jeremiah

THE days are coming, says the LORD, when I will fulfill the promise I made to the house of Israel and Judah. In those days, in that time, I will raise up for David a just shoot; he shall do what is right and just in the land. In those days Judah shall be safe and Jerusalem shall dwell secure; this is what they shall call her: "The LORD our justice."—The word of the Lord. ℟. **Thanks be to God.** ↓

RESPONSORIAL PSALM Ps 25   [Eye on God]

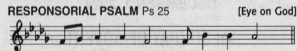

℟. To you, O Lord, I lift my soul.

Your ways, O LORD, make known to me;
   teach me your paths,
guide me in your truth and teach me,
   for you are God my savior,
   and for you I wait all the day.

℟. **To you, O Lord, I lift my soul.**

Good and upright is the LORD;
   thus he shows sinners the way.
He guides the humble to justice,
   and teaches the humble his way.

℟. **To you, O Lord, I lift my soul.**

All the paths of the LORD are kindness and constancy
   toward those who keep his covenant and his decrees.
The friendship of the LORD is with those who fear him,
   and his covenant, for their instruction.

℟. **To you, O Lord, I lift my soul.** ↓

SECOND READING 1 Thes 3:12—4:2   [Lives Pleasing to God]

Paul prays that the Lord will increase his love among the Thessalonians. In turn they must live a life pleasing to God so that they may progress in the way of perfection.

A reading from the first Letter of Saint Paul to
the Thessalonians

BROTHERS and sisters: May the Lord make you increase and abound in love for one another and for all, just as we have for you, so as to strengthen your hearts, to be blameless in holiness before our God and Father at the coming of our Lord Jesus with all his holy ones. Amen.

Finally, brothers and sisters, we earnestly ask and exhort you in the Lord Jesus that, as you received from us how you should conduct yourselves to please God— and as you are conducting yourselves—you do so even more. For you know what instructions we gave you through the Lord Jesus.—The word of the Lord. ℟. **Thanks be to God.** ↓

ALLELUIA Ps 85:8   [God's Salvation]
℟. **Alleluia, alleluia.**
Show us, Lord, your love;
and grant us your salvation.
℟. **Alleluia, alleluia.** ↓

GOSPEL Lk 21:25-28, 34-36   [Prayerful Vigilance]

Jesus tells his disciples that there will be signs for his second coming. The sun, moon, stars, anguish among people, fright—these will warn of his coming. They should watch, pray and stand secure before the Son of Man.

℣. The Lord be with you. ℟. **And with your spirit.**
✛ A reading from the holy Gospel according to Luke.
℟. **Glory to you, O Lord.**

JESUS said to his disciples: "There will be signs in the sun, the moon, and the stars, and on earth nations will be in dismay, perplexed by the roaring of the sea and the waves. People will die of fright in anticipation of what is coming upon the world, for the powers of the heavens will be shaken. And then they will see the Son of Man coming in a cloud with power and great glory. But when these signs begin to happen, stand erect and raise your heads because your redemption is at hand.

"Beware that your hearts do not become drowsy from carousing and drunkenness and the anxieties of daily life, and that day catch you by surprise like a trap. For that day will assault everyone who lives on the face of the earth. Be vigilant at all times and pray that you have the strength to escape the tribulations that are imminent and to stand before the Son of Man."—The Gospel of the Lord. R̸. **Praise to you, Lord Jesus Christ.**   → No. 15, p. 18

PRAYER OVER THE OFFERINGS   [Eternal Redemption]

Accept, we pray, O Lord, these offerings we make,
gathered from among your gifts to us,
and may what you grant us to celebrate devoutly here
    below
gain for us the prize of eternal redemption.
Through Christ our Lord.
R̸. **Amen.**   → No. 21, p. 22 (Pref. P 1)

COMMUNION ANT. Ps 85 (84):13   [God's Bounty]
The Lord will bestow his bounty, and our earth shall yield its increase. ↓

PRAYER AFTER COMMUNION   [Love for Heaven]

May these mysteries, O Lord,
in which we have participated,
profit us, we pray,
for even now, as we walk amid passing things,
you teach us by them
to love the things of heaven
and hold fast to what endures.
Through Christ our Lord.
℟. **Amen.**   → No. 30, p. 77

Optional Solemn Blessings, p. 97, and Prayers over the People, p. 105

"John went throughout the whole region of the Jordan, proclaiming a baptism of repentance."

DECEMBER 8

2nd SUNDAY OF ADVENT

ENTRANCE ANT. Cf. Is 30:19, 30   [Lord of Salvation]

O people of Sion, behold, the Lord will come to save the nations, and the Lord will make the glory of his voice heard in the joy of your heart.

→ No. 2, p. 10 (Omit Gloria)

COLLECT   [Heavenly Wisdom]
Almighty and merciful God,
may no earthly undertaking hinder those
who set out in haste to meet your Son,
but may our learning of heavenly wisdom
gain us admittance to his company.
Who lives and reigns with you in the unity of the Holy
  Spirit,
God, for ever and ever. ℟. **Amen.** ↓

FIRST READING Bar 5:1-9   [God's Favor on Jerusalem]
    Baruch tells Jerusalem of God's favor. God will gather the
    people together that Israel may grow secure in the glory of
    God. He leads in joy, mercy, and justice.

116

A reading from the Book of the Prophet Baruch

JERUSALEM, take off your robe of mourning and
    misery;
    put on the splendor of glory from God forever:
wrapped in the cloak of justice from God,
    bear on your head the mitre
    that displays the glory of the eternal name.
For God will show all the earth your splendor:
    you will be named by God forever
    the peace of justice, the glory of God's worship.

Up, Jerusalem! stand upon the heights;
    look to the east and see your children
gathered from the east and the west
    at the word of the Holy One,
    rejoicing that they are remembered by God.
Led away on foot by their enemies they left you:
    but God will bring them back to you
    borne aloft in glory as on royal thrones.
For God has commanded
    that every lofty mountain be made low,
and that the age-old depths and gorges
    be filled to level ground,
    that Israel may advance secure in the glory of God.
The forests and every fragrant kind of tree
    have overshadowed Israel at God's command;
for God is leading Israel in joy
    by the light of his glory,
    with his mercy and justice for company.
The word of the Lord. ℟. **Thanks be to God.** ↓

RESPONSORIAL PSALM Ps 126   [The Lord's Wonders]

℟. **The Lord has done great things for us; we are filled with joy.**

When the Lord brought back the captives of Zion,
  we were like men dreaming.
Then our mouth was filled with laughter,
  and our tongue with rejoicing.

℞. **The Lord has done great things for us; we are filled
with joy.**

Then they said among the nations,
  "The Lord has done great things for them."
The Lord has done great things for us;
  we are glad indeed.

℞. **The Lord has done great things for us; we are filled
with joy.**

Restore our fortunes, O Lord,
  like the torrents in the southern desert.
Those who sow in tears
  shall reap rejoicing.

℞. **The Lord has done great things for us; we are filled
with joy.**

Although they go forth weeping,
  carrying the seed to be sown,
they shall come back rejoicing,
  carrying their sheaves.

℞. **The Lord has done great things for us; we are filled
with joy.** ↓

SECOND READING Phil 1:4-6, 8-11 [Cooperating with Joy]

Paul rejoices in the progress of faith among the
Philippians. He is sure that God who began this good work
will help it grow. Paul prays that their love may even more
abound that they may be rich in harvest.

A reading from the Letter of Saint Paul
to the Philippians

Brothers and sisters: I pray always with joy in
my every prayer for all of you, because of your

partnership for the gospel from the first day until now. I am confident of this, that the one who began a good work in you will continue to complete it until the day of Christ Jesus. God is my witness, how I long for all of you with the affection of Christ Jesus. And this is my prayer: that your love may increase ever more and more in knowledge and every kind of perception, to discern what is of value, so that you may be pure and blameless for the day of Christ, filled with the fruit of righteousness that comes through Jesus Christ for the glory and praise of God.—The word of the Lord. ℟. **Thanks be to God.** ↓

ALLELUIA Lk 3:4, 6   [Prepare the Way]
℟. **Alleluia, alleluia.**
Prepare the way of the Lord, make straight his paths: all flesh shall see the salvation of God.
℟. **Alleluia, alleluia.** ↓

GOSPEL Lk 3:1-6   [Prepare for the Lord]
Luke outlines some historical facts at the time of John the Baptist's preaching. It is the fulfillment of the prophecy of Isaiah. John prepares the way for the Lord.

℣. The Lord be with you. ℟. **And with your spirit.**
✛ A reading from the holy Gospel according to Luke.
℟. **Glory to you, O Lord.**

IN the fifteenth year of the reign of Tiberius Caesar, when Pontius Pilate was governor of Judea, and Herod was tetrarch of Galilee, and his brother Philip tetrarch of the region of Ituraea and Trachonitis, and Lysanias was tetrarch of Abilene, during the high priesthood of Annas and Caiaphas, the word of God came to John the son of Zechariah in the desert. John went throughout the whole region of the Jordan, pro-claiming a baptism of repentance for the forgiveness

of sins, as it is written in the book of the words of the
prophet Isaiah:

A voice of one crying out in the desert:
"Prepare the way of the Lord,
make straight his paths.
Every valley shall be filled
and every mountain and hill shall be made low.
The winding roads shall be made straight,
and the rough ways made smooth,
and all flesh shall see the salvation of God."

The Gospel of the Lord. ℟. **Praise to you, Lord Jesus
Christ.**   ➙ No. 15, p. 18

PRAYER OVER THE OFFERINGS   [Our Offering]

Be pleased, O Lord, with our humble prayers and
   offerings,
and, since we have no merits to plead our cause,
come, we pray, to our rescue
with the protection of your mercy.
Through Christ our Lord.
℟. **Amen.**   ➙ No. 21, p. 22 (Pref. P 1)

COMMUNION ANT. Bar 5:5; 4:36   [Coming Joy]

**Jerusalem, arise and stand upon the heights, and
behold the joy which comes to you from God.** ↓

PRAYER AFTER COMMUNION   [Wise Judgment]

Replenished by the food of spiritual nourishment,
we humbly beseech you, O Lord,
that, through our partaking in this mystery,
you may teach us to judge wisely the things of earth
and hold firm to the things of heaven.
Through Christ our Lord.
℟. **Amen.**   ➙ No. 30, p. 77

Optional Solemn Blessings, p. 97, Prayers over the People, p. 105

"[John] preached good news to the people."

DECEMBER 15

3rd SUNDAY OF ADVENT

ENTRANCE ANT. Phil 4:4-5   [Mounting Joy]

**Rejoice in the Lord always; again I say, rejoice.
Indeed, the Lord is near.** ➜ No. 2, p. 10 (Omit Gloria)

COLLECT   [Joy of Salvation]

O God, who see how your people
faithfully await the feast of the Lord's Nativity,
enable us, we pray,
to attain the joys of so great a salvation
and to celebrate them always
with solemn worship and glad rejoicing.
Through our Lord Jesus Christ, your Son,
who lives and reigns with you in the unity of the Holy
    Spirit,
God, for ever and ever. ℟. **Amen.** ↓

FIRST READING Zep 3:14-18a [Joy Over the Mighty Savior]

Zephaniah writes that Israel should shout for joy. Her King,
the Lord, is in her midst. The Lord is a mighty savior. Israel
should not be discouraged.

A reading from the Book of the Prophet Zephaniah

S HOUT for joy, O daughter Zion!
  Sing joyfully, O Israel!
Be glad and exult with all your heart,
    O daughter Jerusalem!
The LORD has removed the judgment against you,
    he has turned away your enemies;
the King of Israel, the LORD, is in your midst,
    you have no further misfortune to fear.
On that day, it shall be said to Jerusalem:
    Fear not, O Zion, be not discouraged!
The LORD, your God, is in your midst,
    a mighty savior;
he will rejoice over you with gladness,
    and renew you in his love,
he will sing joyfully because of you,
    as one sings at festivals.
The word of the Lord. ℟. **Thanks be to God.** ↓

RESPONSORIAL PSALM Is 12   [Joy Over the Holy One]

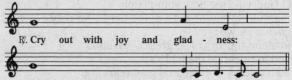

℟. Cry out with joy and gladness: for among you is the great and Holy One of Israel.

God indeed is my savior;
  I am confident and unafraid.
My strength and my courage is the LORD,
  and he has been my savior.
With joy you will draw water
  at the fountain of salvation.

℟. **Cry out with joy and gladness: for among you is the great and Holy One of Israel.**

Give thanks to the LORD, acclaim his name;
   among the nations make known his deeds,
   proclaim how exalted is his name.

℟. **Cry out with joy and gladness: for among you is the
   great and Holy One of Israel.**

Sing praise to the LORD for his glorious achievement;
   let this be known throughout all the earth.
Shout with exultation, O city of Zion,
   for great in your midst
   is the Holy One of Israel!

℟. **Cry out with joy and gladness: for among you is the
   great and Holy One of Israel.** ↓

SECOND READING Phil 4:4-7   [Rejoice in the Lord]

Christians should rejoice in the Lord. They should take
their prayers and petitions to him. God will watch over his
children.

A reading from the Letter of Saint Paul
to the Philippians

B ROTHERS and sisters: Rejoice in the Lord always.
   I shall say it again: rejoice! Your kindness should
be known to all. The Lord is near. Have no anxiety at
all, but in everything, by prayer and petition, with
thanksgiving, make your requests known to God. Then
the peace of God that surpasses all understanding will
guard your hearts and minds in Christ Jesus.—The
word of the Lord. ℟. **Thanks be to God.** ↓

ALLELUIA Is 61:1 (cited in Lk 4:18)   [Glad Tidings]
℟. **Alleluia, alleluia.**
The Spirit of the Lord is upon me,
because he has anointed me
to bring glad tidings to the poor.
℟. **Alleluia, alleluia.** ↓

GOSPEL Lk 3:10-18   [Majesty of the Messiah]

> John preached a law of sharing. He baptized and admonished all to be just and loving and to pray. John tells the people about the majesty of the Messiah.

℣. The Lord be with you. ℟. **And with your spirit.**

✠ A reading from the holy Gospel according to Luke.

℟. **Glory to you, O Lord.**

THE crowds asked John the Baptist,"What should we do?" He said to them in reply, "Whoever has two cloaks should share with the person who has none. And whoever has food should do likewise." Even tax collectors came to be baptized and they said to him,"Teacher, what should we do?"He answered them,"Stop collecting more than what is prescribed." Soldiers also asked him, "And what is it that we should do?"He told them,"Do not practice extortion, do not falsely accuse anyone, and be satisfied with your wages."

Now the people were filled with expectation, and all were asking in their hearts whether John might be the Christ. John answered them all, saying,"I am baptizing you with water, but one mightier than I is coming. I am not worthy to loosen the thongs of his sandals. He will baptize you with the Holy Spirit and fire. His winnowing fan is in his hand to clear his threshing floor and to gather the wheat into his barn, but the chaff he will burn with unquenchable fire."Exhorting them in many other ways, he preached good news to the people.— The Gospel of the Lord. ℟. **Praise to you, Lord Jesus Christ.**   → No. 15, p. 18

PRAYER OVER THE OFFERINGS   [Unceasing Sacrifice]

May the sacrifice of our worship, Lord, we pray,
be offered to you unceasingly,
to complete what was begun in sacred mystery
and powerfully accomplish for us your saving work.

Through Christ our Lord.
R̶/. **Amen.**   ➙ No. 21, p. 22 (Pref. P 1 or 2)

COMMUNION ANT. Cf. Is 35:4   [Trust in God]
**Say to the faint of heart: Be strong and do not fear.
Behold, our God will come, and he will save us.** ↓

PRAYER AFTER COMMUNION   [Preparation for Christ]
We implore your mercy, Lord,
that this divine sustenance may cleanse us of our faults
and prepare us for the coming feasts.
Through Christ our Lord.
R̶/. **Amen.**   ➙ No. 30, p. 77

Optional Solemn Blessings, p. 97, and Prayers over the People, p. 105

*"Blessed are you among women, and blessed is the fruit
of your womb."*

DECEMBER 22

4th SUNDAY OF ADVENT

ENTRANCE ANT. Cf. Is 45:8   [The Advent Plea]
**Drop down dew from above, you heavens, and let the
clouds rain down the Just One; let the earth be opened
and bring forth a Savior.** ➙ No. 2, p. 10 (Omit Gloria)

COLLECT   [From Suffering to Glory]

Pour forth, we beseech you, O Lord,
your grace into our hearts,
that we, to whom the Incarnation of Christ your Son
was made known by the message of an Angel,
may by his Passion and Cross
be brought to the glory of his Resurrection.
Who lives and reigns with you in the unity of the Holy
   Spirit,
God, for ever and ever. ℟. **Amen.** ↓

FIRST READING Mi 5:1-4a   [The Messiah from Bethlehem]

Micah speaks of the glory of Bethlehem, a lone town among the people of Judah. From Bethlehem shall come forth the promised one who shall stand firm and strong in the Lord.

A reading from the Book of the Prophet Micah

T HUS says the LORD:
You, Bethlehem-Ephrathah,
   too small to be among the clans of Judah,
from you shall come forth for me
   one who is to be ruler in Israel;
whose origin is from of old,
   from ancient times.
Therefore the Lord will give them up, until the time
   when she who is to give birth has borne,
and the rest of his kindred shall return
   to the children of Israel.
He shall stand firm and shepherd his flock
   by the strength of the LORD,
   in the majestic name of the LORD, his God;
and they shall remain, for now his greatness
   shall reach to the ends of the earth;
   he shall be peace.
The word of the Lord. ℟. **Thanks be to God.** ↓

RESPONSORIAL PSALM Ps 80   [Turn to the Lord]

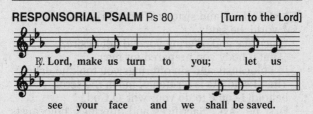

℟. Lord, make us turn to you; let us see your face and we shall be saved.

O shepherd of Israel, hearken,
    from your throne upon the cherubim, shine forth.
Rouse your power,
    and come to save us.

℟. **Lord, make us turn to you; let us see your face and
    we shall be saved.**

Once again, O LORD of hosts,
    look down from heaven, and see;
take care of this vine,
    and protect what your right hand has planted,
    the son of man whom you yourself made strong.

℟. **Lord, make us turn to you; let us see your face and
    we shall be saved.**

May your help be with the man of your right hand,
    with the son of man whom you yourself made
        strong.
Then we will no more withdraw from you;
    give us new life, and we will call upon your name.

℟. **Lord, make us turn to you; let us see your face and
    we shall be saved.** ↓

SECOND READING Heb 10:5-10   [Doing God's Will]
    Jesus said the sacrifices, sin offerings and holocausts did
    not delight the Lord. But he has come to do the will of
    God—to establish a second covenant.

    A reading from the Letter to the Hebrews

B ROTHERS and sisters: When Christ came into the
world, he said:
"Sacrifice and offering you did not desire,
   but a body you prepared for me;
in holocausts and sin offerings you took no delight.
Then I said, 'As is written of me in the scroll,
behold, I come to do your will, O God.'"
First he says, "Sacrifices and offerings, holocausts
and sin offerings, you neither desired nor delighted
in." These are offered according to the law. Then he
says, "Behold, I come to do your will." He takes away
the first to establish the second. By this "will," we have
been consecrated through the offering of the body of
Jesus Christ once for all.—The word of the Lord.
℟. **Thanks be to God.** ↓

ALLELUIA Lk 1:38   [The Lord's Handmaid]
℟. **Alleluia, alleluia.**
Behold, I am the handmaid of the Lord.
May it be done to me according to your word.
℟. **Alleluia, alleluia.** ↓

GOSPEL Lk 1:39-45   [The Visitation]
   Mary went to visit Elizabeth who was also blessed by the
   Holy Spirit. Elizabeth greeted Mary: "Blessed are you
   among women and blessed is the fruit of your womb."

℣. The Lord be with you. ℟. **And with your spirit.**
✠ A reading from the holy Gospel according to Luke.
℟. **Glory to you, O Lord.**

M ARY set out and traveled to the hill country in
haste to a town of Judah, where she entered the
house of Zechariah and greeted Elizabeth. When
Elizabeth heard Mary's greeting, the infant leaped in
her womb, and Elizabeth, filled with the Holy Spirit,
cried out in a loud voice and said, "Blessed are you
among women, and blessed is the fruit of your womb.

And how does this happen to me, that the mother of my Lord should come to me? For at the moment the sound of your greeting reached my ears, the infant in my womb leaped for joy. Blessed are you who believed that what was spoken to you by the Lord would be fulfilled."—The Gospel of the Lord. ℟. **Praise to you, Lord Jesus Christ.**   ➔ No. 15, p. 18

PRAYER OVER THE OFFERINGS   [Power of the Spirit]

May the Holy Spirit, O Lord,
sanctify these gifts laid upon your altar,
just as he filled with his power the womb of the Blessed
  Virgin Mary.
Through Christ our Lord.
℟. **Amen.**   ➔ No. 21, p. 22 (Pref. P 2)

COMMUNION ANT. Is 7:14   [The Virgin Mother]

Behold, a Virgin shall conceive and bear a son; and his name will be called Emmanuel. ↓

PRAYER AFTER COMMUNION   [Worthy Celebration]

Having received this pledge of eternal redemption,
we pray, almighty God,
that, as the feast day of our salvation draws ever nearer,
so we may press forward all the more eagerly
to the worthy celebration of the mystery of your Son's
  Nativity.
Who lives and reigns for ever and ever.
℟. **Amen.**   ➔ No. 30, p. 77

Optional Solemn Blessings, p. 97, and Prayers over the People, p. 105

The Word is made flesh.

DECEMBER 25

THE NATIVITY OF THE LORD [CHRISTMAS]

Solemnity

AT THE MASS DURING THE NIGHT

ENTRANCE ANT. Ps 2:7   **[Son of God]**

The Lord said to me: You are my Son. It is I who have begotten you this day. → No. 2, p. 10

OR   **[True Peace]**

Let us all rejoice in the Lord, for our Savior has been born in the world. Today true peace has come down to us from heaven. → No. 2, p. 10

COLLECT   **[Eternal Gladness]**

O God, who have made this most sacred night
radiant with the splendor of the true light,
grant, we pray, that we, who have known the mysteries
   of his light on earth,
may also delight in his gladness in heaven.
Who lives and reigns with you in the unity of the Holy
   Spirit,
God, for ever and ever. ℟. **Amen.** ↓

FIRST READING Is 9:1-6   [The Messiah's Kingdom]

The spell of darkness, the shame of sin is broken—the Prince of light is born to us.

A reading from the Book of the Prophet Isaiah

T HE people who walked in darkness
have seen a great light;
upon those who dwelt in the land of gloom
a light has shone.
You have brought them abundant joy
and great rejoicing,
as they rejoice before you as at the harvest,
as people make merry when dividing spoils.
For the yoke that burdened them,
the pole on their shoulder,
and the rod of their taskmaster
you have smashed, as on the day of Midian.
For every boot that tramped in battle,
every cloak rolled in blood,
will be burned as fuel for flames.
For a child is born to us, a son is given us;
upon his shoulder dominion rests.
They name him Wonder-Counselor, God-Hero,
Father-Forever, Prince of Peace.
His dominion is vast
and forever peaceful,
from David's throne, and over his kingdom,
which he confirms and sustains
by judgment and justice,
both now and forever.
The zeal of the LORD of hosts will do this!
The word of the Lord. ℟. **Thanks be to God.** ↓

RESPONSORIAL PSALM Ps 96   [Bless the Lord]

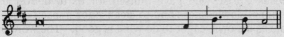

℟. Today is born our Sav - ior, Christ the Lord.

Sing to the LORD a new song;
  sing to the LORD, all you lands.
Sing to the LORD; bless his name.

℟. **Today is born our Savior, Christ the Lord.**

Announce his salvation, day after day.
  Tell his glory among the nations;
  among all peoples, his wondrous deeds.

℟. **Today is born our Savior, Christ the Lord.**

Let the heavens be glad and the earth rejoice;
  let the sea and what fills it resound;
  let the plains be joyful and all that is in them!
Then shall all the trees of the forest exult.

℟. **Today is born our Savior, Christ the Lord.**

They shall exult before the LORD, for he comes;
  for he comes to rule the earth.
He shall rule the world with justice
  and the peoples with his constancy.

℟. **Today is born our Savior, Christ the Lord.** ↓

SECOND READING Ti 2:11-14   [Salvation for All]
  We look to the second coming of Christ in glory. Through
  his Cross we are freed from the darkness of sin.

  A reading from the Letter of Saint Paul to Titus

B ELOVED: The grace of God has appeared, saving
  all and training us to reject godless ways and
worldly desires and to live temperately, justly, and
devoutly in this age, as we await the blessed hope, the
appearance of the glory of our great God and savior
Jesus Christ, who gave himself for us to deliver us
from all lawlessness and to cleanse for himself a people as his own, eager to do what is good.—The word of
the Lord. ℟. **Thanks be to God.** ↓

ALLELUIA Lk 2:10-11   [Great Joy]

℟. **Alleluia, alleluia.**
I proclaim to you good news of great joy:
today a Savior is born for us,
Christ the Lord.
℟. **Alleluia, alleluia.** ↓

GOSPEL Lk 2:1-14   [Birth of Christ]

**Rejoice in the good news—our Savior is born, and he is
revealed to us by the witness of shepherds.**

℣. The Lord be with you. ℟. **And with your spirit.**
✝ A reading from the holy Gospel according to Luke.
℟. **Glory to you, O Lord.**

IN those days a decree went out from Caesar
Augustus that the whole world should be enrolled.
This was the first enrollment, when Quirinius was governor of Syria. So all went to be enrolled, each to his
own town. And Joseph too went up from Galilee from
the town of Nazareth to Judea, to the city of David that
is called Bethlehem, because he was of the house and
family of David, to be enrolled with Mary, his
betrothed, who was with child. While they were there,
the time came for her to have her child, and she gave
birth to her firstborn son. She wrapped him in swaddling clothes and laid him in a manger, because there
was no room for them in the inn.

Now there were shepherds in that region living in
the fields and keeping the night watch over their flock.
The angel of the Lord appeared to them and the glory
of the Lord shone around them, and they were struck
with great fear. The angel said to them, "Do not be
afraid; for behold, I proclaim to you good news of
great joy that will be for all the people. For today in the
city of David a savior has been born for you who is
Christ and Lord. And this will be a sign for you: you

will find an infant wrapped in swaddling clothes and lying in a manger." And suddenly there was a multitude of the heavenly host with the angel, praising God and saying:

"Glory to God in the highest
    and on earth peace to those on whom his favor
    rests."

The Gospel of the Lord. ℟. **Praise to you, Lord Jesus Christ.**   → No. 15, p. 18

The Creed is said. All kneel at the words and by the Holy Spirit was incarnate.

PRAYER OVER THE OFFERINGS   [Become Like Christ]

May the oblation of this day's feast
be pleasing to you, O Lord, we pray,
that through this most holy exchange
we may be found in the likeness of Christ,
in whom our nature is united to you.
Who lives and reigns for ever and ever.
℟. **Amen.**   → No. 21, p. 22 (Pref. P 3-5)

When the Roman Canon is used, the proper form of the Communicantes *(In communion with those) is said.*

COMMUNION ANT. Jn 1:14   [Glory of Christ]
The Word became flesh, and we have seen his glory. ↓

PRAYER AFTER COMMUNION   [Union with Christ]

Grant us, we pray, O Lord our God,
that we, who are gladdened by participation
in the feast of our Redeemer's Nativity,
may through an honorable way of life become worthy of
    union with him.
Who lives and reigns for ever and ever.
℟. **Amen.**   → No. 30, p. 77

Optional Solemn Blessings, p. 97, and Prayers over the People, p. 105

AT THE MASS AT DAWN

ENTRANCE ANT. Cf. Is 9:1, 5; Lk 1:33   [Prince of Peace]
**Today a light will shine upon us, for the Lord is born
for us; and he will be called Wondrous God, Prince of
peace, Father of future ages: and his reign will be
without end.**   ➙ No. 2, p. 10

COLLECT   [Light of Faith]
Grant, we pray, almighty God,
that, as we are bathed in the new radiance of your
    incarnate Word,
the light of faith, which illumines our minds,
may also shine through in our deeds.
Through our Lord Jesus Christ, your Son,
who lives and reigns with you in the unity of the Holy
    Spirit,
God, for ever and ever.
℟. **Amen.** ↓

FIRST READING Is 62:11-12   [The Savior's Birth]
    Our Savior comes. He makes us a holy people and redeems
    us.

    A reading from the Book of the Prophet Isaiah

SEE, the LORD proclaims
    to the ends of the earth:
say to daughter Zion,
    your savior comes!
Here is his reward with him,
    his recompense before him.
They shall be called the holy people,
    the redeemed of the LORD,
and you shall be called "Frequented,"
    a city that is not forsaken.
The word of the Lord. ℟. **Thanks be to God.** ↓

RESPONSORIAL PSALM Ps 97   [Be Glad in the Lord]

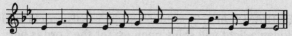

℟. A light will shine on us this day: the Lord is born for us.

The LORD is king; let the earth rejoice;
   let the many isles be glad.
The heavens proclaim his justice,
   and all peoples see his glory.

℟. **A light will shine on us this day: the Lord is born
for us.**

Light dawns for the just;
   and gladness, for the upright of heart.
Be glad in the LORD, you just,
   and give thanks to his holy name.

℟. **A light will shine on us this day: the Lord is born
for us.** ↓

SECOND READING Ti 3:4-7   [Saved by God's Mercy]

**By God's mercy we are saved from sin. Jesus became man
that we might through him receive the Spirit.**

A reading from the Letter of Saint Paul to Titus

BELOVED:
   When the kindness and generous love
      of God our savior appeared,
   not because of any righteous deeds we had done
      but because of his mercy,
   he saved us through the bath of rebirth
      and renewal by the Holy Spirit,
   whom he richly poured out on us
      through Jesus Christ our savior,
   so that we might be justified by his grace
      and become heirs in hope of eternal life.
The word of the Lord. ℟. **Thanks be to God.** ↓

ALLELUIA Lk 2:14   [Glory to God]

℟. **Alleluia, alleluia.**
Glory to God in the highest,
and on earth peace to those
on whom his favor rests.
℟. **Alleluia, alleluia.** ↓

GOSPEL Lk 2:15-20   [Jesus, the God-Man]
The wonder of salvation is revealed to the shepherds and
to us. The love of God is manifest because he is with us.

℣. The Lord be with you. ℟. **And with your spirit.**
✝ A reading from the holy Gospel according to Luke.
℟. **Glory to you, O Lord.**

W HEN the angels went away from them to heaven,
the shepherds said to one another, "Let us go, then,
to Bethlehem to see this thing that has taken place, which
the Lord has made known to us." So they went in haste
and found Mary and Joseph, and the infant lying in the
manger. When they saw this, they made known the message that had been told them about this child. All who
heard it were amazed by what had been told them by the
shepherds. And Mary kept all these things, reflecting on
them in her heart. Then the shepherds returned, glorifying and praising God for all they had heard and seen, just
as it had been told to them.—The Gospel of the Lord.
℟. **Praise to you, Lord Jesus Christ.**   → No. 15, p. 18

The Creed is said. All kneel at the words and by the Holy Spirit
was incarnate.

PRAYER OVER THE OFFERINGS   [Gift of Divine Life]
May our offerings be worthy, we pray, O Lord,
of the mysteries of the Nativity this day,
that, just as Christ was born a man and also shone forth
   as God,
so these earthly gifts may confer on us what is divine.
Through Christ our Lord.
℟. **Amen.**   → No. 21, p. 22 (Pref. P 3-5)

When the Roman Canon is used, the proper form of the Communicantes *(In communion with those) is said.*

COMMUNION ANT. Cf. Zec 9:9   [The Holy One]

Rejoice, O Daughter Sion; lift up praise, Daughter Jerusalem: Behold, your King will come, the Holy One and Savior of the world. ↓

PRAYER AFTER COMMUNION   [Fullness of Faith]

Grant us, Lord, as we honor with joyful devotion
the Nativity of your Son,
that we may come to know with fullness of faith
the hidden depths of this mystery
and to love them ever more and more.
Through Christ our Lord.
℟. **Amen.**   ↦ No. 30, p. 77

Optional Solemn Blessings, p. 97, and Prayers over the People, p. 105

AT THE MASS DURING THE DAY

ENTRANCE ANT. Cf. Is 9:5   [The Gift of God's Son]

A child is born for us, and a son is given to us; his scepter of power rests upon his shoulder, and his name will be called Messenger of great counsel.

↦ No. 2, p. 10

COLLECT   [Share in Christ's Divinity]

O God, who wonderfully created the dignity of human
    nature
and still more wonderfully restored it,
grant, we pray,
that we may share in the divinity of Christ,
who humbled himself to share in our humanity.
Who lives and reigns with you in the unity of the Holy
    Spirit,
God, for ever and ever. ℟. **Amen.** ↓

FIRST READING Is 52:7-10   [Your God Is King]

The good news, the Gospel—the Lord comforts his people by announcing our salvation.

A reading from the Book of the Prophet Isaiah

H OW beautiful upon the mountains
are the feet of him who brings glad tidings,
announcing peace, bearing good news,
     announcing salvation, and saying to Zion,
     "Your God is King!"

Hark! Your sentinels raise a cry,
     together they shout for joy,
for they see directly, before their eyes,
     the LORD restoring Zion.
Break out together in song,
     O ruins of Jerusalem!
For the LORD comforts his people,
     he redeems Jerusalem.
The LORD has bared his holy arm
     in the sight of all the nations;
all the ends of the earth will behold
     the salvation of our God.
The word of the Lord. ℟. **Thanks be to God.** ↓

RESPONSORIAL PSALM Ps 98   [Sing a New Song]

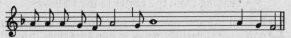

℟. All the ends of the earth have seen the saving   power of God.

Sing to the LORD a new song,
     for he has done wondrous deeds;
his right hand has won victory for him,
     his holy arm.

℟. **All the ends of the earth have seen the saving power of God.**

The LORD has made his salvation known:
  in the sight of the nations he has revealed his jus-
    tice.
He has remembered his kindness and his faithful-
    ness
  toward the house of Israel.

℟. **All the ends of the earth have seen the saving
power of God.**

All the ends of the earth have seen
  the salvation by our God.
Sing joyfully to the LORD, all you lands;
  break into song; sing praise.

℟. **All the ends of the earth have seen the saving
power of God.**

Sing praise to the LORD with the harp,
  with the harp and melodious song.
With trumpets and the sound of the horn
  sing joyfully before the King, the LORD.

℟. **All the ends of the earth have seen the saving
power of God.** ↓

SECOND READING Heb 1:1-6   [God Speaks through Jesus]
  Now God speaks to us more clearly than ever before. His
  Son is with us—God is with us; we are his people.

A reading from the Letter to the Hebrews

BROTHERS and sisters: In times past, God spoke in
partial and various ways to our ancestors through
the prophets; in these last days, he has spoken to us
through the Son, whom he made heir of all things and
through whom he created the universe,
  who is the refulgence of his glory, the very imprint
    of his being,
  and who sustains all things by his mighty word.
  When he had accomplished purification from sins,

he took his seat at the right hand of the Majesty on
   high,
as far superior to the angels
as the name he has inherited is more excellent than
   theirs.

For to which of the angels did God ever say:
   You are my son; this day I have begotten you?
Or again:
   I will be a father to him, and he shall be a son to me?
And again, when he leads the firstborn into the world,
   he says:
   Let all the angels of God worship him.
The word of the Lord. ℟. **Thanks be to God.** ↓

ALLELUIA   [Adore the Lord]
℟. **Alleluia, alleluia.**
A holy day has dawned upon us.
Come, you nations, and adore the Lord.
For today a great light has come upon the earth.
℟. **Alleluia, alleluia.** ↓

GOSPEL Jn 1:1-18 or 1:1-5, 9-14   [The True Light]
**The Word of God is the living Word. The Word became
flesh and lives in our midst.**

*[If the "Shorter Form" is used, the indented text in brackets is
omitted.]*

℣. The Lord be with you. ℟. **And with your spirit.**
✛ A reading from the holy Gospel according to John.
℟. **Glory to you, O Lord.**

IN the beginning was the Word,
   and the Word was with God,
      and the Word was God.
He was in the beginning with God.
All things came to be through him,
   and without him nothing came to be.
What came to be through him was life,
   and this life was the light of the human race;

the light shines in the darkness,
>and the darkness has not overcome it.

>>[A man named John was sent from God. He
>>came for testimony, to testify to the light, so
>>that all might believe through him. He was not
>>the light, but came to testify to the light.]

The true light, which enlightens everyone, was coming
into the world.

>He was in the world,
>>and the world came to be through him,
>>but the world did not know him.

>He came to what was his own,
>>but his own people did not accept him.

But to those who did accept him he gave power to
become children of God, to those who believe in his
name, who were born not by natural generation nor by
human choice nor by a man's decision but of God.

>And the Word became flesh
>>and made his dwelling among us,
>>and we saw his glory,
>>the glory as of the Father's only Son,
>>full of grace and truth.

>>[John testified to him and cried out, saying,
>>"This was he of whom I said, 'The one who is
>>coming after me ranks ahead of me because
>>he existed before me.'" From his fullness we
>>have all received, grace in place of grace,
>>because while the law was given through
>>Moses, grace and truth came through Jesus
>>Christ. No one has ever seen God. The only
>>Son, God, who is at the Father's side, has
>>revealed him.]

The Gospel of the Lord. ℟. **Praise to you, Lord Jesus
Christ.** ➜ No. 15, p. 18

The Creed is said. All kneel at the words and by the Holy Spirit was incarnate.

PRAYER OVER THE OFFERINGS   [Reconciliation]

Make acceptable, O Lord, our oblation on this solemn
     day,
when you manifested the reconciliation
that makes us wholly pleasing in your sight
and inaugurated for us the fullness of divine worship.
Through Christ our Lord.
℟. **Amen.**   → No. 21, p. 22 (Pref. P 3-5)

When the Roman Canon is used, the proper form of the Communicantes *(*In communion with those*) is said.*

COMMUNION ANT. Cf. Ps 98 (97):3   [God's Power]

**All the ends of the earth have seen the salvation of our
God.** ↓

PRAYER AFTER COMMUNION   [Giver of Immortality]

Grant, O merciful God,
that, just as the Savior of the world, born this day,
is the author of divine generation for us,
so he may be the giver even of immortality.
Who lives and reigns for ever and ever.
℟. **Amen.**   → No. 30, p. 77

Optional Solemn Blessings, p. 97, and Prayers over the People, p. 105

"He went down with them and came to Nazareth, and was obedient to them."

DECEMBER 29

THE HOLY FAMILY OF JESUS, MARY AND JOSEPH

Feast

ENTRANCE ANT. Lk 2:16   [Jesus, Mary, and Joseph]

The shepherds went in haste, and found Mary and Joseph and the Infant lying in a manger. → No. 2, p. 10

COLLECT   [Shining Example]

O God, who were pleased to give us
the shining example of the Holy Family,
graciously grant that we may imitate them
in practicing the virtues of family life and in the bonds
   of charity,
and so, in the joy of your house,
delight one day in eternal rewards.
Through our Lord Jesus Christ, your Son,
who lives and reigns with you in the unity of the Holy
   Spirit,
God, for ever and ever. ℟. **Amen.** ↓

The following readings (except the Gospel) are optional. In their place, the readings for Year A, pp. 149-151 may be used.

FIRST READING 1 Sm 1:20-22, 24-28   [God's Creative Love]

This reading teaches us that motherhood and life are a gift of God. The presence of children in a family signals the continuation of life and manifests the newness of God's love, which gives origin to ever new creatures.

A reading from the first Book of Samuel

IN those days Hannah conceived, and at the end of her term bore a son whom she called Samuel, since she had asked the LORD for him. The next time her husband Elkanah was going up with the rest of his household to offer the customary sacrifice to the LORD and to fulfill his vows, Hannah did not go, explaining to her husband, "Once the child is weaned, I will take him to appear before the LORD and to remain there forever; I will offer him as a perpetual nazirite."

Once Samuel was weaned, Hannah brought him up with her, along with a three-year-old bull, an ephah of flour, and a skin of wine, and presented him at the temple of the LORD in Shiloh. After the boy's father had sacrificed the young bull, Hannah, his mother, approached Eli and said: "Pardon, my lord! As you live, my lord, I am the woman who stood near you here, praying to the LORD. I prayed for this child, and the LORD granted my request. Now I, in turn, give him to the LORD; as long as he lives, he shall be dedicated to the LORD." Hannah left Samuel there.—The word of the Lord. ℟. **Thanks be to God.** ↓

RESPONSORIAL PSALM Ps 84   [Love for God's House]

℟. **Blessed   are they who dwell in your house, O Lord.**

How lovely is your dwelling place, O LORD of hosts!
  My soul yearns and pines for the courts of the LORD.
My heart and my flesh cry out for the living God.

℞. **Blessed are they who dwell in your house, O Lord.**

Happy they who dwell in your house!
   Continually they praise you.
Happy the men whose strength you are!
   Their hearts are set upon the pilgrimage.

℞. **Blessed are they who dwell in your house, O Lord.**

O LORD of hosts, hear our prayer;
   hearken, O God of Jacob!
O God, behold our shield,
   and look upon the face of your anointed.

℞. **Blessed are they who dwell in your house, O Lord.** ↓

SECOND READING 1 Jn 3:1-2, 21-24   [Children of God]

Every family must be a mirror of the divine love because
the root of every genuine love is God. Therefore, members
of a family should deal lovingly with one another.

A reading from the first Letter of Saint John

BELOVED: See what love the Father has bestowed
on us that we may be called the children of God.
And so we are. The reason the world does not know us
is that it did not know him. Beloved, we are God's children now; what we shall be has not yet been revealed.
We do know that when it is revealed we shall be like
him, for we shall see him as he is.

   Beloved, if our hearts do not condemn us, we have
confidence in God and receive from him whatever we
ask, because we keep his commandments and do what
pleases him. And his commandment is this: we should
believe in the name of his Son, Jesus Christ, and love
one another just as he commanded us. Those who keep
his commandments remain in him, and he in them,
and the way we know that he remains in us is from the
Spirit he gave us.—The word of the Lord. ℞. **Thanks
be to God.** ↓

ALLELUIA Cf. Acts 16:14b   [Open Hearts]

℟. **Alleluia, alleluia.**
Open our hearts, O Lord,
to listen to the words of your Son.
℟. **Alleluia, alleluia.** ↓

GOSPEL Lk 2:41-52   [Jesus Was Obedient to Them]

> Jesus and his parents go to Jerusalem for the Passover.
> Upon returning, Jesus is separated from them. Mary and
> Joseph find him in the temple teaching. When Mary asked
> why, Jesus replied that he must be doing his Father's work.
> Jesus returned with Mary and Joseph to Nazareth.

℣. The Lord be with you. ℟. **And with your spirit.**
✠ A reading from the holy Gospel according to Luke.
℟. **Glory to you, O Lord.**

EACH year Jesus' parents went to Jerusalem for the
feast of Passover, and when he was twelve years old,
they went up according to festival custom. After they
had completed its days, as they were returning, the boy
Jesus remained behind in Jerusalem, but his parents did
not know it. Thinking that he was in the caravan, they
journeyed for a day and looked for him among their relatives and acquaintances, but not finding him, they
returned to Jerusalem to look for him. After three days
they found him in the temple, sitting in the midst of the
teachers, listening to them and asking them questions,
and all who heard him were astounded at his understanding and his answers. When his parents saw him,
they were astonished, and his mother said to him, "Son,
why have you done this to us? Your father and I have
been looking for you with great anxiety." And he said to
them, "Why were you looking for me? Did you not know
that I must be in my Father's house?" But they did not
understand what he said to them. He went down with
them and came to Nazareth, and was obedient to them;
and his mother kept all these things in her heart. And

Jesus advanced in wisdom and age and favor before God
and man.—The Gospel of the Lord. ℞. **Praise to you,
Lord Jesus Christ.**   → No. 15, p. 18

PRAYER OVER THE OFFERINGS   [Grace and Peace]

We offer you, Lord, the sacrifice of conciliation,
humbly asking that,
through the intercession of the Virgin Mother of God
  and Saint Joseph,
you may establish our families firmly in your grace
  and your peace.
Through Christ our Lord.
℞. **Amen.**   → No. 21, p. 22 (Pref. P 3-5)

*When the Roman Canon is used, the proper form of the Com-
municantes (In communion with those) is said.*

COMMUNION ANT. Bar 3:38   [God with Us]

**Our God has appeared on the earth, and lived among
us.** ↓

PRAYER AFTER COMMUNION   [Imitate Their Example]

Bring those you refresh with this heavenly Sacrament,
most merciful Father,
to imitate constantly the example of the Holy Family,
so that, after the trials of this world,
we may share their company for ever.
Through Christ our Lord.
℞. **Amen.**   → No. 30, p. 77

Optional Solemn Blessings, p. 97, and Prayers over the People, p. 105

*The following readings from Year A may be used in place of
the optional ones given on pp. 145-146.*

FIRST READING Sir 3:2-6, 12-14   [Duties toward Parents]

**Fidelity to Yahweh implies many particular virtues, and
among them Sirach gives precedence to duties toward parents. He promises atonement for sin to those who honor
their parents.**

A reading from the Book of Sirach

GOD sets a father in honor over his children;
a mother's authority he confirms over her sons.
Whoever honors his father atones for sins,
    and preserves himself from them.
When he prays, he is heard;
    he stores up riches who reveres his mother.
Whoever honors his father is gladdened by children,
    and, when he prays, is heard.
Whoever reveres his father will live a long life;
    he obeys his father who brings comfort to his
    mother.

My son, take care of your father when he is old;
    grieve him not as long as he lives.
Even if his mind fail, be considerate of him;
    revile him not all the days of his life;
kindness to a father will not be forgotten,
    firmly planted against the debt of your sins
    —a house raised in justice to you.
The word of the Lord. ℟. **Thanks be to God.** ↓

RESPONSORIAL PSALM Ps 128   [Happiness in Families]

℟. Bles - sed are those who fear the Lord and walk in   his ways.

Blessed is everyone who fears the LORD,
    who walks in his ways!

For you shall eat the fruit of your handiwork;
blessed shall you be, and favored.

℟. **Blessed are those who fear the Lord and walk in his ways.**

Your wife shall be like a fruitful vine
in the recesses of your home;
your children like olive plants
around your table.

℟. **Blessed are those who fear the Lord and walk in his ways.**

Behold, thus is the man blessed
who fears the LORD.
The LORD bless you from Zion:
may you see the prosperity of Jerusalem
all the days of your life.

℟. **Blessed are those who fear the Lord and walk in his ways.** ↓

SECOND READING Col 3:12-21 or 3:12-17

[Plan for Family Life]

Paul describes the life a Christian embraces through Baptism.

[If the "Shorter Form" is used, the indented text in brackets is omitted.]

A reading from the Letter of Saint Paul to the Colossians

BROTHERS and sisters: Put on, as God's chosen ones, holy and beloved, heartfelt compassion, kindness, humility, gentleness, and patience, bearing with one another and forgiving one another, if one has a grievance against another; as the Lord has forgiven you, so must you also do. And over all these put on love, that is, the bond of perfection. And let the peace of Christ control your hearts, the peace into which you were also called in one body. And be thankful. Let the word of Christ dwell in you richly, as in all wisdom you teach and admonish one another, singing psalms, hymns, and spiritual songs with gratitude in your hearts to God. And whatever you do, in word or in deed, do everything in the name of the Lord Jesus, giving thanks to God the Father through him.

     [Wives, be subordinate to your husbands, as is proper in the Lord. Husbands, love your wives, and avoid any bitterness toward them. Children, obey your parents in everything, for this is pleasing to the Lord. Fathers, do not provoke your children, so they may not become discouraged.]

The word of the Lord. ℟. **Thanks be to God.** ↓

ALLELUIA Col 3:15a, 16a   [Peace of Christ]

℟. **Alleluia, alleluia.**
Let the peace of Christ control your hearts;
let the word of Christ dwell in you richly.
℟. **Alleluia, alleluia.**

"He was named Jesus, . . ."

JANUARY 1, 2025

SOLEMNITY OF MARY,
THE HOLY MOTHER OF GOD

ENTRANCE ANT.   [Hail, Holy Mother]

**Hail, Holy Mother, who gave birth to the King who
rules heaven and earth for ever.**   ➡ No. 2, p. 10

OR Cf. Is 9:1, 5; Lk 1:33   [Wondrous God]

**Today a light will shine upon us, for the Lord is born
for us; and he will be called Wondrous God, Prince of
peace, Father of future ages: and his reign will be
without end.**   ➡ No. 2, p. 10

COLLECT   [Mary's Intercession]

O God, who through the fruitful virginity of Blessed
   Mary
bestowed on the human race
the grace of eternal salvation,
grant, we pray,
that we may experience the intercession of her,
through whom we were found worthy
to receive the author of life,
our Lord Jesus Christ, your Son.

Who lives and reigns with you in the unity of the Holy
  Spirit,
God, for ever and ever.
℟. **Amen.** ↓

FIRST READING Nm 6:22-27   [The Aaronic Blessing]
  God speaks to Moses instructing him to have Aaron and
  the Israelites pray that he may answer their prayers with
  blessings.

        A reading from the Book of Numbers

T HE LORD said to Moses: "Speak to Aaron and his
   sons and tell them: This is how you shall bless the
Israelites. Say to them:

  The LORD bless you and keep you!
  The LORD let his face shine upon you, and be gra-
    cious to you!
  The LORD look upon you kindly and give you peace!

So shall they invoke my name upon the Israelites, and
I will bless them."—The word of the Lord. ℟. **Thanks
be to God.** ↓

RESPONSORIAL PSALM Ps 67   [God Bless Us]

  ℟. May   God   bless   us   in   his   mer - cy.

May God have pity on us and bless us;
  may he let his face shine upon us.
So may your way be known upon earth;
  among all nations, your salvation.

℟. **May God bless us in his mercy.**

May the nations be glad and exult
  because you rule the peoples in equity;
  the nations on the earth you guide.

℟. **May God bless us in his mercy.**

May the peoples praise you, O God;
  may all the peoples praise you!
May God bless us,
  and may all the ends of the earth fear him!

℟. **May God bless us in his mercy.** ↓

SECOND READING Gal 4:4-7   [Heirs by God's Design]
  God sent Jesus, his Son, born of Mary, to deliver all from
  the bondage of sin and slavery to the law. By God's choice
  we are heirs of heaven.

A reading from the Letter of Saint Paul to the Galatians

Brothers and sisters: When the fullness of time
had come, God sent his Son, born of a woman,
born under the law, to ransom those under the law, so
that we might receive adoption as sons. As proof that
you are sons, God sent the Spirit of his Son into our
hearts, crying out, "Abba, Father!" So you are no longer
a slave but a son, and if a son then also an heir,
through God.—The word of the Lord. ℟. **Thanks be to
God.** ↓

ALLELUIA Heb 1:1-2   [God Speaks]

℟. **Alleluia, alleluia.**
In the past God spoke to our ancestors through the
  prophets;
in these last days, he has spoken to us through the Son.
℟. **Alleluia, alleluia.** ↓

GOSPEL Lk 2:16-21   [The Name of Jesus]
  When the shepherds came to Bethlehem, they began to
  understand the message of the angels. Mary prayed about
  this great event. Jesus received his name according to the
  Jewish ritual of circumcision.

℣. The Lord be with you. ℟. **And with your spirit.**
✚ A reading from the holy Gospel according to Luke.
℟. **Glory to you, O Lord.**

T HE shepherds went in haste to Bethlehem and found
Mary and Joseph, and the infant lying in the manger.
When they saw this, they made known the message that
had been told them about this child. All who heard it
were amazed by what had been told them by the shepherds. And Mary kept all these things, reflecting on them
in her heart. Then the shepherds returned, glorifying and
praising God for all they had heard and seen, just as it
had been told to them.

When eight days were completed for his circumcision,
he was named Jesus, the name given him by the angel
before he was conceived in the womb.—The Gospel of
the Lord. ℟. **Praise to you, Lord Jesus Christ.**

➜ No. 15, p. 18

PRAYER OVER THE OFFERINGS   [Rejoice in Grace]

O God, who in your kindness begin all good things
and bring them to fulfillment,
grant to us, who find joy in the Solemnity of the holy
    Mother of God,
that, just as we glory in the beginnings of your grace,
so one day we may rejoice in its completion.
Through Christ our Lord. ℟. **Amen.** ↓

PREFACE (P 56)   [Mary, Virgin and Mother]

℣. The Lord be with you. ℟. **And with your spirit.**
℣. Lift up your hearts. ℟. **We lift them up to the Lord.**
℣. Let us give thanks to the Lord our God. ℟. **It is right
and just.**

It is truly right and just, our duty and our salvation,
always and everywhere to give you thanks,
Lord, holy Father, almighty and eternal God,
and to praise, bless, and glorify your name
on the Solemnity of the Motherhood
of the Blessed ever-Virgin Mary.

For by the overshadowing of the Holy Spirit
she conceived your Only Begotten Son,
and without losing the glory of virginity,
brought forth into the world the eternal Light,
Jesus Christ our Lord.

Through him the Angels praise your majesty,
Dominions adore and Powers tremble before you.
Heaven and the Virtues of heaven and the blessed
   Seraphim
worship together with exultation.
May our voices, we pray, join with theirs
in humble praise, as we acclaim: → No. 23, p. 23

When the Roman Canon is used, the proper form of the Communicantes *(In communion with those) is said.*

COMMUNION ANT. Heb 13:8   [Jesus Forever]
Jesus Christ is the same yesterday, today, and for ever. ↓

PRAYER AFTER COMMUNION   [Mother of the Church]

We have received this heavenly Sacrament with joy,
   O Lord:
grant, we pray,
that it may lead us to eternal life,
for we rejoice to proclaim the blessed ever-Virgin Mary
Mother of your Son and Mother of the Church.
Through Christ our Lord.
R̸. **Amen.**   → No. 30, p. 77

Optional Solemn Blessings, p. 97, and Prayers over the People, p. 105

"They prostrated themselves and did him homage."

JANUARY 5

THE EPIPHANY OF THE LORD

Solemnity

AT THE VIGIL MASS (January 4)

ENTRANCE ANT. Cf. Bar 5:5   [Arise, Jerusalem]

Arise, Jerusalem, and look to the East and see your children gathered from the rising to the setting of the sun. → No. 2, p. 10

COLLECT   [Splendor of God's Majesty]

May the splendor of your majesty, O Lord, we pray,
shed its light upon our hearts,
that we may pass through the shadows of this world
and reach the brightness of our eternal home.
Through our Lord Jesus Christ, your Son,
who lives and reigns with you in the unity of the Holy
    Spirit,
God, for ever and ever.
℟. **Amen.** ↓

FIRST READING Is 60:1-6   [Glory of God's Church]

The Lord favors Jerusalem, which kings and peoples will approach. The riches of the earth will be placed at the gates of Jerusalem.

A reading from the Book of the Prophet Isaiah

RISE up in splendor, Jerusalem! Your light has come,
   the glory of the Lord shines upon you.
See, darkness covers the earth,
   and thick clouds cover the peoples;
but upon you the Lord shines,
   and over you appears his glory.
Nations shall walk by your light,
   and kings by your shining radiance.
Raise your eyes and look about;
   they all gather and come to you:
your sons come from afar,
   and your daughters in the arms of their nurses.

Then you shall be radiant at what you see,
   your heart shall throb and overflow,
for the riches of the sea shall be emptied out before you,
   the wealth of nations shall be brought to you.
Caravans of camels shall fill you,
   dromedaries from Midian and Ephah;
all from Sheba shall come
   bearing gold and frankincense,
   and proclaiming the praises of the Lord.
The word of the Lord. ℟. **Thanks be to God.** ↓

RESPONSORIAL PSALM Ps 72   [The Messiah-King]

℟. Lord, every nation on earth will adore you.

O God, with your judgment endow the king,
    and with your justice, the king's son;
he shall govern your people with justice
    and your afflicted ones with judgment.

℟. **Lord, every nation on earth will adore you.**

Justice shall flower in his days,
    and profound peace, till the moon be no more.
May he rule from sea to sea,
    and from the River to the ends of the earth.

℟. **Lord, every nation on earth will adore you.**

The kings of Tarshish and the Isles shall offer gifts;
    the kings of Arabia and Seba shall bring tribute.
All kings shall pay him homage,
    all nations shall serve him.

℟. **Lord, every nation on earth will adore you.**

For he shall rescue the poor man when he cries out,
    and the afflicted when he has no one to help him.
He shall have pity for the lowly and the poor;
    the lives of the poor he shall save.

℟. **Lord, every nation on earth will adore you.** ↓

SECOND READING Eph 3:2-3a, 5-6   [Good News for All]

> **Paul admits that God has revealed the divine plan of salvation to him. Not only the Jews, but also the whole Gentile world, will share in the Good News.**

A reading from the Letter of Saint Paul to the Ephesians

BROTHERS and sisters: You have heard of the stewardship of God's grace that was given to me for your benefit, namely, that the mystery was made known to me by revelation. It was not made known to people in other generations as it has now been revealed to his holy apostles and prophets by the Spirit: that the Gentiles are coheirs, members of the same body, and copartners in the promise in Christ

Jesus through the gospel.—The word of the Lord.
℞. **Thanks be to God.** ↓

ALLELUIA Mt 2:2   [Leading Star]

℞. **Alleluia, alleluia.**
We saw his star at its rising
and have come to do him homage.
℞. **Alleluia, alleluia.** ↓

GOSPEL Mt 2:1-12   [Magi with Gifts]

King Herod, being jealous of his earthly crown, was threat-
ened by the coming of another king. The magi from the
east followed the star to Bethlehem from which a ruler was
to come.

℣. The Lord be with you. ℞. **And with your spirit.**
✛ A reading from the holy Gospel according to
Matthew. ℞. **Glory to you, O Lord.**

WHEN Jesus was born in Bethlehem of Judea, in the
days of King Herod, behold, magi from the east
arrived in Jerusalem, saying, "Where is the newborn
king of the Jews? We saw his star at its rising and have
come to do him homage." When King Herod heard this,
he was greatly troubled, and all Jerusalem with him.
Assembling all the chief priests and the scribes of the
people, he inquired of them where the Christ was to be
born. They said to him, "In Bethlehem of Judea, for thus
it has been written through the prophet:
    And you, Bethlehem, land of Judah,
        are by no means least among the rulers of Judah;
    since from you shall come a ruler,
        who is to shepherd my people Israel."
Then Herod called the magi secretly and ascertained
from them the time of the star's appearance. He sent
them to Bethlehem and said, "Go and search diligently
for the child. When you have found him, bring me
word, that I too may go and do him homage." After

their audience with the king they set out. And behold,
the star that they had seen at its rising preceded them,
until it came and stopped over the place where the
child was. They were overjoyed at seeing the star, and
on entering the house they saw the child with Mary his
mother. They prostrated themselves and did him homage. Then they opened their treasures and offered him
gifts of gold, frankincense, and myrrh. And having
been warned in a dream not to return to Herod, they
departed for their country by another way.—The
Gospel of the Lord. ℟. **Praise to you, Lord Jesus
Christ.**   ➜ No. 15, p. 18

PRAYER OVER THE OFFERINGS   [Render Praise]

Accept we pray, O Lord, our offerings,
in honor of the appearing of your Only Begotten Son
and the first fruits of the nations,
that to you praise may be rendered
and eternal salvation be ours.
Through Christ our Lord. ℟. **Amen.** ↓

PREFACE (P 6)   [Jesus Revealed to All]
℣. The Lord be with you. ℟. **And with your spirit.**
℣. Lift up your hearts. ℟. **We lift them up to the Lord.**
℣. Let us give thanks to the Lord our God. ℟. **It is right
and just.**

It is truly right and just, our duty and our salvation,
always and everywhere to give you thanks,
Lord, holy Father, almighty and eternal God.

For today you have revealed the mystery
of our salvation in Christ
as a light for the nations,
and, when he appeared in our mortal nature,
you made us new by the glory of his immortal nature.

And so, with Angels and Archangels,
with Thrones and Dominions,
and with all the hosts and Powers of heaven,
we sing the hymn of your glory,
as without end we acclaim: → No. 23, p. 23

COMMUNION ANT. Cf. Rev 21:23   [Walking by God's Light]
The brightness of God illumined the holy city Jerusalem, and the nations will walk by its light. ↓

PRAYER AFTER COMMUNION   [True Treasure]

Renewed by sacred nourishment,
we implore your mercy, O Lord,
that the star of your justice
may shine always bright in our minds
and that our true treasure may ever consist in our
   confession of you.
Through Christ our Lord.
℞. **Amen.**   → No. 30, p. 77

Optional Solemn Blessings, p. 97, and Prayers over the People, p. 105

AT THE MASS DURING THE DAY

ENTRANCE ANT. Cf. Mal 3:1; 1 Chr 29:12   [Lord and Ruler]

Behold, the Lord, the Mighty One, has come; and kingship is in his grasp, and power and dominion.

→ No. 2, p. 10

COLLECT   [Behold Glory]

O God, who on this day
revealed your Only Begotten Son to the nations
by the guidance of a star,
grant in your mercy
that we, who know you already by faith,
may be brought to behold the beauty of your sublime
    glory.
Through our Lord Jesus Christ, your Son,
who lives and reigns with you in the unity of the Holy
    Spirit,
God, for ever and ever.
℟. **Amen.** ↓

The readings for this Mass can be found beginning on p. 158.

PRAYER OVER THE OFFERINGS   [Offering of Jesus]

Look with favor, Lord, we pray,
on these gifts of your Church,
in which are offered now not gold or frankincense or
    myrrh,
but he who by them is proclaimed,
sacrificed and received, Jesus Christ.
Who lives and reigns for ever and ever.
℟. **Amen.**   → Pref. P 6, p. 167

When the Roman Canon is used, the proper form of the Com-municantes (In communion with those) is said.

COMMUNION ANT. Cf. Mt 2:2 [Adore the Lord]

We have seen his star in the East, and have come with gifts to adore the Lord. ↓

PRAYER AFTER COMMUNION [Heavenly Light]

Go before us with heavenly light, O Lord,
always and everywhere,
that we may perceive with clear sight
and revere with true affection
the mystery in which you have willed us to participate.
Through Christ our Lord.
℟. **Amen.** → No. 30, p. 77

Optional Solemn Blessings, p. 97, and Prayers over the People, p. 105

"You are my beloved Son; with you I am well pleased."

JANUARY 12

THE BAPTISM OF THE LORD

Feast

ENTRANCE ANT. Cf. Mt 3:16-17   [Beloved Son]
After the Lord was baptized, the heavens were opened,
and the Spirit descended upon him like a dove, and the
voice of the Father thundered: This is my beloved Son,
with whom I am well pleased.   → No. 2, p. 10

COLLECT   [Children by Adoption]
Almighty ever-living God,
who, when Christ had been baptized in the River Jordan
and as the Holy Spirit descended upon him,
solemnly declared him your beloved Son,
grant that your children by adoption,
reborn of water and the Holy Spirit,
may always be well pleasing to you.
Through our Lord Jesus Christ, your Son,
who lives and reigns with you in the unity of the Holy
     Spirit,
God, for ever and ever. ℟. **Amen.** ↓

OR   [God Became Man]

O God, whose Only Begotten Son
has appeared in our very flesh,
grant, we pray, that we may be inwardly transformed
through him whom we recognize as outwardly like
    ourselves.
Who lives and reigns with you in the unity of the Holy
    Spirit,
God, for ever and ever. ℟. **Amen.** ↓

*The following readings (except the Gospel) are optional. In
their place, the readings for Year A, pp. 171-172, may be used.*

FIRST READING Is 40:1-5, 9-11   [Promise of Salvation]

Isaiah's central message is an announcement of salvation
for the people of God. He reveals God as a Shepherd-King,
attracting and ever caring for his people.

A reading from the Book of the Prophet Isaiah

COMFORT, give comfort to my people,
    says your God.
Speak tenderly to Jerusalem, and proclaim to her
    that her service is at an end,
    her guilt is expiated;
indeed, she has received from the hand of the LORD
    double for all her sins.

    A voice cries out:
In the desert prepare the way of the LORD!
    Make straight in the wasteland a highway for our
        God!
Every valley shall be filled in,
    every mountain and hill shall be made low;
the rugged land shall be made a plain,
    the rough country, a broad valley.
Then the glory of the LORD shall be revealed,
    and all people shall see it together;
    for the mouth of the LORD has spoken.

Go up onto a high mountain,
　　Zion, herald of glad tidings;
cry out at the top of your voice,
　　Jerusalem, herald of good news!
Fear not to cry out
　　and say to the cities of Judah:
　　Here is your God!
Here comes with power
　　the Lord GOD,
　　who rules by a strong arm;
here is his reward with him,
　　his recompense before him.
Like a shepherd he feeds his flock;
　　in his arms he gathers the lambs,
carrying them in his bosom,
　　and leading the ewes with care.

The word of the Lord. ℟. **Thanks be to God.** ↓

RESPONSORIAL PSALM Ps 104   [Creator and Redeemer]

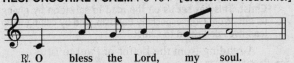

℟. **O   bless   the   Lord,   my   soul.**

O LORD, my God, you are great indeed!
　　you are clothed with majesty and glory,
robed in light as with a cloak.
　　You have spread out the heavens like a tent-cloth.

℟. **O bless the Lord, my soul.**

You have constructed your palace upon the waters.
　　You make the clouds your chariot;
you travel on the wings of the wind.
　　You make the winds your messengers,
and flaming fire your ministers.

℟. **O bless the Lord, my soul.**

How manifold are your works, O LORD!
　　In wisdom you have wrought them all—

the earth is full of your creatures;
  the sea also, great and wide,
in which are schools without number
  of living things both small and great.

℟. **O bless the Lord, my soul.**

They look to you to give them food in due time.
  When you give it to them, they gather it;
when you open your hand, they are filled with good
    things.

℟. **O bless the Lord, my soul.**

If you take away their breath, they perish and return to
    the dust.
  When you send forth your spirit, they are created,
and you renew the face of the earth.

℟. **O bless the Lord, my soul.** ↓

SECOND READING Ti 2:11-14; 3:4-7 [Called through Baptism]

Paul proclaims that the "grace of God has appeared" in
Christ. This has set us on the road to salvation by giving
us gifts from God, especially Baptism, and by calling us to
lead lives dedicated to Christ.

A reading from the Letter of Paul to Titus

BELOVED: The grace of God has appeared, saving
all and training us to reject godless ways and
worldly desires and to live temperately, justly, and
devoutly in this age, as we await the blessed hope, the
appearance of the glory of our great God and savior
Jesus Christ, who gave himself for us to deliver us
from all lawlessness and to cleanse for himself a people as his own, eager to do what is good.

When the kindness and generous love
  of God our savior appeared,
not because of any righteous deeds we had done
  but because of his mercy,
he saved us through the bath of rebirth
  and renewal by the Holy Spirit,

whom he richly poured out on us
    through Jesus Christ our savior,
so that we might be justified by his grace
    and become heirs in hope of eternal life.
The word of the Lord. ℟. **Thanks be to God.** ↓

ALLELUIA Cf. Lk 3:16   **[Baptism with the Spirit]**
℟. **Alleluia, alleluia.**
John said: One mightier than I is coming;
he will baptize you with the Holy Spirit and with fire.
℟. **Alleluia, alleluia.** ↓

GOSPEL Lk 3:15-16, 21-22   **[Beloved Son]**
    The Spirit of God is seen coming upon Christ. The words
    of Isaiah are beginning to be fulfilled.

℣. The Lord be with you. ℟. **And with your spirit.**
✠ A reading from the holy Gospel according to Luke.
℟. **Glory to you, O Lord.**

THE people were filled with expectation, and all were
asking in their hearts whether John might be the
Christ. John answered them all, saying, "I am baptizing
you with water, but one mightier than I is coming. I am
not worthy to loosen the thongs of his sandals. He will
baptize you with the Holy Spirit and fire."
    After all the people had been baptized and Jesus
also had been baptized and was praying, heaven was
opened and the Holy Spirit descended upon him in
bodily form like a dove. And a voice came from heav-
en, "You are my beloved Son; with you I am well
pleased."—The Gospel of the Lord. ℟. **Praise to you,
Lord Jesus Christ.**   ➜ No. 15, p. 18

PRAYER OVER THE OFFERINGS   **[Christ's Revelation]**
Accept, O Lord, the offerings
we have brought to honor the revealing of your
    beloved Son,
so that the oblation of your faithful
may be transformed into the sacrifice of him

who willed in his compassion
to wash away the sins of the world.
Who lives and reigns for ever and ever. ℟. **Amen.** ↓

PREFACE (P 7)   [New Gift of Baptism]

℣. The Lord be with you. ℟. **And with your spirit.**
℣. Lift up your hearts. ℟. **We lift them up to the Lord.**
℣. Let us give thanks to the Lord our God. ℟. **It is right and just.**

It is truly right and just, our duty and our salvation,
always and everywhere to give you thanks,
Lord, holy Father, almighty and eternal God.

For in the waters of the Jordan
you revealed with signs and wonders a new Baptism,
so that through the voice that came down from heaven
we might come to believe in your Word dwelling
    among us,
and by the Spirit's descending in the likeness of a dove
we might know that Christ your Servant
has been anointed with the oil of gladness
and sent to bring the good news to the poor.

And so, with the Powers of heaven,
we worship you constantly on earth,
and before your majesty
without end we acclaim: ➜ No. 23, p. 23

COMMUNION ANT. Jn 1:32, 34   [Witness to God's Son]
Behold the One of whom John said: I have seen and testified that this is the Son of God. ↓

PRAYER AFTER COMMUNION   [Children in Truth]
Nourished with these sacred gifts,
we humbly entreat your mercy, O Lord,
that, faithfully listening to your Only Begotten Son,
we may be your children in name and in truth.
Through Christ our Lord.
℟. **Amen.**   ➜ No. 30, p. 77

Optional Solemn Blessings, p. 97, and Prayers over the People, p. 105

*The following readings from Year A may be used in place of
the optional ones given on pp. 166-169, excluding Gospel.*

FIRST READING Is 42:1-4, 6-7   [Works of the Messiah]

**The prophet Isaiah sees the spirit upon the Lord's servant
who will proclaim the "good news" to the poor, freedom
to prisoners and joy to those in sorrow.**

A reading from the Book of the Prophet Isaiah

T HUS says the LORD:
    Here is my servant whom I uphold,
        my chosen one with whom I am pleased,
    upon whom I have put my spirit;
        he shall bring forth justice to the nations,
    not crying out, not shouting,
        not making his voice heard in the street.
    A bruised reed he shall not break,
        and a smoldering wick he shall not quench,
    until he establishes justice on the earth;
        the coastlands will wait for his teaching.

I, the LORD, have called you for the victory of justice,
        I have grasped you by the hand;
    I formed you, and set you
        as a covenant of the people,
        a light for the nations,
    to open the eyes of the blind,
        to bring out prisoners from confinement,
        and from the dungeon, those who live in darkness.

The word of the Lord. ℟. **Thanks be to God.** ↓

RESPONSORIAL PSALM Ps 29   [Peace for God's People]

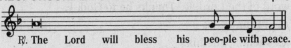

℟. The   Lord   will   bless   his   peo-ple with peace.

Give to the LORD, you sons of God,
    give to the LORD glory and praise,
give to the LORD the glory due his name;
    adore the LORD in holy attire.

℞. **The Lord will bless his people with peace.**

The voice of the LORD is over the waters,
    the LORD, over vast waters.
The voice of the LORD is mighty;
    the voice of the LORD is majestic.

℞. **The Lord will bless his people with peace.**

The God of glory thunders,
    and in his temple all say, "Glory!"
The LORD is enthroned above the flood;
    the LORD is enthroned as king forever.

℞. **The Lord will bless his people with peace.** ↓

SECOND READING Acts 10:34-38   [Anointed to Do Good]
**God anointed Jesus the Savior with the Holy Spirit and
power. Jesus is the Lord of all, and he brought healing to
all who were in the grip of the devil.**

A reading from the Acts of the Apostles

PETER proceeded to speak to those gathered in the
house of Cornelius, saying: "In truth, I see that God
shows no partiality. Rather, in every nation whoever
fears him and acts uprightly is acceptable to him. You
know the word that he sent to the Israelites as he proclaimed peace through Jesus Christ, who is Lord of all,
what has happened all over Judea, beginning in
Galilee after the baptism that John preached, how God
anointed Jesus of Nazareth with the Holy Spirit and
power. He went about doing good and healing all those
oppressed by the devil, for God was with him."—The
word of the Lord. ℞. **Thanks be to God.** ↓

ALLELUIA Cf. Mk 9:7   [Hear Him]
℞. **Alleluia, alleluia.**
The heavens were opened and the voice of the Father
    thundered:
This is my beloved Son, listen to him.
℞. **Alleluia, alleluia.**

"Jesus told them, 'Fill the jars with water.'"

JANUARY 19

2nd SUNDAY IN ORDINARY TIME

ENTRANCE ANT. Ps 66 (65):4   [Proclaim His Glory]
All the earth shall bow down before you, O God, and
shall sing to you, shall sing to your name, O Most
High!   ➡ No. 2, p. 10

COLLECT   [Peace on Our Times]
Almighty ever-living God,
who govern all things,
both in heaven and on earth,
mercifully hear the pleading of your people
and bestow your peace on our times.
Through our Lord Jesus Christ, your Son,
who lives and reigns with you in the unity of the Holy
    Spirit,
God, for ever and ever.
℟. **Amen.** ↓

FIRST READING Is 62:1-5   [God's Love for His People]

"Zion," "Jerusalem," is the people of God and God describes his love and concern for us in terms of the joy of a bridegroom.

A reading from the Book of the Prophet Isaiah

FOR Zion's sake I will not be silent,
  for Jerusalem's sake I will not be quiet,
until her vindication shines forth like the dawn
  and her victory like a burning torch.

Nations shall behold your vindication,
  and all the kings your glory;
you shall be called by a new name
  pronounced by the mouth of the LORD.
You shall be a glorious crown in the hand of the LORD,
  a royal diadem held by your God.
No more shall people call you "Forsaken,"
  or your land "Desolate,"
but you shall be called "My Delight,"
  and your land "Espoused."
For the LORD delights in you
  and makes your land his spouse.
As a young man marries a virgin,
  your Builder shall marry you;
and as a bridegroom rejoices in his bride
  so shall your God rejoice in you.
The word of the Lord. ℟. **Thanks be to God.** ↓

RESPONSORIAL PSALM Ps 96   [Proclaim God's Deeds]

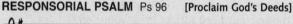
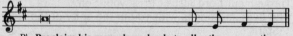

℟. **Proclaim his marvelous deeds to all the na - tions.**

Sing to the LORD a new song;
  sing to the LORD, all you lands.
Sing to the LORD; bless his name.

℟. **Proclaim his marvelous deeds to all the nations.**

Announce his salvation, day after day.
Tell his glory among the nations;
    among all peoples, his wondrous deeds.

℟. **Proclaim his marvelous deeds to all the nations.**

Give to the LORD, you families of nations,
    give to the LORD glory and praise;
    give to the LORD the glory due his name!

℟. **Proclaim his marvelous deeds to all the nations.**

Worship the LORD in holy attire.
    Tremble before him, all the earth;
say among the nations: The LORD is king.
    He governs the peoples with equity.

℟. **Proclaim his marvelous deeds to all the nations.** ↓

SECOND READING 1 Cor 12:4-11 [Gifts of the Holy Spirit]
**The gifts of God come from the same Spirit. The gifts are
diverse but the Spirit is one; and the gifts are given to unite
not separate us.**

A reading from the first Letter of Saint Paul
to the Corinthians

BROTHERS and sisters: There are different kinds of
spiritual gifts but the same Spirit; there are different forms of service but the same Lord; there are different workings but the same God who produces all of
them in everyone. To each individual the manifestation
of the Spirit is given for some benefit. To one is given
through the Spirit the expression of wisdom; to another, the expression of knowledge according to the same
Spirit; to another, faith by the same Spirit; to another,
gifts of healing by the one Spirit; to another, mighty
deeds; to another, prophecy; to another, discernment
of spirits; to another, varieties of tongues; to another,
interpretation of tongues. But one and the same Spirit

produces all of these, distributing them individually to each person as he wishes.—The word of the Lord. ℟. **Thanks be to God.** ↓

ALLELUIA   Cf. 2 Thes 2:14   [We Are Called]
℟. **Alleluia, alleluia.**
God has called us through the Gospel
to possess the glory of our Lord Jesus Christ.
℟. **Alleluia, alleluia.** ↓

In place of the Alleluia which is given for each Sunday in Ordinary Time, another may be selected.

GOSPEL   Jn 2:1-11   [Jesus Reveals His Glory]
Christ the Lord reveals his glory, and the kingdom of God is at hand.

℣. The Lord be with you. ℟. **And with your spirit.**
✠ A reading from the holy Gospel according to John.
℟. **Glory to you, O Lord.**

THERE was a wedding at Cana in Galilee, and the mother of Jesus was there. Jesus and his disciples were also invited to the wedding. When the wine ran short, the mother of Jesus said to him, "They have no wine." And Jesus said to her, "Woman, how does your concern affect me? My hour has not yet come." His mother said to the servers, "Do whatever he tells you." Now there were six stone water jars there for Jewish ceremonial washings, each holding twenty to thirty gallons. Jesus told them, "Fill the jars with water." So they filled them to the brim. Then he told them, "Draw some out now and take it to the headwaiter." So they took it. And when the headwaiter tasted the water that had become wine, without knowing where it came from—although the servers who had drawn the water knew—, the headwaiter called the bridegroom and said to him, "Everyone serves good wine first, and then when people have drunk freely, an inferior one; but you have kept the good wine until now." Jesus did this

as the beginning of his signs at Cana in Galilee and so
revealed his glory, and his disciples began to believe in
him.—The Gospel of the Lord. ℟. **Praise to you, Lord
Jesus Christ.**   → No. 15, p. 18

PRAYER OVER THE OFFERINGS   [Work of Redemption]

Grant us, O Lord, we pray,
that we may participate worthily in these mysteries,
for whenever the memorial of this sacrifice is celebrated
the work of our redemption is accomplished.
Through Christ our Lord.
℟. **Amen.**   → No. 21, p. 22 (Pref. P 29-36)

COMMUNION ANT. Ps 23 (22):5   [Thirst Quenched]
**You have prepared a table before me, and how pre-
cious is the chalice that quenches my thirst.** ↓

OR 1 Jn 4:16   [God's Love]
**We have come to know and to believe in the love that
God has for us.** ↓

PRAYER AFTER COMMUNION   [One in Heart]

Pour on us, O Lord, the Spirit of your love,
and in your kindness
make those you have nourished
by this one heavenly Bread
one in mind and heart.
Through Christ our Lord.
℟. **Amen.**   → No. 30, p. 77

Optional Solemn Blessings, p. 97, and Prayers over the People, p. 105

"The eyes of all in the synagogue looked intently at him."

JANUARY 26

3rd SUNDAY IN ORDINARY TIME

ENTRANCE ANT. Cf. Ps 96 (95):1, 6   [Sing to the Lord]

O sing a new song to the Lord; sing to the Lord, all the earth. In his presence are majesty and splendor, strength and honor in his holy place.   → No. 2, p. 10

COLLECT   [Abound in Good Works]

Almighty ever-living God,
direct our actions according to your good pleasure,
that in the name of your beloved Son
we may abound in good works.
Through our Lord Jesus Christ, your Son,
who lives and reigns with you in the unity of the Holy
   Spirit,
God, for ever and ever.
℟. **Amen.** ↓

FIRST READING Neh 8:2-4a, 5-6, 8-10   [God's Law]

The people of God return to their homeland, rebuild the temple, and now listen to the proclamation of the law of God.

A reading from the Book of the Prophet Nehemiah

EZRA the priest brought the law before the assembly, which consisted of men, women, and those children old enough to understand. Standing at one end of the open place that was before the Water Gate, he read out of the book from daybreak till midday, in the presence of the men, the women, and those children old enough to understand; and all the people listened attentively to the book of the law. Ezra the scribe stood on a wooden platform that had been made for the occasion. He opened the scroll so that all the people might see it—for he was standing higher up than any of the people—; and, as he opened it, all the people rose. Ezra blessed the LORD, the great God, and all the people, their hands raised high, answered, "Amen, amen!" Then they bowed down and prostrated themselves before the LORD, their faces to the ground. Ezra read plainly from the book of the law of God, interpreting it so that all could understand what was read. Then Nehemiah, that is, His Excellency, and Ezra the priest-scribe and the Levites who were instructing the people said to all the people: "Today is holy to the LORD your God. Do not be sad, and do not weep"—for all the people were weeping as they heard the words of the law. He said further: "Go, eat rich foods and drink sweet drinks, and allot portions to those who had nothing prepared; for today is holy to our LORD. Do not be saddened this day, for rejoicing in the LORD must be your strength!"—The word of the Lord. ℟. **Thanks be to God.** ↓

RESPONSORIAL PSALM Ps 19   [Spirit and Life]

℟. Your   words,   Lord,   are   Spir - it   and life.

The law of the LORD is perfect,
  refreshing the soul;

the decree of the LORD is trustworthy,
  giving wisdom to the simple.

℟. **Your words, Lord, are Spirit and life.**

The precepts of the LORD are right,
  rejoicing the heart;
the command of the LORD is clear,
  enlightening the eye.

℟. **Your words, Lord, are Spirit and life.**

The fear of the LORD is pure,
  enduring forever;
the ordinances of the LORD are true,
  all of them just.

℟. **Your words, Lord, are Spirit and life.**

Let the words of my mouth and the thought of my
    heart
  find favor before you,
O LORD, my rock and my redeemer.

℟. **Your words, Lord, are Spirit and life.** ↓

SECOND READING 1 Cor 12:12-30 or 12:12-14, 27 [One Body]
  **By Baptism we begin to become Christians, Christ unites
  himself to us, and we must grow with him.**

*[If the "Shorter Form" is used, the indented text in brackets is
omitted.]*

A reading from the first Letter of Saint Paul
to the Corinthians

BROTHERS and sisters: As a body is one though it
has many parts, and all the parts of the body,
though many, are one body, so also Christ. For in one
Spirit we were all baptized into one body, whether
Jews or Greeks, slaves or free persons, and we were all
given to drink of one Spirit.
  Now the body is not a single part, but many.

[If a foot should say, "Because I am not a hand I do not belong to the body," it does not for this reason belong any less to the body. Or if an ear should say, "Because I am not an eye I do not belong to the body," it does not for this reason belong any less to the body. If the whole body were an eye, where would the hearing be? If the whole body were hearing, where would the sense of smell be? But as it is, God placed the parts, each one of them, in the body as he intended. If they were all one part, where would the body be? But as it is, there are many parts, yet one body. The eye cannot say to the hand, "I do not need you," nor again the head to the feet, "I do not need you." Indeed, the parts of the body that seem to be weaker are all the more necessary, and those parts of the body that we consider less honorable we surround with greater honor, and our less presentable parts are treated with greater propriety, whereas our more presentable parts do not need this. But God has so constructed the body as to give greater honor to a part that is without it, so that there may be no division in the body, but that the parts may have the same concern for one another. If one part suffers, all the parts suffer with it; if one part is honored, all the parts share its joy.]

Now you are Christ's body, and individually parts of it.

[Some people God has designated in the church to be, first, apostles; second, prophets; third, teachers; then, mighty deeds; then gifts of healing, assistance, administration, and varieties of tongues. Are all apostles? Are all prophets? Are all teachers? Do all work mighty deeds? Do all have gifts of healing? Do all speak in tongues? Do all interpret?]

The word of the Lord. ℟. **Thanks be to God.** ↓

ALLELUIA Cf. Lk 4:18   [Glad Tidings]

℟. **Alleluia, alleluia.**

The Lord sent me to bring glad tidings to the poor,
and to proclaim liberty to captives.

℟. **Alleluia, alleluia.** ↓

GOSPEL Lk 1:1-4; 4:14-21   [Proclaiming the Good News]

Jesus proclaims the "good news" to the poor, and announces the fulfillment of the prophetic vision of Isaiah.

℣. The Lord be with you. ℟. **And with your spirit.**

✜ A reading from the holy Gospel according to Luke.

℟. **Glory to you, O Lord.**

SINCE many have undertaken to compile a narrative of the events that have been fulfilled among us, just as those who were eyewitnesses from the beginning and ministers of the word have handed them down to us, I too have decided, after investigating everything accurately anew, to write it down in an orderly sequence for you, most excellent Theophilus, so that you may realize the certainty of the teachings you have received.

Jesus returned to Galilee in the power of the Spirit, and news of him spread throughout the whole region. He taught in their synagogues and was praised by all.

He came to Nazareth, where he had grown up, and went according to his custom into the synagogue on the sabbath day. He stood up to read and was handed a scroll of the prophet Isaiah. He unrolled the scroll and found the passage where it was written:

The Spirit of the Lord is upon me,
because he has anointed me
to bring glad tidings to the poor.
He has sent me to proclaim liberty to captives
and recovery of sight to the blind,
to let the oppressed go free,
and to proclaim a year acceptable to the Lord.

Rolling up the scroll, he handed it back to the attendant and sat down, and the eyes of all in the synagogue looked intently at him. He said to them, "Today
this Scripture passage is fulfilled in your hearing."—
The Gospel of the Lord. ℟. **Praise to you, Lord Jesus
Christ.**   ➜ No. 15, p. 18

PRAYER OVER THE OFFERINGS   [Offerings for Salvation]

Accept our offerings, O Lord, we pray,
and in sanctifying them
grant that they may profit us for salvation.
Through Christ our Lord.
℟. **Amen.**   ➜ No. 21, p. 22 (Pref. P 29-36)

COMMUNION ANT. Cf. Ps 34 (33):6   [Radiance]

**Look toward the Lord and be radiant; let your faces
not be abashed.** ↓

OR Jn 8:12   [Light of Life]

**I am the light of the world, says the Lord; whoever fol-
lows me will not walk in darkness, but will have the
light of life.** ↓

PRAYER AFTER COMMUNION   [New Life]

Grant, we pray, almighty God,
that, receiving the grace
by which you bring us to new life,
we may always glory in your gift.
Through Christ our Lord.
℟. **Amen.**   ➜ No. 30, p. 77

Optional Solemn Blessings, p. 97, and Prayers over the People, p. 105

"This child is destined for the fall and rise of many in Israel."

FEBRUARY 2

THE PRESENTATION OF THE LORD

Feast

The Blessing of Candles and the Procession

FIRST FORM: THE PROCESSION

At an appropriate hour, a gathering takes place at a smaller church or other suitable place other than inside the church to which the procession will go. The faithful hold in their hands unlighted candles.

While the candles are being lit, the following antiphon or another appropriate chant is sung.

[The Lord's Power]

Behold, our Lord will come with power, to enlighten the eyes of his servants, alleluia.

When the chant is concluded, the Priest, facing the people, says: In the name of the Father, and of the Son, and of the Holy Spirit. *Then the Priest greets the people in the usual way, and next he gives an introductory address, encouraging the faithful to celebrate the rite of this feast day actively and consciously. He may use these or similar words:*

184

[Encountering Christ]

Dear brethren (brothers and sisters),
forty days have passed since we celebrated the joyful feast
of the Nativity of the Lord.
Today is the blessed day
when Jesus was presented in the Temple by Mary and Joseph.
Outwardly he was fulfilling the Law,
but in reality he was coming to meet his believing people.
Prompted by the Holy Spirit,
Simeon and Anna came to the Temple.
Enlightened by the same Spirit,
they recognized the Lord
and confessed him with exultation.
So let us also, gathered together by the Holy Spirit,
proceed to the house of God to encounter Christ.
There we shall find him
and recognize him in the breaking of the bread,
until he comes again, revealed in glory.

After the address the Priest blesses the candles, saying, with hands extended:

[Light to the Gentiles]

Let us pray.

O God, source and origin of all light,
who on this day showed to the just man Simeon
the Light for revelation to the Gentiles,
we humbly ask that,
in answer to your people's prayers,
you may be pleased to sanctify with your blessing ✛ these candles,
which we are eager to carry in praise of your name,
so that, treading the path of virtue,
we may reach that light which never fails.
Through Christ our Lord. ℟. **Amen.** ↓

OR   [Light of Glory]

O God, true light, who create light eternal,
spreading it far and wide,
pour, we pray, into the hearts of the faithful
the brilliance of perpetual light,
so that all who are brightened in your holy temple
by the splendor of these candles
may happily reach the light of your glory.
Through Christ our Lord. ℟. **Amen.** ↓

He sprinkles the candles with holy water without saying any-
thing, and puts incense into the thurible for the procession.

Then the Priest receives from the Deacon or a minister the light-
ed candle prepared for him and the procession begins, with the
Deacon announcing (or, if there is no Deacon, the Priest himself):

Let us go in peace to meet the Lord.

OR

Let us go forth in peace.

In this case, all respond: **In the name of Christ. Amen.**

All carry lighted candles. As the procession moves forward,
one or other of the antiphons that follow is sung, namely the
antiphon A light for revelation *with the canticle (Lk 2:29-32),*
or the antiphon Sion, adorn your bridal chamber *or another*
appropriate chant.

I

ANTIPHON   [The Glory of Israel]

A light for revelation to the Gentiles
and the glory of your people Israel.

CANTICLE   [God's Salvation]

Lord, now you let your servant go in peace,
in accordance with your word.

The Antiphon is repeated: "A light for revelation, etc."

For my eyes have seen your salvation.

The Antiphon is repeated: "A light for revelation, etc."

Which you have prepared in the sight of all peoples.

The Antiphon is repeated: "A light for revelation, etc."

II

ANTIPHON

Sion, adorn your bridal chamber and welcome Christ the King; take Mary in your arms, who is the gate of heaven, for she herself is carrying the King of glory and new light. A Virgin she remains, though bringing in her hands the Son before the morning star begotten, whom Simeon, taking in his arms announced to the peoples as Lord of life and death and Savior of the world.

As the procession enters the church, the Entrance Antiphon of the Mass is sung. When the Priest has arrived at the altar, he venerates it and, if appropriate, incenses it. Then he goes to the chair, where he takes off the cope, if he used it in the procession, and puts on a chasuble. After the singing of the hymn Gloria in excelsis *(Glory to God in the highest), he says the Collect as usual. The Mass continues in the usual manner.*

SECOND FORM: THE SOLEMN ENTRANCE

Whenever a procession cannot take place, the faithful gather in church, holding candles in their hands. The Priest, wearing white sacred vestments as for Mass, together with the ministers and a representative group of the faithful, goes to a suitable place, either in front of the church door or inside the church itself, where at least a large part of the faithful can conveniently participate in the rite.

When the Priest reaches the place appointed for the blessing of the candles, candles are lit while the antiphon Behold, our Lord *(p. 184) or another appropriate chant is sung.*

Then, after the greeting and address, the Priest blesses the candles, as above (p. 185); and then the procession to the altar takes place, with singing (p. 186). For Mass, what is indicated above is observed.

AT THE MASS

ENTRANCE ANT. Cf. Ps 48 (47):10-11
[God's Merciful Love]

Your merciful love, O God, we have received in the midst of your temple. Your praise, O God, like your name, reaches the ends of the earth; your right hand is filled with saving justice.   → No. 2, p. 10

COLLECT   [Led into God's Presence]

Almighty ever-living God,
we humbly implore your majesty
that, just as your Only Begotten Son
was presented on this day in the Temple
in the substance of our flesh,
so, by your grace,
we may be presented to you with minds made pure.
Through our Lord Jesus Christ, your Son,
who lives and reigns with you in the unity of the Holy
    Spirit,
God, for ever and ever. ℟. **Amen.** ↓

FIRST READING Mal 3:1-4   [With Purified Hearts]

Malachi speaks of God's great intervention in sacred history—God's speaking to the patriarch (Gn 16:7ff), and to Moses (Ex 3:2), and God's leading the way through the Red Sea (Ex 23:20). These wondrous ways in which God is manifested will be applied to messianic messengers.

A reading from the Book of the Prophet Malachi

T HUS says the Lord GOD:
    Lo, I am sending my messenger
    to prepare the way before me;
And suddenly there will come to the temple
    the LORD whom you seek,
And the messenger of the covenant whom you desire.
    Yes, he is coming, says the LORD of hosts.

But who will endure the day of his coming?
  And who can stand when he appears?
For he is like the refiner's fire,
  or like the fuller's lye.
He will sit refining and purifying silver,
  and he will purify the sons of Levi,
Refining them like gold or like silver
  that they may offer due sacrifice to the LORD.
Then the sacrifice of Judah and Jerusalem
  will please the LORD,
  as in the days of old, as in years gone by.
The word of the Lord. ℟. **Thanks be to God.** ↓

RESPONSORIAL PSALM Ps 24   [The King of Glory]

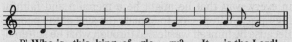

  ℟. Who is this king of glo - ry?   It   is the Lord!

Lift up, O gates, your lintels;
  reach up, you ancient portals,
  that the king of glory may come in!
℟. **Who is this king of glory? It is the Lord!**

Who is this king of glory?
  The LORD, strong and mighty,
  the LORD, mighty in battle.

℟. **Who is this king of glory? It is the Lord!**

Lift up, O gates, your lintels;
  reach up, you ancient portals,
  that the king of glory may come in!

℟. **Who is this king of glory? It is the Lord!**

Who is this king of glory?
  The LORD of hosts; he is the king of glory.

℟. **Who is this king of glory? It is the Lord!** ↓

SECOND READING Heb 2:14-18   [Christ Our Brother]

In the biblical sense, "flesh" means human nature consid-
ered in its weakness. It is contrasted with "spirit" and God.
Because of the connection between sin and death, Christ
overcame the power of death through his priestly work.

A reading from the Letter to the Hebrews

SINCE the children share in blood and flesh, Jesus
likewise shared in them, that through death he might
destroy the one who has the power of death, that is, the
Devil, and free those who through fear of death had
been subject to slavery all their life. Surely he did not
help angels but rather the descendants of Abraham;
therefore, he had to become like his brothers and sisters
in every way, that he might be a merciful and faithful
high priest before God to expiate the sins of the people.
Because he himself was tested through what he suffered,
he is able to help those who are being tested.—The word
of the Lord. ℟. **Thanks be to God.** ↓

ALLELUIA Lk 2:32   [Christ the Light]

℟. **Alleluia, alleluia.**
A light of revelation to the Gentiles
and glory for your people Israel.
℟. **Alleluia, alleluia.** ↓

GOSPEL Lk 2:22-40 or 2:22-32   [The Lord's Salvation]

Mary is seen here, united with Jesus and Joseph in the
Temple ceremony. Jesus is formally recognized as a member of God's chosen people through whom world salvation
was to be achieved.

*[If the "Shorter Form" is used, the indented text in brackets is
omitted.]*

℣. The Lord be with you. ℟. **And with your spirit.**
✢ A reading from the holy Gospel according to Luke.
℟. **Glory to you, O Lord.**

WHEN the days were completed for their purification according to the law of Moses, Mary and Joseph took Jesus up to Jerusalem to present him to the Lord, just as it is written in the law of the Lord, *Every male that opens the womb shall be consecrated to the Lord,* and to offer the sacrifice of *a pair of turtledoves or two young pigeons,* in accordance with the dictate in the law of the Lord.

Now there was a man in Jerusalem whose name was Simeon. This man was righteous and devout, awaiting the consolation of Israel, and the Holy Spirit was upon him. It had been revealed to him by the Holy Spirit that he should not see death before he had seen the Christ of the Lord. He came in the Spirit into the temple; and when the parents brought in the child Jesus to perform the custom of the law in regard to him, he took him into his arms and blessed God, saying:

"Now, Master, you may let your servant go
   in peace, according to your word,
for my eyes have seen your salvation,
   which you prepared in sight of all the peoples,
a light for revelation to the Gentiles,
   and glory for your people Israel."

[The child's father and mother were amazed at what was said about him; and Simeon blessed them and said to Mary his mother, "Behold, this child is destined for the fall and rise of many in Israel, and to be a sign that will be contradicted—and you yourself a sword will pierce—so that the thoughts of many hearts may be revealed." There was also a prophetess, Anna, the daughter of Phanuel, of the tribe of Asher. She was advanced in years, having lived seven years with her husband after her marriage, and then as a widow until she was eighty-four. She never left the temple, but worshiped night and day with fasting and prayer. And coming forward at that very time, she gave thanks to God and spoke about the child to all who were awaiting the redemption of Jerusalem.

When they had fulfilled all the prescriptions of the law of the Lord, they returned to Galilee, to their own town of Nazareth. The child grew and became strong, filled with wisdom; and the favor of God was upon him.]

The Gospel of the Lord. ℞. **Praise to you, Lord Jesus Christ.**   → No. 15, p. 18

PRAYER OVER THE OFFERINGS [Lamb without Blemish]

May the offering made with exultation by your Church
be pleasing to you, O Lord, we pray,
for you willed that your Only Begotten Son
be offered to you for the life of the world
as the Lamb without blemish.
Who lives and reigns for ever and ever. ℞. **Amen.** ↓

PREFACE (P 49)   [Revelation of Christ the Light]

℣. The Lord be with you. ℞. **And with your spirit.**
℣. Lift up your hearts. ℞. **We lift them up to the Lord.** ℣. Let us give thanks to the Lord our God. ℞. **It is right and just.**

It is truly right and just, our duty and our salvation,
always and everywhere to give you thanks,
Lord, holy Father, almighty and eternal God.

For your co-eternal Son was presented on this day in the Temple
and revealed by the Spirit
as the glory of Israel and Light of the nations.

And so, we, too, go forth, rejoicing to encounter your Salvation,
and with the Angels and Saints
praise you, as without end we acclaim:

→ No. 23, p. 23

COMMUNION ANT. Lk 2:30-31   [Sight of Salvation]

My eyes have seen your salvation, which you prepared in the sight of all the peoples. ↓

PRAYER AFTER COMMUNION [Preparing To Meet Christ]

By these holy gifts which we have received, O Lord,
bring your grace to perfection within us,
and, as you fulfilled Simeon's expectation
that he would not see death
until he had been privileged to welcome the Christ,
so may we, going forth to meet the Lord,
obtain the gift of eternal life.
Through Christ our Lord.
℟. **Amen.**   → No. 30, p. 77

Optional Solemn Blessings, p. 97, and Prayers over the People, p. 105

"They caught a great number of fish . . ."

FEBRUARY 9

5th SUNDAY IN ORDINARY TIME

ENTRANCE ANT. Ps 95 (94):6-7   [Adoration]

O come, let us worship God and bow low before the
God who made us, for he is the Lord our God.

→ No. 2, p. 10

COLLECT   [God's Protection]

Keep your family safe, O Lord, with unfailing care,
that, relying solely on the hope of heavenly grace,
they may be defended always by your protection.
Through our Lord Jesus Christ, your Son,
who lives and reigns with you in the unity of the Holy
   Spirit,
God, for ever and ever.
℟. **Amen.** ↓

FIRST READING Is 6:1-2a, 3-8   [Call of Isaiah]

   The prophet, aware of his own unworthiness, is fearful.
   Purged of sin he accepts the call of the Father.

A reading from the Book of the Prophet Isaiah

IN the year King Uzziah died, I saw the Lord seated
on a high and lofty throne, with the train of his garment filling the temple. Seraphim were stationed
above.

They cried one to the other, "Holy, holy, holy is the
LORD of hosts! All the earth is filled with his glory!" At
the sound of that cry, the frame of the door shook and
the house was filled with smoke.

Then I said, "Woe is me, I am doomed! For I am a
man of unclean lips, living among a people of unclean
lips; yet my eyes have seen the King, the LORD of
hosts!" Then one of the seraphim flew to me, holding
an ember that he had taken with tongs from the altar.

He touched my mouth with it, and said, "See, now
that this has touched your lips, your wickedness is
removed, your sin purged."

Then I heard the voice of the Lord saying, "Whom
shall I send? Who will go for us?" "Here I am," I said;
"send me!"—The word of the Lord. ℟. **Thanks be to
God.** ↓

RESPONSORIAL PSALM Ps 138   [Gratitude to God]

℟. In the sight of the an-gels I will sing your praise-es, Lord.

I will give thanks to you, O LORD, with all my heart,
  for you have heard the words of my mouth;
    in the presence of the angels I will sing your praise;
I will worship at your holy temple
  and give thanks to your name.

℟. **In the sight of the angels I will sing your praises,
  Lord.**

Because of your kindness and your truth;
  for you have made great above all things
    your name and your promise.
When I called, you answered me;
  you built up strength within me.

℟. **In the sight of the angels I will sing your praises,
  Lord.**

All the kings of the earth shall give thanks to you,
    O LORD,
  when they hear the words of your mouth;
and they shall sing of the ways of the LORD:
  "Great is the glory of the LORD."

℟. **In the sight of the angels I will sing your praises,
  Lord.**

Your right hand saves me.
  The LORD will complete what he has done for me;
your kindness, O LORD, endures forever;
  forsake not the work of your hands.

℟. **In the sight of the angels I will sing your praises,
  Lord.** ↓

SECOND READING 1 Cor 15:1-11 or 15:3-8, 11

[Content of the Good News]

Through God's favor, the Apostle turned from persecution to preaching the "good news" like Isaiah. Christ has died, Christ is risen, Christ will come again.

[If the "Shorter Form" is used, the indented text in brackets is omitted.]

A reading from the first Letter of Saint Paul
to the Corinthians

[I AM reminding you, brothers and sisters, of the gospel I preached to you, which you indeed received and in which you also stand. Through it you are also being saved, if you hold fast to the word I preached to you, unless you believed in vain.]

For* I handed on to you as of first importance what I also received: that Christ died for our sins in accordance with the Scriptures; that he was buried; that he was raised on the third day in accordance with the Scriptures; that he appeared to Cephas, then to the Twelve. After that, he appeared to more than five hundred brothers at once, most of whom are still living, though some have fallen asleep. After that he appeared to James, then to all the apostles. Last of all, as to one born abnormally, he appeared to me.

[For I am the least of the apostles, not fit to be called an apostle, because I persecuted the church of God. But by the grace of God I am what I am, and his grace to me has not been ineffective. Indeed, I have toiled harder than all of them; not I, however, but the grace of God that is with me.]

Therefore, whether it be I or they, so we preach and so you believed.—The word of the Lord. ℟. **Thanks be to God.** ↓

* *The Shorter Form begins "Brothers and sisters:"*

ALLELUIA Mt 4:19   [Fishers of Men]

℟. **Alleluia, alleluia.**
Come after me
and I will make you fishers of men.
℟. **Alleluia, alleluia.**

GOSPEL Lk 5:1-11   [Call of Peter]

Peter confesses: "I am a sinful man," and is reassured by Christ. Then together with James and John he leaves everything to become his follower.

℣. The Lord be with you. ℟. **And with your spirit.**
✠ A reading from the holy Gospel according to Luke.
℟. **Glory to you, O Lord.**

WHILE the crowd was pressing in on Jesus and listening to the word of God, he was standing by the Lake of Gennesaret. He saw two boats there alongside the lake; the fishermen had disembarked and were washing their nets. Getting into one of the boats, the one belonging to Simon, he asked him to put out a short distance from the shore. Then he sat down and taught the crowds from the boat. After he had finished speaking, he said to Simon, "Put out into deep water and lower your nets for a catch." Simon said in reply, "Master, we have worked hard all night and have caught nothing, but at your command I will lower the nets." When they had done this, they caught a great number of fish and their nets were tearing. They signaled to their partners in the other boat to come to help them. They came and filled both boats so that the boats were in danger of sinking. When Simon Peter saw this, he fell at the knees of Jesus and said, "Depart from me, Lord, for I am a sinful man." For astonishment at the catch of fish they had made seized him and all those with him, and likewise James and John, the sons of Zebedee, who were partners of Simon. Jesus

said to Simon, "Do not be afraid; from now on you will
be catching men." When they brought their boats to the
shore, they left everything and followed him.—The
Gospel of the Lord. ℟. **Praise to you, Lord Jesus
Christ.**   → No. 15, p. 18

PRAYER OVER THE OFFERINGS   [Eternal Life]

O Lord our God,
who once established these created things
to sustain us in our frailty,
grant, we pray,
that they may become for us now
the Sacrament of eternal life.
Through Christ our Lord.
℟. **Amen.**   → No. 21, p. 22 (Pref. P 29-36)

COMMUNION ANT. Cf. Ps 107 (106):8-9   [The Lord's Mercy]
**Let them thank the Lord for his mercy, his wonders
for the children of men, for he satisfies the thirsty
soul, and the hungry he fills with good things.** ↓

OR Mt 5:5-6   [Those Who Mourn]
**Blessed are those who mourn, for they shall be con-
soled. Blessed are those who hunger and thirst for
righteousness, for they shall have their fill.** ↓

PRAYER AFTER COMMUNION   [Salvation and Joy]

O God, who have willed that we be partakers
in the one Bread and the one Chalice,
grant us, we pray, so to live
that, made one in Christ,
we may joyfully bear fruit
for the salvation of the world.
Through Christ our Lord.
℟. **Amen.**   → No. 30, p. 77

Optional Solemn Blessings, p. 97, and Prayers over the People, p. 105

"Blessed are you who are poor, for the kingdom of God is yours."

FEBRUARY 16
6th SUNDAY IN ORDINARY TIME

ENTRANCE ANT. Cf. Ps 31 (30):3-4   **[Protector]**

Be my protector, O God, a mighty stronghold to save me. For you are my rock, my stronghold! Lead me, guide me, for the sake of your name.   → No. 2, p. 10

COLLECT   **[Fashioned by God's Grace]**

O God, who teach us that you abide
in hearts that are just and true,
grant that we may be so fashioned by your grace
as to become a dwelling pleasing to you.
Through our Lord Jesus Christ, your Son,
who lives and reigns with you in the unity of the Holy
    Spirit,
God, for ever and ever.
℟. **Amen.** ↓

FIRST READING Jer 17:5-8   **[Trust in the Lord]**

To put all one's trust in human strength leads to frustration. Let us trust in the Lord and find fulfillment.

A reading from the Book of the Prophet Jeremiah

THUS says the Lord:
Cursed is the one who trusts in human beings,
who seeks his strength in flesh,
whose heart turns away from the Lord.
He is like a barren bush in the desert
that enjoys no change of season,
but stands in a lava waste,
a salt and empty earth.
Blessed is the one who trusts in the Lord,
whose hope is the Lord.
He is like a tree planted beside the waters
that stretches out its roots to the stream:
it fears not the heat when it comes,
its leaves stay green;
in the year of drought it shows no distress,
but still bears fruit.
The word of the Lord. ℟. **Thanks be to God.** ↓

RESPONSORIAL PSALM Ps 1   [Lover of God's Law]

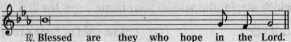

℟. Blessed   are   they   who   hope   in   the   Lord.

Blessed the man who follows not
the counsel of the wicked,
nor walks in the way of sinners,
nor sits in the company of the insolent,
but delights in the law of the Lord
and meditates on his law day and night.

℟. **Blessed are they who hope in the Lord.**

He is like a tree
planted near running water,
that yields its fruit in due season,
and whose leaves never fade.
Whatever he does, prospers.

℟. **Blessed are they who hope in the Lord.**

Not so the wicked, not so;
  they are like chaff which the wind drives away.
For the LORD watches over the way of the just,
  but the way of the wicked vanishes.

℟. **Blessed are they who hope in the Lord.** ↓

SECOND READING 1 Cor 15:12, 16-20   [Hope for Eternity]

If our hopes in Christ are limited to this life only, we are the most pitiable of human beings.

A reading from the first Letter of Saint Paul
to the Corinthians

BROTHERS and sisters: If Christ is preached as raised from the dead, how can some among you say there is no resurrection of the dead? If the dead are not raised, neither has Christ been raised, and if Christ has not been raised, your faith is vain; you are still in your sins. Then those who have fallen asleep in Christ have perished. If for this life only we have hoped in Christ, we are the most pitiable people of all.

  But now Christ has been raised from the dead, the firstfruits of those who have fallen asleep.—The word of the Lord. ℟. **Thanks be to God.** ↓

ALLELUIA Lk 6:23ab   [Heavenly Reward]

℟. **Alleluia, alleluia.**
Rejoice and be glad;
your reward will be great in heaven.
℟. **Alleluia, alleluia.** ↓

GOSPEL Lk 6:17, 20-26   [The Beatitudes]

Happiness and blessing are the rewards of those who accept the Gospel and the Savior. Sorrow and woe await those who take wealth and pleasure as their goal in life.

℣. The Lord be with you. ℟. **And with your spirit.**

✠ A reading from the holy Gospel according to Luke.
℟. **Glory to you, O Lord.**

JESUS came down with the Twelve and stood on a
stretch of level ground with a great crowd of his disciples and a large number of the people from all Judea
and Jerusalem and the coastal region of Tyre and
Sidon. And raising his eyes toward his disciples he
said:

"Blessed are you who are poor,
for the kingdom of God is yours.
Blessed are you who are now hungry,
for you will be satisfied.
Blessed are you who are now weeping,
for you will laugh.
Blessed are you when people hate you,
and when they exclude and insult you,
and denounce your name as evil
on account of the Son of Man.

Rejoice and leap for joy on that day! Behold, your
reward will be great in heaven. For their ancestors
treated the prophets in the same way.

But woe to you who are rich,
for you have received your consolation.
Woe to you who are filled now,
for you will be hungry.
Woe to you who laugh now,
for you will grieve and weep.
Woe to you when all speak well of you,
for their ancestors treated the false prophets in
this way."

The Gospel of the Lord. ℟. **Praise to you, Lord Jesus
Christ.**   ➜ No. 15, p. 18

PRAYER OVER THE OFFERINGS   [Renewal]

May this oblation, O Lord, we pray,
cleanse and renew us
and may it become for those who do your will
the source of eternal reward.
Through Christ our Lord.
℟. **Amen.**   ➥ No. 21, p. 22 (Pref. P 29-36)

COMMUNION ANT. Cf. Ps 78 (77):29-30   [God's Food]

**They ate and had their fill, and what they craved the
Lord gave them; they were not disappointed in what
they craved.** ↓

OR Jn 3:16   [God's Love]

**God so loved the world that he gave his Only Begotten
Son, so that all who believe in him may not perish, but
may have eternal life.** ↓

PRAYER AFTER COMMUNION   [Heavenly Delights]

Having fed upon these heavenly delights,
we pray, O Lord,
that we may always long
for that food by which we truly live.
Through Christ our Lord.
℟. **Amen.**   ➥ No. 30, p. 77

Optional Solemn Blessings, p. 97, and Prayers over the People, p. 105

"Stop judging and you will not be judged."

FEBRUARY 23

7th SUNDAY IN ORDINARY TIME

ENTRANCE ANT. Ps 13 (12):6   [God's Merciful Love]

O Lord, I trust in your merciful love. My heart will
rejoice in your salvation. I will sing to the Lord who
has been bountiful with me.   ➜. No. 2, p. 10

COLLECT   [Word and Deed]

Grant, we pray, almighty God,
that, always pondering spiritual things,
we may carry out in both word and deed
that which is pleasing to you.
Through our Lord Jesus Christ, your Son,
who lives and reigns with you in the unity of the Holy
    Spirit,
God, for ever and ever. ℞. **Amen.** ↓

FIRST READING 1 Sm 26:2, 7-9, 12-13, 22-23
                    [David Spares Saul]

King Saul has condemned David and is trying to cap-
ture him. David has the opportunity to kill Saul, but

204

refuses to harm the king because Saul is anointed by
the LORD.

A reading from the first Book of Samuel

IN those days, Saul went down to the desert of Ziph
with three thousand picked men of Israel, to search
for David in the desert of Ziph. So David and Abishai
went among Saul's soldiers by night and found Saul
lying asleep within the barricade, with his spear thrust
into the ground at his head and Abner and his men
sleeping around him.

Abishai whispered to David: "God has delivered
your enemy into your grasp this day. Let me nail him
to the ground with one thrust of the spear; I will not
need a second thrust!" But David said to Abishai, "Do
not harm him, for who can lay hands on the LORD's
anointed and remain unpunished?" So David took the
spear and the water jug from their place at Saul's
head, and they got away without anyone's seeing or
knowing or awakening. All remained asleep, because
the LORD had put them into a deep slumber.

Going across to an opposite slope, David stood on a
remote hilltop at a great distance from Abner, son of
Ner, and the troops. He said: "Here is the king's spear.
Let an attendant come over to get it. The LORD will
reward each man for his justice and faithfulness.
Today, though the LORD delivered you into my grasp, I
would not harm the LORD's anointed."—The word of
the Lord. ℟. **Thanks be to God.** ↓

RESPONSORIAL PSALM Ps 103   [The Lord's Mercy]

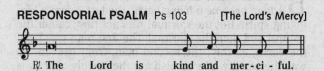

℟. The   Lord   is   kind and mer-ci-ful.

Bless the LORD, O my soul;
  and all my being, bless his holy name.
Bless the LORD, O my soul,
  and forget not all his benefits.

℟. **The Lord is kind and merciful.**

He pardons all your iniquities,
  heals all your ills.
He redeems your life from destruction,
  crowns you with kindness and compassion.

℟. **The Lord is kind and merciful.**

Merciful and gracious is the LORD,
  slow to anger and abounding in kindness.
Not according to our sins does he deal with us,
  nor does he requite us according to our crimes.

℟. **The Lord is kind and merciful.**

As far as the east is from the west,
  so far has he put our transgressions from us.
As a father has compassion on his children,
  so the LORD has compassion on those who fear him.

℟. **The Lord is kind and merciful.** ↓

SECOND READING 1 Cor 15:45-49 [Grace Builds on Nature]

> **Grace builds on nature. In Christ we are formed in the spiritual order.**

A reading from the first Letter of Saint Paul
to the Corinthians

BROTHERS and sisters: It is written, *The first man,
Adam, became a living being*, the last Adam a life-
giving spirit. But the spiritual was not first; rather the
natural and then the spiritual. The first man was from
the earth, earthly; the second man, from heaven. As
was the earthly one, so also are the earthly, and as is
the heavenly one, so also are the heavenly. Just as we

have borne the image of the earthly one, we shall also bear the image of the heavenly one.—The word of the Lord. ℟. **Thanks be to God.** ↓

ALLELUIA Jn 13:34   [Christ's Commandment]
℟. **Alleluia, alleluia.**
I give you a new commandment, says the Lord:
love one another as I have loved you.
℟. **Alleluia, alleluia.** ↓

GOSPEL Lk 6:27-38   [Love for Enemies]
   The supernatural virtues go beyond the natural virtues
   which even sinners practice.

℣. The Lord be with you. ℟. **And with your spirit.**
✛ A reading from the holy Gospel according to Luke.
℟. **Glory to you, O Lord.**

JESUS said to his disciples: "To you who hear I say, love your enemies, do good to those who hate you, bless those who curse you, pray for those who mistreat you. To the person who strikes you on one cheek, offer the other one as well, and from the person who takes your cloak, do not withhold even your tunic. Give to everyone who asks of you, and from the one who takes what is yours do not demand it back. Do to others as you would have them do to you. For if you love those who love you, what credit is that to you? Even sinners love those who love them. And if you do good to those who do good to you, what credit is that to you? Even sinners do the same. If you lend money to those from whom you expect repayment, what credit is that to you? Even sinners lend to sinners, and get back the same amount. But rather, love your enemies and do good to them, and lend expecting nothing back; then your reward will be great and you will be

children of the Most High, for he himself is kind to the
ungrateful and the wicked. Be merciful, just as your
Father is merciful.

"Stop judging and you will not be judged. Stop con-
demning and you will not be condemned. Forgive and
you will be forgiven. Give, and gifts will be given to
you; a good measure, packed together, shaken down,
and overflowing, will be poured into your lap. For the
measure with which you measure will in return be
measured out to you."—The Gospel of the Lord.
℟. **Praise to you, Lord Jesus Christ.**   → No. 15, p. 18

PRAYER OVER THE OFFERINGS   [Celebrate Mysteries]

As we celebrate your mysteries, O Lord,
with the observance that is your due,
we humbly ask you,
that what we offer to the honor of your majesty
may profit us for salvation.
Through Christ our Lord.
℟. **Amen.**   → No. 21, p. 22 (Pref. P 29-36)

COMMUNION ANT. Ps 9:2-3   [Joy in God]
**I will recount all your wonders, I will rejoice in you
and be glad, and sing psalms to your name, O Most
High.** ↓

OR Jn 11:27   [Belief in Christ]
**Lord, I have come to believe that you are the Christ,
the Son of the living God, who is coming into this
world.** ↓

PRAYER AFTER COMMUNION   [Experience Salvation]

Grant, we pray, almighty God,
that we may experience the effects of the salvation

which is pledged to us by these mysteries.
Through Christ our Lord.
℟. **Amen.**   ➞ No. 30, p. 77

Optional Solemn Blessings, p. 97, and Prayers over the People, p. 105

"Every tree is known by its own fruit."

MARCH 2

8th SUNDAY IN ORDINARY TIME

ENTRANCE ANT. Cf. Ps 18 (17):19-20 [God Our Protector]

The Lord became my protector. He brought me out to a place of freedom; he saved me because he delighted in me. → No. 2, p. 10

COLLECT [Peaceful Rule]

Grant us, O Lord, we pray,
that the course of our world
may be directed by your peaceful rule
and that your Church may rejoice,
untroubled in her devotion.
Through our Lord Jesus Christ, your Son,
who lives and reigns with you in the unity of the Holy
   Spirit,
God, for ever and ever. ℟. **Amen.** ↓

FIRST READING Sir 27:4-7   [Revealing Speech]

> The sage indicates that our speech reveals what we really are. In this way, he anticipates the Gospel maxim: "From the fullness of the heart the mouth speaks" (Lk 6:45).

A reading from the Book of Sirach

WHEN a sieve is shaken, the husks appear;
    so do one's faults when one speaks.
As the test of what the potter molds is in the furnace,
    so in tribulation is the test of the just.
The fruit of a tree shows the care it has had;
        so too does one's speech disclose the bent of
        one's mind.
Praise no one before he speaks,
    for it is then that people are tested.
The word of the Lord. ℟. **Thanks be to God.** ↓

RESPONSORIAL PSALM Ps 92 [Thanksgiving of the Just]

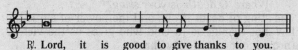

℟. **Lord, it is good to give thanks to you.**

It is good to give thanks to the LORD,
    to sing praise to your name, Most High,
to proclaim your kindness at dawn
    and your faithfulness throughout the night.

℟. **Lord, it is good to give thanks to you.**

The just one shall flourish like the palm tree,
    like a cedar of Lebanon shall he grow.
They that are planted in the house of the LORD
    shall flourish in the courts of our God.

℟. **Lord, it is good to give thanks to you.**

They shall bear fruit even in old age;
    vigorous and sturdy shall they be,

declaring how just is the LORD,
  my rock, in whom there is no wrong.

℟. **Lord, it is good to give thanks to you.** ↓

SECOND READING 1 Cor 15:54-58 [Victory through Christ]

> The Risen Christ is the source of our new life that will pro-
> duce in us all its fruits at the time of our resurrection. We
> must never stop working toward that goal.

A reading from the first Letter of Saint Paul
          to the Corinthians

BROTHERS and sisters: When this which is corruptible clothes itself with incorruptibility and this
which is mortal clothes itself with immortality, then
the word that is written shall come about:
  Death is swallowed up in victory.
  Where, O death, is your victory?
  Where, O death, is your sting?
The sting of death is sin, and the power of sin is the
law. But thanks be to God who gives us the victory
through our Lord Jesus Christ.

  Therefore, my beloved brothers and sisters, be firm,
steadfast, always fully devoted to the work of the Lord,
knowing that in the Lord your labor is not in vain.—
The word of the Lord. ℟. **Thanks be to God.** ↓

ALLELUIA Phil 2:15d, 16a   [Shine with the Word]

℟. **Alleluia, alleluia.**
Shine like lights in the world
as you hold on to the word of life.
℟. **Alleluia, alleluia.** ↓

GOSPEL Lk 6:39-45   [The Heart Speaks]

> We must receive the Word of God with complete open-
> ness. Only then can we draw from our hearts words that
> will lead others to Christ.

℣. The Lord be with you. ℟. **And with your spirit.**

✛ A reading from the holy Gospel according to Luke.
℟. **Glory to you, O Lord.**

JESUS told his disciples a parable, "Can a blind person guide a blind person? Will not both fall into a pit? No disciple is superior to the teacher; but when fully trained, every disciple will be like his teacher. Why do you notice the splinter in your brother's eye, but do not perceive the wooden beam in your own? How can you say to your brother, 'Brother, let me remove that splinter in your eye,' when you do not even notice the wooden beam in your own eye? You hypocrite! Remove the wooden beam from your eye first; then you will see clearly to remove the splinter in your brother's eye.

"A good tree does not bear rotten fruit, nor does a rotten tree bear good fruit. For every tree is known by its own fruit. For people do not pick figs from thornbushes, nor do they gather grapes from brambles. A good person out of the store of goodness in his heart produces good, but an evil person out of a store of evil produces evil; for from the fullness of the heart the mouth speaks."—The Gospel of the Lord. ℟. **Praise to you, Lord Jesus Christ.** ➔ No. 15, p. 18

PRAYER OVER THE OFFERINGS   [Serve with Devotion]

O God, who provide gifts to be offered to your name
and count our oblations as signs
of our desire to serve you with devotion,
we ask of your mercy
that what you grant as the source of merit
may also help us to attain merit's reward.
Through Christ our Lord.
℟. **Amen.**   ➔ No. 21, p. 22 (Pref. P 29-36)

COMMUNION ANT. Cf. Ps 13 (12):6   [God's Bounty]

I will sing to the Lord who has been bountiful with me, sing psalms to the name of the Lord Most High. ↓

OR Mt 28:20   [Christ's Presence]

Behold, I am with you always, even to the end of the age, says the Lord. ↓

PRAYER AFTER COMMUNION   [Life Eternal]

Nourished by your saving gifts,
we beseech your mercy, Lord,
that by this same Sacrament
with which you feed us in the present age,
you may make us partakers of life eternal.
Through Christ our Lord.
℟. **Amen.**   → No. 30, p. 77

Optional Solemn Blessings, p. 97, and Prayers over the People, p. 105

"Jesus said . . . 'You shall not put the Lord, your God, to the test.'"

MARCH 9

1st SUNDAY OF LENT

ENTRANCE ANT. Cf. Ps 91 (90):15-16   [Length of Days]

When he calls on me, I will answer him; I will deliver him and give him glory, I will grant him length of days.

➙ No. 2, p. 10 (Omit Gloria)

COLLECT   [Grow in Understanding]

Grant, almighty God,
through the yearly observances of holy Lent,
that we may grow in understanding
of the riches hidden in Christ
and by worthy conduct pursue their effects.
Through our Lord Jesus Christ, your Son,
who lives and reigns with you in the unity of the Holy
    Spirit,
God, for ever and ever.
℟. **Amen.** ↓

FIRST READING Dt 26:4-10   [Confession of Faith]
> The fruits of our labor are gifts from God. Before we use
> and enjoy them we should first acknowledge his bounty
> with dedication and thanks.

A reading from the Book of Deuteronomy

MOSES spoke to the people, saying: "The priest
shall receive the basket from you and shall set it in
front of the altar of the LORD, your God. Then you shall
declare before the LORD, your God, 'My father was a
wandering Aramean who went down to Egypt with a
small household and lived there as an alien. But there he
became a nation great, strong, and numerous. When the
Egyptians maltreated and oppressed us, imposing hard
labor upon us, we cried to the LORD, the God of our
fathers, and he heard our cry and saw our affliction, our
toil, and our oppression. He brought us out of Egypt with
his strong hand and outstretched arm, with terrifying
power, with signs and wonders; and bringing us into this
country, he gave us this land flowing with milk and
honey. Therefore, I have now brought you the firstfruits
of the products of the soil which you, O LORD, have given
me.' And having set them before the LORD, your God,
you shall bow down in his presence."—The word of the
Lord. ℟. **Thanks be to God.** ↓

RESPONSORIAL PSALM Ps 91   [Call for God's Help]

℟. Be with me, Lord, when I am in trou-ble.

You who dwell in the shelter of the Most High,
    who abide in the shadow of the Almighty,
say to the LORD, "My refuge and fortress,
    my God in whom I trust."

℟. **Be with me, Lord, when I am in trouble.**

No evil shall befall you,
  nor shall affliction come near your tent,
for to his angels he has given command about you,
  that they guard you in all your ways.

℟. **Be with me, Lord, when I am in trouble.**

Upon their hands they shall bear you up,
  lest you dash your foot against a stone.
You shall tread upon the asp and the viper;
  you shall trample down the lion and the dragon.

℟. **Be with me, Lord, when I am in trouble.**

Because he clings to me, I will deliver him;
  I will set him on high because he acknowledges my
    name.
He shall call upon me, and I will answer him;
  I will be with him in distress;
I will deliver him and glorify him.

℟. **Be with me, Lord, when I am in trouble.** ↓

SECOND READING Rom 10:8-13   [Creed of Christians]

Holiness (justification) is rooted in faith. Believe in your
heart that Jesus is raised from the dead.

A reading from the Letter of Saint Paul to the Romans

BROTHERS and sisters: What does Scripture say?
*The word is near you, in your mouth and in your
heart*—that is, the word of faith that we preach—, for, if
you confess with your mouth that Jesus is Lord and
believe in your heart that God raised him from the dead,
you will be saved. For one believes with the heart and so
is justified, and one confesses with the mouth and so is
saved. For the Scripture says, *No one who believes in
him will be put to shame.* For there is no distinction
between Jew and Greek; the same Lord is Lord of all,
enriching all who call upon him. For "everyone who calls
on the name of the Lord will be saved."—The word of the
Lord. ℟. **Thanks be to God.** ↓

VERSE BEFORE THE GOSPEL Mt 4:4b   [Source of Life]

℟. **Praise to you, Lord Jesus Christ, king of endless glory!***

One does not live on bread alone,

but on every word that comes forth from the mouth of God.

℟. **Praise to you, Lord Jesus Christ, king of endless glory!** ↓

GOSPEL Lk 4:1-13   [Practicing Our Creed]

Jesus is fully human and overcomes the temptation of Satan. As Messiah he will not resort to expediency.

℣. The Lord be with you. ℟. **And with your spirit.**

✛ A reading from the holy Gospel according to Luke.

℟. **Glory to you, O Lord.**

F ILLED with the Holy Spirit, Jesus returned from the Jordan and was led by the Spirit into the desert for forty days, to be tempted by the devil. He ate nothing during those days, and when they were over he was hungry. The devil said to him, "If you are the Son of God, command this stone to become bread." Jesus answered him, "It is written, *One does not live on bread alone.*" Then he took him up and showed him all the kingdoms of the world in a single instant. The devil said to him, "I shall give to you all this power and glory; for it has been handed over to me, and I may give it to whomever I wish. All this will be yours, if you worship me." Jesus said to him in reply, "It is written:

You shall worship the Lord, your God,
    and him alone shall you serve."

Then he led him to Jerusalem, made him stand on the parapet of the temple, and said to him, "If you are the Son of God, throw yourself down from here, for it is written:

He will command his angels concerning you,
    to guard you,

* *See p. 16 for other Gospel Acclamations.*

and:
> *With their hands they will support you,*
> *lest you dash your foot against a stone."*

Jesus said to him in reply, "It also says, *You shall not put the Lord, your God, to the test."* When the devil had finished every temptation, he departed from him for a time.—The Gospel of the Lord. ℟. **Praise to you, Lord Jesus Christ.**   ➜ No. 15, p. 18

PRAYER OVER THE OFFERINGS   [Sacred Time]

Give us the right dispositions, O Lord, we pray,
to make these offerings,
for with them we celebrate the beginning
of this venerable and sacred time.
Through Christ our Lord. ℟. **Amen.** ↓

PREFACE (P 12)   [Christ's Abstinence]

℣. The Lord be with you. ℟. **And with your spirit.**
℣. Lift up your hearts. ℟. **We lift them up to the Lord.**
℣. Let us give thanks to the Lord our God. ℟. **It is right and just.**

It is truly right and just, our duty and our salvation,
always and everywhere to give you thanks,
Lord, holy Father, almighty and eternal God,
through Christ our Lord.

By abstaining forty long days from earthly food,
he consecrated through his fast
the pattern of our Lenten observance
and, by overturning all the snares of the ancient serpent,
taught us to cast out the leaven of malice,
so that, celebrating worthily the Paschal Mystery,
we might pass over at last to the eternal paschal feast.

And so, with the company of Angels and Saints,
we sing the hymn of your praise,
as without end we acclaim: ➜ No. 23, p. 23

COMMUNION ANT. Mt 4:4   [Life-Giving Word]

One does not live by bread alone, but by every word that comes forth from the mouth of God. ↓

OR Cf. Ps 91 (90):4   [Refuge in God]

The Lord will conceal you with his pinions, and under his wings you will trust. ↓

PRAYER AFTER COMMUNION   [Heavenly Bread]

Renewed now with heavenly bread,
by which faith is nourished, hope increased,
and charity strengthened,
we pray, O Lord,
that we may learn to hunger for Christ,
the true and living Bread,
and strive to live by every word
which proceeds from your mouth.
Through Christ our Lord.
℟. **Amen.** ↓

The Deacon or, in his absence, the Priest himself, says the invitation: Bow down for the blessing.

PRAYER OVER THE PEOPLE   [Bountiful Blessing]

May bountiful blessing, O Lord, we pray,
come down upon your people,
that hope may grow in tribulation,
virtue be strengthened in temptation,
and eternal redemption be assured.
Through Christ our Lord.
℟. **Amen.**

→ No. 32, p. 77

"And behold, two men were conversing with him, Moses and Elijah."

MARCH 16

2nd SUNDAY OF LENT

ENTRANCE ANT. Cf. Ps 27 (26):8-9   **[God's Face]**

Of you my heart has spoken: Seek his face. It is your face, O Lord, that I seek; hide not your face from me.
     → No. 2, p. 10 (Omit Gloria)

OR Cf. Ps 25 (24):6, 2, 22   **[God's Merciful Love]**

Remember your compassion, O Lord, and your merciful love, for they are from of old. Let not our enemies exult over us. Redeem us, O God of Israel, from all our distress.   → No. 2, p. 10 (Omit Gloria)

COLLECT   **[Nourish Us]**

O God, who have commanded us
to listen to your beloved Son,
be pleased, we pray,
to nourish us inwardly by your word,
that, with spiritual sight made pure,

221

we may rejoice to behold your glory.
Through our Lord Jesus Christ, your Son,
who lives and reigns with you in the unity of the Holy
　　Spirit,
God, for ever and ever. ℞. **Amen.** ↓

FIRST READING Gn 15:5-12, 17-18 [Covenant with Abram]

**By faith Abram finds favor with the Lord. The Lord makes
a covenant, that is, establishes a special relationship, with
Abram and his descendants.**

A reading from the Book of Genesis

THE Lord God took Abram outside and said, "Look
up at the sky and count the stars, if you can. Just
so," he added, "shall your descendants be." Abram put
his faith in the LORD, who credited it to him as an act
of righteousness.

He then said to him, "I am the LORD who brought you
from Ur of the Chaldeans to give you this land as a
possession." "O Lord GOD," he asked, "how am I to
know that I shall possess it?" He answered him, "Bring
me a three-year-old heifer, a three-year-old she-goat, a
three-year-old ram, a turtledove, and a young pigeon."
Abram brought him all these, split them in two, and
placed each half opposite the other; but the birds he
did not cut up. Birds of prey swooped down on the car-
casses, but Abram stayed with them. As the sun was
about to set, a trance fell upon Abram, and a deep, terrifying darkness enveloped him.

When the sun had set and it was dark, there
appeared a smoking fire pot and a flaming torch,
which passed between those pieces. It was on that
occasion that the LORD made a covenant with Abram,
saying: "To your descendants I give this land, from the
Wadi of Egypt to the Great River, the Euphrates."—The
word of the Lord. ℞. **Thanks be to God.** ↓

RESPONSORIAL PSALM Ps 27   [Union with God]

℟. The Lord is my light and my sal - va - tion.

The LORD is my light and my salvation;
   whom should I fear?
The LORD is my life's refuge;
   of whom should I be afraid?

℟. **The Lord is my light and my salvation.**

Hear, O LORD, the sound of my call;
   have pity on me, and answer me.
Of you my heart speaks; you my glance seeks.

℟. **The Lord is my light and my salvation.**

Your presence, O LORD, I seek.
   Hide not your face from me;
do not in anger repel your servant.
   You are my helper: cast me not off.

℟. **The Lord is my light and my salvation.**

I believe that I shall see the bounty of the LORD
   in the land of the living.
Wait for the LORD with courage;
   be stouthearted, and wait for the LORD.

℟. **The Lord is my light and my salvation.** ↓

SECOND READING Phil 3:17—4:1 or 3:20—4:1
                          [Citizenship in Heaven]
**Paul exhorts us to turn away from worldly pleasures and to
reject sin. He reminds us that we are not of this world.**

*[If the "Shorter Form" is used, the indented text in brackets is
omitted.]*

A reading from the Letter of Saint Paul to the Philippians

[**J**OIN with others in being imitators of me,
brothers and sisters, and observe those who

thus conduct themselves according to the model you have in us. For many, as I have often told you and now tell you even in tears, conduct themselves as enemies of the cross of Christ. Their end is destruction. Their God is their stomach; their glory is in their "shame." Their minds are occupied with earthly things.

But] *our citizenship is in heaven, and from it we also await a savior, the Lord Jesus Christ. He will change our lowly body to conform with his glorified body by the power that enables him also to bring all things into subjection to himself.

Therefore, my brothers and sisters, whom I love and long for, my joy and crown, in this way stand firm in the Lord.**—The word of the Lord. ℟. **Thanks be to God.** ↓

VERSE BEFORE THE GOSPEL Cf. Mt 17:5   [Hear Him]
℟. **Praise and honor to you, Lord Jesus Christ!***
From the shining cloud the Father's voice is heard:
This is my beloved Son, hear him.
℟. **Praise and honor to you, Lord Jesus Christ!** ↓

GOSPEL Lk 9:28b-36   [Listen to Jesus]
    The glory of Christ is revealed, and God manifests the special mission of Christ.

℣. The Lord be with you. ℟. **And with your spirit.**
✠ A reading from the holy Gospel according to Luke.
℟. **Glory to you, O Lord.**

JESUS took Peter, John, and James and went up the mountain to pray. While he was praying his face changed in appearance and his clothing became dazzling white. And behold, two men were conversing with him, Moses and Elijah, who appeared in glory

---

* *The Shorter Form adds "Brothers and sisters."*
** *The Shorter Form adds "beloved."*
*** *See p. 16 for other Gospel Acclamations.*

and spoke of his exodus that he was going to accomplish in Jerusalem. Peter and his companions had been
overcome by sleep, but becoming fully awake, they
saw his glory and the two men standing with him. As
they were about to part from him, Peter said to Jesus,
"Master, it is good that we are here; let us make three
tents, one for you, one for Moses, and one for Elijah."
But he did not know what he was saying. While he was
still speaking, a cloud came and cast a shadow over
them, and they became frightened when they entered
the cloud. Then from the cloud came a voice that said,
"This is my chosen Son; listen to him." After the voice
had spoken, Jesus was found alone. They fell silent and
did not at that time tell anyone what they had seen.—
The Gospel of the Lord. ℟. **Praise to you, Lord Jesus
Christ.**   → No. 15, p. 18

PRAYER OVER THE OFFERINGS   [Cleanse Our Faults]

May this sacrifice, O Lord, we pray,
cleanse us of our faults
and sanctify your faithful in body and mind
for the celebration of the paschal festivities.
Through Christ our Lord.
℟. **Amen.** ↓

PREFACE (P 13)   [Jesus in Glory]

℣. The Lord be with you. ℟. **And with your spirit.**
℣. Lift up your hearts. ℟. **We lift them up to the Lord.**
℣. Let us give thanks to the Lord our God. ℟. **It is right
and just.**

It is truly right and just, our duty and our salvation,
always and everywhere to give you thanks,
Lord, holy Father, almighty and eternal God,
through Christ our Lord.

For after he had told the disciples of his coming Death,
on the holy mountain he manifested to them his glory,

to show, even by the testimony of the law and the
    prophets,
that the Passion leads to the glory of the Resurrection.

And so, with the Powers of heaven,
we worship you constantly on earth,
and before your majesty
without end we acclaim: ➔ No. 23, p. 23

COMMUNION ANT. Mt 17:5   [Son of God]
**This is my beloved Son, with whom I am well pleased;
listen to him.** ↓

PRAYER AFTER COMMUNION   [Things of Heaven]
As we receive these glorious mysteries,
we make thanksgiving to you, O Lord,
for allowing us while still on earth
to be partakers even now of the things of heaven.
Through Christ our Lord.
℟. **Amen.** ↓

*The Deacon or, in his absence, the Priest himself, says the
invitation:* Bow down for the blessing.

PRAYER OVER THE PEOPLE   [Faithful to the Gospel]
Bless your faithful, we pray, O Lord,
with a blessing that endures for ever,
and keep them faithful
to the Gospel of your Only Begotten Son,
so that they may always desire and at last attain
that glory whose beauty he showed in his own Body,
to the amazement of his Apostles.
Through Christ our Lord.
℟. **Amen.**   ➔ No. 32, p. 77

————————

"It may bear fruit in the future."

MARCH 23

3rd SUNDAY OF LENT

On this Sunday is celebrated the First Scrutiny in preparation for the Baptism of the catechumens who are to be admitted to the Sacraments of Christian Initiation at the Easter Vigil. The Ritual Mass for the First Scrutiny is found on p. 233.

ENTRANCE ANT. Cf. Ps 25 (24):15-16   **[Eyes on God]**

My eyes are always on the Lord, for he rescues my feet from the snare. Turn to me and have mercy on me, for I am alone and poor. → No. 2, p. 10 (Omit Gloria)

OR Ez 36:23-26   **[A New Spirit]**

When I prove my holiness among you, I will gather you from all the foreign lands; and I will pour clean water upon you and cleanse you from all your impurities, and I will give you a new spirit, says the Lord.

→ No. 2, p. 10 (Omit Gloria)

COLLECT   **[Fasting, Prayer, Almsgiving]**

O God, author of every mercy and of all goodness, who in fasting, prayer and almsgiving

have shown us a remedy for sin,
look graciously on this confession of our lowliness,
that we, who are bowed down by our conscience,
may always be lifted up by your mercy.
Through our Lord Jesus Christ, your Son,
who lives and reigns with you in the unity of the Holy
   Spirit,
God, for ever and ever. ℟. **Amen.** ↓

FIRST READING Ex 3:1-8a, 13-15   **[The Name of God]**

**The Lord God calls Moses to lead his people and reveals
his name to Moses.**

A reading from the Book of Exodus

MOSES was tending the flock of his father-in-law
Jethro, the priest of Midian. Leading the flock
across the desert, he came to Horeb, the mountain of
God. There an angel of the LORD appeared to Moses in
fire flaming out of a bush. As he looked on, he was sur-
prised to see that the bush, though on fire, was not consumed. So Moses decided, "I must go over to look at this
remarkable sight, and see why the bush is not burned."

When the LORD saw him coming over to look at it
more closely, God called out to him from the bush,
"Moses! Moses!" He answered, "Here I am." God said,
"Come no nearer! Remove the sandals from your feet,
for the place where you stand is holy ground. I am the
God of your fathers," he continued, "the God of
Abraham, the God of Isaac, the God of Jacob." Moses
hid his face, for he was afraid to look at God. But the
LORD said, "I have witnessed the affliction of my people
in Egypt and have heard their cry of complaint against
their slave drivers, so I know well what they are suffering. Therefore I have come down to rescue them from
the hands of the Egyptians and lead them out of that
land into a good and spacious land, a land flowing
with milk and honey."

Moses said to God, "But when I go to the Israelites and say to them, 'The God of your fathers has sent me to you,' if they ask me, 'What is his name?' what am I to tell them?" God replied, "I am who am." Then he added, "This is what you shall tell the Israelites: I AM sent me to you."

God spoke further to Moses, "Thus shall you say to the Israelites: The LORD, the God of your fathers, the God of Abraham, the God of Isaac, the God of Jacob, has sent me to you.

"This is my name forever;
      thus am I to be remembered through all genera-
      tions."

The word of the Lord. ℟. **Thanks be to God.** ↓

RESPONSORIAL PSALM Ps 103   [The Lord's Kindness]

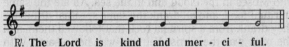

℟. **The Lord is kind and mer - ci - ful.**

Bless the LORD, O my soul;
      and all my being, bless his holy name.
Bless the LORD, O my soul,
      and forget not all his benefits.

℟. **The Lord is kind and merciful.**

He pardons all your iniquities,
      heals all your ills.
He redeems your life from destruction,
      crowns you with kindness and compassion.

℟. **The Lord is kind and merciful.**

The LORD secures justice
      and the rights of all the oppressed.
He has made known his ways to Moses,
      and his deeds to the children of Israel.

℟. **The Lord is kind and merciful.**

Merciful and gracious is the LORD,
  slow to anger and abounding in kindness.
For as the heavens are high above the earth,
  so surpassing is his kindness toward those who fear him.
℟. **The Lord is kind and merciful. ↓**

SECOND READING 1 Cor 10:1-6, 10-12 [Shun Overconfidence]
  We must remain steadfast in our faith. We cannot become
  overconfident even though we are the recipients of God's
  favor and grace.

A reading from the first Letter of Saint Paul
to the Corinthians

I DO not want you to be unaware, brothers and sisters,
that our ancestors were all under the cloud and all
passed through the sea, and all of them were baptized
into Moses in the cloud and in the sea. All ate the same
spiritual food, and all drank the same spiritual drink, for
they drank from a spiritual rock that followed them, and
the rock was the Christ. Yet God was not pleased with
most of them, for they were struck down in the desert.

  These things happened as examples for us, so that
we might not desire evil things, as they did. Do not
grumble as some of them did, and suffered death by
the destroyer. These things happened to them as an
example, and they have been written down as a warn-
ing to us, upon whom the end of the ages has come.
Therefore, whoever thinks he is standing secure
should take care not to fall.—The word of the Lord.
℟. **Thanks be to God. ↓**

VERSE BEFORE THE GOSPEL Mt 4:17   [Repent]
℟. **Glory and praise to you, Lord Jesus Christ!***
Repent, says the Lord;
the kingdom of heaven is at hand.
℟. **Glory and praise to you, Lord Jesus Christ! ↓**

See p. 16 for other Gospel Acclamations.

GOSPEL Lk 13:1-9   [Time To Reform]

Jesus tells us to reform and repent. Time will run out, and
no one can ever count on another year. Now is the time!

℣. The Lord be with you. ℟. **And with your spirit.**
✞ A reading from the holy Gospel according to Luke.
℟. **Glory to you, O Lord.**

SOME people told Jesus about the Galileans whose
blood Pilate had mingled with the blood of their
sacrifices. Jesus said to them in reply, "Do you think
that because these Galileans suffered in this way they
were greater sinners than all other Galileans? By no
means! But I tell you, if you do not repent, you will all
perish as they did! Or those eighteen people who were
killed when the tower at Siloam fell on them—do you
think they were more guilty than everyone else who
lived in Jerusalem? By no means! But I tell you, if you
do not repent, you will all perish as they did!"

And he told them this parable: "There once was a
person who had a fig tree planted in his orchard, and
when he came in search of fruit on it but found none,
he said to the gardener, 'For three years now I have
come in search of fruit on this fig tree but have found
none. So cut it down. Why should it exhaust the soil?'
He said to him in reply, 'Sir, leave it for this year also,
and I shall cultivate the ground around it and fertilize
it; it may bear fruit in the future. If not you can cut it
down.' "—The Gospel of the Lord. ℟. **Praise to you,
Lord Jesus Christ.**   → No. 15, p. 18

PRAYER OVER THE OFFERINGS   [Pardon]

Be pleased, O Lord, with these sacrificial offerings,
and grant that we who beseech pardon for our own sins,
may take care to forgive our neighbor.
Through Christ our Lord.
℟. **Amen.**   → No. 21, p. 22 (Pref. P 8-9)

When the Gospel of the Samaritan Woman is read, see p. 238
for Preface (P 14).

COMMUNION ANT. Ps 84 (83):4-5   [God's House]

The sparrow finds a home, and the swallow a nest for her young: by your altars, O Lord of hosts, my King and my God. Blessed are they who dwell in your house, for ever singing your praise. ↓

When the Gospel of the Samaritan Woman is read:

COMMUNION ANT. Jn 4:13-14   [Water of Eternal Life]

For anyone who drinks it, says the Lord, the water I shall give will become in him a spring welling up to eternal life. ↓

PRAYER AFTER COMMUNION   [Nourishment from Heaven]

As we receive the pledge
of things yet hidden in heaven
and are nourished while still on earth
with the Bread that comes from on high,
we humbly entreat you, O Lord,
that what is being brought about in us in mystery
may come to true completion.
Through Christ our Lord. ℟. **Amen.** ↓

The Deacon or, in his absence, the Priest himself, says the
invitation: Bow down for the blessing.

PRAYER OVER THE PEOPLE   [Love of God and Neighbor]

Direct, O Lord, we pray, the hearts of your faithful,
and in your kindness grant your servants this grace:
that, abiding in the love of you and their neighbor,
they may fulfill the whole of your commands.
Through Christ our Lord.
℟. **Amen.**   → No. 32, p. 77

MASS FOR THE FIRST SCRUTINY

This Mass is celebrated when the First Scrutiny takes place during the Order of Christian Initiation of Adults, usually on the 3rd Sunday of Lent. The readings may be used in any case.

ENTRANCE ANT. Ez 36:23-26   [A New Spirit]

When I prove my holiness among you, I will gather you from all the foreign lands and I will pour clean water upon you and cleanse you from all your impurities, and I will give you a new spirit, says the Lord.

→ No. 2, p. 10 (Omit Gloria)

OR Cf. Is 55:1   [Drink Joyfully]

Come to the waters, you who are thirsty, says the Lord; you who have no money, come and drink joyfully.

→ No. 2, p. 10 (Omit Gloria)

COLLECT   [Fashioned Anew]

Grant, we pray, O Lord,
that these chosen ones may come worthily and wisely
to the confession of your praise,
so that in accordance with that first dignity
which they lost by original sin
they may be fashioned anew through your glory.
Through our Lord Jesus Christ, your Son,
who lives and reigns with you in the unity of the Holy Spirit,
God, for ever and ever. ℟. **Amen.** ↓

FIRST READING Ex 17:3-7   [Water from Rock]

The Israelites murmured against God in their thirst. God directs Moses to strike a rock with his staff, and water issues forth.

A reading from the Book of Exodus

IN those days, in their thirst for water, the people grumbled against Moses, saying, "Why did you ever make us leave Egypt? Was it just to have us die here of thirst with our children and our livestock?" So Moses cried out to the LORD, "What shall I do with this people? A little more and they will stone me!" The LORD answered Moses, "Go over there in

front of the people, along with some of the elders of Israel,
holding in your hand, as you go, the staff with which you
struck the river. I will be standing there in front of you on
the rock in Horeb. Strike the rock, and the water will flow
from it for the people to drink." This Moses did, in the presence of the elders of Israel. The place was called Massah
and Meribah, because the Israelites quarreled there and
tested the LORD, saying, "Is the LORD in our midst or not?"—
The word of the Lord. ℟. **Thanks be to God.** ↓

RESPONSORIAL PSALM Ps 95   [The Lord Our Rock]

℟. **If today you hear his voice, harden not your hearts.**

Come, let us sing joyfully to the LORD;
　　let us acclaim the Rock of our salvation.
Let us come into his presence with thanksgiving;
　　let us joyfully sing psalms to him.—℟.

Come, let us bow down in worship;
　　let us kneel before the LORD who made us.
For he is our God,
　　and we are the people he shepherds, the flock he
　　　guides.—℟.

Oh, that today you would hear his voice:
　　"Harden not your hearts as at Meribah,
　　as in the day of Massah in the desert,
where your fathers tempted me;
　　they tested me though they had seen my works."—℟. ↓

SECOND READING Rom 5:1-2, 5-8   [God's Love for Us]

**Through Jesus we have received the grace of faith. The love of
God has been poured upon us. Jesus laid down his life for us
while we were still sinners.**

A reading from the Letter of Saint Paul to the Romans

BROTHERS and sisters: Since we have been justified
by faith, we have peace with God through our Lord

Jesus Christ, through whom we have gained access by faith to this grace in which we stand, and we boast in hope of the glory of God.

And hope does not disappoint, because the love of God has been poured out into our hearts through the Holy Spirit who has been given to us. For Christ, while we were still helpless, died at the appointed time for the ungodly. Indeed, only with difficulty does one die for a just person, though perhaps for a good person one might even find courage to die. But God proves his love for us in that while we were still sinners Christ died for us.—The word of the Lord. ℟. **Thanks be to God.** ↓

VERSE BEFORE THE GOSPEL Cf. Jn 4:42, 15   [Living Water]

℟. **Glory and praise to you, Lord Jesus Christ!***
Lord, you are truly the Savior of the world;
give me living water, that I may never thirst again.
℟. **Glory and praise to you, Lord Jesus Christ!** ↓

GOSPEL Jn 4:5-42 or 4:5-15, 19b-26, 39, 40-42   [Samaritan Woman]

Jesus speaks to the Samaritan woman at the well. He searches her soul, and she recognizes him as a prophet. Jesus speaks of the water of eternal life. He also notes the fields are ready for harvest.

[If the "Shorter Form" is used, the indented text in brackets is omitted.]

℣. The Lord be with you. ℟. **And with your spirit.**
✛ A reading from the holy Gospel according to John.
℟. **Glory to you, O Lord.**

JESUS came to a town of Samaria called Sychar, near the plot of land that Jacob had given to his son Joseph. Jacob's well was there. Jesus, tired from his journey, sat down there at the well. It was about noon.

A woman of Samaria came to draw water. Jesus said to her, "Give me a drink." His disciples had gone into the

---

* *See p. 16 for other Gospel Acclamations.*

town to buy food. The Samaritan woman said to him, "How can you, a Jew, ask me, a Samaritan woman, for a drink?"—For Jews use nothing in common with Samaritans.—Jesus answered and said to her, "If you knew the gift of God and who is saying to you, 'Give me a drink,' you would have asked him and he would have given you living water." The woman said to him, "Sir, you do not even have a bucket and the cistern is deep; where then can you get this living water? Are you greater than our father Jacob, who gave us this cistern and drank from it himself with his children and his flocks?" Jesus answered and said to her, "Everyone who drinks this water will be thirsty again; but whoever drinks the water I shall give will never thirst; the water I shall give will become in him a spring of water welling up to eternal life." The woman said to him, "Sir, give me this water, so that I may not be thirsty or have to keep coming here to draw water."

[Jesus said to her, "Go call your husband and come back." The woman answered and said to him, "I do not have a husband." Jesus answered her, "You are right in saying, 'I do not have a husband.' For you have had five husbands, and the one you have now is not your husband. What you have said is true."]

[The woman said to him, "Sir,] I can see that you are a prophet. Our ancestors worshiped on this mountain; but you people say that the place to worship is in Jerusalem." Jesus said to her, "Believe me, woman, the hour is coming when you will worship the Father neither on this mountain nor in Jerusalem. You people worship what you do not understand; we worship what we understand, because salvation is from the Jews. But the hour is coming, and is now here, when true worshippers will worship the Father in Spirit and truth; and indeed the Father seeks such people to worship him. God is Spirit, and those who worship him must worship in Spirit and truth." The woman said to him, "I know that the Messiah is coming, the one called the

Christ; when he comes, he will tell us everything." Jesus said to her, "I am he, the one* speaking with you."

[At that moment his disciples returned, and were amazed that he was talking with a woman, but still no one said, "What are you looking for?" or "Why are you talking with her?" The woman left her water jar and went into the town and said to the people, "Come see a man who told me everything I have done. Could he possibly be the Christ?" They went out of the town and came to him. Meanwhile, the disciples urged him, "Rabbi, eat." But he said to them, "I have food to eat of which you do not know." So the disciples said to one another, "Could someone have brought him something to eat?" Jesus said to them, "My food is to do the will of the one who sent me and to finish his work. Do you not say, 'In four months the harvest will be here'? I tell you, look up and see the fields ripe for the harvest. The reaper is already receiving payment and gathering crops for eternal life, so that the sower and reaper can rejoice together. For here the saying is verified that 'One sows and another reaps.' I sent you to reap what you have not worked for; others have done the work, and you are sharing the fruits of their work."]

Many of the Samaritans of that town began to believe in him [because of the word of the woman who testified, "He told me everything I have done."]** When the Samaritans came to him, they invited him to stay with them; and he stayed there two days. Many more began to believe in him because of his word, and they said to the woman, "We no longer believe because of your word; for we have heard for ourselves, and we know that this is truly the savior of the world."—The Gospel of the Lord.
℟. **Praise to you, Lord Jesus Christ.**   ➜ No. 15, p. 18

* *Shorter Form reads: the one who is.*
** *Appears only in Longer Form.*

PRAYER OVER THE OFFERINGS   [Merciful Grace]

May your merciful grace prepare your servants, O Lord,
for the worthy celebration of these mysteries
and lead them to it by a devout way of life.
Through Christ our Lord.
℟. **Amen.** ↓

PREFACE (P 14)   [Gift of Faith]

℣. The Lord be with you. ℟. **And with your spirit.**
℣. Lift up your hearts. ℟. **We lift them up to the Lord.**
℣. Let us give thanks to the Lord our God. ℟. **It is right and just.**

It is truly right and just, our duty and our salvation,
always and everywhere to give you thanks,
Lord, holy Father, almighty and eternal God,
through Christ our Lord.

For when he asked the Samaritan woman for water to
  drink,
he had already created the gift of faith within her
and so ardently did he thirst for her faith,
that he kindled in her the fire of divine love.

And so we, too, give you thanks
and with the Angels
praise your mighty deeds, as we acclaim: → No. 23, p. 23

When the Roman Canon is used, in the section Memento,
Domine (Remember, Lord, your servants) *there is a commemoration of the godparents, and the proper form of the* Hanc igitur *(Therefore, Lord, we pray), is said.*

Remember, Lord, your servants
who are to present your chosen ones
for the holy grace of your Baptism,

(Here the names of the godparents are read out.)

and all gathered here,
whose faith and devotion are known to you . . . (p. 24)

Therefore, Lord, we pray:
graciously accept this oblation
which we make to you for your servants,
whom you have been pleased
to enroll, choose and call for eternal life
and for the blessed gift of your grace.
(Through Christ our Lord. Amen.)

The rest follows the Roman Canon, pp. 25-29.

When Eucharistic Prayer II is used, after the words and all the
clergy, *the following is added:*

Remember also, Lord, your servants
who are to present these chosen ones
at the font of rebirth.

When Eucharistic Prayer III is used, after the words the entire
people you have gained for your own, *the following is added:*

Assist your servants with your grace,
O Lord, we pray,
that they may lead these chosen ones by word and example
to new life in Christ, our Lord.

COMMUNION ANT. Cf. Jn 4:14   [Water of Eternal Life]
**For anyone who drinks it, says the Lord, the water I shall
give will become in him a spring welling up to eternal
life.** ↓

PRAYER AFTER COMMUNION   [God's Protection]
Give help, O Lord, we pray,
by the grace of your redemption
and be pleased to protect and prepare
those you are to initiate
through the Sacraments of eternal life.
Through Christ our Lord.
℟. **Amen.**   → No. 30, p. 77

Optional Solemn Blessings, p. 97, and Prayers over the People, p. 105

"Father, I have sinned against heaven and against you."

MARCH 30

4th SUNDAY OF LENT

*On this Sunday is celebrated the Second Scrutiny in prepara-
tion for the Baptism of the catechumens who are to be admitted to the Sacraments of Christian Initiation at the Easter
Vigil. The Ritual Mass for the Second Scrutiny is found on
p. 246.*

ENTRANCE ANT. Cf. Is 66:10-11   [Rejoice]
**Rejoice, Jerusalem, and all who love her. Be joyful, all
who were in mourning; exult and be satisfied at her
consoling breast.**   ➜ No. 2, p. 10 (Omit Gloria)

COLLECT   [Devotion and Faith]
O God, who through your Word
reconcile the human race to yourself in a wonderful way,
grant, we pray,
that with prompt devotion and eager faith
the Christian people may hasten
toward the solemn celebrations to come.
Through our Lord Jesus Christ, your Son,

who lives and reigns with you in the unity of the Holy
Spirit,
God, for ever and ever. ℟. **Amen.** ↓

FIRST READING Jos 5:9a, 10-12   [Food for the Israelites]
The people of God celebrate the Passover in the promised
land, and as a sign that they are "home," the manna from
heaven is no longer provided.

A reading from the Book of Joshua

THE LORD said to Joshua:"Today I have removed the
reproach of Egypt from you."
While the Israelites were encamped at Gilgal on the
plains of Jericho, they celebrated the Passover on the
evening of the fourteenth of the month. On the day
after the Passover, they ate of the produce of the land
in the form of unleavened cakes and parched grain. On
that same day after the Passover, on which they ate of
the produce of the land, the manna ceased. No longer
was there manna for the Israelites, who that year ate
of the yield of the land of Canaan.—The word of the
Lord. ℟. **Thanks be to God.** ↓

RESPONSORIAL PSALM Ps 34   [The Lord's Goodness]

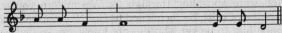

℟. Taste and see   the   goodness   of   the Lord.

I will bless the LORD at all times;
    his praise shall be ever in my mouth.
Let my soul glory in the LORD;
    the lowly will hear me and be glad.

℟. **Taste and see the goodness of the Lord.**

Glorify the LORD with me,
    let us together extol his name.
I sought the LORD, and he answered me
    and delivered me from all my fears.

R̶. **Taste and see the goodness of the Lord.**

Look at him that you may be radiant with joy,
  and your faces may not blush with shame.
When the poor one called out, the LORD heard,
  and from all his distress he saved him.

R̶. **Taste and see the goodness of the Lord.** ↓

SECOND READING 2 Cor 5:17-21   [Reconciliation]

Christ, the ambassador, reconciles all to God. Our transgressions find forgiveness in him so that we might become
the very holiness of God.

A reading from the second Letter of Saint Paul
to the Corinthians

B ROTHERS and sisters: Whoever is in Christ is a new
creation: the old things have passed away; behold,
new things have come. And all this is from God, who has
reconciled us to himself through Christ and given us the
ministry of reconciliation, namely, God was reconciling
the world to himself in Christ, not counting their trespasses against them and entrusting to us the message of
reconciliation. So we are ambassadors for Christ, as if
God were appealing through us. We implore you on
behalf of Christ, be reconciled to God. For our sake he
made him to be sin who did not know sin, so that we
might become the righteousness of God in him.—The
word of the Lord. R̶. **Thanks be to God.** ↓

VERSE BEFORE THE GOSPEL Lk 15:18   [Return Home]

R̶. **Glory to you, Word of God, Lord Jesus Christ!** *
I will get up and go to my Father and shall say to him:
Father, I have sinned against heaven and against you.
R̶. **Glory to you, Word of God, Lord Jesus Christ!** ↓

* See p. 16 for other Gospel Acclamations.

GOSPEL Lk 15:1-3, 11-32   [The Prodigal Son]
Our loving Father is always ready to forgive the truly repentant.

℣. The Lord be with you. ℟. **And with your spirit.**
✠ A reading from the holy Gospel according to Luke.
℟. **Glory to you, O Lord.**

TAX collectors and sinners were all drawing near to listen to Jesus, but the Pharisees and scribes began to complain, saying, "This man welcomes sinners and eats with them." So to them Jesus addressed this parable: "A man had two sons, and the younger son said to his father, 'Father, give me the share of your estate that should come to me.' So the father divided the property between them. After a few days, the younger son collected all his belongings and set off to a distant country where he squandered his inheritance on a life of dissipation. When he had freely spent everything, a severe famine struck that country, and he found himself in dire need. So he hired himself out to one of the local citizens who sent him to his farm to tend the swine. And he longed to eat his fill of the pods on which the swine fed, but nobody gave him any. Coming to his senses he thought, 'How many of my father's hired workers have more than enough food to eat, but here am I, dying from hunger. I shall get up and go to my father and I shall say to him, "Father, I have sinned against heaven and against you. I no longer deserve to be called your son; treat me as you would treat one of your hired workers."' So he got up and went back to his father. While he was still a long way off, his father caught sight of him, and was filled with compassion. He ran to his son, embraced him and kissed him. His son said to him, 'Father, I have sinned against heaven and against you; I no longer deserve to be called your son.' But his father ordered his servants,

'Quickly bring the finest robe and put it on him; put a ring on his finger and sandals on his feet. Take the fattened calf and slaughter it. Then let us celebrate with a feast, because this son of mine was dead, and has come to life again; he was lost, and has been found.' Then the celebration began. Now the older son had been out in the field and, on his way back, as he neared the house, he heard the sound of music and dancing. He called one of the servants and asked what this might mean. The servant said to him, 'Your brother has returned and your father has slaughtered the fattened calf because he has him back safe and sound.' He became angry, and when he refused to enter the house, his father came out and pleaded with him. He said to his father in reply, 'Look, all these years I served you and not once did I disobey your orders; yet you never gave me even a young goat to feast on with my friends. But when your son returns who swallowed up your property with prostitutes, for him you slaughter the fattened calf.' He said to him, 'My son, you are here with me always; everything I have is yours. But now we must celebrate and rejoice, because your brother was dead and has come to life again; he was lost and has been found.' "—The Gospel of the Lord. ℟. **Praise to you, Lord Jesus Christ.** → No. 15, p. 18

PRAYER OVER THE OFFERINGS [Eternal Remedy]

We place before you with joy these offerings,
which bring eternal remedy, O Lord,
praying that we may both faithfully revere them
and present them to you, as is fitting,
for the salvation of all the world.
Through Christ our Lord.
℟. **Amen.** → No. 21, p. 22 (Pref. P 8-9)

When the Gospel of the Man Born Blind is read, see p. 251 for Preface (P 15).

COMMUNION ANT. Lk 15:32   [Rejoice]

You must rejoice, my son, for your brother was dead and has come to life; he was lost and is found. ↓

When the Gospel of the Man Born Blind is read:

COMMUNION ANT. Cf. Jn 9:11, 38   [Spiritual Sight]

The Lord anointed my eyes: I went, I washed, I saw and I believed in God. ↓

PRAYER AFTER COMMUNION   [Illuminate Our Hearts]

O God, who enlighten everyone who comes into this
    world,
illuminate our hearts, we pray,
with the splendor of your grace,
that we may always ponder
what is worthy and pleasing to your majesty
and love you in all sincerity.
Through Christ our Lord.
℟. **Amen.** ↓

The Deacon or, in his absence, the Priest himself, says the invitation: Bow down for the blessing.

PRAYER OVER THE PEOPLE   [Life-Giving Light]

Look upon those who call to you, O Lord,
and sustain the weak;
give life by your unfailing light
to those who walk in the shadow of death,
and bring those rescued by your mercy from every evil
to reach the highest good.
Through Christ our Lord.
℟. **Amen.**   → No. 32, p. 77

MASS FOR THE SECOND SCRUTINY

This Mass is celebrated when the Second Scrutiny takes place during the Order of Christian Initiation of Adults, usually on the 4th Sunday of Lent. The readings may be used in any case.

ENTRANCE ANT. Cf. Ps 25 (24):15-16   **[Have Mercy]**

My eyes are always on the Lord, for he rescues my feet from the snare. Turn to me and have mercy on me, for I am alone and poor.   → No. 2, p. 10 (Omit Gloria)

COLLECT   **[Spiritual Joy]**

Almighty ever-living God,
give to your Church an increase in spiritual joy,
so that those once born of earth
may be reborn as citizens of heaven.
Through our Lord Jesus Christ, your Son,
who lives and reigns with you in the unity of the Holy Spirit,
God, for ever and ever. ℟. Amen. ↓

FIRST READING 1 Sm 16:1b, 6-7, 10-13a   **[The Lord's Anointed]**

God directs Samuel to anoint David king. God looks into the heart of each person.

A reading from the first Book of Samuel

THE LORD said to Samuel: "Fill your horn with oil, and be on your way. I am sending you to Jesse of Bethlehem, for I have chosen my king from among his sons."

As Jesse and his sons came to the sacrifice, Samuel looked at Eliab and thought, "Surely the LORD's anointed is here before him." But the LORD said to Samuel: "Do not judge from his appearance or from his lofty stature, because I have rejected him. Not as man sees does God see, because man sees the appearance but the LORD looks into the heart." In the same way Jesse presented seven sons before Samuel, but Samuel said to Jesse, "The LORD has not chosen any one of these." Then Samuel asked Jesse, "Are these all the sons you have?" Jesse replied, "There is still the youngest, who is tending the sheep." Samuel said to Jesse, "Send for him; we will not begin the sacrificial banquet until he arrives here." Jesse sent and had the young man brought to them. He was ruddy, a youth handsome to behold and making a splendid appearance. The LORD said, "There—anoint him, for this is the one!" Then Samuel, with the horn of oil in hand, anointed him in the presence of his brothers; and from that day on, the spirit of the LORD rushed upon David.—The word of the Lord. ℟. **Thanks be to God.** ↓

RESPONSORIAL PSALM Ps 23   [The Lord's Protection]

℟.   **The Lord is my shep-herd, there is noth-ing I shall want.**

The LORD is my shepherd, I shall not want.
    In verdant pastures he gives me repose;
beside restful waters he leads me;
    he refreshes my soul.—℟.

He guides me in right paths
    for his name's sake.
Even though I walk in the dark valley
    I fear no evil; for you are at my side
with your rod and your staff
    that give me courage.—℟.

You spread the table before me
    in the sight of my foes;
you anoint my head with oil;
    my cup overflows.—℟.

Only goodness and kindness follow me
    all the days of my life;
and I shall dwell in the house of the LORD
    for years to come.—℟. ↓

SECOND READING Eph 5:8-14   [Children of Light]

We are to walk in the light which shows goodness, justice, and truth. Christ gives this light whereby we live.

A reading from the Letter of Saint Paul to the Ephesians

BROTHERS and sisters: You were once darkness, but now you are light in the Lord. Live as children of light, for light produces every kind of goodness and righteousness and truth. Try to learn what is pleasing to the Lord. Take no part in the fruitless works of darkness; rather expose them, for it is shameful even to mention the things done by them in secret; but everything exposed by the light becomes visible, for everything that becomes visible is light. Therefore, it says:
"Awake, O sleeper,
and arise from the dead,
and Christ will give you light."
The word of the Lord. ℟. **Thanks be to God.** ↓

VERSE BEFORE THE GOSPEL Jn 8:12　　　[Light of Life]
℟. **Glory to you, Word of God, Lord Jesus Christ!***
I am the light of the world, says the Lord;
whoever follows me will have the light of life.
℟. **Glory to you, Word of God, Lord Jesus Christ!** ↓

GOSPEL Jn 9:1-41 or 9:1, 6-9, 13-17, 34-38　　[Cure of Blind Man]

> Jesus is the light. He cures a man born blind by bringing him to see. Jesus identifies himself as the Son of Man.

[If the "Shorter Form" is used, the indented text in brackets is omitted.]

℣. The Lord be with you. ℟. **And with your spirit.**
✝ A reading from the holy Gospel according to John.
℟. **Glory to you, O Lord.**

AS Jesus passed by he saw a man blind from birth. [His disciples asked him, "Rabbi, who sinned, this man or his parents, that he was born blind?" Jesus answered, "Neither he nor his parents sinned; it is so that the works of God might be made visible through him. We have to do the works of the one who sent me while it is day. Night is coming when no one can work. While I am in the world, I am the light of the world." When he had said this,]

* *See p. 16 for other Gospel Acclamations.*

he spat on the ground and made clay with the saliva, and smeared the clay on his eyes, and said to him, "Go wash in the Pool of Siloam"—which means Sent—. So he went and washed, and came back able to see.

His neighbors and those who had seen him earlier as a beggar said, "Isn't this the one who used to sit and beg?" Some said, "It is," but others said, "No, he just looks like him." He said, "I am."

[So they said to him, "How were your eyes opened?" He replied, "The man called Jesus made clay and anointed my eyes and told me, 'Go to Siloam and wash.' So I went there and washed and was able to see." And they said to him, "Where is he?" He said, "I don't know."]

They brought the one who was once blind to the Pharisees. Now Jesus had made clay and opened his eyes on a sabbath. So then the Pharisees also asked him how he was able to see. He said to them, "He put clay on my eyes, and I washed, and now I can see." So some of the Pharisees said, "This man is not from God, because he does not keep the sabbath." But others said, "How can a sinful man do such signs?" And there was a division among them. So they said to the blind man again, "What do you have to say about him, since he opened your eyes?" He said, "He is a prophet."

[Now the Jews did not believe that he had been blind and gained his sight until they summoned the parents of the one who had gained his sight. They asked them, "Is this your son, who you say was born blind? How does he now see?" His parents answered and said, "We know that this is our son and that he was born blind. We do not know how he sees now, nor do we know who opened his eyes. Ask him, he is of age; he can speak for himself." His parents said this because they were afraid of the Jews, for the Jews had already agreed that if anyone acknowledged him as the Christ, he would be expelled from the synagogue. For this reason his parents said, "He is of age; question him."

So a second time they called the man who had been blind and said to him, "Give God the praise! We know that this man is a sinner." He replied, "If he is a sinner, I do not know. One thing I do know is that I was blind and now I see." So they said to him, "What did he do to you? How did he open your eyes?" He answered them, "I told you already and you did not listen. Why do you want to hear it again? Do you want to become his disciples, too?" They ridiculed him and said, "You are that man's disciple; we are disciples of Moses! We know that God spoke to Moses, but we do not know where this one is from." The man answered and said to them, "This is what is so amazing, that you do not know where he is from, yet he opened my eyes. We know that God does not listen to sinners, but if one is devout and does his will, he listens to him. It is unheard of that anyone ever opened the eyes of a person born blind. If this man were not from God, he would not be able to do anything."]

They answered and said to him, "You were born totally in sin, and are you trying to teach us?" Then they threw him out.

When Jesus heard that they had thrown him out, he found him and said, "Do you believe in the Son of Man?" He answered and said, "Who is he, sir, that I may believe in him?" Jesus said to him, "You have seen him, and the one speaking with you is he." He said, "I do believe, Lord," and he worshiped him.

[Then Jesus said, "I came into this world for judgment, so that those who do not see might see, and those who do see might become blind."

Some of the Pharisees who were with him heard this and said to him, "Surely we are not also

blind, are we?" Jesus said to them, "If you were blind,
you would have no sin; but now you are saying, 'We
see,' so your sin remains."]

The Gospel of the Lord. ℟. **Praise to you, Lord Jesus
Christ.**   → No. 15, p. 18

PRAYER OVER THE OFFERINGS   [Eternal Remedy]

We place before you with joy these offerings,
which bring eternal remedy, O Lord,
praying that we may both faithfully revere them
and present them to you, as is fitting,
for those who seek salvation.
Through Christ our Lord. ℟. **Amen.** ↓

PREFACE (P 15)   [From Darkness to Radiance]

℣. The Lord be with you. ℟. **And with your spirit.**
℣. Lift up your hearts. ℟. **We lift them up to the Lord.**
℣. Let us give thanks to the Lord our God. ℟. **It is right
and just.**

It is truly right and just, our duty and our salvation,
always and everywhere to give you thanks,
Lord, holy Father, almighty and eternal God,
through Christ our Lord.

By the mystery of the Incarnation,
he has led the human race that walked in darkness
into the radiance of the faith
and has brought those born in slavery to ancient sin
through the waters of regeneration
to make them your adopted children.

Therefore, all creatures of heaven and earth
sing a new song in adoration,
and we, with all the host of Angels,
cry out, and without end acclaim: → No. 23, p. 23

*The commemoration of the godparents in the Eucharistic
Prayers takes place as above (pp. 238, 239) and, if the Roman
Canon is used, the proper form of the* Hanc igitur *(Therefore,*

Lord, we pray*) is said, as in the First Scrutiny (p. 239). The rest follows the Roman Canon, pp. 25-29.*

COMMUNION ANT. Cf. Jn 9:11, 38 [Spiritual Sight]

The Lord anointed my eyes: I went, I washed, I saw and I believed in God. ↓

PRAYER AFTER COMMUNION [God's Kindness]

Sustain your family always in your kindness,
O Lord, we pray,
correct them, set them in order,
graciously protect them under your rule,
and in your unfailing goodness
direct them along the way of salvation.
Through Christ our Lord.
℟. **Amen.**   → No. 30, p. 77

Optional Solemn Blessings, p. 97, and Prayers over the People, p. 105

"Go, and from now on do not sin any more."

APRIL 6

5th SUNDAY OF LENT

On this Sunday is celebrated the Third Scrutiny in prepara-
tion for the Baptism of the catechumens who are to be admit-
ted to the Sacraments of Christian Initiation at the Easter
Vigil. The Ritual Mass for the Third Scrutiny is found on
p. 259.

ENTRANCE ANT. Cf. Ps 43 (42):1-2   **[Rescue Me]**
Give me justice, O God, and plead my cause against a
nation that is faithless. From the deceitful and cun-
ning rescue me, for you, O God, are my strength.

→ No. 2, p. 10 (Omit Gloria)

COLLECT   **[Walk in Charity]**
By your help, we beseech you, Lord our God,
may we walk eagerly in that same charity
with which, out of love for the world,
your Son handed himself over to death.
Through our Lord Jesus Christ, your Son,
who lives and reigns with you in the unity of the Holy
  Spirit,

God, for ever and ever.
℟. **Amen.** ↓

FIRST READING Is 43:16-21   [Hope for the Future]

A call to look with hope to the future. God is not dead. Look around you and see his wonderful works.

A reading from the Book of the Prophet Isaiah

THUS says the LORD,
who opens a way in the sea
    and a path in the mighty waters,
who leads out chariots and horsemen,
    a powerful army,
till they lie prostrate together, never to rise,
    snuffed out and quenched like a wick.
Remember not the events of the past,
    the things of long ago consider not;
see, I am doing something new!
    Now it springs forth, do you not perceive it?
In the desert I make a way,
    in the wasteland, rivers.
Wild beasts honor me,
    jackals and ostriches,
for I put water in the desert
    and rivers in the wasteland
    for my chosen people to drink,
the people whom I formed for myself,
    that they might announce my praise.
The word of the Lord. ℟. **Thanks be to God.** ↓

RESPONSORIAL PSALM Ps 126   [Joy of the Redeemed]

℟. **The Lord has done great things for us;   we are filled with joy.**

When the LORD brought back the captives of Zion,
    we were like men dreaming.

Then our mouth was filled with laughter,
  and our tongue with rejoicing.

℞. **The Lord has done great things for us; we are filled
  with joy.**

Then they said among the nations,
  "The LORD has done great things for them."
The LORD has done great things for us;
  we are glad indeed.

℞. **The Lord has done great things for us; we are filled
  with joy.**

Restore our fortunes, O LORD,
  like the torrents in the southern desert.
Those that sow in tears
  shall reap rejoicing.

℞. **The Lord has done great things for us; we are filled
  with joy.**

Although they go forth weeping,
  carrying the seed to be sown,
they shall come back rejoicing,
  carrying their sheaves.

℞. **The Lord has done great things for us; we are filled
  with joy.** ↓

SECOND READING Phil 3:8-14   [Life in Christ]
  **Faith in Christ is our salvation, but we cannot relax. We
  must continue, while in this life, to strive for the good
  things of life in Christ—heaven.**

A reading from the Letter of Saint Paul to
the Philippians

BROTHERS and sisters: I consider everything as a
loss because of the supreme good of knowing
Christ Jesus my Lord. For his sake I have accepted the
loss of all things and I consider them so much rubbish,
that I may gain Christ and be found in him, not having

any righteousness of my own based on the law but that which comes through faith in Christ, the righteousness from God, depending on faith to know him and the power of his resurrection and the sharing of his sufferings by being conformed to his death, if somehow I may attain the resurrection from the dead.

It is not that I have already taken hold of it or have already attained perfect maturity, but I continue my pursuit in hope that I may possess it, since I have indeed been taken possession of by Christ Jesus. Brothers and sisters, I for my part do not consider myself to have taken possession. Just one thing: forgetting what lies behind but straining forward to what lies ahead, I continue my pursuit toward the goal, the prize of God's upward calling, in Christ Jesus.—The word of the Lord. ℟. **Thanks be to God.** ↓

VERSE BEFORE THE GOSPEL Jl 2:12-13 [Return to God]
℟. **Praise and honor to you, Lord Jesus Christ!***
Even now, says the Lord,
return to me with your whole heart;
for I am gracious and merciful.
℟. **Praise and honor to you, Lord Jesus Christ!** ↓

GOSPEL Jn 8:1-11   [Christ's Forgiveness]
By his example and works the Lord teaches us that God extends his mercy to sinners to free them from slavery to sin.

℣. The Lord be with you. ℟. **And with your spirit.**
✛ A reading from the holy Gospel according to John.
℟. **Glory to you, O Lord.**

JESUS went to the Mount of Olives. But early in the morning he arrived again in the temple area, and all the people started coming to him, and he sat down and taught them. Then the scribes and the Pharisees

---

* *See p. 16 for other Gospel Acclamations.*

brought a woman who had been caught in adultery and made her stand in the middle. They said to him, "Teacher, this woman was caught in the very act of committing adultery. Now in the law, Moses command-ed us to stone such women. So what do you say?" They said this to test him, so that they could have some charge to bring against him. Jesus bent down and began to write on the ground with his finger. But when they continued asking him, he straightened up and said to them, "Let the one among you who is without sin be the first to throw a stone at her." Again he bent down and wrote on the ground. And in response, they went away one by one, beginning with the elders. So he was left alone with the woman before him. Then Jesus straightened up and said to her, "Woman, where are they? Has no one condemned you?" She replied, "No one, sir." Then Jesus said, "Neither do I condemn you. Go, and from now on do not sin any more."—The Gospel of the Lord. ℟. **Praise to you, Lord Jesus Christ.**   ➜ No. 15, p. 18

PRAYER OVER THE OFFERINGS   [Hear Us]

Hear us, almighty God,
and, having instilled in your servants
the teachings of the Christian faith,
graciously purify them
by the working of this sacrifice.
Through Christ our Lord.
℟. **Amen.**   ➜ No. 21, p. 22 (Pref. P 8-9)

When the Gospel of Lazarus is read, see p. 263 for Preface (P 16).

COMMUNION ANT. Jn 8:10-11   [Sin No More]

Has no one condemned you, woman? No one, Lord. Neither shall I condemn you. From now on, sin no more. ↓

When the Gospel of Lazarus is read:

COMMUNION ANT. Cf. Jn 11:26   [Eternal Life]

Everyone who lives and believes in me will not die for ever, says the Lord. ↓

PRAYER AFTER COMMUNION   [Union with Jesus]

We pray, almighty God,
that we may always be counted among the members of
    Christ,
in whose Body and Blood we have communion.
Who lives and reigns for ever and ever.
℟. **Amen.** ↓

*The Deacon or, in his absence, the Priest himself, says the
invitation:* Bow down for the blessing.

PRAYER OVER THE PEOPLE   [Gift of Mercy]

Bless, O Lord, your people,
who long for the gift of your mercy,
and grant that what, at your prompting, they desire
they may receive by your generous gift.
Through Christ our Lord.
℟. **Amen.**

→ No. 32, p. 77

MASS FOR THE THIRD SCRUTINY

*This Mass is celebrated when the Third Scrutiny takes place
during the Order of Christian Initiation of Adults, usually on the
5th Sunday of Lent. The readings may be used in any case.*

ENTRANCE ANT. Cf. Ps 18 (17):5-7   [The Lord Hears Me]

**The waves of death rose about me; the pains of the nether-
world surrounded me. In my anguish I called to the Lord;
and from his holy temple he heard my voice.**

→ No. 2, p. 10 (Omit Gloria)

COLLECT   [Chosen Ones]
Grant, O Lord, to these chosen ones
that, instructed in the holy mysteries,
they may receive new life at the font of Baptism
and be numbered among the members of your Church.
Through our Lord Jesus Christ, your Son,
who lives and reigns with you in the unity of the Holy Spirit,
God, for ever and ever. ℟. **Amen.** ↓

FIRST READING Ez 37:12-14   [The Lord's Promise]

**The Lord promises to bring his people back to their home-
land. He will be with them and they will know him.**

A reading from the Book of the Prophet Ezekiel

T HUS says the Lord GOD: O my people, I will open your
graves and have you rise from them, and bring you back
to the land of Israel. Then you shall know that I am the LORD,
when I open your graves and have you rise from them, O my
people! I will put my spirit in you that you may live, and I will
settle you upon your land; thus you shall know that I am the
LORD. I have promised, and I will do it, says the LORD.—The
word of the Lord. ℟. **Thanks be to God.** ↓

RESPONSORIAL PSALM Ps 130   [Mercy and Redemption]

℟. **With the Lord there is mer-cy   and fullness of redemption.**

Out of the depths I cry to you, O LORD;
  LORD, hear my voice!
Let your ears be attentive
  to my voice in supplication.

R̸. **With the Lord there is mercy and fullness of redemption.**

If you, O LORD, mark iniquities,
  LORD, who can stand?
But with you is forgiveness,
  that you may be revered.—R̸.

I trust in the LORD;
  my soul trusts in his word.
More than sentinels wait for the dawn,
  let Israel wait for the LORD.—R̸.

For with the LORD is kindness
  and with him is plenteous redemption;
and he will redeem Israel
  from all their iniquities.—R̸. ↓

SECOND READING Rom 8:8-11   [Indwelling of Christ's Spirit]

The followers of Jesus live in the Spirit of God. The same Spirit who brought Jesus back to life will bring mortal bodies to life since God's Spirit dwells in them.

A reading from the Letter of Saint Paul to the Romans

BROTHERS and sisters: Those who are in the flesh cannot please God. But you are not in the flesh; on the contrary, you are in the spirit, if only the Spirit of God dwells in you. Whoever does not have the Spirit of Christ does not belong to him. But if Christ is in you, although the body is dead because of sin, the spirit is alive because of righteousness. If the Spirit of the one who raised Jesus from the dead dwells in you, the one who raised Christ from the dead will give life to your mortal bodies also, through his Spirit dwelling in you.—The word of the Lord.
R̸. **Thanks be to God.** ↓

VERSE BEFORE THE GOSPEL Jn 11:25a, 26   [Resurrection]

℟. **Praise and honor to you, Lord Jesus Christ!***
I am the resurrection and the life, says the Lord;
whoever believes in me, even if he dies, will never die.
℟. **Praise and honor to you, Lord Jesus Christ!** ↓

GOSPEL Jn 11:1-45 or 11:3-7, 17, 20-27, 33b-45   [Lazarus]

Lazarus, the brother of Martha and Mary, died and was buried. When Jesus came, he assured them that he was the resurrection and the life. Jesus gave life back to Lazarus.

[If the "Shorter Form" is used, the indented text in brackets is omitted.]

℣. The Lord be with you. ℟. **And with your spirit.**
✙ A reading from the holy Gospel according to John.
℟. **Glory to you, O Lord.**

[NOW a man was ill, Lazarus from Bethany, the village of Mary and her sister Martha. Mary was the one who had anointed the Lord with perfumed oil and dried his feet with her hair; it was her brother Lazarus who was ill.]
[So] the sisters** sent word to Jesus saying, "Master, the one you love is ill." When Jesus heard this he said, "This illness is not to end in death, but is for the glory of God, that the Son of God may be glorified through it." Now Jesus loved Martha and her sister and Lazarus. So when he heard that he was ill, he remained for two days in the place where he was. Then after this he said to his disciples, "Let us go back to Judea."

[The disciples said to him, "Rabbi, the Jews were just trying to stone you, and you want to go back there?" Jesus answered, "Are there not twelve hours in a day? If one walks during the day, he does not stumble, because he sees the light of this world. But if one walks at night, he stumbles, because the light is not in him."

_____
* See p. 16 for other Gospel Acclamations.
** The Shorter Form adds "of Lazarus."

He said this, and then told them, "Our friend Lazarus is asleep, but I am going to awaken him." So the disciples said to him, "Master, if he is asleep, he will be saved." But Jesus was talking about his death, while they thought that he meant ordinary sleep. So then Jesus said to them clearly, "Lazarus has died. And I am glad for you that I was not there, that you may believe. Let us go to him." So Thomas, called Didymus, said to his fellow disciples, "Let us also go to die with him."]

When Jesus arrived, he found that Lazarus had already been in the tomb for four days.

[Now Bethany was near Jerusalem, only about two miles away. And many of the Jews had come to Martha and Mary to comfort them about their brother.]

When Martha heard that Jesus was coming, she went to meet him; but Mary sat at home. Martha said to Jesus, "Lord, if you had been here, my brother would not have died. But even now I know that whatever you ask of God, God will give you." Jesus said to her, "Your brother will rise." Martha said to him, "I know he will rise, in the resurrection on the last day." Jesus told her, "I am the resurrection and the life; whoever believes in me, even if he dies, will live, and everyone who lives and believes in me will never die. Do you believe this?" She said to him, "Yes, Lord. I have come to believe that you are the Christ, the Son of God, the one who is coming into the world."

[When she had said this, she went and called her sister Mary secretly, saying, "The teacher is here and is asking for you." As soon as she heard this, she rose quickly and went to him. For Jesus had not yet come into the village, but was still where Martha had met him. So when the Jews who were with her in the house comforting her saw Mary get up quickly and go out, they followed her, presuming that she was going to the tomb to weep there. When Mary came to where Jesus was and saw him, she fell at his feet and said to him, "Lord, if you had been here, my brother would not

have died." When Jesus saw her weeping and the
    Jews who had come with her weeping,]
he became perturbed and deeply troubled, and said,
"Where have you laid him?" They said to him, "Sir, come
and see." And Jesus wept. So the Jews said, "See how he
loved him." But some of them said, "Could not the one who
opened the eyes of the blind man have done something so
that this man would not have died?"

So Jesus, perturbed again, came to the tomb. It was a
cave, and a stone lay across it. Jesus said, "Take away the
stone." Martha, the dead man's sister, said to him, "Lord,
by now there will be a stench; he has been dead for four
days." Jesus said to her, "Did I not tell you that if you
believe you will see the glory of God?" So they took away
the stone. And Jesus raised his eyes and said, "Father, I
thank you for hearing me. I know that you always hear
me; but because of the crowd here I have said this, that
they may believe that you sent me." And when he had said
this, he cried out in a loud voice, "Lazarus, come out!" The
dead man came out, tied hand and foot with burial bands,
and his face was wrapped in a cloth. So Jesus said to
them, "Untie him and let him go."

Now many of the Jews who had come to Mary and seen
what he had done began to believe in him.—The Gospel
of the Lord. ℟. **Praise to you, Lord Jesus Christ.**

→ No. 15, p. 18

PRAYER OVER THE OFFERINGS   [Hear Us]
Hear us, almighty God,
and, having instilled in your servants
the first fruits of the Christian faith,
graciously purify them by the working of this sacrifice.
Through Christ our Lord. ℟. **Amen.** ↓

PREFACE (P 16)   [God Raised Lazarus]
℣. The Lord be with you. ℟. **And with your spirit.**
℣. Lift up your hearts. ℟. **We lift them up to the Lord.**

℣. Let us give thanks to the Lord our God. ℟. **It is right and just.**

It is truly right and just, our duty and our salvation,
always and everywhere to give you thanks,
Lord, holy Father, almighty and eternal God,
through Christ our Lord.

For as true man he wept for Lazarus his friend
and as eternal God raised him from the tomb,
just as, taking pity on the human race,
he leads us by sacred mysteries to new life.

Through him the host of Angels adores your majesty
and rejoices in your presence for ever.
May our voices, we pray, join with theirs
in one chorus of exultant praise, as we acclaim:

➙ No. 23, p. 23

*The commemoration of the godparents in the Eucharistic
Prayers takes place as above (pp. 238, 239) and, if the Roman
Canon is used, the proper form of the* Hanc igitur *(Therefore,
Lord, we pray) is said, as in the First Scrutiny (p. 239). The rest
follows the Roman Canon, pp. 25-29.*

COMMUNION ANT. Cf. Jn 11:26   [Obtain Grace]
**Everyone who lives and believes in me will not die for
ever, says the Lord.** ↓

PRAYER AFTER COMMUNION   [Joy at Salvation]
May your people be at one, O Lord, we pray,
and in wholehearted submission to you
may they obtain this grace:
that, safe from all distress,
they may readily live out their joy at being saved
and remember in loving prayer those to be reborn.
Through Christ our Lord.
℟. **Amen.**

➙ No. 30, p. 77

Optional Solemn Blessings, p. 97, and Prayers over the People, p. 105

*"Blessed are you, who have come
in your abundant mercy!"*

APRIL 13

PALM SUNDAY OF THE PASSION
OF THE LORD

*On this day the Church recalls the entrance of Christ the Lord
into Jerusalem to accomplish his Paschal Mystery. Accordingly, the memorial of this entrance of the Lord takes place at
all Masses, by means of the Procession or the Solemn Entrance
before the principal Mass or the Simple Entrance before other
Masses. The Solemn Entrance, but not the Procession, may be
repeated before other Masses that are usually celebrated with
a large gathering of people.*

*It is desirable that, where neither the Procession nor the Solemn
Entrance can take place, there be a sacred celebration of the
Word of God on the messianic entrance and on the Passion of the
Lord, either on Saturday evening or on Sunday at a convenient
time.*

The Commemoration of the Lord's Entrance
into Jerusalem

FIRST FORM: THE PROCESSION

*At an appropriate hour, a gathering takes place at a smaller
church or other suitable place other than inside the church to*

265

which the procession will go. The faithful hold branches in their hands.

Meanwhile, the following antiphon or another appropriate chant is sung.

ANTIPHON Mt 21:9   [Hosanna]

**Hosanna to the Son of David;
blessed is he who comes
in the name of the Lord,
the King of Israel.
Hosanna in the highest.**

After this, the Priest and people sign themselves, while the Priest says: In the name of the Father, and of the Son, and of the Holy Spirit. *Then he greets the people in the usual way. A brief address is given, in which the faithful are invited to participate actively and consciously in the celebration of this day, in these or similar words:*

Dear brethren (brothers and sisters),
since the beginning of Lent until now
we have prepared our hearts by penance and charitable
   works.
Today we gather together to herald with the whole
   Church
the beginning of the celebration
of our Lord's Paschal Mystery,
that is to say, of his Passion and Resurrection.
For it was to accomplish this mystery
that he entered his own city of Jerusalem.
Therefore, with all faith and devotion,
let us commemorate
the Lord's entry into the city for our salvation,
following in his footsteps,
so that, being made by his grace partakers of the Cross,
we may have a share also in his Resurrection and in his
   life.

After the address, the Priest says one of the following prayers with hands extended.

PRAYER   [Following Christ]

Let us pray.
Almighty ever-living God,
sanctify ✠ these branches with your blessing,
that we, who follow Christ the King in exultation,
may reach the eternal Jerusalem through him.
Who lives and reigns for ever and ever. ℟. **Amen.** ↓

OR   [Christ in Triumph]

Increase the faith of those who place their hope in you,
    O God,
and graciously hear the prayers of those who call on you,
that we, who today hold high these branches
to hail Christ in his triumph,
may bear fruit for you by good works accomplished in
    him.
Who lives and reigns for ever and ever.
℟. **Amen.** ↓

*The Priest sprinkles the branches with holy water without say-
ing anything.*

*Then a Deacon or, if there is no Deacon, a Priest, proclaims in
the usual way the Gospel concerning the Lord's entrance
according to one of the four Gospels.*

GOSPEL Lk 19:28-40   [Jesus' Triumphal Entry]

> In triumphant glory Jesus comes into Jerusalem. The peo-
> ple spread their cloaks on the ground for him, wave olive
> branches, and sing in his honor.

℣. The Lord be with you. ℟. **And with your spirit.**
✠ A reading from the holy Gospel according to Luke.
℟. **Glory to you, O Lord.**

JESUS proceeded on his journey up to Jerusalem. As
he drew near to Bethphage and Bethany at the place
called the Mount of Olives, he sent two of his disciples.
He said, "Go into the village opposite you, and as you
enter it you will find a colt tethered on which no one has

ever sat. Untie it and bring it here. And if anyone should ask you, 'Why are you untying it?' you will answer, 'The Master has need of it.'" So those who had been sent went off and found everything just as he had told them. And as they were untying the colt, its owners said to them, "Why are you untying this colt?" They answered, "The Master has need of it." So they brought it to Jesus, threw their cloaks over the colt, and helped Jesus to mount. As he rode along, the people were spreading their cloaks on the road; and now as he was approaching the slope of the Mount of Olives, the whole multitude of his disciples began to praise God aloud with joy for all the mighty deeds they had seen. They proclaimed:

"Blessed is the king who comes
      in the name of the Lord.
Peace in heaven
      and glory in the highest."

Some of the Pharisees in the crowd said to him, "Teacher, rebuke your disciples." He said in reply, "I tell you, if they keep silent, the stones will cry out!"—The Gospel of the Lord. ℟. **Praise to you, Lord Jesus Christ**.

After the Gospel, a brief homily may be given. Then, to begin the Procession, an invitation may be given by a Priest or a Deacon or a lay minister, in these or similar words:

Dear brethren (brothers and sisters),
like the crowds who acclaimed Jesus in Jerusalem,
let us go forth in peace.

OR

Let us go forth in peace.
℟. **In the name of Christ. Amen**.

The Procession to the church where Mass will be celebrated then sets off in the usual way. If incense is used, the thurifer goes first, carrying a thurible with burning incense, then an acolyte or another minister, carrying a cross decorated with palm branches according to local custom, between two ministers with lighted candles. Then follow the Deacon carrying the

Book of the Gospels, the Priest with the ministers, and, after them, all the faithful carrying branches.

As the Procession moves forward, the following or other suitable chants in honor of Christ the King are sung by the choir and people.

ANTIPHON 1   [Hosanna]

The children of the Hebrews, carrying olive branches, went to meet the Lord, crying out and saying: Hosanna in the highest.

If appropriate, this antiphon is repeated between the strophes [stanzas] of the following Psalm.

PSALM 24 (23)   [The King of Glory]

The LORD's is the earth and its fullness, the world, and those who dwell in it. It is he who set it on the seas; on the rivers he made it firm. *(The antiphon is repeated.)*

Who shall climb the mountain of the LORD? Who shall stand in his holy place? The clean of hands and pure of heart, whose soul is not set on vain things, who has not sworn deceitful words.
(The antiphon is repeated.)

Blessings from the LORD shall he receive, and right reward from the God who saves him. Such are the people who seek him, who seek the face of the God of Jacob.
(The antiphon is repeated.)

O gates, lift high your heads; grow higher, ancient doors. Let him enter, the king of glory! *(The antiphon is repeated.)*

Who is this king of glory? The LORD, the mighty, the valiant; the LORD, the valiant in war. *(The antiphon is repeated.)*

O gates, lift high your heads; grow higher, ancient doors. Let him enter, the king of glory! *(The antiphon is repeated.)*

Who is this king of glory?
He, the LORD of hosts,
he is the king of glory.   *(The antiphon is repeated.)*

ANTIPHON 2   [Hosanna]

The children of the Hebrews spread their garments on
    the road,
crying out and saying: Hosanna to the Son of David;
blessed is he who comes in the name of the Lord.

If appropriate, this antiphon is repeated between the strophes
[stanzas] of the following Psalm.

PSALM 47 (46)   [The Great King]

All peoples, clap your hands.
Cry to God with shouts of joy!
For the LORD, the Most High, is awesome,
the great king over all the earth.   *(The antiphon is repeated.)*

He humbles peoples under us
and nations under our feet.
Our heritage he chose for us,
the pride of Jacob whom he loves.
                        (The antiphon is repeated.)

God has gone up with shouts of joy.
The LORD goes up with trumpet blast.
Sing praise for God; sing praise!
Sing praise to our king; sing praise!
                        (The antiphon is repeated.)

For God is king of all the earth.
Sing praise with a hymn.
God is reigning over nations.
God sits upon his holy throne.   *(The antiphon is repeated.)*

The princes of the peoples are assembled
with the people of the God of Abraham.
The rulers of the earth belong to God,
who is greatly exalted.   *(The antiphon is repeated.)*

Hymn to Christ the King

Chorus:

Glory and honor and praise be to you, Christ, King and Redeemer,

to whom young children cried out loving Hosannas with joy.

All repeat: **Glory and honor ...**

Chorus:

Israel's King are you, King David's magnificent offspring;

you are the ruler who come blest in the name of the Lord.

All repeat: **Glory and honor ...**

Chorus:

Heavenly hosts on high unite in singing your praises;

men and women on earth and all creation join in.

All repeat: **Glory and honor ...**

Chorus:

Bearing branches of palm, Hebrews came crowding to greet you;

see how with prayers and hymns we come to pay you our vows.

All repeat: **Glory and honor ...**

Chorus:

They offered gifts of praise to you, so near to your Passion;

see how we sing this song now to you reigning on high.

All repeat: **Glory and honor ...**

Chorus:

Those you were pleased to accept; now accept our gifts of devotion,

good and merciful King, lover of all that is good.

All repeat: **Glory and honor ...**

As the procession enters the church, there is sung the following responsory or another chant, which should speak of the Lord's entrance.

RESPONSORY

℟. As the Lord entered the holy city, the children of the Hebrews proclaimed the resurrection of life. Waving their branches of palm, they cried: Hosanna in the Highest.

℣. When the people had heard that Jesus was coming to Jerusalem, they went out to meet him. Waving their branches of palm, they cried: Hosanna in the Highest.

When the Priest arrives at the altar, he venerates it and, if appropriate, incenses it. Then he goes to the chair, where he puts aside the cope, if he has worn one, and puts on the chasuble. Omitting the other Introductory Rites of the Mass and, if appropriate, the Kyrie (Lord, have mercy), *he says the Collect of the Mass, and then continues the Mass in the usual way.*

SECOND FORM: THE SOLEMN ENTRANCE

When a procession outside the church cannot take place, the entrance of the Lord is celebrated inside the church by means of a Solemn Entrance before the principal Mass.

Holding branches in their hands, the faithful gather either outside, in front of the church door, or inside the church itself. The Priest and ministers and a representative group of the faithful go to a suitable place in the church outside the sanctuary, where at least the greater part of the faithful can see the rite.

While the Priest approaches the appointed place, the antiphon Hosanna *or another appropriate chant is sung. Then the blessing of branches and the proclamation of the Gospel of the Lord's entrance into Jerusalem take place as above (pp. 267-268). After the Gospel, the Priest processes solemnly with the ministers and the representative group of the faithful through the church to the sanctuary, while the responsory* As the Lord entered *(above) or another appropriate chant is sung.*

Arriving at the altar, the Priest venerates it. He then goes to the chair and, omitting the Introductory Rites of the Mass and, if appropriate, the Kyrie (Lord, have mercy), *he says the Collect of the Mass, and then continues the Mass in the usual way.*

THIRD FORM: THE SIMPLE ENTRANCE

At all other Masses of this Sunday at which the Solemn Entrance is not held, the memorial of the Lord's entrance into Jerusalem takes place by means of a Simple Entrance.

While the Priest proceeds to the altar, the Entrance Antiphon with its Psalm (below) or another chant on the same theme is sung. Arriving at the altar, the Priest venerates it and goes to the chair. After the Sign of the Cross, he greets the people and continues the Mass in the usual way.

At other Masses, in which singing at the entrance cannot take place, the Priest, as soon as he has arrived at the altar and venerated it, greets the people, reads the Entrance Antiphon, and continues the Mass in the usual way.

ENTRANCE ANT. Cf. Jn 12:1, 12-13; Ps 24 (23): 9-10
[Hosanna in the Highest]

Six days before the Passover, when the Lord came into the city of Jerusalem, the children ran to meet him; in their hands they carried palm branches and with a loud voice cried out: Hosanna in the highest! Blessed are you, who have come in your abundant mercy!

O gates, lift high your heads; grow higher, ancient doors. Let him enter, the king of glory! Who is this king of glory? He, the Lord of hosts, he is the king of glory. Hosanna in the highest! Blessed are you, who have come in your abundant mercy!

AT THE MASS

After the Procession or Solemn Entrance the Priest begins the Mass with the Collect.

COLLECT   [Patient Suffering]

Almighty ever-living God,
who as an example of humility for the human race to
   follow
caused our Savior to take flesh and submit to the Cross,
graciously grant that we may heed his lesson of patient
   suffering
and so merit a share in his Resurrection.
Who lives and reigns with you in the unity of the Holy
   Spirit,
God, for ever and ever.
℟. **Amen.** ↓

FIRST READING Is 50:4-7   [Christ's Suffering]

The sufferings of God's servant will not deter him from faith in God.

A reading from the Book of the Prophet Isaiah

THE Lord GOD has given me
   a well-trained tongue,
that I might know how to speak to the weary
   a word that will rouse them.
Morning after morning
   he opens my ear that I may hear;
and I have not rebelled,
   have not turned back.
I gave my back to those who beat me,
   my cheeks to those who plucked my beard;
my face I did not shield
   from buffets and spitting.

The Lord GOD is my help,
   therefore I am not disgraced;
I have set my face like flint,
   knowing that I shall not be put to shame.
The word of the Lord. ℟. **Thanks be to God.** ↓

RESPONSORIAL PSALM Ps 22   [Christ's Abandonment]

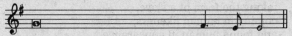

℟. My God, my God, why have you a-ban - doned me?

All who see me scoff at me;
    they mock me with parted lips, they wag their
        heads:
"He relied on the LORD; let him deliver him,
    let him rescue him, if he loves him."

℟. **My God, my God, why have you abandoned me?**

Indeed, many dogs surround me,
    a pack of evildoers closes in upon me;
they have pierced my hands and my feet;
    I can count all my bones.

℟. **My God, my God, why have you abandoned me?**

They divide my garments among them,
    and for my vesture they cast lots.
But you, O LORD, be not far from me;
    O my help, hasten to aid me.

℟. **My God, my God, why have you abandoned me?**

I will proclaim your name to my brethren;
    in the midst of the assembly I will praise you:
"You who fear the LORD, praise him;
    all you descendants of Jacob, give glory to him;
    revere him, all you descendants of Israel!"

℟. **My God, my God, why have you abandoned me?** ↓

SECOND READING Phil 2:6-11   [Humility]

Jesus Christ is Lord!

A reading from the Letter of Saint Paul
to the Philippians

CHRIST Jesus, though he was in the form of God,
    did not regard equality with God
something to be grasped.

Rather, he emptied himself,
  taking the form of a slave,
  coming in human likeness;
  and found human in appearance,
  he humbled himself,
  becoming obedient to the point of death,
  even death on a cross.
Because of this, God greatly exalted him
  and bestowed on him the name
  which is above every name,
  that at the name of Jesus
  every knee should bend,
  of those in heaven and on earth and under the earth,
  and every tongue confess that
  Jesus Christ is Lord,
  to the glory of God the Father.
The word of the Lord. ℟. **Thanks be to God.** ↓

VERSE BEFORE THE GOSPEL Phil 2:8-9 [Obedient to Death]

℟. **Praise to you, Lord Jesus Christ, King of endless glory!***

Christ became obedient to the point of death,
even death on the cross.
Because of this, God greatly exalted him
and bestowed on him the name which is above every
  name.

℟. **Praise to you, Lord Jesus Christ, King of endless glory!** ↓

GOSPEL Lk 22:14—23:56 or 23:1-49   [The Passion]
**Attend to the account of Christ's last days, and consider
how he suffered that we might have faith. By his Holy
Cross he has saved the world.**

When the Shorter Form is read, see pp. 281-284.

* *See p. 16 for other Gospel Acclamations.*

The fourteen subheadings introduced into the reading enable those who so desire to meditate on this text while making the Stations of the Cross.

The Passion may be read by lay readers, with the part of Christ, if possible, read by a Priest. The Narrator is noted by N, the words of Jesus by a ✢ and the words of others by V (Voice) and C (Crowd). The parts of the Crowd (C) printed in boldface type may be recited by the people.

We participate in the Passion narrative in several ways: by reading it and reflecting on it during the week ahead; by listening with faith as it is proclaimed; by respectful posture during the narrative; by reverent silence after the passage about Christ's Death. We do not hold the palms during the reading on Palm Sunday.

The message of the liturgy in proclaiming the Passion narratives in full is to enable the assembly to see vividly the love of Christ for each person, despite their sins, a love that even death could not vanquish. The crimes during the Passion of Christ cannot be attributed indiscriminately to all Jews of that time, nor to Jews today. The Jewish people should not be referred to as though rejected or cursed, as if this view followed from Scripture. The Church ever keeps in mind that Jesus, his Mother Mary, and the Apostles were Jewish. As the Church has always held, Christ freely suffered his Passion and Death because of the sins of all, that all might be saved.

This week we are challenged by the Passion narrative to reflect on the way we are living up to our baptismal promises of dying with Christ to sin and living with him for God.

N. **T**HE Passion of our Lord Jesus Christ according to Luke.

1. THE HOLY EUCHARIST

N. **W**HEN the hour came, Jesus took his place at table with the apostles. He said to them, ✢ "I have eagerly desired to eat this Passover with you before I suffer, for, I tell you, I shall not eat it again until there is fulfillment in the kingdom of God."

N. Then he took a cup, gave thanks, and said, ✤ "Take this and share it among yourselves; for I tell you that from this time on I shall not drink of the fruit of the vine until the kingdom of God comes." **N.** Then he took the bread, said the blessing, broke it, and gave it to them, saying, ✤ "This is my body, which will be given for you; do this in memory of me." **N.** And likewise the cup after they had eaten, saying, ✤ "This cup is the new covenant in my blood, which will be shed for you.

2. THE BETRAYER

✤ "**A**ND yet behold, the hand of the one who is to betray me is with me on the table; for the Son of Man indeed goes as it has been determined; but woe to that man by whom he is betrayed." **N.** And they began to debate among themselves who among them would do such a deed.

3. WHO IS GREATEST?

N. **T**HEN an argument broke out among them about which of them should be regarded as the greatest. He said to them, ✤ "The kings of the Gentiles lord it over them and those in authority over them are addressed as 'Benefactors'; but among you it shall not be so. Rather, let the greatest among you be as the youngest, and the leader as the servant. For who is greater: the one seated at table or the one who serves? Is it not the one seated at table? I am among you as the one who serves. It is you who have stood by me in my trials; and I confer a kingdom on you, just as my Father has conferred one on me, that you may eat and drink at my table in my kingdom; and you will sit on thrones judging the twelve tribes of Israel.

4. PETER'S DENIALS FORETOLD

✤ "**S**IMON, Simon, behold Satan has demanded to sift all of you like wheat, but I have prayed that your own faith may not fail; and once you have turned back, you must strengthen your brothers." **N.** He said to him, **V.** "Lord, I am prepared to go to prison and to die with you." **N.** But he replied, ✠ "I tell you, Peter, before the cock crows this day, you will deny three times that you know me."

N. He said to them, ✠ "When I sent you forth without a money bag or a sack or sandals, were you in need of anything?" **C.** "No, nothing," **N.** they replied. He said to them, ✠ "But now one who has a money bag should take it, and likewise a sack, and one who does not have a sword should sell his cloak and buy one. For I tell you that this Scripture must be fulfilled in me, namely, *He was counted among the wicked;* and indeed what is written about me is coming to fulfillment." **N.** Then they said, **C.** "Lord, look, there are two swords here." **N.** But he replied, ✠ "It is enough!"

5. THE AGONY IN THE GARDEN

N. THEN going out, he went, as was his custom, to the Mount of Olives, and the disciples followed him. When he arrived at the place he said to them, ✠ "Pray that you may not undergo the test." **N.** After withdrawing about a stone's throw from them and kneeling, he prayed, saying, ✠ "Father, if you are willing, take this cup away from me; still, not my will but yours be done." **N.** And to strengthen him an angel from heaven appeared to him. He was in such agony and he prayed so fervently that his sweat became like drops of blood falling on the ground. When he rose from prayer and returned to his disciples, he found them sleeping from grief. He said to them, ✠ "Why are you sleeping? Get up and pray that you may not undergo the test."

6. JESUS ARRESTED

N. WHILE he was still speaking, a crowd approached and in front was one of the Twelve, a man named Judas. He went up to Jesus to kiss him. Jesus said to him, ✠ "Judas, are you betraying the Son of Man with a kiss?" **N.** His disciples realized what was about to happen, and they asked, **C. "Lord, shall we strike with a sword?" N.** And one of them struck the high priest's servant and cut off his right ear. But Jesus said in reply, ✠ "Stop, no more of this!" **N.** Then he touched the servant's ear and healed him. And Jesus said to the chief priests and temple guards and elders who had come for him, ✠ "Have you come out as against a robber, with swords and clubs? Day after day I was with you in the temple area, and you did not seize me; but this is your hour, the time for the power of darkness."

7. PETER'S DENIAL

N. **A**FTER arresting him they led him away and took him into the house of the high priest; Peter was following at a distance. They lit a fire in the middle of the courtyard and sat around it, and Peter sat down with them. When a maid saw him seated in the light, she looked intently at him and said, **C. "This man too was with him." N.** But he denied it saying, **V.** "Woman, I do not know him." **N.** A short while later someone else saw him and said, **C. "You too are one of them"; N.** but Peter answered, **V.** "My friend, I am not." **N.** About an hour later, still another insisted, **C. "Assuredly, this man too was with him, for he also is a Galilean." N.** But Peter said, **V.** "My friend, I do not know what you are talking about." **N.** Just as he was saying this, the cock crowed, and the Lord turned and looked at Peter; and Peter remembered the word of the Lord, how he had said to him, "Before the cock crows today, you will deny me three times." He went out and began to weep bitterly.

[8. JESUS BEFORE THE SANHEDRIN]

N. The men who held Jesus in custody were ridiculing and beating him. They blindfolded him and questioned him, saying, **C. "Prophesy! Who is it that struck you?"**

N. And they reviled him in saying many other things against him.

When day came the council of elders of the people met, both chief priests and scribes, and they brought him before their Sanhedrin. They said, **C. "If you are the Christ, tell us,"** **N.** but he replied to them, ✝ "If I tell you, you will not believe, and if I question, you will not respond. But from this time on the Son of Man will be seated at the right hand of the power of God." **N.** They all asked, **C. "Are you then the Son of God?"** **N.** He replied to them, ✝ "You say that I am." **N.** Then they said, **C. "What further need have we for testimony? We have heard it from his own mouth."**

[Beginning of Shorter Form]

9. JESUS BEFORE PILATE

N.* **T**HE elders of the people, chief priests and scribes arose and brought him before Pilate. They brought charges against him, saying, **C. "We found this man misleading our people; he opposes the payment of taxes to Caesar and maintains that he is the Christ, a king."** **N.** Pilate asked him, **V.** "Are you the king of the Jews?" **N.** He said to him in reply, ✝ "You say so." **N.** Pilate then addressed the chief priests and the crowds, **V.** "I find this man not guilty." **N.** But they were adamant and said, **C. "He is inciting the people with his teaching throughout all Judea, from Galilee where he began even to here."**

N. On hearing this Pilate asked if the man was a Galilean; and upon learning that he was under Herod's jurisdiction, he sent him to Herod who was in Jerusalem at that time. Herod was very glad to see Jesus; he had been wanting to see him for a long time, for he had heard about him and had been hoping to see him perform some sign. He questioned him at length, but he gave him no

---

* *The Longer Form reads: "Then the whole assembly of them . . . ."*

answer. The chief priests and scribes, meanwhile, stood by accusing him harshly. Herod and his soldiers treated him contemptuously and mocked him, and after clothing him in resplendent garb, he sent him back to Pilate. Herod and Pilate became friends that very day, even though they had been enemies formerly.

[10. JESUS AGAIN BEFORE PILATE]

N. Pilate then summoned the chief priests, the rulers, and the people and said to them, **V.** "You brought this man to me and accused him of inciting the people to revolt. I have conducted my investigation in your presence and have not found this man guilty of the charges you have brought against him, nor did Herod, for he sent him back to us. So no capital crime has been committed by him. Therefore I shall have him flogged and then release him."

N. BUT all together they shouted out, **C.** "**Away with this man! Release Barabbas to us.**" **N.**—Now Barabbas had been imprisoned for a rebellion that had taken place in the city and for murder.—Again Pilate addressed them, still wishing to release Jesus, but they continued their shouting, **C.** "**Crucify him! Crucify him!**" **N.** Pilate addressed them a third time, **V.** "What evil has this man done? I found him guilty of no capital crime. Therefore I shall have him flogged and then release him." **N.** With loud shouts, however, they persisted in calling for his crucifixion, and their voices prevailed. The verdict of Pilate was that their demand should be granted. So he released the man who had been imprisoned for rebellion and murder, for whom they asked, and he handed Jesus over to them to deal with as they wished.

11. THE WAY OF THE CROSS

N. AS they led him away they took hold of a certain Simon, a Cyrenian, who was coming in from the country; and after laying the cross on him, they made him carry it behind Jesus. A large crowd of people followed Jesus, including many women who mourned and lamented him. Jesus turned to them and said, ✚ "Daughters of Jerusalem, do not weep for me; weep instead for yourselves and for your children, for indeed, the days are coming when people will say, 'Blessed are the barren, the wombs that never bore and the breasts that never nursed.' At that time people will say to the mountains, 'Fall upon us!' and to the hills, 'Cover us!' for if these things are done when the wood is green what will happen when it is dry?"

[12. THE CRUCIFIXION]

N. Now two others, both criminals, were led away with him to be executed.

WHEN they came to the place called the Skull, they crucified him and the criminals there, one on his right, the other on his left. Then Jesus said, ✚ "Father, forgive them, they know not what they do." **N.** They divided his garments by casting lots. The people stood by and watched; the rulers, meanwhile, sneered at him and said, **C.** "He saved others, let him save himself if he is the chosen one, the Christ of God." **N.** Even the soldiers jeered at him. As they approached to offer him wine they called out, **C.** "If you are King of the Jews, save yourself." **N.** Above him there was an inscription that read, "This is the King of the Jews."

Now one of the criminals hanging there reviled Jesus, saying, **V.** "Are you not the Christ? Save yourself and us." **N.** The other, however, rebuking him, said in reply, **V.** "Have you no fear of God, for you are subject to the same condemnation? And indeed, we have been condemned justly, for the sentence we received corresponds to our crimes, but this man has done nothing criminal." **N.** Then he said, **V.** "Jesus, remember me when you come into your kingdom." **N.** He replied to him, ✚ "Amen, I say to you, today you will be with me in Paradise."

13. JESUS DIES ON THE CROSS

N. **I**T was now about noon and darkness came over the whole land until three in the afternoon because of an eclipse of the sun. Then the veil of the temple was torn down the middle. Jesus cried out in a loud voice, ✚ "Father, into your hands I commend my spirit"; **N.** and when he had said this he breathed his last.

Here all kneel and pause for a short time.

The centurion who witnessed what had happened glorified God and said, **V.** "This man was innocent beyond doubt." **N.** When all the people who had gathered for this spectacle saw what had happened, they returned home beating their breasts; but all his acquaintances stood at a distance, including the women who had followed him from Galilee and saw these events.

[End of Shorter Form]

14. THE BURIAL

N. **N**OW there was a virtuous and righteous man named Joseph who, though he was a member of the council, had not consented to their plan of action. He came from the Jewish town of Arimathea and was awaiting the kingdom of God. He went to Pilate and asked for the body of Jesus. After he had taken the body down, he wrapped it in a linen cloth and laid him in a rock-hewn tomb in which no one had yet been buried. It was the day of preparation, and the sabbath was about to begin. The women who had come from Galilee with him followed behind, and when they had seen the tomb and the way in which his body was laid in it, they returned and prepared spices and perfumed oils. Then they rested on the sabbath according to the commandment.—The Gospel of the Lord. ℟. **Praise to you Lord Jesus Christ.**   → No. 15, p. 18

After the narrative of the Passion, a brief homily should take place, if appropriate. A period of silence may also be observed.

PRAYER OVER THE OFFERINGS   [Reconciled with God]

Through the Passion of your Only Begotten Son, O Lord,
may our reconciliation with you be near at hand,
so that, though we do not merit it by our own deeds,
yet by this sacrifice made once for all,
we may feel already the effects of your mercy.
Through Christ our Lord. ℟. **Amen.** ↓

PREFACE (P 19)   [Purchased Our Justification]

℣. The Lord be with you. ℟. **And with your spirit.**
℣. Lift up your hearts. ℟. **We lift them up to the Lord.**
℣. Let us give thanks to the Lord our God. ℟. **It is right and just.**

It is truly right and just, our duty and our salvation,
always and everywhere to give you thanks,
Lord, holy Father, almighty and eternal God,
through Christ our Lord.

For, though innocent, he suffered willingly for sinners
and accepted unjust condemnation to save the guilty.
His Death has washed away our sins,
and his Resurrection has purchased our justification.

And so, with all the Angels,
we praise you, as in joyful celebration we acclaim:

→ No. 23, p. 23

COMMUNION ANT. Mt 26:42   [God's Will]
Father, if this chalice cannot pass without my drinking it, your will be done. ↓

PRAYER AFTER COMMUNION   [Nourishing Gifts]

Nourished with these sacred gifts,
we humbly beseech you, O Lord,

that, just as through the death of your Son
you have brought us to hope for what we believe,
so by his Resurrection
you may lead us to where you call.
Through Christ our Lord.
R̸. **Amen.** ↓

*The Deacon or, in his absence, the Priest himself, says the
invitation:* Bow down for the blessing.

PRAYER OVER THE PEOPLE   [God's Family]

Look, we pray, O Lord, on this your family,
for whom our Lord Jesus Christ
did not hesitate to be delivered into the hands of the
    wicked
and submit to the agony of the Cross.
Who lives and reigns for ever and ever.
R̸. **Amen.**   → No. 32, p. 77

"The Spirit of the Lord is upon me."

APRIL 17

THURSDAY OF HOLY WEEK
[HOLY THURSDAY]

THE CHRISM MASS

This Mass, which the Bishop concelebrates with his presbyterate, should be, as it were, a manifestation of the Priests' communion with their Bishop. Accordingly it is desirable that all the Priests participate in it, insofar as is possible, and during it receive Communion even under both kinds. To signify the unity of the presbyterate of the diocese, the Priests who concelebrate with the Bishop should be from different regions of the diocese.

In accord with traditional practice, the blessing of the Oil of the Sick takes place before the end of the Eucharistic Prayer, but the blessing of the Oil of Catechumens and the consecration of the Chrism take place after Communion. Nevertheless, for pastoral reasons, it is permitted for the entire rite of blessing to take place after the Liturgy of the Word.

ENTRANCE ANT. Rev 1:6   [Kingdom of Priests]
Jesus Christ has made us into a kingdom, priests for his God and Father. To him be glory and power for ever and ever. Amen. ➜ No. 2, p. 10

The Gloria *is said.*

COLLECT   [Faithful Witnesses]

O God, who anointed your Only Begotten Son with the
    Holy Spirit
and made him Christ and Lord,
graciously grant
that, being made sharers in his consecration,
we may bear witness to your Redemption in the world.
Through our Lord Jesus Christ, your Son,
who lives and reigns with you in the unity of the Holy
    Spirit,
God, for ever and ever. ℟. **Amen.** ↓

FIRST READING Is 61:1-3ab, 6a, 8b-9   [The Lord's Anointed]

**The prophet, anointed by God to bring the Good News to
the poor, proclaims a message filled with hope. It is one
that replaces mourning with gladness.**

A reading from the Book of the Prophet Isaiah

THE Spirit of the Lord GOD is upon me,
    because the LORD has anointed me;
He has sent me to bring glad tidings to the lowly,
    to heal the brokenhearted,
To proclaim liberty to the captives
    and release to the prisoners,
To announce a year of favor from the LORD
    and a day of vindication by our God,
    to comfort all who mourn;
To place on those who mourn in Zion
    a diadem instead of ashes,
To give them oil of gladness in place of mourning,
    a glorious mantle instead of a listless spirit.

You yourselves shall be named priests of the LORD,
    ministers of our God you shall be called.

I will give them their recompense faithfully,
    a lasting covenant I will make with them.

Their descendants shall be renowned among the
    nations,
  and their offspring among the peoples;
All who see them shall acknowledge them
    as a race the Lord has blessed.
The word of the Lord. ℟. **Thanks be to God.** ↓

RESPONSORIAL PSALM Ps 89   [God the Savior]

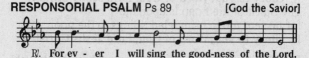

    ℟. For ev - er I will sing the good-ness of the Lord.

"I have found David, my servant;
  with my holy oil I have anointed him,
that my hand may be always with him,
    and that my arm may make him strong."—℟.

"My faithfulness and my kindness shall be with him,
  and through my name shall his horn be exalted.
He shall say of me, 'You are my father,
  my God, the Rock my savior.' "—℟. ↓

SECOND READING Rv 1:5-8   [The Alpha and the Omega]
    **God says, "I am the Alpha and the Omega, the one who is
    and who was and who is to come, the almighty!" All shall
    see God as he comes amid the clouds.**

    A reading from the Book of Revelation

[G]RACE to you and peace] from Jesus Christ, who is
the faithful witness, the firstborn of the dead and
ruler of the kings of the earth. To him who loves us and
has freed us from our sins by his Blood, who has made
us into a Kingdom, priests for his God and Father, to
him be glory and power forever and ever! Amen.
  Behold, he is coming amid the clouds,
    and every eye will see him,
    even of those who pierced him.
All the peoples of the earth will lament him.
    Yes. Amen.

"I am the Alpha and the Omega," says the Lord God, "the one who is and who was and who is to come, the Almighty!"—The word of the Lord. ℟. **Thanks be to God.** ↓

VERSE BEFORE THE GOSPEL Is 61:1 (cited in Lk 4:18)
[Glad Tidings]

℟. **Glory to you, Word of God, Lord Jesus Christ!***
The Spirit of the LORD is upon me
for he sent me to bring glad tidings to the poor.
℟. **Glory to you, Word of God, Lord Jesus Christ!** ↓

GOSPEL Lk 4:16-21   [Christ the Messiah]

Jesus reads in the synagogue at Nazareth the words of Isaiah quoted in the first reading. Jesus is the Anointed One. He tells the people that today Isaiah's prophecy is fulfilled.

℣. The Lord be with you. ℟. **And with your spirit.**
✚ A reading from the holy Gospel according to Luke.
℟. **Glory to you, O Lord.**

JESUS came to Nazareth, where he had grown up, and went according to his custom into the synagogue on the sabbath day. He stood up to read and was handed a scroll of the prophet Isaiah. He unrolled the scroll and found the passage where it was written:

The Spirit of the Lord is upon me,
because he has anointed me
    to bring glad tidings to the poor.
He has sent me to proclaim liberty to captives
    and recovery of sight to the blind,
    to let the oppressed go free,
and to proclaim a year acceptable to the Lord.

Rolling up the scroll, he handed it back to the attendant and sat down, and the eyes of all in the synagogue looked intently at him. He said to them, "Today this Scripture passage is fulfilled in your hearing."—

---

* See p. 16 for other Gospel Acclamations.

The Gospel of the Lord. ℟. **Praise to you, Lord Jesus Christ.** ↓

After the reading of the Gospel, the Bishop preaches the Homily in which, taking his starting point from the text of the readings proclaimed in the Liturgy of the Word, he speaks to the people and to his Priests about priestly anointing, urging the Priests to be faithful in their office and calling on them to renew publicly their priestly promises.

Renewal of Priestly Promises

After the Homily, the Bishop speaks with the Priests in these or similar words.

Beloved sons,
on the anniversary of that day
when Christ our Lord conferred his priesthood
on his Apostles and on us,
are you resolved to renew,
in the presence of your Bishop and God's holy people,
the promises you once made?
Priests: I am.

Bishop:
Are you resolved to be more united with the Lord Jesus
and more closely conformed to him,
denying yourselves and confirming those promises
about sacred duties towards Christ's Church
which, prompted by love of him,
you willingly and joyfully pledged
on the day of your priestly ordination?
Priests: I am.

Bishop:
Are you resolved to be faithful stewards of the mysteries
    of God
in the Holy Eucharist and the other liturgical rites
and to discharge faithfully the sacred office of teaching,
following Christ the Head and Shepherd,
not seeking any gain,

but moved only by zeal for souls?

Priests: I am.

Then, turned towards the people, the Bishop continues:

As for you, dearest sons and daughters,
pray for your Priests,
that the Lord may pour out his gifts abundantly upon
   them,
and keep them faithful as ministers of Christ, the High
   Priest,
so that they may lead you to him,
who is the source of salvation.

People: Christ, hear us. Christ, graciously hear us.

Bishop:
And pray also for me,
that I may be faithful to the apostolic office
entrusted to me in my lowliness
and that in your midst I may be made day by day
a living and more perfect image of Christ,
the Priest, the Good Shepherd,
the Teacher and the Servant of all.

People: Christ, hear us. Christ, graciously hear us.

Bishop:
May the Lord keep us all in his charity
and lead all of us,
shepherds and flock,
to eternal life.

All: Amen.

The Creed is not said.   ➜ No. 17, p. 20

PRAYER OVER THE OFFERINGS   [New Life]

May the power of this sacrifice, O Lord, we pray,
mercifully wipe away what is old in us
and increase in us grace of salvation and newness of life.
Through Christ our Lord.
℟. **Amen.** ↓

PREFACE (P 20)   [Continuation of Christ's Priesthood]

℣. The Lord be with you. ℟. **And with your spirit.**

℣. Lift up your hearts. ℟. **We lift them up to the Lord.**

℣. Let us give thanks to the Lord our God. ℟. **It is right and just.**

It is truly right and just, our duty and our salvation,
always and everywhere to give you thanks,
Lord, holy Father, almighty and eternal God.

For by the anointing of the Holy Spirit
you made your Only Begotten Son
High Priest of the new and eternal covenant,
and by your wondrous design were pleased to decree
that his one Priesthood should continue in the Church.

For Christ not only adorns with a royal priesthood
the people he has made his own,
but with a brother's kindness he also chooses men
to become sharers in his sacred ministry
through the laying on of hands.

They are to renew in his name
the sacrifice of human redemption,
to set before your children the paschal banquet,
to lead your holy people in charity,
to nourish them with the word
and strengthen them with the Sacraments.

As they give up their lives for you
and for the salvation of their brothers and sisters,
they strive to be conformed to the image of Christ
  himself
and offer you a constant witness of faith and love.

And so, Lord, with all the Angels and Saints,
we, too, give you thanks, as in exultation we acclaim:

→ No. 23, p. 23

COMMUNION ANT. Ps 89 (88):2   [The Lord's Fidelity]

I will sing for ever of your mercies, O Lord; through all ages my mouth will proclaim your fidelity. ↓

PRAYER AFTER COMMUNION   [Renewed in Christ]

We beseech you, almighty God,
that those you renew by your Sacraments
may merit to become the pleasing fragrance of Christ.
Who lives and reigns for ever and ever.
℟. **Amen.**   → No. 30, p. 77

Optional Solemn Blessings, p. 97, and Prayers over the People, p. 105

———————

"Do this in remembrance of me."

THE SACRED PASCHAL TRIDUUM
APRIL 17

THURSDAY OF THE LORD'S SUPPER
[HOLY THURSDAY]

AT THE EVENING MASS

The Evening Mass of the Lord's Supper commemorates the institution of the Holy Eucharist and the Sacrament of Holy Orders. It was at this Mass that Jesus changed bread and wine into his Body and

Blood. He then directed his disciples to carry out this same ritual: "Do this in remembrance of me."

ENTRANCE ANT. Cf. Gal 6:14   [Glory in the Cross]

We should glory in the Cross of our Lord Jesus Christ, in whom is our salvation, life and resurrection, through whom we are saved and delivered.

→ No. 2, p. 10

The Gloria in excelsis *(Glory to God in the highest) is said. While the hymn is being sung, bells are rung, and when it is finished, they remain silent until the* Gloria in excelsis *of the Easter Vigil, unless, if appropriate, the Diocesan Bishop has decided otherwise. Likewise, during this same period, the organ and other musical instruments may be used only so as to support the singing.*

COLLECT   [Fullness of Charity]

O God, who have called us to participate
in this most sacred Supper,
in which your Only Begotten Son,
when about to hand himself over to death,
entrusted to the Church a sacrifice new for all eternity,
the banquet of his love,
grant, we pray,
that we may draw from so great a mystery,
the fullness of charity and of life.
Through our Lord Jesus Christ, your Son,
who lives and reigns with you in the unity of the Holy
    Spirit,
God, for ever and ever. ℟. **Amen.** ↓

FIRST READING Ex 12:1-8, 11-14   [The First Passover]

For the protection of the Jewish people, strict religious and dietary instructions are given to Moses by God. The law of the Passover meal requires that the doorposts and lintels of each house be marked with the blood of the sacrificial animal so that the LORD can "go through Egypt striking down every firstborn of the land, both man and beast."

A reading from the Book of Exodus

THE LORD said to Moses and Aaron in the land of Egypt, "This month shall stand at the head of your calendar; you shall reckon it the first month of the year. Tell the whole community of Israel: On the tenth of this month every one of your families must procure for itself a lamb, one apiece for each household. If a family is too small for a whole lamb, it shall join the nearest household in procuring one and shall share in the lamb in proportion to the number of persons who partake of it. The lamb must be a year-old male and without blemish. You may take it from either the sheep or the goats. You shall keep it until the fourteenth day of this month, and then, with the whole assembly of Israel present, it shall be slaughtered during the evening twilight. They shall take some of its blood and apply it to the two doorposts and the lintel of every house in which they partake of the lamb. That same night they shall eat its roasted flesh with unleavened bread and bitter herbs.

"This is how you are to eat it: with your loins girt, sandals on your feet and your staff in hand, you shall eat like those who are in flight. It is the Passover of the LORD. For on this same night I will go through Egypt, striking down every firstborn of the land, both man and beast, and executing judgment on all the gods of Egypt—I, the LORD! But the blood will mark the houses where you are. Seeing the blood, I will pass over you; thus, when I strike the land of Egypt, no destructive blow will come upon you.

"This day shall be a memorial feast for you, which all your generations shall celebrate with pilgrimage to the LORD, as a perpetual institution."—The word of the Lord. ℟. **Thanks be to God.** ↓

RESPONSORIAL PSALM Ps 116   [Thanksgiving]

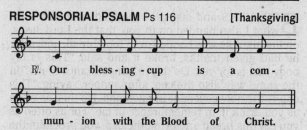

℟. Our bless-ing-cup is a com-mun-ion with the Blood of Christ.

How shall I make a return to the LORD
  for all the good he has done for me?
The cup of salvation I will take up,
  and I will call upon the name of the LORD.

℟. **Our blessing-cup is a communion with the Blood of
  Christ.**

Precious in the eyes of the LORD
  is the death of his faithful ones.
I am your servant, the son of your handmaid;
  you have loosed my bonds.

℟. **Our blessing-cup is a communion with the Blood of
  Christ.**

To you will I offer sacrifice of thanksgiving,
  and I will call upon the name of the LORD.
My vows to the LORD I will pay
  in the presence of all his people.

℟. **Our blessing-cup is a communion with the Blood of
  Christ.** ↓

SECOND READING 1 Cor 11:23-26   [The Lord's Supper]

Paul recounts the events of the Last Supper which were
handed down to him. The changing of bread and wine into
the Body and Blood of the Lord proclaimed again his
death. It was to be a sacrificial meal.

A reading from the first Letter of Saint Paul
                to the Corinthians

B ROTHERS and sisters: I received from the Lord what I also handed on to you, that the Lord Jesus, on the night he was handed over, took bread, and, after he had given thanks, broke it and said, "This is my body that is for you. Do this in remembrance of me." In the same way also the cup, after supper, saying, "This cup is the new covenant in my blood. Do this, as often as you drink it, in remembrance of me." For as often as you eat this bread and drink the cup, you proclaim the death of the Lord until he comes.—The word of the Lord. ℟. **Thanks be to God.** ↓

VERSE BEFORE THE GOSPEL Jn 13:34 [Love One Another]

℟. **Praise to you, Lord Jesus Christ, King of endless glory!***

I give you a new commandment, says the Lord:
love one another as I have loved you.

℟. **Praise to you, Lord Jesus Christ, King of endless glory!** ↓

GOSPEL Jn 13:1-15   [Love and Service]

Jesus washes the feet of his disciples to prove to them his sincere love and great humility which they should imitate.

℣. The Lord be with you. ℟. **And with your spirit.**

✤ A reading from the holy Gospel according to John.

℟. **Glory to you, O Lord.**

B EFORE the feast of Passover, Jesus knew that his hour had come to pass from this world to the Father. He loved his own in the world and he loved them to the end. The devil had already induced Judas, son of Simon the Iscariot, to hand him over. So, during supper, fully aware that the Father had put everything into his power and that he had come from God and was returning to God, he rose from supper and took off his outer gar-

* See p. 16 for other Gospel Acclamations.

ments. He took a towel and tied it around his waist. Then he poured water into a basin and began to wash the disciples' feet and dry them with the towel around his waist. He came to Simon Peter, who said to him, "Master, are you going to wash my feet?" Jesus answered and said to him, "What I am doing, you do not understand now, but you will understand later." Peter said to him, "You will never wash my feet." Jesus answered him, "Unless I wash you, you will have no inheritance with me." Simon Peter said to him, "Master, then not only my feet, but my hands and head as well." Jesus said to him, "Whoever has bathed has no need except to have his feet washed, for he is clean all over; so you are clean, but not all." For he knew who would betray him; for this reason, he said, "Not all of you are clean."

So when he had washed their feet and put his garments back on and reclined at table again, he said to them, "Do you realize what I have done for you? You call me 'teacher' and 'master,' and rightly so, for indeed I am. If I, therefore, the master and teacher, have washed your feet, you ought to wash one another's feet. I have given you a model to follow, so that as I have done for you, you should also do."—The Gospel of the Lord. ℟. **Praise to you, Lord Jesus Christ.**

After the proclamation of the Gospel, the Priest gives a homily in which light is shed on the principal mysteries that are commemorated in this Mass, namely, the institution of the Holy Eucharist and of the priestly Order, and the commandment of the Lord concerning fraternal charity.

The Washing of Feet

After the Homily, where a pastoral reason suggests it, the Washing of Feet follows.

Those who are chosen from among the people of God are led by the ministers to seats prepared in a suitable place. Then the Priest (removing his chasuble if necessary) goes to each one, and, with the help of the ministers, pours water over each one's feet and then dries them.

Meanwhile some of the following antiphons or other appropriate chants are sung.

ANTIPHON 1 Cf. Jn 13:4, 5, 15   [Jesus' Example]

After the Lord had risen from supper,
he poured water into a basin
and began to wash the feet of his disciples:
he left them this example.

ANTIPHON 2 Cf. Jn 13:12, 13, 15   [Do Likewise]

The Lord Jesus, after eating supper with his disciples,
washed their feet and said to them:
Do you know what I, your Lord and Master, have done
   for you?
I have given you an example, that you should do likewise.

ANTIPHON 3 Jn 13:6, 7, 8   [Peter's Understanding]

Lord, are you to wash my feet? Jesus said to him in
   answer:
If I do not wash your feet, you will have no share with
   me.

℣. So he came to Simon Peter and Peter said to him:
—Lord.

℣. What I am doing, you do not know for now,
but later you will come to know.
—Lord.

ANTIPHON 4 Cf. Jn 13:14   [Service]

If I, your Lord and Master, have washed your feet,
how much more should you wash each other's feet?

ANTIPHON 5 Jn 13:35   [Identified by Love]

This is how all will know that you are my disciples:
if you have love for one another.

℣. Jesus said to his disciples:
—This is how.

ANTIPHON 6 Jn 13:34   [New Commandment]

I give you a new commandment,
that you love one another
as I have loved you, says the Lord.

ANTIPHON 7 1 Cor 13:13   [Greatest Is Charity]

Let faith, hope and charity, these three, remain among
    you,
but the greatest of these is charity.

℣. Now faith, hope and charity, these three, remain;
but the greatest of these is charity.
—Let.

*After the Washing of Feet, the Priest washes and dries his
hands, puts the chasuble back on, and returns to the chair,
and from there he directs the Universal Prayer.*

The Creed is not said.

The Liturgy of the Eucharist

*At the beginning of the Liturgy of the Eucharist, there may be
a procession of the faithful in which gifts for the poor may be
presented with the bread and wine.*

*Meanwhile the following, or another appropriate chant, is
sung.*

[Christ's Love]

Ant. Where true charity is dwelling, God is present there.

℣. By the love of Christ we have been brought to-
        gether:
℣. let us find in him our gladness and our pleasure;
℣. may we love him and revere him, God the living,
℣. and in love respect each other with sincere hearts.

Ant. Where true charity is dwelling, God is present there.

℣. So when we as one are gathered all together,
℣. let us strive to keep our minds free of division;
℣. may there be an end to malice, strife and quarrels,
℣. and let Christ our God be dwelling here among us.

Ant. Where true charity is dwelling, God is present there.

℣. May your face thus be our vision, bright in glory,
℣. Christ our God, with all the blessed Saints in heaven:
℣. such delight is pure and faultless, joy unbounded,
℣. which endures through countless ages world without end. Amen.   → No. 17, p. 20

PRAYER OVER THE OFFERINGS [Work of Redemption]

Grant us, O Lord, we pray,
that we may participate worthily in these mysteries,
for whenever the memorial of this sacrifice is celebrated
the work of our redemption is accomplished.
Through Christ our Lord.
℟. Amen.   → No. 21, p. 22 (Pref. P 47)

*When the Roman Canon is used, this special form of it is said,
with proper formulas for the* Communicantes *(In communion
with those),* Hanc igitur *(Therefore, Lord, we pray), and* Qui
pridie *(On the day before he was to suffer).*

To you, therefore, most merciful Father,
we make humble prayer and petition
through Jesus Christ, your Son, our Lord:
that you accept
and bless ✠ these gifts, these offerings,
these holy and unblemished sacrifices,
which we offer you firstly
for your holy catholic Church.
Be pleased to grant her peace,
to guard, unite and govern her

throughout the whole world,
together with your servant N. our Pope
and N. our Bishop,
and all those who, holding to the truth,
hand on the catholic and apostolic faith.

Remember, Lord, your servants N. and N.
and all gathered here,
whose faith and devotion are known to you.
For them we offer you this sacrifice of praise
or they offer it for themselves
and all who are dear to them:
for the redemption of their souls,
in hope of health and well-being,
and paying their homage to you,
the eternal God, living and true.

Celebrating the most sacred day
on which our Lord Jesus Christ
was handed over for our sake,
and in communion with those whose memory we
    venerate,
especially the glorious ever-Virgin Mary,
Mother of our God and Lord, Jesus Christ,
and † blessed Joseph, her Spouse,
your blessed Apostles and Martyrs
Peter and Paul, Andrew,
(James, John,
Thomas, James, Philip,
Bartholomew, Matthew, Simon and Jude;
Linus, Cletus, Clement, Sixtus,
Cornelius, Cyprian,
Lawrence, Chrysogonus,
John and Paul,
Cosmas and Damian)
and all your Saints;
we ask that through their merits and prayers,
in all things we may be defended

by your protecting help.
(Through Christ our Lord. Amen.)

Therefore, Lord, we pray:
graciously accept this oblation of our service,
that of your whole family,
which we make to you
as we observe the day
on which our Lord Jesus Christ
handed on the mysteries of his Body and Blood
for his disciples to celebrate;
order our days in your peace,
and command that we be delivered from eternal
   damnation
and counted among the flock of those you have chosen.
(Through Christ our Lord. Amen.)

Be pleased, O God, we pray,
to bless, acknowledge,
and approve this offering in every respect;
make it spiritual and acceptable,
so that it may become for us
the Body and Blood of your most beloved Son,
our Lord Jesus Christ.

On the day before he was to suffer
for our salvation and the salvation of all,
that is today,
he took bread in his holy and venerable hands,
and with eyes raised to heaven
to you, O God, his almighty Father,
giving you thanks, he said the blessing,
broke the bread
and gave it to his disciples, saying:

Take this, all of you, and eat of it,
for this is my Body,
which will be given up for you.

In a similar way, when supper was ended,
he took this precious chalice
in his holy and venerable hands,
and once more giving you thanks, he said the blessing
and gave the chalice to his disciples, saying:

Take this, all of you, and drink from it,
for this is the chalice of my Blood,
the Blood of the new and eternal covenant,
which will be poured out for you and for many
for the forgiveness of sins.

Do this in memory of me.

The rest follows the Roman Canon, pp. 26-29.

COMMUNION ANT. 1 Cor 11:24-25   [In Memory of Christ]

This is the Body that will be given up for you; this is the Chalice of the new covenant in my Blood, says the Lord; do this, whenever you receive it, in memory of me. ↓

After the distribution of Communion, a ciborium with hosts for Communion on the following day is left on the altar. The Priest, standing at the chair, says the Prayer after Communion.

PRAYER AFTER COMMUNION   [Renewed]

Grant, almighty God,
that, just as we are renewed
by the Supper of your Son in this present age,
so we may enjoy his banquet for all eternity.
Who lives and reigns for ever and ever. ℟. **Amen.**

The Transfer of the Most Blessed Sacrament

After the Prayer after Communion, the Priest puts incense in the thurible while standing, blesses it and then, kneeling, incenses the Blessed Sacrament three times. Then, having put on a white humeral veil, he rises, takes the ciborium, and covers it with the ends of the veil.

A procession is formed in which the Blessed Sacrament, accompanied by torches and incense, is carried through the church to a place of repose prepared in a part of the church or in a chapel suitably decorated. A lay minister with a cross, standing between two other ministers with lighted candles leads off. Others carrying lighted candles follow. Before the Priest carrying the Blessed Sacrament comes the thurifer with a smoking thurible. Meanwhile, the hymn Pange, lingua *(exclusive of the last two stanzas) or another eucharistic chant is sung.*

PANGE LINGUA

[Adoring the Lord]

Sing my tongue, the Savior's glory,
Of his flesh the mystery sing;
Of his blood all price exceeding,
Shed by our immortal king,
Destined for the world's redemption,
From a noble womb to spring.

Of a pure and spotless Virgin
Born for us on earth below,
He, as man with man conversing,
Stayed the seeds of truth to sow;
Then he closed in solemn order
Wondrously his life of woe.

On the night of that Last Supper,
Seated with his chosen band,
He, the paschal victim eating,
First fulfills the law's command;
Then as food to all his brethren
Gives himself with his own hand.

Word made Flesh, the bread of nature,
By his word to flesh he turns;
Wine into his blood he changes:
What though sense no change discerns,
Only be the heart in earnest,
Faith her lesson quickly learns.

When the procession reaches the place of repose, the Priest, with the help of the Deacon if necessary, places the ciborium in the tabernacle, the door of which remains open. Then he puts incense in the thurible and, kneeling, incenses the Blessed Sacrament, while Tantum ergo Sacramentum *or*

*another eucharistic chant is sung. Then the Deacon or the
Priest himself places the Sacrament in the tabernacle and
closes the door.*

Down in adoration falling,
Lo! the sacred host we
  hail,
Lo! o'er ancient forms departing
Newer rites of grace pre-
  vail;
Faith for all defects supplying,
Where the feeble senses
  fail.

To the everlasting Father,
And the Son who reigns on
  high
With the Holy Spirit pro-
  ceeding
Forth from each eternally,
Be salvation, honor, bless-
  ing,
Might and endless majesty.
  Amen.

*After a period of adoration in silence, the Priest and ministers
genuflect and return to the sacristy.*

*At an appropriate time, the altar is stripped and, if possible,
the crosses are removed from the church. It is expedient that
any crosses which remain in the church be veiled.*

*The faithful are invited to continue adoration before the
Blessed Sacrament for a suitable length of time during the
night, according to local circumstances, but after midnight the
adoration should take place without solemnity.*

"And bowing his head, [Jesus] handed over the spirit."

APRIL 18

FRIDAY OF THE PASSION OF THE LORD [GOOD FRIDAY]

CELEBRATION OF THE PASSION OF THE LORD

The liturgy of Good Friday recalls graphically the Passion and Death of Jesus. The reading of the Passion describes the suffering and Death of Jesus. Today we show great reverence for the crucifix, the sign of our redemption.

On this and the following day, by a most ancient tradition, the Church does not celebrate the Sacraments at all, except for Penance and the Anointing of the Sick. On the afternoon of this day, about three o'clock (unless a later hour is chosen for a pastoral reason), there takes place the celebration of the Lord's Passion.

The Priest and the Deacon, if a Deacon is present, wearing red vestments as for Mass, go to the altar in silence and, after making a reverence to the altar, prostrate themselves or, if appropriate, kneel and pray in silence for a while. All others kneel. Then the Priest, with the ministers, goes to the chair where, facing the people, who are standing, he says, with hands extended, one of the following prayers, omitting the invitation Let us pray.

PRAYER   [Sanctify Your Servants]
Remember your mercies, O Lord,
and with your eternal protection sanctify your servants,
for whom Christ your Son,
by the shedding of his Blood,
established the Paschal Mystery.
Who lives and reigns for ever and ever. ℟. **Amen.** ↓

OR   [Image of Christ]
O God, who by the Passion of Christ your Son, our Lord,
abolished the death inherited from ancient sin
by every succeeding generation,
grant that just as, being conformed to him,
we have borne by the law of nature
the image of the man of earth,
so by the sanctification of grace
we may bear the image of the Man of heaven.
Through Christ our Lord. ℟. **Amen.** ↓

FIRST PART: THE LITURGY OF THE WORD

FIRST READING Is 52:13—53:12   [Suffering and Glory]
**The suffering Servant shall be raised up and exalted. The
Servant remains one with all people in sorrow and yet dis-
tinct from each of them in innocence of life and total service to God. The doctrine of expiatory suffering finds
supreme expression in these words.**

A reading from the Book of the Prophet Isaiah

SEE, my servant shall prosper,
he shall be raised high and greatly exalted.
Even as many were amazed at him—
   so marred was his look beyond human semblance
   and his appearance beyond that of the sons of
      man—
so shall he startle many nations,
   because of him kings shall stand speechless;
for those who have not been told shall see,
   those who have not heard shall ponder it.

Who would believe what we have heard?
    To whom has the arm of the LORD been revealed?
He grew up like a sapling before him,
    like a shoot from the parched earth;
there was in him no stately bearing to make us look
        at him,
    nor appearance that would attract us to him.
He was spurned and avoided by people,
    a man of suffering, accustomed to infirmity,
one of those from whom people hide their faces,
    spurned, and we held him in no esteem.

Yet it was our infirmities that he bore,
    our sufferings that he endured,
while we thought of him as stricken,
    as one smitten by God and afflicted.
But he was pierced for our offenses,
    crushed for our sins;
upon him was the chastisement that makes us whole,
    by his stripes we were healed.
We had all gone astray like sheep,
    each following his own way;
but the LORD laid upon him
    the guilt of us all.

Though he was harshly treated, he submitted
    and opened not his mouth;
like a lamb led to the slaughter
    or a sheep before the shearers,
    he was silent and opened not his mouth.
Oppressed and condemned, he was taken away,
        and who would have thought any more of his
        destiny?
When he was cut off from the land of the living,
    and smitten for the sin of his people,
a grave was assigned him among the wicked
    and a burial place with evildoers,
though he had done no wrong
    nor spoken any falsehood.

But the LORD was pleased
  to crush him in infirmity.

If he gives his life as an offering for sin,
  he shall see his descendants in a long life,
    and the will of the LORD shall be accomplished
      through him.

Because of his affliction
  he shall see the light in fullness of days;
through his suffering, my servant shall justify many,
  and their guilt he shall bear.

Therefore I will give him his portion among the great,
  and he shall divide the spoils with the mighty,
because he surrendered himself to death
  and was counted among the wicked;
and he shall take away the sins of many,
  and win pardon for their offenses.

The word of the Lord. ℟. **Thanks be to God.** ↓

RESPONSORIAL PSALM Ps 31   [Trust in God]

℟. Fa - ther, in - to your hands I com - mend my spir - it.

In you, O LORD, I take refuge;
  let me never be put to shame.
In your justice rescue me.
Into your hands I commend my spirit;
  you will redeem me, O LORD, O faithful God.

℟. **Father, into your hands I commend my spirit.**

For all my foes I am an object of reproach,
  a laughingstock to my neighbors, and a dread to my
    friends;
  they who see me abroad flee from me.
I am forgotten like the unremembered dead;
  I am like a dish that is broken.

R̂). **Father, into your hands I commend my spirit.**

But my trust is in you, O LORD;
  I say, "You are my God."
In your hands is my destiny; rescue me
  from the clutches of my enemies and my persecutors.

R̂). **Father, into your hands I commend my spirit.**

Let your face shine upon your servant;
  save me in your kindness.
Take courage and be stouthearted,
  all you who hope in the LORD.

R̂). **Father, into your hands I commend my spirit.** ↓

SECOND READING Heb 4:14-16; 5:7-9   [Access to Christ]

The theme of the compassionate high priest appears again
in this passage. In him the Christian can approach God
confidently and without fear. Christ learned obedience
from his sufferings whereby he became the source of eternal life for all.

A reading from the Letter to the Hebrews

BROTHERS and sisters: Since we have a great high
priest who has passed through the heavens, Jesus,
the Son of God, let us hold fast to our confession. For
we do not have a high priest who is unable to sympa-
thize with our weaknesses, but one who has similarly
been tested in every way, yet without sin. So let us confidently approach the throne of grace to receive mercy
and to find grace for timely help.

In the days when Christ was in the flesh, he offered
prayers and supplications with loud cries and tears to
the one who was able to save him from death, and he
was heard because of his reverence. Son though he
was, he learned obedience from what he suffered; and
when he was made perfect, he became the source of
eternal salvation for all who obey him.—The word of
the Lord. R̂). **Thanks be to God.** ↓

VERSE BEFORE THE GOSPEL Phil 2:8-9 [Obedient for Us]

℟. **Praise and honor to you, Lord Jesus Christ!***
Christ became obedient to the point of death,
even death on a cross.
Because of this, God greatly exalted him
and bestowed on him the name which is above every
    other name.

℟. **Praise and honor to you, Lord Jesus Christ!**

GOSPEL Jn 18:1—19:42   [Christ's Passion]

*The Passion is read as on the preceding Sunday. See the note
on p. 276-277.*

*The passion narratives are proclaimed in full so that all see
vividly the love of Christ for each person. In light of this, the
crimes during the Passion of Christ cannot be attributed, in
either preaching or catechesis, indiscriminately to all Jews of
that time, nor to Jews today. The Jewish people should not be
referred to as though rejected or cursed, as if this view followed from Scripture. The Church ever keeps in mind that
Jesus, his mother Mary, and the apostles all were Jewish. As
the Church has always held, Christ freely suffered his passion
and death because of the sins of all, that all might be saved.*

N. **T**HE Passion of our Lord Jesus Christ according
to John

1. JESUS IS ARRESTED

N. **J**ESUS went out with his disciples across the
Kidron valley to where there was a garden, into
which he and his disciples entered. Judas his betrayer
also knew the place, because Jesus had often met
there with his disciples. So Judas got a band of soldiers and guards from the chief priests and the
Pharisees and went there with lanterns, torches, and
weapons. Jesus, knowing everything that was going to
happen to him, went out and said to them, ✠ "Whom
are you looking for?" N. They answered him, C. **"Jesus
the Nazorean."** N. He said to them, ✠ "I AM." N. Judas
his betrayer was also with them. When he said

* *See p. 16 for other Gospel Acclamations.*

to them, "I AM," they turned away and fell to the ground. So he again asked them, ✠ "Whom are you looking for?" **N.** They said, **C. "Jesus the Nazorean."** **N.** Jesus answered, ✠ "I told you that I AM. So if you are looking for me, let these men go." **N.** This was to fulfill what he had said, "I have not lost any of those you gave me." Then Simon Peter, who had a sword, drew it, struck the high priest's slave, and cut off his right ear. The slave's name was Malchus. Jesus said to Peter, ✠ "Put your sword into its scabbard. Shall I not drink the cup that the Father gave me?"

N. So the band of soldiers, the tribune, and the Jewish guards seized Jesus, bound him, and brought him to Annas first. He was the father-in-law of Caiaphas, who was high priest that year. It was Caiaphas who had counseled the Jews that it was better that one man should die rather than the people.

2. PETER'S FIRST DENIAL

N. SIMON Peter and another disciple followed Jesus. Now the other disciple was known to the high priest, and he entered the courtyard of the high priest with Jesus. But Peter stood at the gate outside. So the other disciple, the acquaintance of the high priest, went out and spoke to the gatekeeper and brought Peter in. Then the maid who was the gatekeeper said to Peter, **C. "You are not one of this man's disciples, are you?"** **N.** He said, **V.** "I am not." **N.** Now the slaves and the guards were standing around a charcoal fire that they had made, because it was cold, and were warming themselves. Peter was also standing there keeping warm.

3. THE INQUIRY BEFORE ANNAS

N. THE high priest questioned Jesus about his disciples and about his doctrine. Jesus answered him, ✠ "I have spoken publicly to the world. I have always taught in a synagogue or in the temple area where all the Jews gather, and in secret I have said nothing. Why ask me? Ask those who heard me what I said to them. They know what I said." **N.** When he had said this, one of the temple guards standing there struck Jesus and said, **V.** "Is this the way you answer the high priest?" **N.** Jesus answered him, ✠ "If I have spoken wrongly, testify to the wrong; but if I have spoken rightly, why do you strike me?" **N.** Then Annas sent him bound to Caiaphas the high priest.

4. THE FURTHER DENIALS

N. **N**OW Simon Peter was standing there keeping warm. And they said to him, **C.** **"You are not one of his disciples, are you?"** **N.** He denied it and said, **V.** "I am not." **N.** One of the slaves of the high priest, a relative of the one whose ear Peter had cut off, said, **C.** **"Didn't I see you in the garden with him?"** **N.** Again Peter denied it. And immediately the cock crowed.

5. JESUS BROUGHT BEFORE PILATE

N. **T**HEN they brought Jesus from Caiaphas to the praetorium. It was morning. And they themselves did not enter the praetorium, in order not to be defiled so that they could eat the Passover. So Pilate came out to them and said, **V.** "What charge do you bring against this man?" **N.** They answered and said to him, **C.** **"If he were not a criminal, we would not have handed him over to you."** **N.** At this, Pilate said to them, **V.** "Take him yourselves, and judge him according to your law." **N.** The Jews answered him, **C.** **"We do not have the right to execute anyone,"** **N.** in order that the word of Jesus might be fulfilled that he said indicating the kind of death he would die.

[6. JESUS QUESTIONED BY PILATE]

So Pilate went back into the praetorium and summoned Jesus and said to him, **V.** "Are you the King of the Jews?" **N.** Jesus answered, ✠ "Do you say this on your own or have others told you about me?" **N.** Pilate answered, **V.** "I am not a Jew, am I? Your own nation and the chief priests handed you over to me. What have you done?" **N.** Jesus answered, ✠ "My kingdom does not belong to this world. If my kingdom did belong to this world, my attendants would be fighting to keep me from being handed over to the Jews. But as it is, my kingdom is not here." **N.** So Pilate said to him, **V.** "Then you are a king?" **N.** Jesus answered, ✠ "You say I am a king. For this I was born and for this I came into the world, to testify to the truth. Everyone who belongs to the truth listens to my voice." **N.** Pilate said to him, **V.** "What is truth?"

7. BARABBAS CHOSEN OVER JESUS

N. WHEN he had said this, he again went out to the Jews and said to them, **V.** "I find no guilt in him. But you have a custom that I release one prisoner to you at Passover. Do you want me to release to you the King of the Jews?" **N.** They cried out again, **C.** **"Not this one but Barabbas!"** **N.** Now Barabbas was a revolutionary.

8. JESUS IS SCOURGED

N. THEN Pilate took Jesus and had him scourged. And the soldiers wove a crown out of thorns and placed it on his head, and clothed him in a purple cloak, and they came to him and said, **C.** **"Hail, King of the Jews!"** **N.** And they struck him repeatedly.

[9. JESUS IS PRESENTED TO THE CROWD]

Once more Pilate went out and said to them, **V.** "Look, I am bringing him out to you, so that you may know that I find no guilt in him." **N.** So Jesus came out, wearing the crown of thorns and the purple cloak. And Pilate said to them, **V.** "Behold, the man!" **N.** When the chief priests and the guards saw him they cried out, **C.** **"Crucify him, crucify him!"** N. Pilate said to them, **V.** "Take him yourselves and crucify him. I find no guilt in him." **N.** The Jews answered, **C. "We have a law, and according to that law he ought to die, because he made himself the Son of God."**

[*10. JESUS AGAIN QUESTIONED BY PILATE*]

N. Now when Pilate heard this statement, he became even more afraid, and went back into the praetorium and said to Jesus, **V.** "Where are you from?" **N.** Jesus did not answer him. So Pilate said to him, **V.** "Do you not speak to me? Do you not know that I have power to release you and I have power to crucify you?" [**N.** Jesus answered him,] ✠ "You would have no power over me if it had not been given to you from above. For this reason the one who handed me over to you has the greater sin."

[*11. JESUS SENTENCED TO BE CRUCIFIED*]

N. Consequently, Pilate tried to release him; but the Jews cried out, **C. "If you release him, you are not a Friend of Caesar. Everyone who makes himself a king opposes Caesar."**

N. When Pilate heard these words he brought Jesus out and seated him on the judge's bench in the place called Stone Pavement, in Hebrew, Gabbatha. It was preparation day for Passover, and it was about noon. And he said to the Jews, **V.** "Behold, your king!" **N.** They cried out, **C. "Take him away, take him away! Crucify him!"** **N.** Pilate said to them, **V.** "Shall I crucify your king?" **N.** The chief priests answered, **C. "We have no king but Caesar."** **N.** Then he handed him over to them to be crucified.

12. CRUCIFIXION AND DEATH

N. SO they took Jesus, and, carrying the cross himself, he went out to what is called the Place of the Skull, in Hebrew, Golgotha. There they crucified him, and with him two others, one on either side, with Jesus in the middle. Pilate also had an inscription written and put on the cross. It read, "Jesus the Nazorean, the King of the Jews." Now many of the Jews read this inscription, because the place where Jesus was crucified was near the city; and it was written in Hebrew, Latin, and Greek. So the chief priests of the Jews said to Pilate, **C.** **"Do not write 'The King of the Jews,' but that he said, 'I am the King of the Jews.' "** **N.** Pilate answered, **V.** "What I have written, I have written."

N. When the soldiers had crucified Jesus, they took his clothes and divided them into four shares, a share for each soldier. They also took his tunic, but the tunic was seamless, woven in one piece from the top down. So they said to one another, **C.** **"Let's not tear it, but cast lots for it to see whose it will be,"** **N.** in order that the passage of Scripture might be fulfilled that says:

They divided my garments among them,
and for my vesture they cast lots.

This is what the soldiers did. Standing by the cross of Jesus were his mother and his mother's sister, Mary the wife of Clopas, and Mary of Magdala. When Jesus saw his mother and the disciple there whom he loved he said to his mother, ✠ "Woman, behold, your son." **N.** Then he said to the disciple, ✠ "Behold, your mother." **N.** And from that hour the disciple took her into his home.

After this, aware that everything was now finished, in order that the Scripture might be fulfilled, Jesus said, ✠ "I thirst." **N.** There was a vessel filled with common wine. So they put a sponge soaked in wine on a sprig of hyssop and put it up to his mouth. When Jesus had taken the wine, he said, ✠ "It is finished." And bowing his head, he handed over the spirit.

Here all kneel and pause for a short time.

13. THE BLOOD AND WATER

N. **N**OW since it was preparation day, in order that the bodies might not remain on the cross on the sabbath, for the sabbath day of that week was a solemn one, the Jews asked Pilate that their legs be broken and that they be taken down. So the soldiers came and broke the legs of the first and then of the other one who was crucified with Jesus. But when they came to Jesus and saw that he was already dead, they did not break his legs, but one soldier thrust his lance into his side, and immediately blood and water flowed out. An eyewitness has testified, and his testimony is true; he knows that he is speaking the truth, so that you also may come to believe. For this happened so that the Scripture passage might be fulfilled:

Not a bone of it will be broken.

And again another passage says:

They will look upon him whom they have pierced.

14. BURIAL OF JESUS

N. **A**FTER this, Joseph of Arimathea, secretly a disciple of Jesus for fear of the Jews, asked Pilate if he could remove the body of Jesus. And Pilate permitted it. So he came and took his body. Nicodemus, the one who had first come to him at night, also came bringing a mixture of myrrh and aloes weighing about one hundred pounds. They took the body of Jesus and bound it with burial cloths along with the spices, according to the Jewish burial custom. Now in the place where he had been crucified there was a garden, and in the garden a new tomb, in which no one had yet been buried. So they laid Jesus there because of the Jewish preparation day; for the tomb was close by.— The Gospel of the Lord. ℟. **Praise to you, Lord Jesus Christ.**

THE SOLEMN INTERCESSIONS

*The Liturgy of the Word concludes with the Solemn
Intercessions, which take place in this way: the Deacon, if a
Deacon is present, or if he is not, a lay minister, stands at the
ambo, and sings or says the invitation in which the intention
is expressed. Then all pray in silence for a while, and afterwards the Priest, standing at the chair or, if appropriate, at
the altar, with hands extended, sings or says the prayer. The
faithful may remain either kneeling or standing throughout
the entire period of the prayers. Before the Priest's prayer, in
accord with tradition, it is permissible to use the Deacon's
invitations* Let us kneel—Let us stand, *with all kneeling for
silent prayer.*

I. For Holy Church

Let us pray, dearly beloved, for the holy Church of God,
that our God and Lord be pleased to give her peace,
to guard her and to unite her throughout the whole
    world
and grant that, leading our life in tranquility and quiet,
we may glorify God the Father almighty.

Prayer in silence. Then the Priest says:

Almighty ever-living God,
who in Christ revealed your glory to all the nations,
watch over the works of your mercy,
that your Church, spread throughout all the world,
may persevere with steadfast faith in confessing your
    name.
Through Christ our Lord. ℟. **Amen.** ↓

II. For the Pope

Let us pray also for our most Holy Father Pope N.,
that our God and Lord,
who chose him for the Order of Bishops,
may keep him safe and unharmed for the Lord's holy
    Church,
to govern the holy People of God.

Prayer in silence. Then the Priest says:

Almighty ever-living God,
by whose decree all things are founded,
look with favor on our prayers
and in your kindness protect the Pope chosen for us,
that, under him, the Christian people,
governed by you their maker,
may grow in merit by reason of their faith.
Through Christ our Lord. ℟. **Amen.** ↓

III. For all orders and degrees of the faithful

Let us pray also for our Bishop N.,
for all Bishops, Priests, and Deacons of the Church
and for the whole of the faithful people.

Prayer in silence. Then the Priest says:

Almighty ever-living God,
by whose Spirit the whole body of the Church
is sanctified and governed,
hear our humble prayer for your ministers,
that, by the gift of your grace,
all may serve you faithfully.
Through Christ our Lord. ℟. **Amen.** ↓

IV. For catechumens

Let us pray also for (our) catechumens,
that our God and Lord
may open wide the ears of their inmost hearts
and unlock the gates of his mercy,
that, having received forgiveness of all their sins
through the waters of rebirth,
they, too, may be one with Christ Jesus our Lord.

Prayer in silence. Then the Priest says:

Almighty ever-living God,
who make your Church ever fruitful with new offspring,
increase the faith and understanding of (our)
    catechumens,
that, reborn in the font of Baptism,

they may be added to the number of your adopted
children.
Through Christ our Lord. ℟. **Amen.** ↓

V. For the unity of Christians

Let us pray also for all our brothers and sisters who
believe in Christ,
that our God and Lord may be pleased,
as they live the truth,
to gather them together and keep them in his one
Church.

Prayer in silence. Then the Priest says:

Almighty ever-living God,
who gather what is scattered
and keep together what you have gathered,
look kindly on the flock of your Son,
that those whom one Baptism has consecrated
may be joined together by integrity of faith
and united in the bond of charity.
Through Christ our Lord. ℟. **Amen.** ↓

VI. For the Jewish people

Let us pray also for the Jewish people,
to whom the Lord our God spoke first,
that he may grant them to advance in love of his name
and in faithfulness to his covenant.

Prayer in silence. Then the Priest says:

Almighty ever-living God,
who bestowed your promises on Abraham and his
descendants,
graciously hear the prayers of your Church,
that the people you first made your own
may attain the fullness of redemption.
Through Christ our Lord. ℟. **Amen.** ↓

VII. For those who do not believe in Christ

Let us pray also for those who do not believe in Christ,
that, enlightened by the Holy Spirit,
they, too, may enter on the way of salvation.

Prayer in silence. Then the Priest says:

Almighty ever-living God,
grant to those who do not confess Christ
that, by walking before you with a sincere heart,
they may find the truth
and that we ourselves, being constant in mutual love
and striving to understand more fully the mystery of
     your life,
may be made more perfect witnesses to your love in the
     world.
Through Christ our Lord.
℟. **Amen.** ↓

VIII. For those who do not believe in God

Let us pray also for those who do not acknowledge God,
that, following what is right in sincerity of heart,
they may find the way to God himself.

Prayer in silence. Then the Priest says:

Almighty ever-living God,
who created all people
to seek you always by desiring you
and, by finding you, come to rest,
grant, we pray,
that, despite every harmful obstacle,
all may recognize the signs of your fatherly love
and the witness of the good works
done by those who believe in you,
and so in gladness confess you,
the one true God and Father of our human race.
Through Christ our Lord. ℟. **Amen.** ↓

IX. For all in public office

Let us pray also for those in public office,
that our God and Lord
may direct their minds and hearts according to his will
for the true peace and freedom of all.

Prayer in silence. Then the Priest says:

Almighty ever-living God,
in whose hand lies every human heart
and the rights of peoples,
look with favor, we pray,
on those who govern with authority over us,
that throughout the whole world,
the prosperity of peoples,
the assurance of peace,
and freedom of religion
may through your gift be made secure.
Through Christ our Lord. ℟. **Amen.** ↓

X. For those in tribulation

Let us pray, dearly beloved,
to God the Father almighty,
that he may cleanse the world of all errors,
banish disease, drive out hunger,
unlock prisons, loosen fetters,
granting to travelers safety, to pilgrims return,
health to the sick, and salvation to the dying.

Prayer in silence. Then the Priest says:

Almighty ever-living God,
comfort of mourners, strength of all who toil,
may the prayers of those who cry out in any tribulation
come before you,
that all may rejoice,
because in their hour of need
your mercy was at hand.
Through Christ our Lord. ℟. **Amen.** ↓

***SECOND PART:* THE ADORATION OF THE HOLY CROSS**

After the Solemn Intercessions, the solemn Adoration of the Holy Cross takes place. Of the two forms of the showing of the Cross presented here, the more appropriate one, according to pastoral needs, should be chosen.

The Showing of the Holy Cross: First Form

The Deacon accompanied by ministers, or another suitable minister, goes to the sacristy, from which, in procession, accompanied by two ministers with lighted candles, he carries the Cross, covered with a violet veil, through the church to the middle of the sanctuary.

The Priest, standing before the altar and facing the people, receives the Cross, uncovers a little of its upper part and elevates it while beginning the Ecce lignum Crucis (Behold the wood of the Cross). *He is assisted in singing by the Deacon or, if need be, by the choir. All respond,* Come, let us adore. *At the end of the singing, all kneel and for a brief moment adore in silence, while the Priest stands and holds the Cross raised.*

Behold the wood of the Cross,
on which hung the salvation of the world.

℞. **Come, let us adore.**

Then the Priest uncovers the right arm of the Cross and again, raising up the Cross, begins, Behold the wood of the Cross *and everything takes place as above.*

Finally, he uncovers the Cross entirely and, raising it up, he begins the invitation Behold the wood of the Cross *a third time and everything takes place like the first time.*

The Showing of the Holy Cross: Second Form

The Priest or the Deacon accompanied by ministers, or another suitable minister, goes to the door of the church, where he receives the unveiled Cross, and the ministers take lighted candles; then the procession sets off through the church to the sanctuary. Near the door, in the middle of the church and before the entrance of the sanctuary, the one who carries the Cross elevates it, singing, Behold the wood of the Cross, *to which all respond,* Come, let us adore. *After each response all kneel and for a brief moment adore in silence, as above.*

The Adoration of the Holy Cross

Then, accompanied by two ministers with lighted candles, the Priest or the Deacon carries the Cross to the entrance of the sanctuary or to another suitable place and there puts it down or hands it over to the ministers to hold. Candles are placed on the right and left sides of the Cross.

For the Adoration of the Cross, first the Priest Celebrant alone approaches, with the chasuble and his shoes removed, if appropriate. Then the clergy, the lay ministers, and the faithful approach, moving as if in procession, and showing reverence to the Cross by a simple genuflection or by some other sign appropriate to the usage of the region, for example, by kissing the Cross.

Only one Cross should be offered for adoration. If, because of the large number of people, it is not possible for all to approach individually, the Priest, after some of the clergy and faithful have adored, takes the Cross and, standing in the middle before the altar, invites the people in a few words to adore the Holy Cross and afterwards holds the Cross elevated higher for a brief time, for the faithful to adore it in silence.

While the adoration of the Holy Cross is taking place, the antiphon Crucem tuam adoramus (We adore your Cross, O Lord), *the Reproaches, the hymn* Crux fidelis (Faithful Cross) *or other suitable chants are sung, during which all who have already adored the Cross remain seated.*

Chants to Be Sung during
the Adoration of the Holy Cross

ANTIPHON [Holy Cross]

Ant. We adore your Cross, O Lord,
we praise and glorify your holy Resurrection,
for behold, because of the wood of a tree
joy has come to the whole world.

May God have mercy on us and bless us;
may he let his face shed its light upon us
and have mercy on us.   Cf. Ps 67 (66):2

And the antiphon is repeated: **We adore . . .**

THE REPROACHES

Parts assigned to one of the two choirs separately are indicat-
ed by the numbers 1 (first choir) and 2 (second choir); parts
sung by both choirs together are marked: 1 and 2. Some of the
verses may also be sung by two cantors.

I

1 and 2: **My people, what have I done to you?**
          Or how have I grieved you? Answer me!

1: **Because I led you out of the land of Egypt,**
    you have prepared a Cross for your Savior.

1: **Hagios o Theos,**

2: **Holy is God,**

1: **Hagios Ischyros,**

2: **Holy and Mighty,**

1: **Hagios Athanatos, eleison himas.**

2: **Holy and Immortal One, have mercy on us.**

1 and 2: **Because I led you out through the desert forty**
          years
          and fed you with manna and brought you into
          a land of plenty,
          you have prepared a Cross for your Savior.

1: **Hagios o Theos,**

2: **Holy is God,**

1: **Hagios Ischyros,**

2: **Holy and Mighty,**

1: **Hagios Athanatos, eleison himas.**

2: **Holy and Immortal One, have mercy on us.**

1 and 2: **What more should I have done for you and have not done?**
   Indeed, I planted you as my most beautiful chosen vine
   and you have turned very bitter for me,
   for in my thirst you gave me vinegar to drink
   and with a lance you pierced your Savior's side.

1: **Hagios o Theos,**

2: **Holy is God,**

1: **Hagios Ischyros,**

2: **Holy and Mighty,**

1: **Hagios Athanatos, eleison himas.**

2: **Holy and Immortal One, have mercy on us.**

II

Cantors:

I scourged Egypt for your sake with its firstborn sons,
and you scourged me and handed me over.

1 and 2 repeat:

My people, what have I done to you?
Or how have I grieved you? Answer me!

Cantors:

I led you out from Egypt as Pharaoh lay sunk in the Red Sea,
and you handed me over to the chief priests.

1 and 2 repeat:

My people . . .

Cantors:

I opened up the sea before you,
and you opened my side with a lance.

1 and 2 repeat:

My people . . .

Cantors:

**I went before you in a pillar of cloud,
and you led me into Pilate's palace.**

1 and 2 repeat:

My people . . .

Cantors:

**I fed you with manna in the desert,
and on me you rained blows and lashes.**

1 and 2 repeat:

My people . . .

Cantors:

**I gave you saving water from the rock to drink,
and for drink you gave me gall and vinegar.**

1 and 2 repeat:

My people . . .

Cantors:

**I struck down for you the kings of the Canaanites,
and you struck my head with a reed.**

1 and 2 repeat:

My people . . .

Cantors:

**I put in your hand a royal scepter,
and you put on my head a crown of thorns.**

1 and 2 repeat:

My people . . .

Cantors:

**I exalted you with great power,
and you hung me on the scaffold of the Cross.**

1 and 2 repeat:

My people . . .

HYMN [Faithful Cross]

All:

Faithful Cross the Saints rely on,
Noble tree beyond compare!
Never was there such a scion,
Never leaf or flower so rare.
Sweet the timber, sweet the iron,
Sweet the burden that they bear!

Cantors:

Sing, my tongue, in exultation
Of our banner and device!
Make a solemn proclamation
Of a triumph and its price:
How the Savior of creation
Conquered by his sacrifice!

All:

Faithful Cross the Saints rely on,
Noble tree beyond compare!
Never was there such a scion,
Never leaf or flower so rare.

Cantors:

For, when Adam first offended,
Eating that forbidden fruit,
Not all hopes of glory ended
With the serpent at the root:
Broken nature would be mended
By a second tree and shoot.

All:

Sweet the timber, sweet the iron,
Sweet the burden that they bear!

Cantors:

Thus the tempter was outwitted
By a wisdom deeper still:
Remedy and ailment fitted,
Means to cure and means to kill;

That the world might be
  acquitted,
Christ would do his Father's will.

All:

Faithful Cross the Saints rely on,
Noble tree beyond compare!
Never was there such a scion,
Never leaf or flower so rare.

Cantors:

So the Father, out of pity
For our self-inflicted doom,
Sent him from the heavenly city
When the holy time had come:
He, the Son and the Almighty,
Took our flesh in Mary's womb.

All:

Sweet the timber, sweet the iron,
Sweet the burden that they bear!

Cantors:

Hear a tiny baby crying,
Founder of the seas and strands;
See his virgin Mother tying
Cloth around his feet and hands;
Find him in a manger lying
Tightly wrapped in swaddling-
  bands!

All:

Faithful Cross the Saints rely on,
Noble tree beyond compare!
Never was there such a scion,
Never leaf or flower so rare.

Cantors:

So he came, the long-expected,
Not in glory, not to reign;
Only born to be rejected,

Choosing hunger, toil and pain,
Till the scaffold was erected
And the Paschal Lamb was slain.

All:
Sweet the timber, sweet the iron,
Sweet the burden that they bear!

Cantors:
No disgrace was too abhorrent:
Nailed and mocked and parched
    he died;
Blood and water, double war-
    rant,
Issue from his wounded side,
Washing in a mighty torrent
Earth and stars and oceantide.

All:
Faithful Cross the Saints rely on,
Noble tree beyond compare!
Never was there such a scion,
Never leaf or flower so rare.

Cantors:
Lofty timber, smooth your
    roughness,
Flex your boughs for blossom-
    ing;
Let your fibers lose their tough-
    ness,
Gently let your tendrils cling;

Lay aside your native gruffness,
Clasp the body of your King!

All:
Sweet the timber, sweet the iron,
Sweet the burden that they bear!

Cantors:
Noblest tree of all created,
Richly jeweled and embossed:
Post by Lamb's blood conse-
    crated;
Spar that saves the tempest-
    tossed;
Scaffold-beam which, elevated,
Carries what the world has cost!

All:
Faithful Cross the Saints rely on,
Noble tree beyond compare!
Never was there such a scion,
Never leaf or flower so rare.

*The following conclusion is never
to be omitted:*

All:
Wisdom, power, and adoration
To the blessed Trinity
For redemption and salvation
Through the Paschal Mystery,
Now, in every generation,
And for all eternity. Amen.

*In accordance with local circumstances or popular traditions
and if it is pastorally appropriate, the* Stabat Mater *may be
sung, as found in the* Graduale Romanum, *or another suitable
chant in memory of the compassion of the Blessed Virgin Mary.*

*When the adoration has been concluded, the Cross is carried
by the Deacon or a minister to its place at the altar. Lighted
candles are placed around or on the altar or near the Cross.*

THIRD PART: HOLY COMMUNION

A cloth is spread on the altar, and a corporal and the Missal put in place. Meanwhile the Deacon or, if there is no Deacon, the Priest himself, putting on a humeral veil, brings the Blessed Sacrament back from the place of repose to the altar by a shorter route, while all stand in silence. Two ministers with lighted candles accompany the Blessed Sacrament and place their candlesticks around or upon the altar.

When the Deacon, if a Deacon is present, has placed the Blessed Sacrament upon the altar and uncovered the ciborium, the Priest goes to the altar and genuflects.

Then the Priest, with hands joined, says aloud:

At the Savior's command
and formed by divine teaching,
we dare to say:

The Priest, with hands extended says, and all present continue:

Our Father . . .

With hands extended, the Priest continues alone:

Deliver us, Lord, we pray, from every evil,
graciously grant peace in our days,
that, by the help of your mercy,
we may be always free from sin
and safe from all distress,
as we await the blessed hope
and the coming of our Savior, Jesus Christ.

The people conclude the prayer, acclaiming:

For the kingdom, the power and the glory are yours now and for ever.

Then the Priest, with hands joined, says quietly:

May the receiving of your Body and Blood,
Lord Jesus Christ,
not bring me to judgment and condemnation,
but through your loving mercy

be for me protection in mind and body
and a healing remedy.

*The Priest then genuflects, takes a particle, and, holding it
slightly raised over the ciborium, while facing the people, says
aloud:*

Behold the Lamb of God,
behold him who takes away the sins of the world.
Blessed are those called to the supper of the Lamb.

And together with the people he adds once:

**Lord, I am not worthy
that you should enter under my roof,
but only say the word
and my soul shall be healed.**

*And facing the altar, he reverently consumes the Body of
Christ, saying quietly:* May the Body of Christ keep me safe for
eternal life.

*He then proceeds to distribute Communion to the faithful.
During Communion, Psalm 22 (21) or another appropriate
chant may be sung.*

*When the distribution of Communion has been completed, the
ciborium is taken by the Deacon or another suitable minister
to a place prepared outside the church or, if circumstances so
require, it is placed in the tabernacle.*

Then the Priest says: Let us pray, *and, after a period of sacred
silence, if circumstances so suggest, has been observed, he
says the Prayer after Communion.*

[Devoted to God]

Almighty ever-living God,
who have restored us to life
by the blessed Death and Resurrection of your Christ,
preserve in us the work of your mercy,
that, by partaking of this mystery,
we may have a life unceasingly devoted to you.
Through Christ our Lord.
℟. **Amen.** ↓

For the Dismissal the Deacon or, if there is no Deacon, the Priest himself, may say the invitation Bow down for the blessing.

Then the Priest, standing facing the people and extending his hands over them, says this:

PRAYER OVER THE PEOPLE   [Redemption Secured]

May abundant blessing, O Lord, we pray,
descend upon your people,
who have honored the Death of your Son
in the hope of their resurrection:
may pardon come,
comfort be given,
holy faith increase,
and everlasting redemption be made secure.
Through Christ our Lord.

℟. **Amen.** ↓

And all, after genuflecting to the Cross, depart in silence.

After the celebration, the altar is stripped, but the Cross remains on the altar with two or four candlesticks.

APRIL 19

HOLY SATURDAY

On Holy Saturday the Church waits at the Lord's tomb in prayer and fasting, meditating on his Passion and Death and on his Descent into Hell, and awaiting his Resurrection.

The Church abstains from the Sacrifice of the Mass, with the sacred table left bare, until after the solemn Vigil, that is, the anticipation by night of the Resurrection, when the time comes for paschal joys, the abundance of which overflows to occupy fifty days.

"He is not here, but he has been raised."

APRIL 19

THE EASTER VIGIL IN THE HOLY NIGHT

By most ancient tradition, this is the night of keeping vigil for the Lord (Ex 12:42), in which, following the Gospel admonition (Lk 12:35-37), the faithful, carrying lighted lamps in their hands, should be like those looking for the Lord when he returns, so that at his coming he may find them awake and have them sit at his table.

Of this night's Vigil, which is the greatest and most noble of all solemnities, there is to be only one celebration in each church. It is arranged, moreover, in such a way that after the Lucernarium and Easter Proclamation (which constitutes the first part of this Vigil), Holy Church meditates on the wonders the Lord God has done for his people from the beginning, trusting in his word and promise (the second part, that is, the Liturgy of the Word) until, as day approaches, with new members reborn in Baptism (the third part), the Church is called to the table the Lord has prepared for his people, the memorial of his Death and Resurrection until he comes again (the fourth part).

Candles should be prepared for all who participate in the Vigil. The lights of the church are extinguished.

FIRST PART:
THE SOLEMN BEGINNING OF THE VIGIL
OR LUCERNARIUM

The Blessing of the Fire and Preparation of the Candle

A blazing fire is prepared in a suitable place outside the church. When the people are gathered there, the Priest approaches with the ministers, one of whom carries the paschal candle. The processional Cross and candles are not carried.

Where, however, a fire cannot be lit outside the church, the rite is carried out as below, p. 338.

The Priest and faithful sign themselves while the Priest says:
In the name of the Father, and of the Son, and of the Holy Spirit, *and then he greets the assembled people in the usual way and briefly instructs them about the night vigil in these or similar words:*

[Keeping the Lord's Paschal Solemnity]

Dear brethren (brothers and sisters),
on this most sacred night,
in which our Lord Jesus Christ
passed over from death to life,
the Church calls upon her sons and daughters,
scattered throughout the world,
to come together to watch and pray.
If we keep the memorial
of the Lord's paschal solemnity in this way,
listening to his word and celebrating his mysteries,
then we shall have the sure hope
of sharing his triumph over death
and living with him in God.

Then the Priest blesses the fire, saying with hands extended:
Let us pray.   [Fire of God's Glory]

O God, who through your Son
bestowed upon the faithful the fire of your glory,

sanctify ✠ this new fire, we pray,
and grant that,
by these paschal celebrations,
we may be so inflamed with heavenly desires,
that with minds made pure
we may attain festivities of unending splendor.
Through Christ our Lord. ℟. **Amen.** ↓

*After the blessing of the new fire, one of the ministers brings
the paschal candle to the Priest, who cuts a cross into the
candle with a stylus. Then he makes the Greek letter Alpha
above the cross, the letter Omega below, and the four numer-
als of the current year between the arms of the cross, saying
meanwhile:*

1. Christ yesterday and today *(he cuts a vertical line);*

2. the Beginning and the End *(he cuts a horizontal
    line);*

3. the Alpha *(he cuts the letter Alpha above the verti-
    cal line);*

4. and the Omega *(he cuts the letter Omega below
    the vertical line).*

5. All time belongs to him *(he cuts the first numeral of
    the current year in the upper left corner of the
    cross);*

6. and all the ages *(he cuts the second numeral of the
    current year in the upper right corner of the cross).*

7. To him be glory and power *(he cuts the
    third numeral of the current year in the
    lower left corner of the cross);*

8. through every age and for ever. Amen *(he
    cuts the fourth numeral of the current
    year in the lower right corner of the cross).*

```
      A
 2  |  0
 ───┼───
 2  |  5
      Ω
```

*When the cutting of the cross and of the other signs has been
completed, the Priest may insert five grains of incense into the
candle in the form of a cross, meanwhile saying:*

1. By his holy
2. and glorious wounds,
3. may Christ the Lord
4. guard us
5. and protect us. Amen.

1

4 2 5

3

Where, because of difficulties that may occur, a fire is not lit, the blessing of fire is adapted to the circumstances. When the people are gathered in the church as on other occasions, the Priest comes to the door of the church, along with the ministers carrying the paschal candle. The people, insofar as is possible, turn to face the Priest.

The greeting and address take place as above, p. 336; then the fire is blessed and the candle is prepared, as above, pp. 336-338.

The Priest lights the paschal candle from the new fire, saying:

May the light of Christ rising in glory
dispel the darkness of our hearts and minds.

Procession

When the candle has been lit, one of the ministers takes burning coals from the fire and places them in the thurible, and the Priest puts incense into it in the usual way. The Deacon or, if there is no Deacon, another suitable minister, takes the paschal candle and a procession forms. The thurifer with the smoking thurible precedes the Deacon or other minister who carries the paschal candle. After them follows the Priest with the ministers and the people, all holding in their hands unlit candles.

At the door of the church the Deacon, standing and raising up the candle, sings:

The Light of Christ.

And all reply:

Thanks be to God.

The Priest lights his candle from the flame of the paschal candle.

Then the Deacon moves forward to the middle of the church and, standing and raising up the candle, sings a second time:

The Light of Christ.

And all reply:

Thanks be to God.

All light their candles from the flame of the paschal candle and continue in procession.

When the Deacon arrives before the altar, he stands facing the people, raises up the candle and sings a third time:

The Light of Christ.

And all reply:

Thanks be to God.

Then the Deacon places the paschal candle on a large candle-stand prepared next to the ambo or in the middle of the sanctuary.

And lights are lit throughout the church, except for the altar candles.

The Easter Proclamation (Exsultet)

Arriving at the altar, the Priest goes to his chair, gives his candle to a minister, puts incense into the thurible and blesses the incense as at the Gospel at Mass. The Deacon goes to the Priest and saying, Your blessing, Father, *asks for and receives a blessing from the Priest, who says in a low voice:*

May the Lord be in your heart and on your lips,
that you may proclaim his paschal praise worthily and
    well,
in the name of the Father and of the Son, ✠ and of the
    Holy Spirit.

The Deacon replies: Amen. ↓

This blessing is omitted if the Proclamation is made by someone who is not a Deacon.

The Deacon, after incensing the book and the candle, proclaims the Easter Proclamation (Exsultet) at the ambo or at a lectern, with all standing and holding lighted candles in their hands.

The Easter Proclamation may be made, in the absence of a Deacon, by the Priest himself or by another concelebrating Priest. If, however, because of necessity, a lay cantor sings the Proclamation, the words Therefore, dearest friends *up to the end of the invitation are omitted, along with the greeting* The Lord be with you.

[When the Shorter Form is used, omit the italicized parts.]

Exult, let them exult, the hosts of heaven,
exult, let Angel ministers of God exult,
let the trumpet of salvation
sound aloud our mighty King's triumph!
Be glad, let earth be glad, as glory floods her,
ablaze with light from her eternal King,
let all corners of the earth be glad,
knowing an end to gloom and darkness.
Rejoice, let Mother Church also rejoice,
arrayed with the lightning of his glory,
let this holy building shake with joy,
filled with the mighty voices of the peoples.
*(Therefore, dearest friends,
standing in the awesome glory of this holy light,
invoke with me, I ask you,
the mercy of God almighty,
that he, who has been pleased to number me,
though unworthy, among the Levites,
may pour into me his light unshadowed,
that I may sing this candle's perfect praises).*

(℣. The Lord be with you. ℟. **And with your spirit.**)
℣. Lift up your hearts. ℟. **We lift them up to the Lord.**
℣. Let us give thanks to the Lord our God. ℟. **It is right and just.**

It is truly right and just,
with ardent love of mind and heart
and with devoted service of our voice,
to acclaim our God invisible, the almighty Father,
and Jesus Christ, our Lord, his Son, his Only Begotten.

Who for our sake paid Adam's debt to the eternal Father,
and, pouring out his own dear Blood,
wiped clean the record of our ancient sinfulness.

These then are the feasts of Passover,
in which is slain the Lamb, the one true Lamb,
whose Blood anoints the doorposts of believers.

This is the night,
when once you led our forebears, Israel's children,
from slavery in Egypt
and made them pass dry-shod through the Red Sea.

This is the night
that with a pillar of fire
banished the darkness of sin.

This is the night
that even now, throughout the world,
sets Christian believers apart from worldly vices
and from the gloom of sin,
leading them to grace
and joining them to his holy ones.

This is the night,
when Christ broke the prison-bars of death
and rose victorious from the underworld.

Our birth would have been no gain,
had we not been redeemed.
O wonder of your humble care for us!
O love, O charity beyond all telling,
to ransom a slave you gave away your Son!

O truly necessary sin of Adam,
destroyed completely by the Death of Christ!

O happy fault
that earned so great, so glorious a Redeemer!

O truly blessed night,
worthy alone to know the time and hour
when Christ rose from the underworld!

This is the night
of which it is written:
The night shall be as bright as day,
dazzling is the night for me,
and full of gladness.

The sanctifying power of this night
dispels wickedness, washes faults away,
restores innocence to the fallen, and joy to mourners,
drives out hatred, fosters concord, and brings down the
mighty.

On this, your night of grace, O holy Father,
accept this candle, a solemn offering,
the work of bees and of your servants' hands,
an evening sacrifice of praise,
this gift from your most holy Church.

But now we know the praises of this pillar,
which glowing fire ignites for God's honor,
a fire into many flames divided,
yet never dimmed by sharing of its light,
for it is fed by melting wax,
drawn out by mother bees
to build a torch so precious.

O truly blessed night,
when things of heaven are wed to those of earth,
and divine to the human.

> *Shorter Form only:*
> On this, your night of grace, O holy Father,
> accept this candle, a solemn offering,
> the work of bees and of your servants' hands,
> an evening sacrifice of praise,
> this gift from your most holy Church.

Therefore, O Lord,
we pray you that this candle,

hallowed to the honor of your name,
may persevere undimmed,
to overcome the darkness of this night.
Receive it as a pleasing fragrance,
and let it mingle with the lights of heaven.
May this flame be found still burning
by the Morning Star:
the one Morning Star who never sets,
Christ your Son,
who, coming back from death's domain,
has shed his peaceful light on humanity,
and lives and reigns for ever and ever.
℟. **Amen.** ↓

SECOND PART:
THE LITURGY OF THE WORD

*In this Vigil, the mother of all Vigils, nine readings are provid-
ed, namely seven from the Old Testament and two from the New
(the Epistle and Gospel), all of which should be read whenever
this can be done, so that the character of the Vigil, which demands an extended period of time, may be preserved.*

*Nevertheless, where more serious pastoral circumstances
demand it, the number of readings from the Old Testament
may be reduced, always bearing in mind that the reading of
the Word of God is a fundamental part of this Easter Vigil. At
least three readings should be read from the Old Testament,
both from the Law and from the Prophets, and their respective
Responsorial Psalms should be sung. Never, moreover, should
the reading of chapter 14 of Exodus with its canticle be
omitted.*

*After setting aside their candles, all sit. Before the readings
begin, the Priest instructs the people in these or similar words:*

[Listen with Quiet Hearts]

Dear brethren (brothers and sisters),
now that we have begun our solemn Vigil,
let us listen with quiet hearts to the Word of God.

Let us meditate on how God in times past saved his
   people
and in these, the last days, has sent us his Son as our
   Redeemer.
Let us pray that our God may complete this paschal
   work of salvation
by the fullness of redemption.

*Then the readings follow. A reader goes to the ambo and pro-
claims the reading. Afterwards a psalmist or a cantor sings or
says the Psalm with the people making the response. Then all
rise, the Priest says,* Let us pray *and, after all have prayed for
a while in silence, he says the prayer corresponding to the
reading. In place of the Responsorial Psalm a period of sacred
silence may be observed, in which case the pause after* Let us
pray *is omitted.*

FIRST READING Gn 1:1—2:2 or 1:1, 26-31a **[God Our Creator]**

**God created the world and all that is in it. He saw that it
was good. This reading from the first book of the Bible
shows that God loved all that he made.**

*[If the "Shorter Form" is used, the indented text in brackets is
omitted.]*

A reading from the Book of Genesis

IN the beginning, when God created the heavens and
the earth,
[the earth was a formless wasteland, and darkness
covered the abyss, while a mighty wind swept over
the waters.

    Then God said, "Let there be light," and there
was light. God saw how good the light was. God
then separated the light from the darkness. God
called the light "day," and the darkness he called
"night." Thus evening came, and morning followed—the first day.

    Then God said, "Let there be a dome in the
middle of the waters, to separate one body of
water from the other." And so it happened: God

made the dome, and it separated the water above the dome from the water below it. God called the dome "the sky." Evening came, and morning followed—the second day.

Then God said, "Let the water under the sky be gathered into a single basin, so that the dry land may appear." And so it happened: the water under the sky was gathered into its basin, and the dry land appeared. God called the dry land "the earth," and the basin of the water he called "the sea." God saw how good it was. Then God said, "Let the earth bring forth vegetation: every kind of plant that bears seed and every kind of fruit tree on earth that bears fruit with its seed in it." And so it happened: the earth brought forth every kind of plant that bears seed and every kind of fruit tree on earth that bears fruit with its seed in it. God saw how good it was. Evening came, and morning followed—the third day.

Then God said: "Let there be lights in the dome of the sky, to separate day from night. Let them mark the fixed times, the days and the years, and serve as luminaries in the dome of the sky, to shed light upon the earth." And so it happened: God made the two great lights, the greater one to govern the day, and the lesser one to govern the night; and he made the stars. God set them in the dome of the sky, to shed light upon the earth, to govern the day and the night, and to separate the light from the darkness. God saw how good it was. Evening came, and morning followed—the fourth day.

Then God said, "Let the water teem with an abundance of living creatures, and on the earth let birds fly beneath the dome of the sky." And so it happened: God created the great sea monsters and all kinds of swimming creatures with which the water teems, and all kinds of winged birds. God saw how good it was, and God blessed them, saying, "Be fertile, multiply, and fill the water of the seas; and let the birds multiply on the earth." Evening came, and morning followed—the fifth day.

Then God said, "Let the earth bring forth all kinds of living creatures: cattle, creeping things, and wild animals of all kinds." And so it happened: God made all kinds of wild animals, all kinds of cattle, and all kinds of creeping things of the earth. God saw how good it was. Then]

God said: "Let us make man in our image, after our likeness. Let them have dominion over the fish of the sea, the birds of the air, and the cattle, and over all the wild animals and all the creatures that crawl on the ground."

God created man in his image;
in the divine image he created him;
male and female he created them.

God blessed them, saying: "Be fertile and multiply; fill the earth and subdue it. Have dominion over the fish of the sea, the birds of the air, and all the living things that move on the earth." God also said: "See, I give you every seed-bearing plant all over the earth and every tree that has seed-bearing fruit on it to be your food; and to all the animals of the land, all the birds of the air, and all the living creatures that crawl on the ground, I give all the green plants for food." And so it happened. God looked at everything he had made, and he found it very good.

[Evening came, and morning followed—the sixth day.

Thus the heavens and the earth and all their array were completed. Since on the seventh day God was finished with the work he had been doing, he rested on the seventh day from all the work he had undertaken.]

The word of the Lord. ℟. **Thanks be to God.** ↓

RESPONSORIAL PSALM Ps 104   [Come, Holy Spirit]

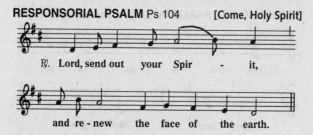

℟. Lord, send out your Spir - it,

and re - new the face of the earth.

Bless the LORD, O my soul!
  O LORD, my God, you are great indeed!
You are clothed with majesty and glory,
  robed in light as with a cloak.—℟.

You fixed the earth upon its foundation,
  not to be moved forever;
with the ocean, as with a garment, you covered it;
  above the mountains the waters stood.—℟.

You send forth springs into the watercourses
  that wind among the mountains.
Beside them the birds of heaven dwell;
  from among the branches they send forth their
    song.—℟.

You water the mountains from your palace;
  the earth is replete with the fruit of your works.
You raise grass for the cattle,
  and vegetation for men's use,
producing bread from the earth.—℟.

How manifold are your works, O LORD!
  In wisdom you have wrought them all—
the earth is full of your creatures.
  Bless the LORD, O my soul!—℟. ↓

OR

RESPONSORIAL PSALM Ps 33   [The Lord's Goodness]

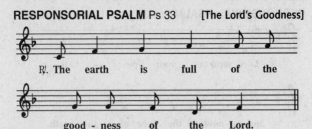

℟. The earth is full of the good - ness of the Lord.

Upright is the word of the LORD,
  and all his works are trustworthy.
He loves justice and right;
  of the kindness of the LORD the earth is full.—℟.

By the word of the LORD the heavens were made;
  by the breath of his mouth all their host.
He gathers the waters of the sea as in a flask;
  in cellars he confines the deep.—℟.

Blessed the nation whose God is the LORD,
  the people he has chosen for his own inheritance.
From heaven the LORD looks down;
  he sees all mankind.—℟.

Our soul waits for the LORD,
  who is our help and our shield.
May your kindness, O LORD, be upon us
  who have put our hope in you.—℟. ↓

PRAYER   [Creation in the Beginning]
Let us pray.

Almighty ever-living God,
who are wonderful in the ordering of all your works,
may those you have redeemed understand
that there exists nothing more marvelous
than the world's creation in the beginning
except that, at the end of the ages,

Christ our Passover has been sacrificed.
Who lives and reigns for ever and ever. ℟. **Amen.** ↓

OR

PRAYER (On the creation of man)   [Eternal Joys]

O God, who wonderfully created human nature
and still more wonderfully redeemed it,
grant us, we pray,
to set our minds against the enticements of sin,
that we may merit to attain eternal joys.
Through Christ our Lord. ℟. **Amen.** ↓

SECOND READING Gn 22:1-18 or 22:1-2, 9a, 10-13, 15-18
[Obedience to God]

**Abraham is obedient to the will of God. Because God asks
him, without hesitation he prepares to sacrifice his son
Isaac. In the new order, God sends his Son to redeem man
by his death on the Cross.**

*[If the "Shorter Form" is used, the indented text in brackets is
omitted.]*

A reading from the Book of Genesis

GOD put Abraham to the test. He called to him,
"Abraham!" "Here I am," he replied. Then God
said: "Take your son Isaac, your only one, whom you
love, and go to the land of Moriah. There you shall
offer him up as a holocaust on a height that I will point
out to you."

[Early the next morning Abraham saddled
his donkey, took with him his son Isaac, and two
of his servants as well, and with the wood that he
had cut for the holocaust, set out for the place of
which God had told him.

On the third day Abraham got sight of the
place from afar. Then he said to his servants: "Both
of you stay here with the donkey, while the boy

and I go on over yonder. We will worship and then
come back to you." Thereupon Abraham took the
wood for the holocaust and laid it on his son
Isaac's shoulders, while he himself carried the fire
and the knife. As the two walked on together,
Isaac spoke to his father Abraham. "Father!" Isaac
said. "Yes, son," he replied. Isaac continued, "Here
are the fire and the wood, but where is the sheep
for the holocaust?" "Son," Abraham answered,
"God himself will provide the sheep for the holocaust." Then the two continued going forward.]

When they came to the place of which God had told
him, Abraham built an altar there and arranged the
wood on it.

[Next he tied up his son Isaac, and put him on top
of the wood on the altar.]

Then he reached out and took the knife to slaughter
his son. But the LORD's messenger called to him from
heaven, "Abraham, Abraham!" "Here I am," he
answered. "Do not lay your hand on the boy," said the
messenger. "Do not do the least thing to him. I know
now how devoted you are to God, since you did not
withhold from me your own beloved son." As Abraham
looked about, he spied a ram caught by its horns in the
thicket. So he went and took the ram and offered it up
as a holocaust in place of his son.

[Abraham named the site Yahweh-yireh; hence
people now say, "On the mountain the LORD will
see."]

Again the LORD's messenger called to Abraham
from heaven and said: "I swear by myself, declares the
LORD, that because you acted as you did in not with-
holding from me your beloved son, I will bless you
abundantly and make your descendants as countless
as the stars of the sky and the sands of the seashore;
your descendants shall take possession of the gates of

their enemies, and in your descendants all the nations of the earth shall find blessing—all this because you obeyed my command."—The word of the Lord. ℟. **Thanks be to God.** ↓

RESPONSORIAL PSALM Ps 16 [God Our Hope]

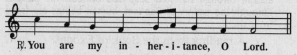

℟. You are my in - her - i - tance, O Lord.

O LORD, my allotted portion and my cup,
  you it is who hold fast my lot.
I set the LORD ever before me;
  with him at my right I shall not be disturbed.—℟.

Therefore my heart is glad and my soul rejoices,
  my body, too, abides in confidence;
because you will not abandon my soul to the nether-
    world,
  nor will you suffer your faithful one to undergo cor-
    ruption.—℟.

You will show me the path to life,
  fullness of joys in your presence,
  the delights at your right hand forever.—℟. ↓

PRAYER [Entering into Grace]

Let us pray.

O God, supreme Father of the faithful,
who increase the children of your promise
by pouring out the grace of adoption
throughout the whole world
and who through the Paschal Mystery
make your servant Abraham father of nations,
as once you swore,
grant, we pray,
that your peoples may enter worthily
into the grace to which you call them.

Through Christ our Lord.

℟. **Amen.** ↓

THIRD READING Ex 14:15—15:1 [Exodus]

Moses leads the Israelites out of Egypt. He opens a path of escape through the Red Sea. God protects his people. Through the waters of Baptism, human beings are freed from sin.

A reading from the Book of Exodus

THE LORD said to Moses, "Why are you crying out to me? Tell the Israelites to go forward. And you, lift up your staff and, with hand outstretched over the sea, split the sea in two, that the Israelites may pass through it on dry land. But I will make the Egyptians so obstinate that they will go in after them. Then I will receive glory through Pharaoh and all his army, his chariots and charioteers. The Egyptians shall know that I am the LORD, when I receive glory through Pharaoh and his chariots and charioteers."

The angel of God, who had been leading Israel's camp, now moved and went around behind them. The column of cloud also, leaving the front, took up its place behind them, so that it came between the camp of the Egyptians and that of Israel. But the cloud now became dark, and thus the night passed without the rival camps coming any closer together all night long. Then Moses stretched out his hand over the sea, and the LORD swept the sea with a strong east wind throughout the night and so turned it into dry land. When the water was thus divided, the Israelites marched into the midst of the sea on dry land, with the water like a wall to their right and to their left.

The Egyptians followed in pursuit; all Pharaoh's horses and chariots and charioteers went after them right into the midst of the sea. In the night watch just before dawn the LORD cast through the column of the

fiery cloud upon the Egyptian force a glance that
threw it into a panic; and he so clogged their chariot
wheels that they could hardly drive. With that the
Egyptians sounded the retreat before Israel, because
the LORD was fighting for them against the Egyptians.

Then the LORD told Moses, "Stretch out your hand
over the sea, that the water may flow back upon the
Egyptians, upon their chariots and their charioteers."
So Moses stretched out his hand over the sea, and at
dawn the sea flowed back to its normal depth. The
Egyptians were fleeing head on toward the sea, when
the LORD hurled them into its midst. As the water
flowed back, it covered the chariots and the charioteers of Pharaoh's whole army which had followed the
Israelites into the sea. Not a single one of them
escaped. But the Israelites had marched on dry land
through the midst of the sea, with the water like a wall
to their right and to their left. Thus the LORD saved
Israel on that day from the power of the Egyptians.
When Israel saw the Egyptians lying dead on the
seashore and beheld the great power that the LORD
had shown against the Egyptians, they feared the
LORD and believed in him and in his servant Moses.

Then Moses and the Israelites sang this song to the
LORD:

I will sing to the LORD, for he is gloriously triumphant;

horse and chariot he has cast into the sea.

The word of the Lord. ℟. **Thanks be to God.** ↓

RESPONSORIAL PSALM Ex 15   [God the Savior]

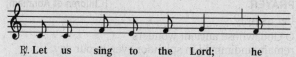

℟. Let   us   sing   to   the   Lord;   he

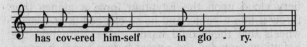
has cov-ered him-self in glo - ry.

I will sing to the LORD, for he is gloriously triumphant;
   horse and chariot he has cast into the sea.
My strength and my courage is the LORD,
   and he has been my savior.
He is my God, I praise him;
   the God of my father, I extol him.

R⫽. **Let us sing to the Lord; he has covered himself in
glory.**

The LORD is a warrior,
   LORD is his name!
Pharaoh's chariots and army he hurled into the sea;
   the elite of his officers were submerged into the Red
      Sea.—R⫽.

The flood waters covered them,
   they sank into the depths like a stone.
Your right hand, O LORD, magnificent in power,
   your right hand, O LORD, has shattered the enemy.
      —R⫽.

You brought in the people you redeemed
   and planted them on the mountain of your inheri-
      tance—
the place where you made your seat, O LORD,
   the sanctuary, O LORD, which your hands estab-
      lished.
The LORD shall reign forever and ever.—R⫽. ↓

PRAYER [Children of Abraham]

Let us pray.

O God, whose ancient wonders
remain undimmed in splendor even in our day,
for what you once bestowed on a single people,

freeing them from Pharaoh's persecution
by the power of your right hand,
now you bring about as the salvation of the nations
through the waters of rebirth,
grant, we pray, that the whole world
may become children of Abraham
and inherit the dignity of Israel's birthright.
Through Christ our Lord. ℟. **Amen.** ↓

OR

PRAYER   [Reborn]
O God, who by the light of the New Testament
have unlocked the meaning
of wonders worked in former times,
so that the Red Sea prefigures the sacred font
and the nation delivered from slavery
foreshadows the Christian people,
grant, we pray, that all nations,
obtaining the privilege of Israel by merit of faith,
may be reborn by partaking of your Spirit.
Through Christ our Lord. ℟. **Amen.** ↓

FOURTH READING Is 54:5-14   [God's Love]
> For a time, God hid from his people, but his love for them
> is everlasting. He takes pity on them and promises them
> prosperity.

A reading from the Book of the Prophet Isaiah

THE One who has become your husband is your
    Maker;
    his name is the LORD of hosts;
your redeemer is the Holy One of Israel,
    called God of all the earth.
The LORD calls you back,
    like a wife forsaken and grieved in spirit,
    a wife married in youth and then cast off,
    says your God.
For a brief moment I abandoned you,
    but with great tenderness I will take you back.

In an outburst of wrath, for a moment
    I hid my face from you;
but with enduring love I take pity on you,
    says the LORD, your redeemer.
This is for me like the days of Noah,
    when I swore that the waters of Noah
    should never again deluge the earth;
so I have sworn not to be angry with you,
    or to rebuke you.
Though the mountains leave their place
    and the hills be shaken,
my love shall never leave you
    nor my covenant of peace be shaken,
    says the LORD, who has mercy on you.
O afflicted one, storm-battered and unconsoled,
    I lay your pavements in carnelians,
    and your foundations in sapphires;
I will make your battlements of rubies,
    your gates of carbuncles,
    and all your walls of precious stones.
All your children shall be taught by the LORD,
    and great shall be the peace of your children.
In justice shall you be established,
    far from the fear of oppression,
    where destruction cannot come near you.
The word of the Lord. ℟. **Thanks be to God.** ↓

RESPONSORIAL PSALM Ps 30   [God Our Help]

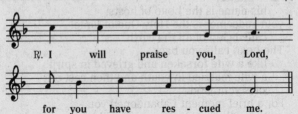

℟. I will praise you, Lord,
for you have res - cued me.

I will extol you, O Lord, for you drew me clear
   and did not let my enemies rejoice over me.
O Lord, you brought me up from the netherworld;
   you preserved me from among those going down
      into the pit.—℟.

Sing praise to the Lord, you his faithful ones,
   and give thanks to his holy name.
For his anger lasts but a moment;
   a lifetime, his good will.
At nightfall, weeping enters in,
   but with the dawn, rejoicing.—℟.

Hear, O Lord, and have pity on me;
   O Lord, be my helper.
You changed my mourning into dancing;
   O Lord, my God, forever will I give you thanks.—℟. ↓

PRAYER   [Fulfillment of God's Promise]

Let us pray.

Almighty ever-living God,
surpass, for the honor of your name,
what you pledged to the Patriarchs by reason of their
   faith,
and through sacred adoption increase the children of
   your promise,
so that what the Saints of old never doubted would come
   to pass
your Church may now see in great part fulfilled.
Through Christ our Lord. ℟. **Amen.** ↓

Alternatively, other prayers may be used from among those
which follow the readings that have been omitted.

FIFTH READING Is 55:1-11   [God of Forgiveness]
   God is a loving Father and he calls his people back. He
   promises an everlasting covenant with them. God is mer-
   ciful, generous, and forgiving.

A reading from the Book of the Prophet Isaiah

THUS says the LORD:
All you who are thirsty,
    come to the water!
You who have no money,
    come, receive grain and eat;
come, without paying and without cost,
    drink wine and milk!
Why spend your money for what is not bread;
    your wages for what fails to satisfy?
Heed me, and you shall eat well,
    you shall delight in rich fare.
Come to me heedfully,
    listen, that you may have life.
I will renew with you the everlasting covenant,
    the benefits assured to David.
As I made him a witness to the peoples,
    a leader and commander of nations,
so shall you summon a nation you knew not,
    and nations that knew you not shall run to you,
because of the LORD, your God,
    the Holy One of Israel, who has glorified you.

Seek the LORD while he may be found,
    call him while he is near.
Let the scoundrel forsake his way,
    and the wicked man his thoughts;
let him turn to the LORD for mercy;
    to our God, who is generous in forgiving.
For my thoughts are not your thoughts,
    nor are your ways my ways, says the LORD.
As high as the heavens are above the earth,
    so high are my ways above your ways,
    and my thoughts above your thoughts.

For just as from the heavens
    the rain and snow come down

and do not return there
    till they have watered the earth,
    making it fertile and fruitful,
giving seed to the one who sows
    and bread to the one who eats,
so shall my word be
    that goes forth from my mouth;
my word shall not return to me void,
    but shall do my will,
    achieving the end for which I sent it.
The word of the Lord. ℟. **Thanks be to God.** ↓

RESPONSORIAL PSALM Is 12   [Make Known God's Deeds]

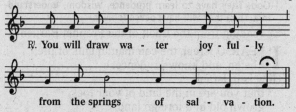

℟. You will draw water joyfully from the springs of salvation.

God indeed is my savior;
    I am confident and unafraid.
My strength and my courage is the LORD,
    and he has been my savior.
With joy you will draw water
    at the fountain of salvation.—℟.

Give thanks to the LORD, acclaim his name;
    among the nations make known his deeds,
    proclaim how exalted is his name.—℟.

Sing praise to the LORD for his glorious achievement;
    let this be known throughout all the earth.
Shout with exultation, O city of Zion,
    for great in your midst
    is the Holy One of Israel!—℟. ↓

PRAYER   [Progress in Virtue]

Let us pray.

Almighty ever-living God,
sole hope of the world,
who by the preaching of your Prophets
unveiled the mysteries of this present age,
graciously increase the longing of your people,
for only at the prompting of your grace
do the faithful progress in any kind of virtue.
Through Christ our Lord. ℟. **Amen.** ↓

SIXTH READING Bar 3:9-15, 32—4:4 [Walk in God's Ways]

> Baruch tells the people of Israel to walk in the ways of
> God. They have to learn prudence, wisdom, understand-
> ing. Then they will have peace forever.

A reading from the Book of the Prophet Baruch

HEAR, O Israel, the commandments of life:
listen, and know prudence!
How is it, Israel,
    that you are in the land of your foes,
    grown old in a foreign land,
defiled with the dead,
    accounted with those destined for the netherworld?
You have forsaken the fountain of wisdom!
    Had you walked in the way of God,
    you would have dwelt in enduring peace.
Learn where prudence is,
    where strength, where understanding;
that you may know also
    where are length of days, and life,
    where light of the eyes, and peace.
Who has found the place of wisdom,
    who has entered into her treasuries?

The One who knows all things knows her;
    he has probed her by his knowledge—

the One who established the earth for all time,
 and filled it with four-footed beasts;
he who dismisses the light, and it departs,
 calls it, and it obeys him trembling;
before whom the stars at their posts
 shine and rejoice;
when he calls them, they answer, "Here we are!"
 shining with joy for their Maker.
Such is our God;
 no other is to be compared to him:
he has traced out all the way of understanding,
 and has given her to Jacob, his servant,
 to Israel, his beloved son.

Since then she has appeared on earth,
 and moved among people.
She is the book of the precepts of God,
 the law that endures forever;
all who cling to her will live,
 but those will die who forsake her.
Turn, O Jacob, and receive her:
 walk by her light toward splendor.
Give not your glory to another,
 your privileges to an alien race.
Blessed are we, O Israel;
 for what pleases God is known to us!
The word of the Lord. ℟. **Thanks be to God.** ↓

RESPONSORIAL PSALM Ps 19 [Words of Eternal Life]

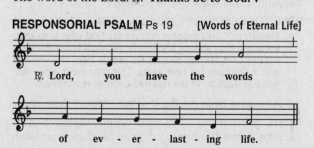

℟. Lord, you have the words of ev-er-last-ing life.

The law of the LORD is perfect,
    refreshing the soul;
the decree of the LORD is trustworthy,
    giving wisdom to the simple.

℟. **Lord, you have the words of everlasting life.**

The precepts of the LORD are right,
    rejoicing the heart;
the command of the LORD is clear,
    enlightening the eye.—℟.

The fear of the LORD is pure,
    enduring forever;
the ordinances of the LORD are true,
    all of them just.—℟.

They are more precious than gold,
    than a heap of purest gold;
sweeter also than syrup
    or honey from the comb.—℟. ↓

PRAYER   [Unfailing Protection]

Let us pray.
O God, who constantly increase your Church
by your call to the nations,
graciously grant
to those you wash clean in the waters of Baptism
the assurance of your unfailing protection.
Through Christ our Lord. ℟. **Amen.** ↓

SEVENTH READING Ez 36:16-17a, 18-28   [God's People]

Ezekiel, as God's prophet, speaks for God who is to keep
his name holy among his people. All shall know the holiness of God. He will cleanse his people from idol worship
and make them his own again. This promise is again fulfilled in Baptism in the restored order of redemption.

A reading from the Book of the Prophet Ezekiel

THE word of the LORD came to me, saying: Son of
man, when the house of Israel lived in their land,

they defiled it by their conduct and deeds. Therefore I poured out my fury upon them because of the blood that they poured out on the ground, and because they defiled it with idols. I scattered them among the nations, dispersing them over foreign lands; according to their conduct and deeds I judged them. But when they came among the nations wherever they came, they served to profane my holy name, because it was said of them: "These are the people of the LORD, yet they had to leave their land." So I have relented because of my holy name which the house of Israel profaned among the nations where they came. Therefore say to the house of Israel: Thus says the Lord GOD: Not for your sakes do I act, house of Israel, but for the sake of my holy name, which you profaned among the nations to which you came. I will prove the holiness of my great name, profaned among the nations, in whose midst you have profaned it. Thus the nations shall know that I am the LORD, says the Lord GOD, when in their sight I prove my holiness through you. For I will take you away from among the nations, gather you from all the foreign lands, and bring you back to your own land. I will sprinkle clean water upon you to cleanse you from all your impurities, and from all your idols I will cleanse you. I will give you a new heart and place a new spirit within you, taking from your bodies your stony hearts and giving you natural hearts. I will put my spirit within you and make you live by my statutes, careful to observe my decrees. You shall live in the land I gave your fathers; you shall be my people, and I will be your God.—The word of the Lord. ℟. **Thanks be to God.** ↓

When Baptism is celebrated, Responsorial Psalm 42 is used; when Baptism is not celebrated, Is 12 or Ps 51 is used.

RESPONSORIAL PSALM Ps 42   [Longing for God]

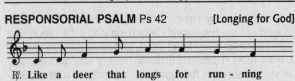

℟. Like a deer that longs for run-ning streams, my soul longs for you, my God.

Athirst is my soul for God, the living God.
    When shall I go and behold the face of God?—℟.

I went with the throng
    and led them in procession to the house of God,
amid loud cries of joy and thanksgiving,
    with the multitude keeping festival.—℟.

Send forth your light and your fidelity;
    they shall lead me on
and bring me to your holy mountain,
    to your dwelling-place.—℟.

Then will I go into the altar of God,
    the God of my gladness and joy;
then will I give you thanks upon the harp,
    O God, my God!—℟. ↓

OR

*When Baptism is not celebrated, the Responsorial Psalm after
the Fifth Reading (Is 12:2-3, 4bcd, 5-6) as above, p. 359, may
be used; or the following:*

RESPONSORIAL PSALM Ps 51   [A Clean Heart]

℟. Cre-ate a clean heart in me, O God.

A clean heart create for me, O God,
  and a steadfast spirit renew within me.
Cast me not out from your presence,
  and your Holy Spirit take not from me.—℟.

Give me back the joy of your salvation,
  and a willing spirit sustain in me.
I will teach transgressors your ways,
  and sinners shall return to you.—℟.

For you are not pleased with sacrifices;
  should I offer a holocaust, you would not accept it.
My sacrifice, O God, is a contrite spirit;
  a heart contrite and humbled, O God, you will not
    spurn.—℟. ↓

PRAYER   [Human Salvation]
Let us pray.

O God of unchanging power and eternal light,
look with favor on the wondrous mystery of the whole
    Church
and serenely accomplish the work of human salvation,
which you planned from all eternity;
may the whole world know and see
that what was cast down is raised up,
what had become old is made new,
and all things are restored to integrity through Christ,
just as by him they came into being.
Who lives and reigns for ever and ever. ℟. **Amen.** ↓

OR

PRAYER   [Confirm Our Hope]
O God, who by the pages of both Testaments
instruct and prepare us to celebrate the Paschal Mystery,
grant that we may comprehend your mercy,
so that the gifts we receive from you this night

may confirm our hope of the gifts to come.
Through Christ our Lord. ℟. **Amen.** ↓

After the last reading from the Old Testament with its Responsorial Psalm and its prayer, the altar candles are lit, and the Priest intones the hymn Gloria in excelsis Deo (Glory to God in the highest), *which is taken up by all, while bells are rung, according to local custom.*

COLLECT   [Renewed in Body and Mind]
Let us pray.
O God, who make this most sacred night radiant
with the glory of the Lord's Resurrection,
stir up in your Church a spirit of adoption,
so that, renewed in body and mind,
we may render you undivided service.
Through our Lord Jesus Christ, your Son,
who lives and reigns with you in the unity of the Holy
    Spirit,
God, for ever and ever. ℟. **Amen.** ↓

Then the reader proclaims the reading from the Apostle.

EPISTLE Rom 6:3-11   [Alive in Christ]
By Baptism the Christian is not merely identified with the dying Christ, who has won a victory over sin, but is introduced into the very act by which Christ died to sin.

A reading from the Letter of Saint Paul to the Romans

BROTHERS and sisters: Are you unaware that we who were baptized into Christ Jesus were baptized into his death? We were indeed buried with him through baptism into death, so that, just as Christ was raised from the dead by the glory of the Father, we too might live in newness of life.

For if we have grown into union with him through a death like his, we shall also be united with him in the resurrection. We know that our old self was crucified with him, so that our sinful body might be done away with, that we might no longer be in slavery to sin. For a dead person has been absolved from sin. If, then, we have died with Christ, we believe that we shall also live with him. We know that Christ, raised from the dead, dies no more; death no longer has power over him. As to his death, he died to sin once and for all; as to his life, he lives for God. Consequently, you too must think of yourselves as being dead to sin and living for God in Christ Jesus.—The word of the Lord. ℟. **Thanks be to God.** ↓

After the Epistle has been read, all rise, then the Priest solemnly intones the Alleluia *three times, raising his voice by a step each time, with all repeating it. If necessary, the psalmist intones the* Alleluia.

RESPONSORIAL PSALM Ps 118   [God's Mercy]

℟. **Al - le - lu - ia.   Al - le - lu - ia.   Al - le - lu - ia.**

Give thanks to the LORD, for he is good,
    for his mercy endures forever.
Let the house of Israel say,
    "His mercy endures forever."—℟.

The right hand of the LORD has struck with power;
    the right hand of the LORD is exalted.
I shall not die, but live,
    and declare the works of the LORD.—℟.

The stone which the builders rejected
    has become the cornerstone.
By the LORD has this been done;
    it is wonderful in our eyes.—℟. ↓

The Priest, in the usual way, puts incense in the thurible and blesses the Deacon. At the Gospel lights are not carried, but only incense.

GOSPEL Lk 24:1-12 [The Resurrection]

> Christ has died, Christ has risen, Christ will come again!
> God's mercy brings us forgiveness and salvation.

℣. The Lord be with you. ℟. **And with your spirit.**
✛ A reading from the holy Gospel according to Luke.
℟. **Glory to you, O Lord.**

AT daybreak on the first day of the week the women who had come from Galilee with Jesus took the spices they had prepared and went to the tomb. They found the stone rolled away from the tomb; but when they entered, they did not find the body of the Lord Jesus. While they were puzzling over this, behold, two men in dazzling garments appeared to them. They were terrified and bowed their faces to the ground. They said to them, "Why do you seek the living one among the dead? He is not here, but he has been raised. Remember what he said to you while he was still in Galilee, that the Son of Man must be handed over to sinners and be crucified, and rise on the third day." And they remembered his words. Then they returned from the tomb and announced all these things to the eleven and to all the others. The women were Mary Magdalene, Joanna, and Mary the mother of James; the others who accompanied them also told this to the apostles, but their story seemed like some nonsense and they did not believe them. But Peter got up and ran to the tomb, bent down, and saw the burial cloths alone; then he went home amazed at what had happened.—The Gospel of the Lord. ℟. **Praise to you, Lord Jesus Christ.**

After the Gospel, the Homily, even if brief, is not to be omitted.

THIRD PART:
CELEBRATION OF THE SACRAMENTS OF INITIATION

The following is adapted from the Order of Christian Initiation of Adults.

Celebration of Baptism

PRESENTATION OF THE CANDIDATES

An assisting Deacon or other minister calls the the elect forward and their godparents present them. The Invitation to Prayer and the Litany of the Saints follow.

INVITATION TO PRAYER   [Supportive Prayer]

The Priest addresses the following or a similar invitation for the assembly to join in prayer for the elect.

Dearly beloved,
with one heart and one soul, let us by our prayers
come to the aid of these our brothers and sisters in their
    blessed hope,
so that, as they approach the font of rebirth,
the almighty Father may bestow on them
all his merciful help.

LITANY OF THE SAINTS   [Petitioning the Saints]

In the Litany the names of some Saints may be added, especially the Titular Saint of the church and the Patron Saints of the place and of those to be baptized.

Lord, have mercy.
Lord, have mercy.

Christ, have mercy.
Christ, have mercy.

Lord, have mercy.
Lord, have mercy.

Holy Mary, Mother of God,
    pray for us.
Saint Michael, **pray for us.**

Holy Angels of God, **pray for us.**
Saint John the Baptist, **pray for us.**
Saint Joseph, **pray for us.**
Saint Peter and Saint Paul, **pray for us.**
Saint Andrew, **pray for us.**
Saint John, **pray for us.**

Saint Mary Magdalene, **pray for us.**

Saint Stephen, **pray for us.**

Saint Ignatius of Antioch, **pray for us.**

Saint Lawrence, **pray for us.**

Saint Perpetua and Saint Felicity, **pray for us.**

Saint Agnes, **pray for us.**

Saint Gregory, **pray for us.**

Saint Augustine, **pray for us.**

Saint Athanasius, **pray for us.**

Saint Basil, **pray for us.**

Saint Martin, **pray for us.**

Saint Benedict, **pray for us.**

Saint Francis and Saint Dominic, **pray for us.**

Saint Francis Xavier, **pray for us.**

Saint John Vianney, **pray for us.**

Saint Catherine of Siena, **pray for us.**

Saint Teresa of Jesus, **pray for us.**

All holy men and women, Saints of God, **pray for us.**

Lord, be merciful, **Lord, deliver us, we pray.**

From all evil, **Lord, deliver us, we pray.**

From every sin, **Lord, deliver us, we pray.**

From everlasting death, **Lord, deliver us, we pray.**

By your Incarnation, **Lord, deliver us, we pray.**

By your Death and Resurrection, **Lord, deliver us, we pray.**

By the outpouring of the Holy Spirit, **Lord, deliver us, we pray.**

Be merciful to us sinners, **Lord, we ask you, hear our prayer.**

Bring these chosen ones to new birth through the grace of Baptism, **Lord, we ask you, hear our prayer.**

Jesus, Son of the living God, **Lord, we ask you, hear our prayer.**

Christ, hear us.
Christ, hear us.

Christ, graciously hear us.
Christ, graciously hear us.

BLESSING OF BAPTISMAL WATER [Grace-Filled Water]

The Priest then blesses the baptismal water, saying the follow-
ing prayer with hands extended:

O God, who by invisible power
accomplish a wondrous effect
through sacramental signs
and who in many ways have prepared water, your
    creation,
to show forth the grace of Baptism;

O God, whose Spirit
in the first moments of the world's creation
hovered over the waters,
so that the very substance of water
would even then take to itself the power to sanctify;

O God, who by the outpouring of the flood
foreshadowed regeneration,
so that from the mystery of one and the same element of
    water
would come an end to vice and a beginning of virtue;

O God, who caused the children of Abraham
to pass dry-shod through the Red Sea,
so that the chosen people,
set free from slavery to Pharaoh,
would prefigure the people of the baptized;

O God, whose Son,
baptized by John in the waters of the Jordan,
was anointed with the Holy Spirit,
and, as he hung upon the Cross,
gave forth water from his side along with blood,
and after his Resurrection, commanded his disciples:
"Go forth, teach all nations, baptizing them
in the name of the Father and of the Son and of the Holy
    Spirit,"
look now, we pray, upon the face of your Church
and graciously unseal for her the fountain of Baptism.

May this water receive by the Holy Spirit
the grace of your Only Begotten Son,
so that human nature, created in your image
and washed clean through the Sacrament of Baptism
from all the squalor of the life of old,
may be found worthy to rise to the life of newborn
  children
through water and the Holy Spirit.

*And, if appropriate, lowering the paschal candle into the
water either once or three times, he continues:*

May the power of the Holy Spirit,
O Lord, we pray,
come down through your Son
into the fullness of this font,

and, holding the candle in the water, he continues:

so that all who have been buried with Christ
by Baptism into death
may rise again to life with him.
Who lives and reigns with you in the unity of the Holy
  Spirit,
God, for ever and ever. ℟. **Amen.**

*Then the candle is lifted out of the water, as the people
acclaim:*

**Springs of water, bless the Lord;
praise and exalt him above all for ever.**

THE BLESSING OF WATER   [Memorial of Baptism]

*If no one present is to be baptized and the font is not to be
blessed, the Priest introduces the faithful to the blessing of
water, saying:*

Dear brothers and sisters,
let us humbly beseech the Lord our God
to bless this water he has created,
which will be sprinkled upon us
as a memorial of our Baptism.

May he graciously renew us,
that we may remain faithful to the Spirit
whom we have received.

*And after a brief pause in silence, he proclaims the following
prayer, with hands extended:*

Lord our God,
in your mercy be present to your people
who keep vigil on this most sacred night,
and, for us who recall the wondrous work of our creation
and the still greater work of our redemption,
graciously bless this water.
For you created water to make the fields fruitful
and to refresh and cleanse our bodies.
You also made water the instrument of your mercy:
for through water you freed your people from slavery
and quenched their thirst in the desert;
through water the Prophets proclaimed the new
    covenant
you were to enter upon with the human race;
and last of all,
through water, which Christ made holy in the Jordan,
you have renewed our corrupted nature
in the bath of regeneration.

Therefore, may this water be for us
a memorial of the Baptism we have received,
and grant that we may share
in the gladness of our brothers and sisters,
who at Easter have received their Baptism.
Through Christ our Lord.
℟. **Amen.**

RENUNCIATION OF SIN AND PROFESSION OF FAITH
[Witnessing to Our Faith]

*If Baptism is to take place, the Priest, in a series of questions
to which the elect reply,* **I do,** *asks the elect to renounce sin
and profess their faith.*

BAPTISM [Children of God]

The Priest baptizes the elect either by immersion or by the pouring of water.

N., I baptize you in the name of the Father, and of the Son, and of the Holy Spirit.

EXPLANATORY RITES

The celebration of Baptism continues with the explanatory rites, after which the celebration of Confirmation normally follows.

ANOINTING AFTER BAPTISM [Chrism of Salvation]

If the Confirmation of those baptized is separated from their Baptism, the Priest anoints them with Chrism immediately after Baptism.

Almighty God, the Father of our Lord Jesus Christ,
has given you new birth by water and the Holy Spirit,
granted you the remission of all sins,
and joined you to his people.
He now anoints you with the Chrism of salvation,
so that you may remain members of Christ, Priest,
   Prophet and King,
unto eternal life.

Newly baptized: **Amen.**

In silence each of the newly baptized is anointed with Chrism on the crown of the head.

CLOTHING WITH A WHITE GARMENT
[Clothed in Christ]

The garment used in this Rite may be white or of a color that conforms to local custom. If circumstances suggest, this Rite may be omitted.

N. and N., you have become a new creation
and have clothed yourselves in Christ.

Receive, therefore, the white garment
and bring it unstained
before the judgment seat of our Lord Jesus Christ,
that you may have eternal life.

Newly baptized: **Amen.**

HANDING ON OF A LIGHTED CANDLE   [Light of Christ]

The Priest takes the Easter candle in his hands or touches it,
saying:

Come forward, godfathers and godmothers,
that you may hand on the light to the newly baptized.

A godparent of each of the newly baptized goes to the Priest,
lights a candle from the Easter candle, then presents it to the
newly baptized.

You have been made light in Christ.
Walk always as children of light,
that persevering in faith
you may run to meet the Lord when he comes
with all the Saints in the heavenly court.

Newly baptized: **Amen.**

The Renewal of Baptismal Promises

INVITATION   [Call to Renewal]

After the celebration of Baptism, the Priest addresses the com-
munity, in order to invite those present to the renewal of their
baptismal promises; the candidates for reception into full com-
munion join the rest of the community in this renunciation of sin
and profession of faith. All stand and hold lighted candles.

The Priest addresses the faithful in these or similar words.

Dear brethren (brothers and sisters), through the
    Paschal Mystery
we have been buried with Christ in Baptism,
so that we may walk with him in newness of life.
And so, now that our Lenten observance is concluded,
let us renew the promises of Holy Baptism,

by which we once renounced Satan and his works
and promised to serve God in the holy catholic Church.
And so I ask you:

A   [Reject Evil]

Priest: Do you renounce Satan?
All: **I do.**

Priest: And all his works?
All: **I do.**

Priest: And all his empty show?
All: **I do.**

B

Priest: Do you renounce sin,
   so as to live in the freedom of the children of God?
All: **I do.**

Priest: Do you renounce the lure of evil,
   so that sin may have no mastery over you?
All: **I do.**

Priest: Do you renounce Satan,
   the author and prince of sin?
All: **I do.**

PROFESSION OF FAITH   [I Believe]

Then the Priest continues:

Priest: Do you believe in God,
         the Father almighty,
         Creator of heaven and earth?
All: **I do.**

Priest: Do you believe in Jesus Christ, his only Son, our
         Lord,
         who was born of the Virgin Mary,
         suffered death and was buried,
         rose again from the dead
         and is seated at the right hand of the Father?
All: **I do.**

Priest: Do you believe in the Holy Spirit,
the holy catholic Church,
the communion of saints,
the forgiveness of sins,
the resurrection of the body,
and life everlasting?

All: **I do.**

And the Priest concludes:

And may almighty God, the Father of our Lord Jesus
  Christ,
who has given us new birth by water and the Holy Spirit
and bestowed on us forgiveness of our sins,
keep us by his grace,
in Christ Jesus our Lord,
for eternal life.

All: **Amen.**

SPRINKLING WITH BAPTISMAL WATER   [Water of Life]

*The Priest sprinkles all the people with the blessed baptismal
water, while all sing the following song or any other that is
baptismal in character.*

Antiphon

**I saw water flowing from the Temple,
from its right-hand side, alleluia;
and all to whom this water came were saved
and shall say: Alleluia, alleluia.**

Celebration of Reception

INVITATION   [Call To Come Forward]

*If Baptism has been celebrated at the font, the Priest, the
assisting ministers, and the newly baptized with their godparents proceed to the sanctuary. As they do so the assembly may
sing a suitable song.*

*Then in the following or similar words the Priest invites the
candidates for reception, along with their sponsors, to come
into the sanctuary and before the community to make a profession of faith.*

N. and N., since after mature deliberation in the Holy Spirit
and of your own free will
you have asked to be received
into the full communion of the Catholic Church,
I now invite you to come forward with your sponsor
and in the presence of this community
to profess the Catholic faith.
In this faith, today for the first time
you will partake with us at the eucharistic table of the
  Lord Jesus,
by which the unity of the Church is signified.

PROFESSION BY THE CANDIDATES   [Belief in Church]

When the candidates for reception and their sponsors have
taken their places in the sanctuary, the Priest asks the candi-
dates to make the following profession of faith. The candi-
dates say:

I believe and profess
all that the holy Catholic Church
believes, teaches, and proclaims as revealed by God.

FORMULA OF RECEPTION   [Full Communion]

Then the candidates with their sponsors go individually to the
Priest, who says to each candidate (laying his right hand on
the head of any candidate who is not to receive Confirmation):

N., the Lord receives you into the Catholic Church.
In his mercy he has led you here,
so that in the Holy Spirit
you may have full communion with us
in the faith you have professed before this his family.

Celebration of Confirmation

INVITATION   [Strength in the Spirit]

The newly baptized with their godparents and, if they have
not received the Sacrament of Confirmation, the newly

*received with their sponsors, stand before the Priest. He first
speaks briefly to the newly baptized and the newly received in
these or similar words.*

Dear candidates for Confirmation,
you have been born again in Christ,
and have become members of Christ and of his
    Priestly people.
Now you are to share
in the outpouring among us of the Holy Spirit,
who was sent by the Lord upon the Apostles at Pentecost
to be given by them and their successors to the baptized.

Therefore, you also are to receive the promised power
    of the Holy Spirit,
so that, being more perfectly conformed to Christ,
you may bear witness to the Lord's Passion and
    Resurrection
and become an active member of the Church
for the building up of the Body of Christ in faith and
    charity.

Dearly beloved,
let us pray to God the almighty Father,
that he will graciously pour out the Holy Spirit
upon these candidates for Confirmation
to confirm them with his abundant gifts,
and through his anointing
conform them more fully to Christ, the Son of God.

All pray briefly in silence.

THE LAYING ON OF HANDS   [Gifts of the Spirit]

*The Priest holds his hands outstretched over the entire group
of those to be confirmed and says the following prayer.*

Almighty God, Father of our Lord Jesus Christ,
who brought these your servants to new birth
by water and the Holy Spirit,
freeing them from sin:

send upon them, O Lord, the Holy Spirit, the Paraclete;
give them the spirit of wisdom and understanding,
the spirit of counsel and fortitude,
the spirit of knowledge and piety;
fill them with the spirit of the fear of the Lord.
Through Christ our Lord.
℟. **Amen.**

THE ANOINTING WITH CHRISM　　　[Sealed in the Spirit]

Either or both godparents and sponsors place the right hand on the shoulder of the one to be confirmed, and a godparent or a sponsor of the one to be confirmed gives his (her) name to the minister of the Sacrament. During the conferral of the Sacrament an appropriate song may be sung.

The minister of the Sacrament dips his right thumb in the Chrism and makes the Sign of the Cross on the forehead of the one to be confirmed as he says:

N., be sealed with the Gift of the Holy Spirit.
Newly confirmed: **Amen.**
Minister: Peace be with you.
Newly confirmed: **And with your spirit.**

After all have received the Sacrament, the newly confirmed as well as the godparents and sponsors are led to their places in the assembly.

[Since the Profession of Faith is not said, the Universal Prayer (no. 16, p. 19) begins immediately and for the first time the neophytes take part in it.]

FOURTH PART:

THE LITURGY OF THE EUCHARIST

The Priest goes to the altar and begins the Liturgy of the Eucharist in the usual way.

It is desirable that the bread and wine be brought forward by the newly baptized or, if they are children, by their parents or godparents.

PRAYER OVER THE OFFERINGS   [God's Saving Work]

Accept, we ask, O Lord,
the prayers of your people
with the sacrificial offerings,
that what has begun in the paschal mysteries
may, by the working of your power,
bring us to the healing of eternity.
Through Christ our Lord.
℟. **Amen.**

> → No. 21, p. 22 (Pref P 21: on this night above all)

*In the Eucharistic Prayer, a commemoration is made of the
baptized and their godparents in accord with the formulas
which are found in the Roman Missal and Roman Ritual for
each of the Eucharistic Prayers.*

COMMUNION ANT. 1 Cor 5:7-8   [Purity and Truth]

**Christ our Passover has been sacrificed; therefore let
us keep the feast with the unleavened bread of purity
and truth, alleluia. ↓**

Psalm 118 (117) may appropriately be sung.

PRAYER AFTER COMMUNION   [One in Mind and Heart]

Pour out on us, O Lord, the Spirit of your love,
and in your kindness make those you have nourished
by this paschal Sacrament
one in mind and heart.
Through Christ our Lord. ℟. **Amen.**

SOLEMN BLESSING   [God's Blessings]

May almighty God bless you
through today's Easter Solemnity
and, in his compassion,
defend you from every assault of sin. ℟. **Amen.**

And may he, who restores you to eternal life
in the Resurrection of his Only Begotten,
endow you with the prize of immortality. ℟. **Amen.**
Now that the days of the Lord's Passion have drawn to a
    close,
may you who celebrate the gladness of the Paschal Feast
come with Christ's help, and exulting in spirit,
to those feasts that are celebrated in eternal joy.
℟. **Amen.**

And may the blessing of almighty God,
the Father, and the Son, ✠ and the Holy Spirit,
come down on you and remain with you for ever.
℟. **Amen.** ↓

*The final blessing formula from the Rite of Baptism of Adults
or of Children may also be used, according to circumstances.*

*To dismiss the people the Deacon or, if there is no Deacon, the
Priest himself sings or says:*

Go forth, the Mass is ended, alleluia, alleluia.

Or:

Go in peace, alleluia, alleluia.

℟. **Thanks be to God, alleluia, alleluia.**

This practice is observed throughout the Octave of Easter.

"I have risen, and I am with you still."

APRIL 20

EASTER SUNDAY

ENTRANCE ANT. Cf. Ps 139 (138):18, 5-6
[Christ's Resurrection]

I have risen, and I am with you still, alleluia. You have
laid your hand upon me, alleluia. Too wonderful for
me, this knowledge, alleluia, alleluia. → No. 2, p. 10

OR Lk 24:34; cf. Rv 1:6 **[Glory and Power]**

The Lord is truly risen, alleluia. To him be glory and
power for all the ages of eternity, alleluia, alleluia.
→ No. 2, p. 10

COLLECT **[Renewal]**

O God, who on this day,
through your Only Begotten Son,
have conquered death
and unlocked for us the path to eternity,
grant, we pray, that we who keep
the solemnity of the Lord's Resurrection
may, through the renewal brought by your Spirit,
rise up in the light of life.
Through our Lord Jesus Christ, your Son,

who lives and reigns with you in the unity of the Holy
   Spirit,
God, for ever and ever. ℟. **Amen.** ↓

FIRST READING Acts 10:34a, 37-43   [Salvation in Christ]

> In his sermon Peter sums up the "Good News," the
> Gospel. Salvation comes through Christ, the beloved Son
> of the Father, the anointed of the Holy Spirit.

A reading from the Acts of the Apostles

PETER proceeded to speak and said: "You know
what has happened all over Judea, beginning in
Galilee after the baptism that John preached, how God
anointed Jesus of Nazareth with the Holy Spirit and
power. He went about doing good and healing all those
oppressed by the devil, for God was with him. We are
witnesses of all that he did both in the country of the
Jews and in Jerusalem. They put him to death by hanging him on a tree. This man God raised on the third day
and granted that he be visible, not to all the people, but
to us, the witnesses chosen by God in advance, who ate
and drank with him after he rose from the dead. He
commissioned us to preach to the people and testify
that he is the one appointed by God as judge of the living and the dead. To him all the prophets bear witness,
that everyone who believes in him will receive forgiveness of sins through his name."—The word of the Lord.
℟. **Thanks be to God.** ↓

RESPONSORIAL PSALM Ps 118   [The Day of the Lord]

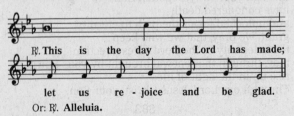

℟. This is the day the Lord has made;
let us re - joice and be glad.
Or: ℟. **Alleluia.**

Give thanks to the LORD, for he is good,
  for his mercy endures forever.
Let the house of Israel say,
  "His mercy endures forever."

℟. **This is the day the Lord has made; let us rejoice
  and be glad.**

Or: ℟. **Alleluia.**

"The right hand of the LORD has struck with power;
  the right hand of the LORD is exalted.
I shall not die, but live,
  and declare the works of the LORD."

℟. **This is the day the Lord has made; let us rejoice
  and be glad.**

Or: ℟. **Alleluia.**

The stone which the builders rejected
  has become the cornerstone.
By the LORD has this been done;
  it is wonderful in our eyes.

℟. **This is the day the Lord has made; let us rejoice
  and be glad.** ↓

Or: ℟. **Alleluia.** ↓

*One of the following texts may be chosen as the Second
Reading.*

SECOND READING Col 3:1-4   [Seek Heavenly Things]

**Look to the glory of Christ in which we share because our
lives are hidden in him (through Baptism) and we are destined to share in the glory.**

A reading from the Letter of Saint Paul to the Colossians

BROTHERS and sisters: If then you were raised with
Christ, seek what is above, where Christ is seated
at the right hand of God. Think of what is above, not of
what is on earth. For you have died, and your life is
hidden with Christ in God. When Christ your life
appears, then you too will appear with him in glory.—
The word of the Lord. ℟. **Thanks be to God.** ↓

OR

SECOND READING 1 Cor 5:6b-8   [Change of Heart]

Turn away from your old ways, from sin. Have a change of heart; be virtuous.

A reading from the first Letter of Saint Paul
to the Corinthians

BROTHERS and sisters: Do you not know that a little yeast leavens all the dough? Clear out the old yeast, so that you may become a fresh batch of dough, inasmuch as you are unleavened. For our paschal lamb, Christ, has been sacrificed. Therefore, let us celebrate the feast, not with the old yeast, the yeast of malice and wickedness, but with the unleavened bread of sincerity and truth.—The word of the Lord. ℟. **Thanks be to God.** ↓

SEQUENCE (Victimae paschali laudes)   [Hymn to the Victor]

Christians, to the Paschal Victim
    Offer your thankful praises!
A Lamb the sheep redeems;
    Christ, Who only is sinless,
    Reconciles sinners to the Father.
Death and life have contended in that combat stupendous:
    The Prince of life, who died, reigns immortal.
Speak, Mary, declaring
    What you saw, wayfaring.
"The tomb of Christ, who is living,
    The glory of Jesus' resurrection;
Bright angels attesting,
    The shroud and napkin resting.
Yes, Christ my hope is arisen;
    To Galilee he goes before you."
Christ indeed from death is risen, our new life obtaining.
    Have mercy, victor King, ever reigning!
    Amen. Alleluia. ↓

ALLELUIA Cf. 1 Cor 5:7b-8a   [Joy in the Lord]

℟. **Alleluia, alleluia.**
Christ, our paschal lamb, has been sacrificed;
let us then feast with joy in the Lord.
℟. **Alleluia, alleluia.** ↓

(For Morning Mass)

GOSPEL Jn 20:1-9   [Renewed Faith]

> Let us discover the empty tomb and ponder this mystery, and
> like Christ's first followers be strengthened in our faith.

℣. The Lord be with you. ℟. **And with your spirit.**
✛ A reading from the holy Gospel according to John.
℟. **Glory to you, O Lord.**

O N the first day of the week, Mary of Magdala came
to the tomb early in the morning, while it was still
dark, and saw the stone removed from the tomb. So she
ran and went to Simon Peter and to the other disciple
whom Jesus loved, and told them, "They have taken the
Lord from the tomb, and we don't know where they put
him." So Peter and the other disciple went out and came
to the tomb. They both ran, but the other disciple ran
faster than Peter and arrived at the tomb first; he bent
down and saw the burial cloths there, but did not go in.
When Simon Peter arrived after him, he went into the
tomb and saw the burial cloths there, and the cloth that
had covered his head, not with the burial cloths but rolled
up in a separate place. Then the other disciple also went
in, the one who had arrived at the tomb first, and he saw
and believed. For they did not yet understand the
Scripture that he had to rise from the dead.—The Gospel
of the Lord. ℟. **Praise to you, Lord Jesus Christ.**

→ No. 15, p. 18

*However, in Easter Sunday Masses which are celebrated with
a congregation, the rite of the renewal of baptismal promises
may take place after the Homily, according to the text used at
the Easter Vigil (p. 375). In that case the Creed is omitted.*

OR

GOSPEL Lk 24:1-12   [The Resurrection]
See p. 368.

(For an Afternoon or Evening Mass)

GOSPEL Lk 24:13-35   [The Messiah's Need To Suffer]
Let us accept the testimony of these two witnesses that
our hearts may burn with the fire of faith.

℣. The Lord be with you. ℟. **And with your spirit.**
✠ A reading from the holy Gospel according to Luke.
℟. **Glory to you, O Lord.**

THAT very day, the first day of the week, two of
Jesus' disciples were going to a village seven miles
from Jerusalem called Emmaus, and they were conversing about all the things that had occurred. And it
happened that while they were conversing and debat-
ing, Jesus himself drew near and walked with them,
but their eyes were prevented from recognizing him.
He asked them, "What are you discussing as you walk
along?" They stopped, looking downcast. One of them,
named Cleopas, said to him in reply, "Are you the only
visitor to Jerusalem who does not know of the things
that have taken place there in these days?" And he
replied to them, "What sort of things?" They said to
him, "The things that happened to Jesus the Nazarene,
who was a prophet mighty in deed and word before
God and all the people, how our chief priests and
rulers both handed him over to a sentence of death
and crucified him. But we were hoping that he would
be the one to redeem Israel; and besides all this, it is
now the third day since this took place. Some women
from our group, however, have astounded us: they
were at the tomb early in the morning and did not find
his body; they came back and reported that they had

indeed seen a vision of angels who announced that he
was alive. Then some of those with us went to the tomb
and found things just as the women had described, but
him they did not see." And he said to them, "Oh, how
foolish you are! How slow of heart to believe all that
the prophets spoke! Was is not necessary that the
Christ should suffer these things and enter into his
glory?" Then beginning with Moses and all the
prophets, he interpreted to them what referred to him
in all the Scriptures. As they approached the village to
which they were going, he gave the impression that he
was going on farther. But they urged him, "Stay with
us, for it is nearly evening and the day is almost over."
So he went in to stay with them. And it happened that,
while he was with them at table, he took bread, said
the blessing, broke it, and gave it to them. With that
their eyes were opened and they recognized him, but
he vanished from their sight. They said to each other,
"Were not our hearts burning within us while he spoke
to us on the way and opened the Scriptures to us?" So
they set out at once and returned to Jerusalem where
they found gathered together the eleven and those
with them who were saying, "The Lord has truly been
raised and has appeared to Simon!" Then the two
recounted what had taken place on the way and how
he was made known to them in the breaking of
bread.—The Gospel of the Lord. ℟. **Praise to you, Lord
Jesus Christ.**   → No. 15, p. 18

*However, in Easter Sunday Masses which are celebrated with
a congregation, the rite of the renewal of baptismal promises
may take place after the Homily, according to the text used at
the Easter Vigil (p. 375). In that case the Creed is omitted.*

PRAYER OVER THE OFFERINGS [Reborn and Nourished]

Exultant with paschal gladness, O Lord,
we offer the sacrifice

by which your Church
is wondrously reborn and nourished.
Through Christ our Lord. ℟. **Amen.**

→ No. 21, p. 22 (Pref. P 21: on this day above all)

When the Roman Canon is used, the proper forms of the Communicantes *(*In communion with those*) and* Hanc igitur
*(*Therefore, Lord, we pray*) are said.*

COMMUNION ANT. 1 Cor 5:7-8   [Purity and Truth]

**Christ our Passover has been sacrificed, alleluia;
therefore let us keep the feast with the unleavened
bread of purity and truth, alleluia, alleluia.** ↓

PRAYER AFTER COMMUNION   [Glory of Resurrection]

Look upon your Church, O God,
with unfailing love and favor,
so that, renewed by the paschal mysteries,
she may come to the glory of the resurrection.
Through Christ our Lord.
℟. **Amen.**   → No. 30, p. 77

*To impart the blessing at the end of Mass, the Priest may
appropriately use the formula of Solemn Blessing for the
Mass of the Easter Vigil, p. 381.*

For the dismissal of the people, there is sung or said:

Go forth, the Mass is ended, alleluia, alleluia.

OR

Go in peace, alleluia, alleluia.

℟. **Thanks be to God, alleluia, alleluia.**

"Thomas answered . . . , 'My Lord and my God!' "

APRIL 27

2nd SUNDAY OF EASTER
(or of Divine Mercy)

ENTRANCE ANT. 1 Pt 2:2   [Long for Spiritual Milk]

Like newborn infants, you must long for the pure, spiritual milk, that in him you may grow to salvation, alleluia.   ➜ No. 2, p. 10

OR 4 Esdr 2:36-37   [Give Thanks]

Receive the joy of your glory, giving thanks to God, who has called you into the heavenly Kingdom, alleluia.   ➜ No. 2, p. 10

COLLECT   [Kindle Faith]

God of everlasting mercy,
who in the very recurrence of the paschal feast
kindle the faith of the people you have made your own,
increase, we pray, the grace you have bestowed,
that all may grasp and rightly understand
in what font they have been washed,
by whose Spirit they have been reborn,

by whose Blood they have been redeemed.
Through our Lord Jesus Christ, your Son,
who lives and reigns with you in the unity of the Holy
   Spirit,
God, for ever and ever. ℟. **Amen.** ↓

FIRST READING Acts 5:12-16   [Signs and Wonders]

**Through signs and wonders—miracles—the Lord supports
the work of the Apostles and leads people to the Faith.**

A reading from the Acts of the Apostles

MANY signs and wonders were done among the
people at the hands of the apostles. They were all
together in Solomon's portico. None of the others
dared to join them, but the people esteemed them. Yet
more than ever, believers in the Lord, great numbers of
men and women, were added to them. Thus they even
carried the sick out into the streets and laid them on
cots and mats so that when Peter came by, at least his
shadow might fall on one or another of them. A large
number of people from the towns in the vicinity of
Jerusalem also gathered, bringing the sick and those
disturbed by unclean spirits, and they were all
cured.—The word of the Lord. ℟. **Thanks be to God.** ↓

RESPONSORIAL PSALM Ps 118 [The Lord's Goodness]

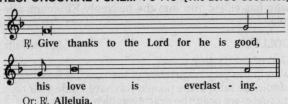

℟. Give thanks to the Lord for he is good,

his love is   everlast - ing.

Or: ℟. **Alleluia.**

Let the house of Israel say,
   "His mercy endures forever."
Let the house of Aaron say,
   "His mercy endures forever."

Let those who fear the LORD say,
   "His mercy endures forever."

℟. **Give thanks to the Lord for he is good, his love is
   everlasting.**

Or: ℟. **Alleluia.**

I was hard pressed and was falling,
   but the LORD helped me.
My strength and my courage is the LORD,
   and he has been my savior.
The joyful shout of victory
   in the tents of the just:

℟. **Give thanks to the Lord for he is good, his love is
   everlasting.**

Or: ℟. **Alleluia.**

The stone which the builders rejected
   has become the cornerstone.
By the LORD has this been done;
   it is wonderful in our eyes.
This is the day the LORD has made;
   let us be glad and rejoice in it.

℟. **Give thanks to the Lord for he is good, his love is
   everlasting.** ↓

Or: ℟. **Alleluia.** ↓

SECOND READING Rv 1:9-11a, 12-13, 17-19
[The First and the Last]

In symbol and allegory the glory of the Lord is depicted.

A reading from the Book of Revelation

I, JOHN, your brother, who share with you the distress, the kingdom, and the endurance we have
in Jesus, found myself on the island called Patmos
because I proclaimed God's word and gave testimony
to Jesus. I was caught up in spirit on the Lord's day
and heard behind me a voice as loud as a trumpet,

which said, "Write on a scroll what you see." Then I turned to see whose voice it was that spoke to me, and when I turned, I saw seven gold lampstands and in the midst of the lampstands one like a son of man, wearing an ankle-length robe, with a gold sash around his chest.

When I caught sight of him, I fell down at his feet as though dead. He touched me with his right hand and said, "Do not be afraid. I am the first and the last, the one who lives. Once I was dead, but now I am alive forever and ever. I hold the keys to death and the netherworld. Write down, therefore, what you have seen, and what is happening, and what will happen afterwards."—The word of the Lord. ℞. **Thanks be to God. ↓**

ALLELUIA Jn 20:29   [Blind Faith]

℞. **Alleluia, alleluia.**
You believe in me, Thomas, because you have seen me,
    says the Lord;
blessed are they who have not seen me, but still believe!
℞. **Alleluia, alleluia. ↓**

GOSPEL Jn 20:19-31   [Living Faith]
    **Jesus is risen; he comes and stands before his disciples. He
    encourages them and strengthens their faith.**

℣. The Lord be with you. ℞. **And with your spirit.**
✛ A reading from the holy Gospel according to John.
℞. **Glory to you, O Lord.**

ON the evening of that first day of the week, when the doors were locked, where the disciples were, for fear of the Jews, Jesus came and stood in their midst and said to them, "Peace be with you." When he had said this, he showed them his hands and his side. The disciples rejoiced when they saw the Lord. Jesus said to them again, "Peace be with you. As the Father has sent me, so

I send you." And when he had said this, he breathed on them and said to them, "Receive the Holy Spirit. Whose sins you forgive are forgiven them, and whose sins you retain are retained."

Thomas, called Didymus, one of the Twelve, was not with them when Jesus came. So the other disciples said to him, "We have seen the Lord." But he said to them, "Unless I see the mark of the nails in his hands and put my finger into the nailmarks and put my hand into his side, I will not believe."

Now a week later his disciples were again inside and Thomas was with them. Jesus came, although the doors were locked, and stood in their midst and said, "Peace be with you." Then he said to Thomas, "Put your finger here and see my hands, and bring your hand and put it into my side, and do not be unbelieving, but believe." Thomas answered and said to him, "My Lord and my God!" Jesus said to him, "Have you come to believe because you have seen me? Blessed are those who have not seen and have believed."

Now Jesus did many other signs in the presence of his disciples that are not written in this book. But these are written that you may come to believe that Jesus is the Christ, the Son of God, and that through this belief you may have life in his name.—The Gospel of the Lord. ℟. **Praise to you, Lord Jesus Christ.**   ➤ No. 15, p. 18

PRAYER OVER THE OFFERINGS   [Unending Happiness]

Accept, O Lord, we pray,
the oblations of your people
(and of those you have brought to new birth),
that, renewed by confession of your name and by
    Baptism,
they may attain unending happiness.
Through Christ our Lord. ℟. **Amen.**
    ➤ No. 21, p. 22 (Pref. P 21: on this day above all)

When the Roman Canon is used, the proper forms of the Communicantes *(*In communion with those*) and* Hanc igitur *(*Therefore, Lord, we pray*) are said.*

COMMUNION ANT. Cf. Jn 20:27   [Believe]

Bring your hand and feel the place of the nails, and do not be unbelieving but believing, alleluia. ↓

PRAYER AFTER COMMUNION   [Devout Reception]

Grant, we pray, almighty God,
that our reception of this paschal Sacrament
may have a continuing effect
in our minds and hearts.
Through Christ our Lord.
℟. **Amen.**   → No. 30, p. 77

Optional Solemn Blessings, p. 97, and Prayers over the People, p. 105

For the dismissal of the people, there is sung or said: Go forth, the Mass is ended alleluia, alleluia. *Or:* Go in peace, alleluia, alleluia. *The people respond:* **Thanks be to God, alleluia, alleluia.**

"He said to them, 'Cast the net over the right side of the boat.'"

MAY 4

3rd SUNDAY OF EASTER

ENTRANCE ANT. Cf. Ps 66 (65):1-2   [Praise the Lord]
Cry out with joy to God, all the earth; O sing to the
glory of his name. O render him glorious praise,
alleluia.   → No. 2, p. 10

COLLECT   [Hope of Resurrection]
May your people exult for ever, O God,
in renewed youthfulness of spirit,
so that, rejoicing now in the restored glory of our
    adoption,
we may look forward in confident hope
to the rejoicing of the day of resurrection.
Through our Lord Jesus Christ, your Son,
who lives and reigns with you in the unity of the Holy
    Spirit,
God, for ever and ever. ℟. **Amen.** ↓

FIRST READING Acts 5:27-32, 40b-41 [Preaching the Name]

With a strong faith the Apostles persevere in the mission that Christ gave them.

A reading from the Acts of the Apostles

WHEN the captain and the court officers had brought the apostles in and made them stand before the Sanhedrin, the high priest questioned them, "We gave you strict orders, did we not, to stop teaching in that name? Yet you have filled Jerusalem with your teaching and want to bring this man's blood upon us." But Peter and the apostles said in reply, "We must obey God rather than men. The God of our ancestors raised Jesus, though you had him killed by hanging him on a tree. God exalted him at his right hand as leader and savior to grant Israel repentance and forgiveness of sins. We are witnesses of these things, as is the Holy Spirit whom God has given to those who obey him."

The Sanhedrin ordered the apostles to stop speaking in the name of Jesus, and dismissed them. So they left the presence of the Sanhedrin, rejoicing that they had been found worthy to suffer dishonor for the sake of the name.—The word of the Lord. ℟. **Thanks be to God.** ↓

RESPONSORIAL PSALM Ps 30   [Divine Security]

℟. I will praise you, Lord, for you have res-cued me.
Or: ℟. **Alleluia.**

I will extol you, O LORD, for you drew me clear
    and did not let my enemies rejoice over me.
O LORD, you brought me up from the netherworld;
    you preserved me from among those going down
        into the pit.
℟. **I will praise you, Lord, for you have rescued me.**
Or: ℟. **Alleluia.**

Sing praise to the LORD, you his faithful ones,
  and give thanks to his holy name.
For his anger lasts but a moment;
  a lifetime, his good will.
At nightfall, weeping enters in,
  but with the dawn, rejoicing.

℟. **I will praise you, Lord, for you have rescued me.**
Or: ℟. **Alleluia.**

Hear, O LORD, and have pity on me;
  O LORD, be my helper.
You changed my mourning into dancing;
  O LORD, my God, forever will I give you thanks.

℟. **I will praise you, Lord, for you have rescued me.** ↓
Or: ℟. **Alleluia.** ↓

SECOND READING Rv 5:11-14   [The Throne of God]
  **The power and the glory of God are acclaimed by his cre-
  ation.**

A reading from the Book of Revelation

I, JOHN, looked and heard the voices of many angels
who surrounded the throne and the living creatures and the elders. They were countless in number,
and they cried out in a loud voice:
  "Worthy is the Lamb that was slain
    to receive power and riches, wisdom and strength,
    honor and glory and blessing."
Then I heard every creature in heaven and on earth
and under the earth and in the sea, everything in the
universe, cry out:
  "To the one who sits on the throne and to the Lamb
    be blessing and honor, glory and might,
    forever and ever."
The four living creatures answered, "Amen," and the
elders fell down and worshiped.—The word of the
Lord. ℟. **Thanks be to God.** ↓

ALLELUIA   [Creator of All]

℟. **Alleluia, alleluia.**
Christ is risen, creator of all;
he has shown pity on all people.
℟. **Alleluia, alleluia.** ↓

GOSPEL Jn 21:1-19 or 21:1-14   [Christ Is Lord]

**Again the risen Savior appears to his disciples in a very
human way. Peter in three affirmations rejects his triple
denial and again hears the call "Follow me."**

*[If the "Shorter Form" is used, the indented text in brackets is
omitted.]*

℣. The Lord be with you. ℟. **And with your spirit.**
✝ A reading from the holy Gospel according to John.
℟. **Glory to you, O Lord.**

AT that time, Jesus revealed himself again to his
disciples at the Sea of Tiberias. He revealed himself in this way. Together were Simon Peter, Thomas
called Didymus, Nathanael from Cana in Galilee,
Zebedee's sons, and two others of his disciples. Simon
Peter said to them, "I am going fishing." They said to
him, "We also will come with you." So they went out
and got into the boat, but that night they caught nothing. When it was already dawn, Jesus was standing on
the shore; but the disciples did not realize that it was
Jesus. Jesus said to them, "Children, have you caught
anything to eat?" They answered him, "No." So he said
to them, "Cast the net over the right side of the boat
and you will find something." So they cast it, and were
not able to pull it in because of the number of fish. So
the disciple whom Jesus loved said to Peter, "It is the
Lord." When Simon Peter heard that it was the Lord,
he tucked in his garment, for he was lightly clad, and
jumped into the sea. The other disciples came in the
boat, for they were not far from shore, only about a
hundred yards, dragging the net with the fish. When

they climbed out on shore, they saw a charcoal fire with fish on it and bread. Jesus said to them, "Bring some of the fish you just caught." So Simon Peter went over and dragged the net ashore full of one hundred fifty-three large fish. Even though there were so many, the net was not torn. Jesus said to them, "Come, have breakfast." And none of the disciples dared to ask him, "Who are you?" because they realized it was the Lord. Jesus came over and took the bread and gave it to them, and in like manner the fish. This was now the third time Jesus was revealed to his disciples after being raised from the dead.

[When they had finished breakfast, Jesus said to Simon Peter, "Simon, son of John, do you love me more than these?" Simon Peter answered him, "Yes, Lord, you know that I love you." Jesus said to him, "Feed my lambs." He then said to Simon Peter a second time, "Simon, son of John, do you love me?" Simon Peter answered him, "Yes, Lord, you know that I love you." Jesus said to him, "Tend my sheep." Jesus said to him the third time, "Simon, son of John, do you love me?" Peter was distressed that Jesus had said to him a third time, "Do you love me?" and he said to him, "Lord, you know everything; you know that I love you." Jesus said to him, "Feed my sheep. Amen, amen, I say to you, when you were younger, you used to dress yourself and go where you wanted; but when you grow old, you will stretch out your hands, and someone else will dress you and lead you where you do not want to go." He said this signifying by what kind of death he would glorify God. And when he had said this, he said to him, "Follow me."]

The Gospel of the Lord. ℟. **Praise to you, Lord Jesus Christ.**   ➜ No. 15, p. 18

PRAYER OVER THE OFFERINGS [Exultant Church]

Receive, O Lord, we pray,
these offerings of your exultant Church,
and, as you have given her cause for such great
  gladness,
grant also that the gifts we bring
may bear fruit in perpetual happiness.
Through Christ our Lord.
℞. **Amen.** → No. 21, p. 22 (Pref. P 21-25)

COMMUNION ANT. Cf. Lk 24:35 [Christ's Presence]

**The disciples recognized the Lord Jesus in the break-
ing of the bread, alleluia.** ↓

OR Cf. Jn 21:12-13 [Come and Eat]

**Jesus said to his disciples: Come and eat. And he took
bread and gave it to them, alleluia.** ↓

PRAYER AFTER COMMUNION [The Lord's Kindness]

Look with kindness upon your people, O Lord,
and grant, we pray,
that those you were pleased to renew by eternal
  mysteries
may attain in their flesh
the incorruptible glory of the resurrection.
Through Christ our Lord.
℞. **Amen.** → No. 30, p. 77

Optional Solemn Blessings, p. 97, and Prayers over the People, p. 105

"My sheep hear my voice."

MAY 11

4th SUNDAY OF EASTER

ENTRANCE ANT. Cf. Ps 33 (32):5-6   [God the Creator]
The merciful love of the Lord fills the earth; by the word of the Lord the heavens were made, alleluia.

→ No. 2, p. 10

COLLECT   [Joys of Heaven]

Almighty ever-living God,
lead us to a share in the joys of heaven,
so that the humble flock may reach
where the brave Shepherd has gone before.
Who lives and reigns with you in the unity of the Holy
    Spirit,
God, for ever and ever.
℞. **Amen.** ↓

FIRST READING   Acts 13:14, 43-52   [Salvation in Jesus]

As missionaries, Paul and Barnabas meet with some suc-
cess and encounter strong opposition. Steadfastness in
faith is a source of joy.

A reading from the Acts of the Apostles

PAUL and Barnabas continued on from Perga and reached Antioch in Pisidia. On the sabbath they entered the synagogue and took their seats. Many Jews and worshipers who were converts to Judaism followed Paul and Barnabas, who spoke to them and urged them to remain faithful to the grace of God.

On the following sabbath almost the whole city gathered to hear the word of the Lord. When the Jews saw the crowds, they were filled with jealousy and with violent abuse contradicted what Paul said. Both Paul and Barnabas spoke out boldly and said, "It was necessary that the word of God be spoken to you first, but since you reject it and condemn yourselves as unworthy of eternal life, we now turn to the Gentiles. For so the Lord has commanded us, *I have made you a light to the Gentiles, that you may be an instrument of salvation to the ends of the earth.*"

The Gentiles were delighted when they heard this and glorified the word of the Lord. All who were destined for eternal life came to believe, and the word of the Lord continued to spread through the whole region. The Jews, however, incited the women of prominence who were worshipers and the leading men of the city, stirred up a persecution against Paul and Barnabas, and expelled them from their territory. So they shook the dust from their feet in protest against them, and went to Iconium. The disciples were filled with joy and the Holy Spirit.—The word of the Lord. ℟. **Thanks be to God.** ↓

RESPONSORIAL PSALM Ps 100   [The Lord Is God]

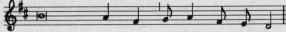

℟. **We are his peo - ple, the sheep of his flock.**
Or: ℟. **Alleluia.**

Sing joyfully to the LORD, all you lands;
  serve the LORD with gladness;
  come before him with joyful song.

℟. **We are his people, the sheep of his flock.**

Or: ℟. **Alleluia.**

Know that the LORD is God;
  he made us, his we are;
  his people, the flock he tends.

℟. **We are his people, the sheep of his flock.**

Or: ℟. **Alleluia.**

The LORD is good:
  his kindness endures forever,
  and his faithfulness, to all generations.

℟. **We are his people, the sheep of his flock.** ↓

Or: ℟. **Alleluia.** ↓

SECOND READING Rv 7:9, 14b-17 **[The Blood of the Lamb]**
  **Those who remain faithful despite severe persecution will
  find their reward is to be with God and restored to peace.**

A reading from the Book of Revelation

I, JOHN, had a vision of a great multitude, which no
  one could count, from every nation, race, people,
and tongue. They stood before the throne and before
the Lamb, wearing white robes and holding palm
branches in their hands.

Then one of the elders said to me, "These are the
ones who have survived the time of great distress; they
have washed their robes and made them white in the
blood of the Lamb.

"For this reason they stand before God's throne
  and worship him day and night in his temple.
The one who sits on the throne will shelter them.
They will not hunger or thirst anymore,
  nor will the sun or any heat strike them.

For the Lamb who is in the center of the throne
  will shepherd them
    and lead them to springs of life-giving water,
    and God will wipe away every tear from their eyes."
The word of the Lord. ℟. **Thanks be to God.** ↓

ALLELUIA Jn 10:14   [God's Sheep]
℟. **Alleluia, alleluia.**
I am the good shepherd, says the Lord;
I know my sheep, and mine know me.
℟. **Alleluia, alleluia.**

GOSPEL Jn 10:27-30   [The Good Shepherd]
Jesus proclaims his oneness with the Father. His love for
us is so great that he brings us eternal life.

℣. The Lord be with you. ℟. **And with your spirit.**
✜ A reading from the holy Gospel according to John.
℟. **Glory to you, O Lord.**

JESUS said: "My sheep hear my voice. I know them,
and they follow me. I give them eternal life, and
they shall never perish. No one can take them out of
my hand. My Father, who has given them to me, is
greater than all, and no one can take them out of the
Father's hand. The Father and I are one."—The Gospel
of the Lord. ℟. **Praise to you, Lord Jesus Christ.**

→ No. 15, p. 18

PRAYER OVER THE OFFERINGS   [Unending Joy]
Grant, we pray, O Lord,
that we may always find delight in these paschal
  mysteries,
so that the renewal constantly at work within us
may be the cause of our unending joy.
Through Christ our Lord.
℟. **Amen.**   → No. 21, p. 22 (Pref. P 21-25)

COMMUNION ANT.   [The Risen Shepherd]

The Good Shepherd has risen, who laid down his life for his sheep and willingly died for his flock, alleluia. ↓

PRAYER AFTER COMMUNION   [Kind Shepherd]

Look upon your flock, kind Shepherd,
and be pleased to settle in eternal pastures
the sheep you have redeemed
by the Precious Blood of your Son.
Who lives and reigns for ever and ever.
℟. **Amen.**   →   No. 30, p. 77

Optional Solemn Blessings, p. 97, and Prayers over the People, p. 105

"I give you a new commandment: love one another."

MAY 18

5th SUNDAY OF EASTER

ENTRANCE ANT. Cf. Ps 98 (97):1-2   [Wonders of the Lord]

O sing a new song to the Lord, for he has worked wonders; in the sight of the nations he has shown his deliverance, alleluia.   → No. 2, p. 10

COLLECT   [Much Fruit]

Almighty ever-living God,
constantly accomplish the Paschal Mystery within us,
that those you were pleased to make new in Holy
    Baptism
may, under your protective care, bear much fruit
and come to the joys of life eternal.
Through our Lord Jesus Christ, your Son,
who lives and reigns with you in the unity of the Holy
    Spirit,
God, for ever and ever.
℟. **Amen.** ↓

FIRST READING Acts 14:21-27   [Conversion of the Gentiles]

The life we have through Faith is not easy. We must struggle against many difficulties, even temptations, on our journey to eternal life.

A reading from the Acts of the Apostles

A FTER Paul and Barnabas had proclaimed the good news to that city and made a considerable number of disciples, they returned to Lystra and to Iconium and to Antioch. They strengthened the spirits of the disciples and exhorted them to persevere in the faith, saying, "It is necessary for us to undergo many hardships to enter the kingdom of God." They appointed elders for them in each church and, with prayer and fasting, commended them to the Lord in whom they had put their faith. Then they traveled through Pisidia and reached Pamphylia. After proclaiming the word at Perga they went down to Attalia. From there they sailed to Antioch, where they had been commended to the grace of God for the work they had now accomplished. And when they arrived, they called the church together and reported what God had done with them and how he had opened the door of faith to the Gentiles.—The word of the Lord. ℟. **Thanks be to God.** ↓

RESPONSORIAL PSALM Ps 145   [The Kingdom of God]

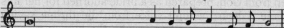

℟. **I will praise your name for ev - er, my king and my God.**
Or: ℟. **Alleluia.**

The LORD is gracious and merciful,
    slow to anger and of great kindness.
The LORD is good to all
    and compassionate toward all his works.

℟. **I will praise your name for ever, my king and my God.**
Or: ℟. **Alleluia.**

Let all your works give you thanks, O LORD,
  and let your faithful ones bless you.
Let them discourse of the glory of your kingdom
  and speak of your might.

℟. **I will praise your name for ever, my king and my God.**

Or: ℟. **Alleluia.**

Let them make known your might to the children
  of Adam,
  and the glorious splendor of your kingdom.
Your kingdom is a kingdom for all ages,
  and your dominion endures through all generations.

℟. **I will praise your name for ever, my king and my God.** ↓

Or: ℟. **Alleluia.** ↓

SECOND READING Rv 21:1-5a   [God's Dwelling]
  In the Kingdom of God all things are made new.

A reading from the Book of Revelation

THEN I, John, saw a new heaven and a new earth.
The former heaven and the former earth had
passed away, and the sea was no more. I also saw the
holy city, a new Jerusalem, coming down out of heav-
en from God, prepared as a bride adorned for her husband. I heard a loud voice from the throne saying,
"Behold, God's dwelling is with the human race. He
will dwell with them and they will be his people and
God himself will always be with them as their God. He
will wipe every tear from their eyes, and there shall be
no more death or mourning, wailing or pain, for the
old order has passed away."

The One who sat on the throne said, "Behold, I make
all things new."—The word of the Lord. ℟. **Thanks be
to God.** ↓

ALLELUIA Jn 13:34   [Love One Another]

℞. **Alleluia, alleluia.**

I give you a new commandment, says the Lord:
love one another as I have loved you.

℞. **Alleluia, alleluia.** ↓

GOSPEL Jn 13:31-33a, 34-35   [The New Commandment]

**Jesus is about to be betrayed yet he teaches us the way to
glory—the way he will go. It is the way of love.**

℣. The Lord be with you. ℞. **And with your spirit.**

✝ A reading from the holy Gospel according to John.

℞. **Glory to you, O Lord.**

WHEN Judas had left them, Jesus said, "Now is the
Son of Man glorified, and God is glorified
in him. If God is glorified in him, God will also glorify
him in himself, and God will glorify him at once. My children, I will be with you only a little while longer. I give
you a new commandment: love one another. As I have
loved you, so you also should love one another. This is
how all will know that you are my disciples, if you have
love for one another."—The Gospel of the Lord. ℞. **Praise
to you, Lord Jesus Christ.**   → No. 15, p. 18

PRAYER OVER THE OFFERINGS [Guided by God's Truth]

O God, who by the wonderful exchange effected in this
    sacrifice
have made us partakers of the one supreme Godhead,
grant, we pray,
that, as we have come to know your truth,
we may make it ours by a worthy way of life.
Through Christ our Lord.

℞. **Amen.**   → No. 21, p. 22 (Pref. P 21-25)

COMMUNION ANT. Cf. Jn 15:1, 5   [Union with Christ]

**I am the true vine and you are the branches, says the
Lord. Whoever remains in me, and I in him, bears fruit
in plenty, alleluia.** ↓

PRAYER AFTER COMMUNION   [New Life]

Graciously be present to your people, we pray, O Lord,
and lead those you have imbued with heavenly
  mysteries
to pass from former ways to newness of life.
Through Christ our Lord.
R̶). **Amen.**   → No. 30, p. 77

Optional Solemn Blessings, p. 97, and Prayers over the People, p. 105

"The Father will send [the Holy Spirit] in my name."

MAY 25

6th SUNDAY OF EASTER

ENTRANCE ANT. Cf. Is 48:20   [Spiritual Freedom]

**Proclaim a joyful sound and let it be heard; proclaim
to the ends of the earth: The Lord has freed his people,
alleluia.**   → No. 2, p. 10

COLLECT   [Heartfelt Devotion]

Grant, almighty God,
that we may celebrate with heartfelt devotion these
  days of joy,

which we keep in honor of the risen Lord,
and that what we relive in remembrance
we may always hold to in what we do.
Through our Lord Jesus Christ, your Son,
who lives and reigns with you in the unity of the Holy
     Spirit,
God, for ever and ever. ℟. **Amen.** ↓

FIRST READING Acts 15:1-2, 22-29   [Settling a Dispute]

**The Church faces its first test caused by inner dissensions
and she shows how, guided by the Spirit, charity will prevail.**

A reading from the Acts of the Apostles

SOME who had come down from Judea were
instructing the brothers, "Unless you are circum-
cised according to the Mosaic practice, you cannot be
saved." Because there arose no little dissension and
debate by Paul and Barnabas with them, it was decided that Paul, Barnabas, and some of the others should
go up to Jerusalem to the apostles and elders about
this question.

   The apostles and elders, in agreement with the whole
church, decided to choose representatives and to send
them to Antioch with Paul and Barnabas. The ones chosen were Judas, who was called Barsabbas, and Silas,
leaders among the brothers. This is the letter delivered
by them:

   "The apostles and the elders, your brothers, to the
brothers in Antioch, Syria, and Cilicia of Gentile origin:
greetings. Since we have heard that some of our number
who went out without any mandate from us have upset
you with their teachings and disturbed your peace of
mind, we have with one accord decided to choose representatives and to send them to you along with our
beloved Barnabas and Paul, who have dedicated their
lives to the name of our Lord Jesus Christ. So we are
sending Judas and Silas who will also convey this same

message by word of mouth: 'It is the decision of the Holy
Spirit and of us not to place on you any burden beyond
these necessities, namely, to abstain from meat sacrificed to idols, from blood, from meats of strangled animals, and from unlawful marriage. If you keep free of
these, you will be doing what is right. Farewell.' "—The
word of the Lord. ℟. **Thanks be to God.** ↓

RESPONSORIAL PSALM Ps 67   [Praise of God]

   ℟. **O God, let all the na-tions praise you!**
   Or: ℟. **Alleluia.**

May God have pity on us and bless us;
   may he let his face shine upon us.
So may your way be known upon earth;
   among all nations, your salvation.

℟. **O God, let all the nations praise you!**

Or: ℟. **Alleluia.**

May the nations be glad and exult
   because you rule the peoples in equity;
   the nations on the earth you guide.

℟. **O God, let all the nations praise you!**

Or: ℟. **Alleluia.**

May the peoples praise you, O God;
   may all the peoples praise you!
May God bless us,
   and may all the ends of the earth fear him!

℟. **O God, let all the nations praise you!** ↓

Or: ℟. **Alleluia.** ↓

SECOND READING Rv 21:10-14, 22-23 [The City of God]
   In symbolic language the Church is depicted as a wonderful
   glorious city, repenting and caught up in the glory of God.

A reading from the Book of Revelation

THE angel took me in spirit to a great, high mountain and showed me the holy city Jerusalem coming down out of heaven from God. It gleamed with the splendor of God. Its radiance was like that of a precious stone, like jasper, clear as crystal. It had a massive, high wall, with twelve gates where twelve angels were stationed and on which names were inscribed, the names of the twelve tribes of the Israelites. There were three gates facing east, three north, three south, and three west. The wall of the city had twelve courses of stones as its foundation, on which were inscribed the twelve names of the twelve apostles of the Lamb.

I saw no temple in the city for its temple is the Lord God almighty and the Lamb. The city had no need of sun or moon to shine on it, for the glory of God gave it light, and its lamp was the Lamb.—The word of the Lord. ℟. **Thanks be to God.** ↓

ALLELUIA Jn 14:23   [Divine Love]
℟. **Alleluia, alleluia.**
Whoever loves me will keep my word, says the Lord, and my Father will love him and we will come to him.
℟. **Alleluia, alleluia.** ↓

GOSPEL Jn 14:23-29   [The Gift of Peace]
In saying farewell Jesus has not deserted us. In his name the Father sends the Holy Spirit to aid us bearing witness to Jesus.

℣. The Lord be with you. ℟. And with your spirit.
✝ A reading from the holy Gospel according to John.
℟. **Glory to you, O Lord.**

JESUS said to his disciples: "Whoever loves me will keep my word, and my Father will love him, and we will come to him and make our dwelling with him. Whoever does not love me does not keep my words;

yet the word you hear is not mine but that of the Father who sent me.

"I have told you this while I am with you. The Advocate, the Holy Spirit, whom the Father will send in my name, will teach you everything and remind you of all that I told you. Peace I leave with you; my peace I give to you. Not as the world gives do I give it to you. Do not let your hearts be troubled or afraid. You heard me tell you, 'I am going away and I will come back to you.' If you loved me, you would rejoice that I am going to the Father; for the Father is greater than I. And now I have told you this before it happens, so that when it happens you may believe."—The Gospel of the Lord.
℟. **Praise to you, Lord Jesus Christ.**   → No. 15, p. 18

PRAYER OVER THE OFFERINGS   [God's Mighty Love]

May our prayers rise up to you, O Lord,
together with the sacrificial offerings,
so that, purified by your graciousness,
we may be conformed to the mysteries of your mighty
    love.
Through Christ our Lord.
℟. **Amen.**   → No. 21, p. 22 (Pref. P 21-25)

COMMUNION ANT. Jn 14:15-16   [Role of the Paraclete]

If you love me, keep my commandments, says the Lord, and I will ask the Father and he will send you another Paraclete, to abide with you for ever, alleluia. ↓

PRAYER AFTER COMMUNION   [Eucharistic Strength]

Almighty ever-living God,
who restore us to eternal life in the Resurrection of
    Christ,
increase in us, we pray, the fruits of this paschal
    Sacrament
and pour into our hearts the strength of this saving food.

Through Christ our Lord.
R̶. **Amen.**   → No. 30, p. 77

Optional Solemn Blessings, p. 97, and Prayers over the People, p. 105

"And behold I am sending the promise of my Father upon you."

*In those dioceses in which the Ascension is celebrated on
Sunday, the Mass of the Ascension (Vigil Mass, below, or Mass
during the Day, p. 423) is celebrated in place of the Mass of
the 7th Sunday of Easter that appears on p. 425.*

MAY 29

THE ASCENSION OF THE LORD

Solemnity

AT THE VIGIL MASS (May 28)

ENTRANCE ANT. Ps 68 (67): 33, 35   [Praise the Lord]
**You kingdoms of the earth, sing to God; praise the Lord,
who ascends above the highest heavens; his majesty
and might are in the skies, alleluia.**   → No. 2, p. 10

COLLECT   [Jesus' Promise]

O God, whose Son today ascended to the heavens
as the Apostles looked on,

grant, we pray, that, in accordance with his promise,
we may be worthy for him to live with us always on
   earth,
and we with him in heaven.
Who lives and reigns with you in the unity of the Holy
   Spirit,
God, for ever and ever. ℟. **Amen.** ↓

FIRST READING Acts 1:1-11   [Christ's Ascension]

   **Christ is divine! He will come again! Our Faith affirms this
   for us. We live in the era of the Holy Spirit.**

A reading from the Acts of the Apostles

IN the first book, Theophilus, I dealt with all that
   Jesus did and taught until the day he was taken up,
after giving instructions through the Holy Spirit to the
apostles whom he had chosen. He presented himself
alive to them by many proofs after he had suffered,
appearing to them during forty days and speaking about
the kingdom of God. While meeting with them, he
enjoined them not to depart from Jerusalem, but to wait
for "the promise of the Father about which you have
heard me speak; for John baptized with water, but in a
few days you will be baptized with the Holy Spirit."

When they had gathered together they asked him,
"Lord, are you at this time going to restore the kingdom to Israel?" He answered them, "It is not for you to
know the times or seasons that the Father has established by his own authority. But you will receive power
when the Holy Spirit comes upon you, and you will be
my witnesses in Jerusalem, throughout Judea and
Samaria, and to the ends of the earth." When he had
said this, as they were looking on, he was lifted up, and
a cloud took him from their sight. While they were
looking intently at the sky as he was going, suddenly
two men dressed in white garments stood beside them.
They said, "Men of Galilee, why are you standing there

looking at the sky? This Jesus who has been taken up from you into heaven will return in the same way as you have seen him going into heaven."—The word of the Lord. ℟. **Thanks be to God.** ↓

RESPONSORIAL PSALM Ps 47   [Praise to the Lord]

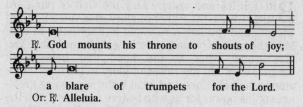

℟. **God mounts his throne to shouts of joy;**
a **blare of trumpets for the Lord.**
Or: ℟. **Alleluia.**

All you peoples, clap your hands,
 shout to God with cries of gladness.
For the Lord, the Most High, the awesome,
 is the great king over all the earth.

℟. **God mounts his throne to shouts of joy: a blare of trumpets for the Lord.**

Or: ℟. **Alleluia.**

God mounts his throne amid shouts of joy;
 the Lord, amid trumpet blasts.
Sing praise to God, sing praise;
 sing praise to our king, sing praise.

℟. **God mounts his throne to shouts of joy: a blare of trumpets for the Lord.**

Or: ℟. **Alleluia.**

For king of all the earth is God;
 sing hymns of praise.
God reigns over the nations,
 God sits upon his holy throne.

℟. **God mounts his throne to shouts of joy: a blare of trumpets for the Lord.** ↓

Or: ℟. **Alleluia.** ↓

SECOND READING Eph 1:17-23   [Glorification of Jesus]

Our hope is in God. He is our strength. With Christ our head, we his people will receive the gift of wisdom and insight.

A reading from the Letter of Saint Paul to the Ephesians

BROTHERS and sisters: May the God of our Lord Jesus Christ, the Father of glory, give you a Spirit of wisdom and revelation resulting in knowledge of him. May the eyes of your hearts be enlightened, that you may know what is the hope that belongs to his call, what are the riches of glory in his inheritance among the holy ones, and what is the surpassing greatness of his power for us who believe, in accord with the exercise of his great might, which he worked in Christ, raising him from the dead and seating him at his right hand in the heavens, far above every principality, authority, power, and dominion, and every name that is named not only in this age but also in the one to come. And he put all things beneath his feet and gave him as head over all things to the church, which is his body, the fullness of the one who fills all things in every way.—The word of the Lord. ℞. **Thanks be to God.** ↓

OR

SECOND READING Heb 9:24-28; 10:19-23

[The Ascension and Us]

Christ's Ascension gives us hope. He who made the promise is trustworthy.

A reading from the Letter to the Hebrews

CHRIST did not enter into a sanctuary made by hands, a copy of the true one, but heaven itself, that he might now appear before God on our behalf. Not that he might offer himself repeatedly, as the high priest enters each year into the sanctuary with blood that is not his own; if that were so, he would have had to suffer repeatedly from the foundation of the world. But now once for all he has appeared at the end of the ages to take away sin by his sacrifice. Just as it is appointed that men and women die once, and after this the judgment, so also Christ, offered once to take away the sins of many, will appear a second time, not to take away sin but to bring salvation to those who eagerly await him.

Therefore, brothers and sisters, since through the blood of Jesus we have confidence of entrance into the sanctuary by the new and living way he opened for us through the veil, that is, his flesh, and since we have "a great priest over the house of God," let us approach with a sincere heart and in absolute trust, with our hearts sprinkled clean from an evil conscience and our bodies washed in pure water. Let us hold unwaveringly to our confession that gives us hope, for he who made the promise is trustworthy.—The word of the Lord. ℟. **Thanks be to God.** ↓

ALLELUIA Mt 28:19a, 20b   [Christ's Abiding Presence]
℟. **Alleluia, alleluia.**
Go and teach all nations, says the Lord;
I am with you always, until the end of the world.
℟. **Alleluia, alleluia.** ↓

GOSPEL Lk 24:46-53   [The Ascension]
  We are called to penance for the remission of sins.

℣. The Lord be with you. ℟. **And with your spirit.**
✛ A reading from the holy Gospel according to Luke.
℟. **Glory to you, O Lord.**

JESUS said to his disciples: "Thus it is written that the Christ would suffer and rise from the dead on the third day and that repentance, for the forgiveness of sins, would be preached in his name to all the nations, beginning from Jerusalem. You are witnesses of these things. And behold I am sending the promise of my Father upon you; but stay in the city until you are clothed with power from on high."

Then he led them out as far as Bethany, raised his hands, and blessed them. As he blessed them he parted from them and was taken up to heaven. They did him homage and then returned to Jerusalem with great joy, and they were continually in the temple praising God.—The Gospel of the Lord. ℟. **Praise to you, Lord Jesus Christ.**   → No. 15, p. 18

PRAYER OVER THE OFFERINGS   [Obtain Mercy]

O God, whose Only Begotten Son, our High Priest,
is seated ever-living at your right hand to intercede for
    us,
grant that we may approach with confidence the
    throne of grace
and there obtain your mercy.
Through Christ our Lord.
℟. **Amen.**   → No. 21, p. 22 (Pref. P 26-27)

When the Roman Canon is used, the proper form of the Communicantes *(In communion with those) is said.*

COMMUNION ANT. Cf. Heb 10:12
                        [Christ at God's Right Hand]
Christ, offering a single sacrifice for sins, is seated for ever at God's right hand, alleluia. ↓

PRAYER AFTER COMMUNION   [Longing for Heaven]

May the gifts we have received from your altar, Lord,
kindle in our hearts a longing for the heavenly
    homeland
and cause us to press forward, following in the
    Savior's footsteps,

to the place where for our sake he entered before us.
Who lives and reigns for ever and ever.
℟. **Amen.**   → No. 30, p. 77

Optional Solemn Blessings, p. 97, and Prayers over the People, p. 105

AT THE MASS DURING THE DAY

ENTRANCE ANT. Acts 1:11   [The Lord Will Return]
**Men of Galilee, why gaze in wonder at the heavens?
This Jesus whom you saw ascending into heaven will
return as you saw him go, alleluia.**   → No. 2, p. 10

COLLECT   [Thankful for the Ascension]
Gladden us with holy joys, almighty God,
and make us rejoice with devout thanksgiving,
for the Ascension of Christ your Son
is our exaltation,
and, where the Head has gone before in glory,
the Body is called to follow in hope.
Through our Lord Jesus Christ, your Son,
who lives and reigns with you in the unity of the Holy
    Spirit,
God, for ever and ever. ℟. **Amen.** ↓

OR   [Belief in the Ascension]
Grant, we pray, almighty God,
that we, who believe that your Only Begotten Son, our
    Redeemer,
ascended this day to the heavens,
may in spirit dwell already in heavenly realms.
Who lives and reigns with you in the unity of the Holy
    Spirit,
God, for ever and ever. ℟. **Amen.** ↓

The readings for this Mass can be found beginning on p. 418.

PRAYER OVER THE OFFERINGS

[Rise to Heavenly Realms]

We offer sacrifice now in supplication, O Lord,
to honor the wondrous Ascension of your Son:
grant, we pray,
that through this most holy exchange
we, too, may rise up to the heavenly realms.
Through Christ our Lord.
℟. **Amen.** → No. 21, p. 22 (Pref. P 26-27)

When the Roman Canon is used, the proper form of the Communicantes *(In communion with those) is said.*

COMMUNION ANT. Mt 28:20 [Christ's Presence]

**Behold, I am with you always, even to the end of the
age, alleluia.** ↓

PRAYER AFTER COMMUNION [United with Christ]

Almighty ever-living God,
who allow those on earth to celebrate divine mysteries,
grant, we pray,
that Christian hope may draw us onward
to where our nature is united with you.
Through Christ our Lord.
℟. **Amen.** → No. 30, p. 77

Optional Solemn Blessings, p. 97, and Prayers over the People, p. 105

*"Righteous Father, the world also does not know you,
but I know you."*

*In those dioceses in which the Ascension is celebrated on
Sunday, the Mass of the Ascension (Vigil Mass, p. 417, or
Mass during the Day, p. 423) is celebrated in place of the fol-
lowing Mass of the 7th Sunday of Easter.*

JUNE 1

7th SUNDAY OF EASTER

ENTRANCE ANT. Cf. Ps 27 (26):7-9　　　[Seek the Lord]

O Lord, hear my voice, for I have called to you; of you
my heart has spoken: Seek his face; hide not your face
from me, alleluia.　　　　　　　　　　→ No. 2, p. 10

COLLECT　　　　　　　　　[Experience Christ among Us]

Graciously hear our supplications, O Lord,
so that we, who believe that the Savior of the human race
is with you in your glory,
may experience, as he promised,
until the end of the world,
his abiding presence among us.
Who lives and reigns with you in the unity of the Holy
　Spirit,
God, for ever and ever. ℟. **Amen.** ↓

FIRST READING Acts 7:55-60   [Stephen's Martyrdom]

Deacon Stephen, the first martyr, proclaims the glory of Jesus.

A reading from the Acts of the Apostles

STEPHEN, filled with the Holy Spirit, looked up intently to heaven and saw the glory of God and Jesus standing at the right hand of God, and Stephen said, "Behold, I see the heavens opened and the Son of Man standing at the right hand of God." But they cried out in a loud voice, covered their ears, and rushed upon him together. They threw him out of the city, and began to stone him. The witnesses laid down their cloaks at the feet of a young man named Saul. As they were stoning Stephen, he called out, "Lord Jesus, receive my spirit." Then he fell to his knees and cried out in a loud voice, "Lord, do not hold this sin against them"; and when he said this, he fell asleep.—The word of the Lord. ℟. **Thanks be to God.** ↓

RESPONSORIAL PSALM Ps 97   [The Glory of God]

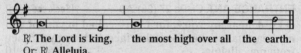

℟. **The Lord is king,**   the most high over all   the earth.
Or: ℟. **Alleluia.**

The LORD is king; let the earth rejoice;
    let the many isles be glad.
Justice and judgment are the foundation of his throne.

℟. **The Lord is king, the most high over all the earth.**

Or: ℟. **Alleluia.**

The heavens proclaim his justice,
    and all peoples see his glory.
All gods are prostrate before him.

℟. **The Lord is king, the most high over all the earth.**

Or: ℟. **Alleluia.**

You, O Lord, are the Most High over all the earth,
  exalted far above all gods.

℟. **The Lord is king, the most high over all the earth.** ↓

Or: ℟. **Alleluia.** ↓

SECOND READING Rv 22:12-14, 16-17, 20 [Come, Lord Jesus]
> He will come soon to judge each one of us. Now is the
> time to repent (symbolically wash our robes).

A reading from the Book of Revelation

I, JOHN, heard a voice saying to me: "Behold, I am
coming soon. I bring with me the recompense I will
give to each according to his deeds. I am the Alpha and
the Omega, the first and the last, the beginning and the
end."

Blessed are they who wash their robes so as to have
the right to the tree of life and enter the city through
its gates.

"I, Jesus, sent my angel to give you this testimony
for the churches. I am the root and offspring of David,
the bright morning star."

The Spirit and the bride say, "Come." Let the hearer
say, "Come." Let the one who thirsts come forward, and
the one who wants it receive the gift of life-giving
water.

The one who gives this testimony says, "Yes, I am
coming soon." Amen! Come, Lord Jesus!—The word of
the Lord. ℟. **Thanks be to God.** ↓

ALLELUIA Cf. Jn 14:18   [Joyous Return]

℟. **Alleluia, alleluia.**
I will not leave you orphans, says the Lord.
I will come back to you, and your hearts will rejoice.
℟. **Alleluia, alleluia.** ↓

GOSPEL Jn 17:20-26   [One in the Lord]
> Jesus prays for us—who believe in him—that our faith will
> unite us to each other, to him, and in him to the Father.

℣. The Lord be with you. ℟. **And with your spirit.**
✠ A reading from the holy Gospel according to John.
℟. **Glory to you, O Lord.**

L IFTING up his eyes to heaven, Jesus prayed, saying:
"Holy Father, I pray not only for them, but also for
those who will believe in me through their word, so that
they may all be one, as you, Father, are in me and I in
you, that they also may be in us, that the world may
believe that you sent me. And I have given them the
glory you gave me, so that they may be one, as we are
one, I in them and you in me, that they may be brought
to perfection as one, that the world may know that you
sent me, and that you loved them even as you loved me.
Father, they are your gift to me. I wish that where I am
they also may be with me, that they may see my glory
that you gave me, because you loved me before the foundation of the world. Righteous Father, the world also
does not know you, but I know you, and they know that
you sent me. I made known to them your name and I will
make it known, that the love with which you loved me
may be in them and I in them."—The Gospel of the
Lord. ℟. **Praise to you, Lord Jesus Christ.**

→ No. 15, p. 18

PRAYER OVER THE OFFERINGS   [Glory of Heaven]

Accept, O Lord, the prayers of your faithful
with the sacrificial offerings,
that through these acts of devotedness
we may pass over to the glory of heaven.
Through Christ our Lord.
℟. **Amen.**   → No. 21, p. 22 (Pref. P 21-25 or P 26-27)

COMMUNION ANT. Jn 17:22   [Christian Unity]

**Father, I pray that they may be one as we also are one,
alleluia.** ↓

PRAYER AFTER COMMUNION   [Grant Us Confidence]

Hear us, O God our Savior,
and grant us confidence,
that through these sacred mysteries
there will be accomplished in the body of the whole
   Church
what has already come to pass in Christ her Head.
Who lives and reigns for ever and ever.
R̸. **Amen.**   ➜ No. 30, p. 77

Optional Solemn Blessings, p. 97, and Prayers over the People, p. 105

"They were all filled with the Holy Spirit."

JUNE 8

PENTECOST SUNDAY

Solemnity

AT THE VIGIL MASS (June 7) (Simple Form)

ENTRANCE ANT. Rom 5:5; cf. 8:11   [Love-Imparting Spirit]

**The love of God has been poured into our hearts
through the Spirit of God dwelling within us, alleluia.**
                                        ➜ No. 2, p. 10

COLLECT   **[Heavenly Grace]**

Almighty ever-living God,
who willed the Paschal Mystery
to be encompassed as a sign in fifty days,
grant that from out of the scattered nations
the confusion of many tongues
may be gathered by heavenly grace
into one great confession of your name.
Through our Lord Jesus Christ, your Son,
who lives and reigns with you in the unity of the Holy
    Spirit,
God, for ever and ever. ℟. **Amen.** ↓

OR   **[New Birth in the Spirit]**

Grant, we pray, almighty God,
that the splendor of your glory
may shine forth upon us
and that, by the bright rays of the Holy Spirit,
the light of your light may confirm the hearts
of those born again by your grace.
Through our Lord Jesus Christ, your Son,
who lives and reigns with you in the unity of the Holy
    Spirit,
God, for ever and ever. ℟. **Amen.** ↓

FIRST READING

A Gn 11:1-9   **[Dangers of Human Pride]**
   **Those who put their trust in pride, and human ability, are
   bound to fail.**

A reading from the Book of Genesis

THE whole world spoke the same language, using
the same words. While the people were migrating
in the east, they came upon a valley in the land of
Shinar and settled there. They said to one another,
"Come, let us mold bricks and harden them with fire."

They used bricks for stone, and bitumen for mortar.
Then they said, "Come, let us build ourselves a city and
a tower with its top in the sky, and so make a name for
ourselves; otherwise we shall be scattered all over the
earth."

The LORD came down to see the city and the tower
that the people had built. Then the LORD said: "If now,
while they are one people, all speaking the same language, they have started to do this, nothing will later
stop them from doing whatever they presume to do. Let
us then go down there and confuse their language, so
that one will not understand what another says." Thus
the LORD scattered them from there all over the earth,
and they stopped building the city. That is why it was
called Babel, because there the LORD confused the
speech of all the world. It was from that place that he
scattered them all over the earth.—The word of the Lord.
℞. **Thanks be to God.** ↓

OR

B Ex 19:3-8a, 16-20b   [The Lord on Mount Sinai]
**The Lord God covenants with the Israelites—they are to be
a holy nation, a princely kingdom.**

A reading from the Book of Exodus

MOSES went up the mountain to God. Then the
LORD called to him and said, "Thus shall you say
to the house of Jacob; tell the Israelites: You have seen
for yourselves how I treated the Egyptians and how I
bore you up on eagle wings and brought you here to
myself. Therefore, if you hearken to my voice and keep
my covenant, you shall be my special possession, dear-
er to me than all other people, though all the earth is
mine. You shall be to me a kingdom of priests, a holy
nation. That is what you must tell the Israelites." So
Moses went and summoned the elders of the people.
When he set before them all that the LORD had ordered

him to tell them, the people all answered together,
"Everything the LORD has said, we will do."

On the morning of the third day there were peals of
thunder and lightning, and a heavy cloud over the
mountain, and a very loud trumpet blast, so that all the
people in the camp trembled. But Moses led the people
out of the camp to meet God, and they stationed themselves at the foot of the mountain. Mount Sinai was all
wrapped in smoke, for the LORD came down upon it in
fire. The smoke rose from it as though from a furnace,
and the whole mountain trembled violently. The trumpet blast grew louder and louder, while Moses was
speaking and God answering him with thunder.

When the LORD came down to the top of Mount
Sinai, he summoned Moses to the top of the mountain.—The word of the Lord. ℟. **Thanks be to God.** ↓

OR

C Ez 37:1-14   [Life-Giving Spirit]

In a vision, the prophet sees God's power—the band of the living and the dead, as he describes the resurrection of the dead.

A reading from the Book of the Prophet Ezekiel

THE hand of the LORD came upon me, and he led me
out in the spirit of the LORD and set me in the center
of the plain, which was now filled with bones. He made
me walk among the bones in every direction so that I
saw how many they were on the surface of the plain.
How dry they were! He asked me: Son of man, can these
bones come to life? I answered, "Lord GOD, you alone
know that." Then he said to me: Prophesy over these
bones, and say to them: Dry bones, hear the word of the
LORD! Thus says the Lord GOD to these bones: See! I will
bring spirit into you, that you may come to life. I will put
sinews upon you, make flesh grow over you, cover you
with skin, and put spirit in you so that you may come to

life and know that I am the LORD. I, Ezekiel, prophesied as I had been told, and even as I was prophesying I heard a noise; it was a rattling as the bones came together, bone joining bone. I saw the sinews and the flesh come upon them, and the skin cover them, but there was no spirit in them. Then the LORD said to me: Prophesy to the spirit, prophesy, son of man, and say to the spirit: Thus says the Lord GOD: From the four winds come, O spirit, and breathe into these slain that they may come to life. I prophesied as he told me, and the spirit came into them; they came alive and stood upright, a vast army. Then he said to me: Son of man, these bones are the whole house of Israel. They have been saying, "Our bones are dried up, our hope is lost, and we are cut off." Therefore, prophesy and say to them: Thus says the Lord GOD: O my people, I will open your graves and have you rise from them, and bring you back to the land of Israel. Then you shall know that I am the LORD, when I open your graves and have you rise from them, O my people! I will put my spirit in you that you may live, and I will settle you upon your land; thus you shall know that I am the LORD. I have promised, and I will do it, says the LORD.—The word of the Lord. ℟. **Thanks be to God.** ↓

OR

D Jl 3:1-5   [Signs of the Spirit]

At the end of time, the Day of the Lord, Judgment Day, those who persevere in faith will be saved.

A reading from the Book of the Prophet Joel

THUS says the LORD:
    I will pour out my spirit upon all flesh.
Your sons and daughters shall prophesy,
    your old men shall dream dreams,
    your young men shall see visions;
even upon the servants and the handmaids,
    in those days, I will pour out my spirit.

And I will work wonders in the heavens and on the
    earth,
    blood, fire, and columns of smoke;
the sun will be turned to darkness,
    and the moon to blood,
at the coming of the day of the LORD,
    the great and terrible day.
Then everyone shall be rescued
    who calls on the name of the LORD;
for on Mount Zion there shall be a remnant,
    as the LORD has said,
and in Jerusalem survivors
    whom the LORD shall call.
The word of the Lord. ℟. **Thanks be to God.** ↓

RESPONSORIAL PSALM Ps 104   **[Send Out Your Spirit]**

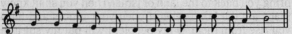

℟.   Lord, send out your Spir - it,   and re-new the face of the earth.

Or: ℟. **Alleluia.**

Bless the LORD, O my soul!
    O LORD, my God, you are great indeed!
You are clothed with majesty and glory,
    robed in light as with a cloak.—℟.

How manifold are your works, O LORD!
    In wisdom you have wrought them all—
the earth is full of your creatures;
    bless the LORD, O my soul! Alleluia.—℟.

Creatures all look to you
    to give them food in due time.
When you give it to them, they gather it;
    when you open your hand, they are filled with good
        things.—℟.

If you take away their breath, they perish
    and return to their dust.

When you send forth your spirit, they are created,
  and you renew the face of the earth.—℟. ↓

SECOND READING Rom 8:22-27   [The Spirit Our Helper]
  Be patient and have hope. The Spirit intercedes for us.

A reading from the Letter of Saint Paul to the Romans

BROTHERS and sisters: We know that all creation is groaning in labor pains even until now; and not only that, but we ourselves, who have the firstfruits of the Spirit, we also groan within ourselves as we wait for adoption, the redemption of our bodies. For in hope we were saved. Now hope that sees is not hope. For who hopes for what one sees? But if we hope for what we do not see, we wait with endurance.

In the same way, the Spirit too comes to the aid of our weakness; for we do not know how to pray as we ought, but the Spirit himself intercedes with inexpressible groanings. And the one who searches hearts knows what is the intention of the Spirit, because he intercedes for the holy ones according to God's will.— The word of the Lord. ℟. **Thanks be to God.** ↓

ALLELUIA   [Fire of the Spirit's Love]
℟. **Alleluia, alleluia.**
Come, Holy Spirit, fill the hearts of your faithful
and kindle in them the fire of your love.
℟. **Alleluia, alleluia.** ↓

GOSPEL Jn 7:37-39   [Prediction of the Spirit]
  The Spirit is the source of life for those who have faith and believe.

℣. The Lord be with you. ℟. **And with your spirit.**
✠ A reading from the holy Gospel according to John.
℟. **Glory to you, O Lord.**

O N the last and greatest day of the feast, Jesus stood up and exclaimed, "Let anyone who thirsts come to me and drink. As Scripture says:

Rivers of living water will flow from within him
    who believes in me."

He said this in reference to the Spirit that those who came to believe in him were to receive. There was, of course, no Spirit yet, because Jesus had not yet been glorified.—The Gospel of the Lord. ℟. **Praise to you, Lord Jesus Christ.**   → No. 15, p. 18

PRAYER OVER THE OFFERINGS [Manifestation of Salvation]
Pour out upon these gifts the blessing of your Spirit, we pray, O Lord,
so that through them your Church may be imbued with such love
that the truth of your saving mystery
may shine forth for the whole world.
Through Christ our Lord.
℟. **Amen.**   → Pref. P 28, p. 451

When the Roman Canon is used, the proper form of the Communicantes *(In communion with those) is said.*

COMMUNION ANT. Jn 7:37   [Thirst for the Spirit]
On the last day of the festival, Jesus stood and cried out: If anyone is thirsty, let him come to me and drink, alleluia. ↓

PRAYER AFTER COMMUNION   [Aflame with the Spirit]
May these gifts we have consumed
benefit us, O Lord,
that we may always be aflame with the same Spirit,
whom you wondrously poured out on your Apostles.
Through Christ our Lord.
℟. **Amen.**   → No. 30, p. 77

Optional Solemn Blessings, p. 97, and Prayers over the People, p. 105

(At the end of the Dismissal the people respond: "**Thanks be to God, alleluia, alleluia.**"*)*

AT THE VIGIL MASS (June 7) (Extended Form)

ENTRANCE ANT. Rom 5:5; cf. 8:11   [Love-Imparting Spirit]
**The love of God has been poured into our hearts
through the Spirit of God dwelling within us, alleluia.**

➜ No. 2, p. 10

Grant, we pray, almighty God,
that the splendor of your glory
may shine forth upon us
and that, by the bright rays of the Holy Spirit,
the light of your light may confirm the hearts
of those born again by your grace.
Through our Lord Jesus Christ, your Son,
who lives and reigns with you in the unity of the Holy
    Spirit,
God, for ever and ever. ℟. **Amen.** ↓

*Then the Priest may address the people in these or similar
words:*

Dear brethren (brothers and sisters), [God's Great Deeds]
we have now begun our Pentecost Vigil,
after the example of the Apostles and disciples,
who with Mary, the Mother of Jesus, persevered in
    prayer,
awaiting the Spirit promised by the Lord;
like them, let us, too, listen with quiet hearts to the
    Word of God.
Let us meditate on how many great deeds
God in times past did for his people
and let us pray that the Holy Spirit,
whom the Father sent as the first fruits for those who
    believe,
may bring to perfection his work in the world.

FIRST READING

See p. 430, A. ↓

RESPONSORIAL PSALM Ps 33   [God's People]

℟. **Blessed the people the Lord has chosen to be his own.**

The LORD brings to nought the plans of nations;
  he foils the designs of peoples.
But the plan of the LORD stands forever;
  the design of his heart, through all generations.—℟.

Blessed the nation whose God is the LORD,
  the people he has chosen for his own inheritance.
From heaven the LORD looks down;
  he sees all mankind.—℟.

From his fixed throne he beholds
  all who dwell on the earth,
He who fashioned the heart of each,
  he who knows all their works.—℟. ↓

All rise.

PRAYER   [Church Formed as One]
Let us pray.

Grant, we pray, almighty God,
that your Church may always remain that holy people,
formed as one by the unity of Father, Son and Holy
  Spirit,
which manifests to the world
the Sacrament of your holiness and unity
and leads it to the perfection of your charity.
Through Christ our Lord.
℟. **Amen.** ↓

SECOND READING

See p. 431, B. ↓

RESPONSORIAL PSALM Dn 3   [Praiseworthy and Exalted]

℟. **Glory and praise for ever!**

"Blessed are you, O Lord, the God of our fathers,
  praiseworthy and exalted above all forever;

And blessed is your holy and glorious name,
   praiseworthy and exalted above all for all ages."—℟.

"Blessed are you in the temple of your holy glory,
   praiseworthy and glorious above all forever."—℟.

"Blessed are you on the throne of your Kingdom,
   praiseworthy and exalted above all forever."—℟.

"Blessed are you who look into the depths
   from your throne upon the cherubim,
   praiseworthy and exalted above all forever."—℟.

"Blessed are you in the firmament of heaven,
   praiseworthy and glorious forever."—℟. ↓

OR

Ps 19   [The Lord's Words]

℟. **Lord, you have the words of everlasting life.**

The law of the Lord is perfect,
   refreshing the soul;
The decree of the Lord is trustworthy,
   giving wisdom to the simple.—℟.

The precepts of the Lord are right,
   rejoicing the heart;
The command of the Lord is clear,
   enlightening the eye.—℟.

The fear of the Lord is pure,
   enduring forever;
The ordinances of the Lord are true,
   all of them just.—℟.

They are more precious than gold,
   than a heap of purest gold;
Sweeter also than syrup
   or honey from the comb.—℟.

All rise.

PRAYER [Fire of the Spirit]

Let us pray.

O God, who in fire and lightning
gave the ancient Law to Moses on Mount Sinai
and on this day manifested the new covenant
in the fire of the Spirit,
grant, we pray,
that we may always be aflame with that same Spirit
whom you wondrously poured out on your Apostles,
and that the new Israel,
gathered from every people,
may receive with rejoicing
the eternal commandment of your love.
Through Christ our Lord.
℟. **Amen.** ↓

THIRD READING

See p. 432, C. ↓

RESPONSORIAL PSALM Ps 107 [God's Love]

℟. **Give thanks to the Lord; his love is everlasting.**

Or: ℟. **Alleluia.**

Let the redeemed of the Lord say,
  those whom he has redeemed from the hand of the
    foe
And gathered from the lands,
  from the east and the west, from the north and the
    south.—℟.

They went astray in the desert wilderness;
  the way to an inhabited city they did not find.
Hungry and thirsty,
  their life was wasting away within them.—℟.

They cried to the Lord in their distress;
  from their straits he rescued them.
And he led them by a direct way
  to reach an inhabited city.—℟.

Let them give thanks to the LORD for his mercy
  and his wondrous deeds to the children of men,
Because he satisfied the longing soul
  and filled the hungry soul with good things.—R̸.

All rise.

PRAYER   [God Restores]
Let us pray.

Lord, God of power,
who restore what has fallen
and preserve what you have restored,
increase, we pray, the peoples
to be renewed by the sanctification of your name,
that all who are washed clean by holy Baptism
may always be directed by your prompting.
Through Christ our Lord.
R̸. **Amen.** ↓

OR

O God, who have brought us to rebirth by the word of
  life,
pour out upon us your Holy Spirit,
that, walking in oneness of faith,
we may attain in our flesh
the incorruptible glory of the resurrection.
Through Christ our Lord.
R̸. **Amen.** ↓

OR

May your people exult for ever, O God,
in renewed youthfulness of spirit,
so that, rejoicing now in the restored glory of our
  adoption,
we may look forward in confident hope
to the rejoicing of the day of resurrection.
Through Christ our Lord.
R̸. **Amen.** ↓

FOURTH READING

See p. 433, D. ↓

RESPONSORIAL PSALM Ps 104   [Send Out Your Spirit]

See p. 434. ↓

All rise.

PRAYER   [Witnesses]

Let us pray.

Fulfill for us your gracious promise,
O Lord, we pray, so that by his coming
the Holy Spirit may make us witnesses before the
    world
to the Gospel of our Lord Jesus Christ.
Who lives and reigns for ever and ever.
℟. **Amen.** ↓

Then the Priest intones the hymn Gloria in excelsis Deo *(Glory
to God in the highest).*

COLLECT   [Heavenly Grace]

Almighty ever-living God,
who willed the Paschal Mystery
to be encompassed as a sign in fifty days,
grant that from out of the scattered nations
the confusion of many tongues
may be gathered by heavenly grace
into one great confession of your name.
Through our Lord Jesus Christ, your Son,
who lives and reigns with you in the unity of the Holy
    Spirit,
God, for ever and ever. ℟. **Amen.** ↓

EPISTLE

See p. 435, Second Reading.

The Mass continues as in the Simple Form (pp. 435-436).

———————

AT THE MASS DURING THE DAY

ENTRANCE ANT. Wis 1:7 ·   [The Spirit in the World]

The Spirit of the Lord has filled the whole world and that which contains all things understands what is said, alleluia.   → No. 2, p. 10

OR Rom 5:5; cf. 8:11   [God's Love for Us]

The love of God has been poured into our hearts through the Spirit of God dwelling within us, alleluia.   → No. 2, p. 10

COLLECT   [Gifts of the Spirit]

O God, who by the mystery of today's great feast
sanctify your whole Church in every people and
    nation,
pour out, we pray, the gifts of the Holy Spirit
across the face of the earth
and, with the divine grace that was at work
when the Gospel was first proclaimed,
fill now once more the hearts of believers.
Through our Lord Jesus Christ, your Son,
who lives and reigns with you in the unity of the Holy
    Spirit,
God, for ever and ever. ℟. **Amen.** ↓

FIRST READING Acts 2:1-11   [Coming of the Spirit]

On this day the Holy Spirit in fiery tongues descended upon the Apostles and the Mother of Jesus. Today the law of grace and purification from sin was announced. Three thousand were baptized.

A reading from the Acts of the Apostles

W HEN the time for Pentecost was fulfilled, they were all in one place together. And suddenly there came from the sky a noise like a strong driving wind, and it filled the entire house in which they were. Then there appeared to them tongues as of fire, which parted and

came to rest on each of them. And they were all filled
with the Holy Spirit and began to speak in different
tongues, as the Spirit enabled them to proclaim.

Now there were devout Jews from every nation under
heaven staying in Jerusalem. At this sound, they gathered
in a large crowd, but they were confused because each
one heard them speaking in his own language. They were
astounded, and in amazement they asked, "Are not all
these people who are speaking Galileans? Then how does
each of us hear them in his native language? We are
Parthians, Medes, and Elamites, inhabitants of Mes-
opotamia, Judea and Cappadocia, Pontus and Asia,
Phrygia and Pamphylia, Egypt, and the districts of Libya
near Cyrene, as well as travelers from Rome, both Jews
and converts to Judaism, Cretans and Arabs, yet we hear
them speaking in our own tongues of the mighty acts of
God."—The word of the Lord. ℟. **Thanks be to God.** ↓

RESPONSORIAL PSALM Ps 104   [Renewal by the Spirit]

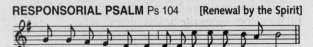

℟. Lord, send out your Spir - it, and re-new the face of the earth.

Or: ℟. Alleluia.

Bless the LORD, O my soul!
  O LORD, my God, you are great indeed!
How manifold are your works, O LORD!
  the earth is full of your creatures.

℟. **Lord, send out your Spirit, and renew the face of
  the earth.**

Or: ℟. **Alleluia.**

May the glory of the LORD endure forever;
  may the LORD be glad in his works!
Pleasing to him be my theme;
  I will be glad in the LORD.

R̂. **Lord, send out your Spirit, and renew the face of the earth.**

Or: R̂. **Alleluia.**

If you take away their breath, they perish
   and return to their dust.
When you send forth your spirit, they are created,
   and you renew the face of the earth.

R̂. **Lord, send out your Spirit, and renew the face of the earth.** ↓

Or: R̂. **Alleluia.** ↓

SECOND READING 1 Cor 12:3b-7, 12-13 [Grace of the Spirit]

No one can confess the divinity and sovereignty of Jesus
unless inspired by the Holy Spirit. Different gifts and min-
istries are given but all for the one body with Jesus.

A reading from the first Letter of Saint Paul
to the Corinthians

BROTHERS and sisters: No one can say: "Jesus is
Lord," except by the Holy Spirit.

There are different kinds of spiritual gifts but the same
Spirit; there are different forms of service but the same
Lord; there are different workings but the same God who
produces all of them in everyone. To each individual the
manifestation of the Spirit is given for some benefit.

As a body is one though it has many parts, and all the
parts of the body, though many, are one body, so also
Christ. For in one Spirit we were all baptized into one
body, whether Jews or Greeks, slaves or free persons, and
we are all given to drink of one Spirit.—The word of the
Lord. R̂. **Thanks be to God.** ↓

OR

SECOND READING Rom 8:8-17   [Living with Christ]

The Spirit places us in a filial relationship with God, enabling
us to invoke him, as Jesus did, with the name of Father.

A reading from the Letter of Saint Paul to the Romans

BROTHERS and sisters: Those who are in the flesh cannot please God. But you are not in the flesh; on the contrary, you are in the spirit, if only the Spirit of God dwells in you. Whoever does not have the Spirit of Christ does not belong to him. But if Christ is in you, although the body is dead because of sin, the spirit is alive because of righteousness. If the Spirit of the one who raised Jesus from the dead dwells in you, the one who raised Christ from the dead will give life to your mortal bodies also, through his Spirit that dwells in you. Consequently, brothers and sisters, we are not debtors to the flesh, to live according to the flesh. For if you live according to the flesh, you will die, but if by the Spirit you put to death the deeds of the body, you will live.

For those who are led by the Spirit of God are sons of God. For you did not receive a spirit of slavery to fall back into fear, but you received a Spirit of adoption, through whom we cry, "Abba, Father!" The Spirit himself bears witness with our spirit that we are children of God, and if children, then heirs, heirs of God and joint heirs with Christ, if only we suffer with him so that we may also be glorified with him.—The word of the Lord. ℟. **Thanks be to God.** ↓

SEQUENCE *(Veni, Sancte Spiritus)*   [Come, Holy Spirit]

Come, Holy Spirit, come!
And from your celestial home
    Shed a ray of light divine!
Come, Father of the poor!
Come, source of all our store!
    Come, within our bosoms shine!
You, of comforters the best;
You, the soul's most welcome guest;
    Sweet refreshment here below;

In our labor, rest most sweet;
Grateful coolness in the heat;
  Solace in the midst of woe.
O most blessed Light divine,
Shine within these hearts of yours,
  And our inmost being fill!
Where you are not, we have naught,
Nothing good in deed or thought,
  Nothing free from taint of ill.
Heal our wounds, our strength renew;
On our dryness pour your dew;
  Wash the stains of guilt away:
Bend the stubborn heart and will;
Melt the frozen, warm the chill;
  Guide the steps that go astray.
On the faithful, who adore
And confess you, evermore
  In your sevenfold gift descend;
Give them virtue's sure reward;
Give them your salvation, Lord;
  Give them joys that never end. Amen.
  Alleluia. ↓

ALLELUIA   [Fire of God's Love]

℟. Alleluia, alleluia.
Come, Holy Spirit, fill the hearts of your faithful
and kindle in them the fire of your love.
℟. Alleluia, alleluia. ↓

GOSPEL Jn 20:19-23   [Christ Imparts the Spirit]

Jesus breathes on the disciples to indicate the conferring
of the Holy Spirit. Here we see the origin of power over
sin, the Sacrament of Penance. This shows the power of
the Holy Spirit in the hearts of human beings.

℣. The Lord be with you. ℟. **And with your spirit.**
✛ A reading from the holy Gospel according to John.
℟. **Glory to you, O Lord.**

O N the evening of that first day of the week, when the doors were locked, where the disciples were, for fear of the Jews, Jesus came and stood in their midst and said to them, "Peace be with you." When he had said this, he showed them his hands and his side. The disciples rejoiced when they saw the Lord. Jesus said to them again, "Peace be with you. As the Father has sent me, so I send you." And when he had said this, he breathed on them and said to them, "Receive the Holy Spirit. Whose sins you forgive are forgiven them, and whose sins you retain are retained."—The Gospel of the Lord. ℟. **Praise to you, Lord Jesus Christ.**   ↠ No. 15, p. 18

OR

GOSPEL Jn 14:15-16, 23b-26   **[Fruits of the Spirit]**

Jesus tells his disciples that the Holy Spirit, the Spirit of truth, will reveal everything to them. The Holy Spirit will be their new Advocate.

℣. The Lord be with you. ℟. **And with your spirit.**
✛ A reading from the holy Gospel according to John.
℟. **Glory to you, O Lord.**

J ESUS said to his disciples: "If you love me, you will keep my commandments. And I will ask the Father, and he will give you another Advocate to be with you always.

"Whoever loves me will keep my word, and my Father will love him, and we will come to him and make our dwelling with him. Those who do not love me do not keep my words; yet the word you hear is not mine but that of the Father who sent me.

"I have told you this while I am with you. The
Advocate, the Holy Spirit whom the Father will send in
my name, will teach you everything and remind you of
all that I told you."—The Gospel of the Lord. ℟. **Praise
to you, Lord Jesus Christ.**   → No. 15, p. 18

PRAYER OVER THE OFFERINGS   [All Truth]

Grant, we pray, O Lord,
that, as promised by your Son,
the Holy Spirit may reveal to us more abundantly
the hidden mystery of this sacrifice
and graciously lead us into all truth.
Through Christ our Lord. ℟. **Amen.** ↓

PREFACE (P 28)   [Coming of the Spirit]

℣. The Lord be with you. ℟. **And with your spirit.**
℣. Lift up your hearts. ℟. **We lift them up to the Lord.**
℣. Let us give thanks to the Lord our God. ℟. **It is right
and just.**

It is truly right and just, our duty and our salvation,
always and everywhere to give you thanks,
Lord, holy Father, almighty and eternal God.

For, bringing your Paschal Mystery to completion,
you bestowed the Holy Spirit today
on those you made your adopted children
by uniting them to your Only Begotten Son.
This same Spirit, as the Church came to birth,
opened to all peoples the knowledge of God
and brought together the many languages of the earth
in profession of the one faith.

Therefore, overcome with paschal joy,
every land, every people exults in your praise
and even the heavenly Powers, with the angelic hosts,
sing together the unending hymn of your glory,
as they acclaim: → No. 23, p. 23

When the Roman Canon is used, the proper form of the Communicantes *(*In communion with those*) is said.*

COMMUNION ANT. Acts 2:4, 11   [Filled with the Spirit]

They were all filled with the Holy Spirit and spoke of the marvels of God, alleluia. ↓

PRAYER AFTER COMMUNION   [Safeguard Grace]

O God, who bestow heavenly gifts upon your Church,
safeguard, we pray, the grace you have given,
that the gift of the Holy Spirit poured out upon her
may retain all its force
and that this spiritual food
may gain her abundance of eternal redemption.
Through Christ our Lord.
℟. **Amen.**   → No. 30, p. 77

Optional Solemn Blessings, p. 97, and Prayers over the People, p. 105

(At the end of the Dismissal the people respond: **"Thanks be to God, alleluia, alleluia."***)*

"Glory to the Father, the Son, and the Holy Spirit."

JUNE 15

THE MOST HOLY TRINITY

Solemnity

ENTRANCE ANT. [Blessed Trinity]

Blest be God the Father, and the Only Begotten Son of God, and also the Holy Spirit, for he has shown us his merciful love. → No. 2, p. 10

COLLECT [Witnessing to the Trinity]

God our Father, who by sending into the world
the Word of truth and the Spirit of sanctification
made known to the human race your wondrous
   mystery,
grant us, we pray, that in professing the true faith,
we may acknowledge the Trinity of eternal glory
and adore your Unity, powerful in majesty.
Through our Lord Jesus Christ, your Son,
who lives and reigns with you in the unity of the Holy
   Spirit,
God, for ever and ever.
℞. **Amen.** ↓

FIRST READING Prv 8:22-31   [God's Wisdom]

In a messianic application, the "Wisdom of God" who speaks in this reading foreshadowed the revelation of the Second Person of the Trinity.

A reading from the Book of Proverbs

THUS says the wisdom of God:
"The LORD possessed me, the beginning of his ways,
  the forerunner of his prodigies of long ago;
from of old I was poured forth,
  at the first, before the earth.
When there were no depths I was brought forth,
  when there were no fountains or springs of water;
before the mountains were settled into place,
  before the hills, I was brought forth;
while as yet the earth and fields were not made,
  nor the first clods of the world.

"When the Lord established the heavens I was there,
    when he marked out the vault over the face of the
      deep;
when he made firm the skies above,
    when he fixed fast the foundations of the earth;
when he set for the sea its limit,
    so that the waters should not transgress his
      command;
then was I beside him as his craftsman,
    and I was his delight day by day,
playing before him all the while,
    playing on the surface of his earth;
    and I found delight in the human race."
The word of the Lord. ℟. **Thanks be to God.** ↓

RESPONSORIAL PSALM Ps 8   [The Power of God]

℟. O Lord, our God, how wonderful your name in all the earth!

When I behold your heavens, the work of your
    fingers,
  the moon and the stars which you set in place—
what is man that you should be mindful of him,
  or the son of man that you should care for him?

℟. **O Lord, our God, how wonderful your name in all
  the earth!**

You have made him little less than the angels,
  and crowned him with glory and honor.
You have given him rule over the works of your hands,
  putting all things under his feet:

℟. **O Lord, our God, how wonderful your name in all
  the earth!**

All sheep and oxen,
  yes, and the beasts of the field,
the birds of the air, the fishes of the sea,
  and whatever swims the paths of the seas.

℟. **O Lord, our God, how wonderful your name in all
  the earth!** ↓

SECOND READING Rom 5:1-5   [Justification by Faith]
   **Our hope, our faith, will be fulfilled because the Holy
   Spirit has been given to us.**

A reading from the Letter of Saint Paul to the Romans

B ROTHERS and sisters: Therefore, since we have
been justified by faith, we have peace with God
through our Lord Jesus Christ, through whom we have
gained access by faith to this grace in which we stand,
and we boast in hope of the glory of God. Not only
that, but we even boast of our afflictions, knowing that
affliction produces endurance, and endurance, proven
character, and proven character, hope, and hope does
not disappoint, because the love of God has been

poured out into our hearts through the Holy Spirit that
has been given to us.—The word of the Lord.
℟. **Thanks be to God.** ↓

ALLELUIA Cf. Rv 1:8   [Triune God]
℟. **Alleluia, alleluia.**
Glory to the Father, the Son, and the Holy Spirit;
to God who is, who was, and who is to come.
℟. **Alleluia, alleluia.** ↓

GOSPEL Jn 16:12-15   [The Spirit of Truth]
All that the Father has belongs to Jesus. The Spirit of truth
will guide us and announce to us the things to come. The
Apostles lived in the time of Christ, and lead us into the
era of the Spirit.

℣. The Lord be with you. ℟. **And with your spirit.**
✝ A reading from the holy Gospel according to John.
℟. **Glory to you, O Lord.**

JESUS said to his disciples: "I have much more to tell
you, but you cannot bear it now. But when he
comes, the Spirit of truth, he will guide you to all truth.
He will not speak on his own, but he will speak what
he hears, and will declare to you the things that are
coming. He will glorify me, because he will take from
what is mine and declare it to you. Everything that the
Father has is mine; for this reason I told you that he
will take from what is mine and declare it to you."—
The Gospel of the Lord. ℟. **Praise to you, Lord Jesus
Christ.**   → No. 15, p. 18

PRAYER OVER THE OFFERINGS   [Eternal Offering]
Sanctify by the invocation of your name,
we pray, O Lord our God,
this oblation of our service,
and by it make of us an eternal offering to you.

Through Christ our Lord.
℟. **Amen.** ↓

PREFACE (P 43)   [Mystery of the One Godhead]
℣. The Lord be with you. ℟. **And with your spirit.**
℣. Lift up your hearts. ℟. **We lift them up to the Lord.**
℣. Let us give thanks to the Lord our God. ℟. **It is right and just.**

It is truly right and just, our duty and our salvation,
always and everywhere to give you thanks,
Lord, holy Father, almighty and eternal God.

For with your Only Begotten Son and the Holy Spirit
you are one God, one Lord:
not in the unity of a single person,
but in a Trinity of one substance.

For what you have revealed to us of your glory
we believe equally of your Son
and of the Holy Spirit,
so that, in the confessing of the true and eternal
    Godhead,
you might be adored in what is proper to each Person,
their unity in substance,
and their equality in majesty.

For this is praised by Angels and Archangels,
Cherubim, too, and Seraphim,
who never cease to cry out each day,
as with one voice they acclaim: → No. 23, p. 23

COMMUNION ANT. Gal 4:6   [Abba, Father]
**Since you are children of God, God has sent into your
hearts the Spirit of his Son, the Spirit who cries out:
Abba, Father.** ↓

PRAYER AFTER COMMUNION   [Eternal Trinity]
May receiving this Sacrament, O Lord our God,
bring us health of body and soul,

as we confess your eternal holy Trinity and undivided
  Unity.
Through Christ our Lord.
℟. **Amen.**   → No. 30, p. 77

Optional Solemn Blessings, p. 97, and Prayers over the People, p. 105

*"[Jesus] said the blessing [over the loaves and fish],
and gave them to the disciples to set before the crowd."*

[In the Dioceses of the United States]

JUNE 22

THE MOST HOLY
BODY AND BLOOD OF CHRIST
(CORPUS CHRISTI)

Solemnity

ENTRANCE ANT. Cf. Ps 81 (80):17 [Finest Wheat and Honey]

**He fed them with the finest wheat and satisfied them
with honey from the rock.**   → No. 2, p. 10

COLLECT   [Memorial of Christ's Passion]

O God, who in this wonderful Sacrament
have left us a memorial of your Passion,

grant us, we pray,
so to revere the sacred mysteries of your Body and
    Blood
that we may always experience in ourselves
the fruits of your redemption.
Who live and reign with God the Father
in the unity of the Holy Spirit,
God, for ever and ever. ℟. **Amen.** ↓

FIRST READING Gn 14:18-20   [Blessing of Melchizedek]
> Sharing bread and wine, a foreshadowing of the Eucharistic elements, Abram is blessed and God is praised.

A reading from the Book of Genesis

IN those days, Melchizedek, king of Salem, brought
out bread and wine, and being a priest of God Most
High, he blessed Abram with these words:
    "Blessed be Abram by God Most High,
        the creator of heaven and earth;
    and blessed be God Most High,
        who delivered your foes into your hand."
Then Abram gave him a tenth of everything.—The
word of the Lord. ℟. **Thanks be to God.** ↓

RESPONSORIAL PSALM Ps 110   [Eternal Priesthood]

℟. You are a priest for ev - er, in the line   of Mel-chi-ze-dek.

The LORD said to my Lord: "Sit at my right hand
    till I make your enemies your footstool."
℟. **You are a priest for ever, in the line of Mel-
    chizedek.**
The scepter of your power the LORD will stretch forth
        from Zion:
    "Rule in the midst of your enemies."

℟. **You are a priest for ever, in the line of Mel-chizedek.**

"Yours is princely power in the day of your birth, in holy splendor;
  before the daystar, like the dew, I have begotten you."

℟. **You are a priest for ever, in the line of Mel-chizedek.**

The LORD has sworn, and he will not repent:
  "You are a priest forever, according to the order of Melchizedek."

℟. **You are a priest for ever, in the line of Mel-chizedek.** ↓

SECOND READING 1 Cor 11:23-26   [The First Eucharist]
When we eat this bread and drink this cup, we proclaim your glory, Lord Jesus, until you come again.

A reading from the first Letter of Saint Paul
to the Corinthians

BROTHERS and sisters: I received from the Lord what I also handed on to you, that the Lord Jesus, on the night he was handed over, took bread, and, after he had given thanks, broke it and said, "This is my body that is for you. Do this in remembrance of me." In the same way also the cup, after supper, saying, "This cup is the new covenant in my blood. Do this, as often as you drink it, in remembrance of me." For as often as you eat this bread and drink the cup, you proclaim the death of the Lord until he comes.—The word of the Lord. ℟. **Thanks be to God.** ↓

SEQUENCE (*Lauda Sion*)   [Praise of the Eucharist]
The Sequence Laud, O Zion (*Lauda Sion*), *or the Shorter Form beginning with the verse* Lo! the angel's food is given, *may be sung optionally before the Alleluia.*

Laud, O Zion, your salvation,
Laud with hymns of exultation,
Christ, your king and shep-
herd true:

Bring him all the praise you
know,
He is more than you bestow,
Never can you reach his due.

Special theme for glad thanks-
giving
Is the quick'ning and the living
Bread today before you set:

From his hands of old partak-
en,
As we know, by faith unshak-
en,
Where the Twelve at supper
met.

Full and clear ring out your
chanting,
Joy nor sweetest grace be
wanting,
From your heart let praises
burst:

For today the feast is holden,
When the institution olden
Of that supper was rehearsed.

Here the new law's new obla-
tion,
By the new king's revelation,
Ends the form of ancient rite:

Now the new the old effaces,
Truth away the shadow chases,
Light dispels the gloom of
night.

What he did at supper seated,
Christ ordained to be repeated,
His memorial ne'er to cease:

And his rule for guidance taking,
Bread and wine we hallow,
making
Thus our sacrifice of peace.

This the truth each Christian
learns,
Bread into his flesh he turns,
To his precious blood the
wine:

Sight has fail'd, nor thought
conceives,
But a dauntless faith believes,
Resting on a pow'r divine.

Here beneath these signs are
hidden
Priceless things to sense forbidden;
Signs, not things are all we
see:

Blood is poured and flesh is
broken,
Yet in either wondrous token
Christ entire we know to be.

Whoso of this food partakes,
Does not rend the Lord nor
breaks;
Christ is whole to all that
taste:

Thousands are, as one, re-
ceivers,
One, as thousands of be-
lievers,
Eats of him who cannot
waste.

Bad and good the feast are
sharing,

Of what divers dooms prepar-
ing,
Endless death, or endless life.

Life to these, to those damna-
tion,
See how like participation
Is with unlike issues rife.

When the sacrament is broken,
Doubt not, but believe 'tis spoken,

That each sever'd outward
token
doth the very whole contain.

Nought the precious gift di-
vides,
Breaking but the sign betides,
Jesus still the same abides,
still unbroken does remain.

The Shorter Form of the Sequence begins here.

Lo! the angel's food is given
To the pilgrim who has
striven;
See the children's bread
from heaven,
which on dogs may not be
spent.

Truth the ancient types fulfilling,
Isaac bound, a victim willing,
Paschal lamb, its life blood
spilling,
manna to the fathers sent.

Very bread, good shepherd,
tend us,

Jesu, of your love befriend us,
You refresh us, you defend
us,
Your eternal goodness send
us
In the land of life to see.

You who all things can and
know,
Who on earth such food
bestow,
Grant us with your saints,
though lowest,
Where the heav'nly feast
you show,
Fellow heirs and guests to be.
Amen. Alleluia. ↓

ALLELUIA Jn 6:51   [Living Bread]

℟. **Alleluia, alleluia.**
I am the living bread that came down from heaven,
says the Lord;
whoever eats this bread will live forever.
℟. **Alleluia, alleluia.** ↓

GOSPEL Lk 9:11b-17   [Loaves and Fishes]

Jesus feeds the people through the Apostles. It all foreshadows the Eucharist.

℣. The Lord be with you. ℟. **And with your spirit.**

✝ A reading from the holy Gospel according to Luke.

℟. **Glory to you, O Lord.**

JESUS spoke to the crowds about the kingdom of God, and he healed those who needed to be cured. As the day was drawing to a close, the Twelve approached him and said, "Dismiss the crowd so that they can go to the surrounding villages and farms and find lodging and provisions; for we are in a deserted place here." He said to them, "Give them some food yourselves." They replied, "Five loaves and two fish are all we have, unless we ourselves go and buy food for all these people." Now the men there numbered about five thousand. Then he said to his disciples, "Have them sit down in groups of about fifty." They did so and made them all sit down. Then taking the five loaves and the two fish, and looking up to heaven, he said the blessing over them, broke them, and gave them to the disciples to set before the crowd. They all ate and were satisfied. And when the leftover fragments were picked up, they filled twelve wicker baskets.—The Gospel of the Lord. ℟. **Praise to you, Lord Jesus Christ.**   ➜ No. 15, p. 18

PRAYER OVER THE OFFERINGS   [Unity and Peace]

Grant your Church, O Lord, we pray,
the gifts of unity and peace,
whose signs are to be seen in mystery
in the offerings we here present.
Through Christ our Lord.

℟. **Amen.**   ➜ No. 21, p. 22 (Pref. P 47-48)

COMMUNION ANT. Jn 6:57   [Eucharistic Life]

Whoever eats my flesh and drinks my blood remains in me and I in him, says the Lord. ↓

PRAYER AFTER COMMUNION   [Divine Life]

Grant, O Lord, we pray,
that we may delight for all eternity
in that share in your divine life,
which is foreshadowed in the present age
by our reception of your precious Body and Blood.
Who live and reign for ever and ever.
℟. **Amen.**   → No. 30, p. 77

Optional Solemn Blessings, p. 97, and Prayers over the People, p. 105

*"You are Peter, and upon this rock
I will build my church."*

JUNE 29

STS. PETER AND PAUL, APOSTLES

Solemnity

AT THE VIGIL MASS (June 28)

ENTRANCE ANT. [Role of Peter and Paul]

**Peter the Apostle, and Paul the teacher of the Gentiles,
these have taught us your law, O Lord.** → No. 2, p. 10

COLLECT [Salvation through Intercession of Apostles]

Grant, we pray, O Lord our God,
that we may be sustained
by the intercession of the blessed Apostles Peter and Paul,
that, as through them you gave your Church
the foundations of her heavenly office,
so through them you may help her to eternal salvation.
Through our Lord Jesus Christ, your Son,
who lives and reigns with you in the unity of the Holy
  Spirit,
God, for ever and ever. ℟. **Amen.** ↓

FIRST READING Acts 3:1-10   [The Power of Jesus' Name]

St. Peter cures the crippled man not in his own name, but in the name of Christ. We may see in this cure an image of ourselves. We are crippled by sin, but we are lifted up by Christ's power into human dignity and spiritual health.

A reading from the Acts of the Apostles

PETER and John were going up to the temple area for the three o'clock hour of prayer. And a man crippled from birth was carried and placed at the gate of the temple called "the Beautiful Gate" every day to beg for alms from the people who entered the temple. When he saw Peter and John about to go into the temple, he asked for alms. But Peter looked intently at him, as did John, and said, "Look at us." He paid attention to them, expecting to receive something from them. Peter said, "I have neither silver nor gold, but what I do have I give you: in the name of Jesus Christ the Nazorean, rise and walk." Then Peter took him by the right hand and raised him up, and immediately his feet and ankles grew strong. He leaped up, stood, and walked around, and went into the temple with them, walking and jumping and praising God. When all the people saw the man walking and praising God, they recognized him as the one who used to sit begging at the Beautiful Gate of the temple, and they were filled with amazement and astonishment at what had happened to him.—The word of the Lord. ℟. **Thanks be to God.** ↓

RESPONSORIAL PSALM Ps 19   [Creation Praises God]

℟. Their message goes out through all the earth.

The heavens declare the glory of God,
   and the firmament proclaims his handiwork.

Day pours out the word to day,
    and night to night imparts knowledge.

℟. **Their message goes out through all the earth.**

Not a word nor a discourse
    whose voice is not heard;
through all the earth their voice resounds,
    and to the ends of the world, their message.

℟. **Their message goes out through all the earth.** ↓

SECOND READING Gal 1:11-20   [God's Call]

St. Paul explains how he and the other apostles can claim
such authority for their teaching. The message comes from
Christ and is delivered by those whom the Lord has chosen.

A reading from the Letter of Saint Paul to the Galatians

I want you to know, brothers and sisters, that the
Gospel preached by me is not of human origin. For I
did not receive it from a human being, nor was I taught
it, but it came through a revelation of Jesus Christ.

For you heard of my former way of life in Judaism,
how I persecuted the Church of God beyond measure
and tried to destroy it, and progressed in Judaism
beyond many of my contemporaries among my race,
since I was even more a zealot for my ancestral traditions. But when God, who from my mother's womb
had set me apart and called me through his grace, was
pleased to reveal his Son to me, so that I might proclaim him to the Gentiles, I did not immediately con-
sult flesh and blood, nor did I go up to Jerusalem to
those who were apostles before me; rather, I went into
Arabia and then returned to Damascus.

Then after three years I went up to Jerusalem to
confer with Cephas and remained with him for fifteen
days. But I did not see any other of the Apostles, only
James the brother of the Lord.—As to what I am writ-
ing to you, behold, before God, I am not lying.—The
word of the Lord. ℟. **Thanks be to God.** ↓

ALLELUIA Jn 21:17 [Love for Christ]

℟. **Alleluia, alleluia.**
Lord, you know everything;
you know that I love you.
℟. **Alleluia, alleluia.** ↓

GOSPEL Jn 21:15-19 [The Primacy Bestowed on Peter]

The words of Jesus to Peter indicate the dignity bestowed on
him, but also the great responsibility. Peter must tend the
flock of Christ, even to the point of sacrificing his life. Today's
Holy Father must do the same, and deserves our prayers.

℣. The Lord be with you. ℟. **And with your spirit.**
✙ A reading from the holy Gospel according to John.
℟. **Glory to you, O Lord.**

JESUS revealed himself to his disciples and, when
they had finished breakfast, said to Simon Peter,
"Simon, son of John, do you love me more than these?"
He answered him, "Yes, Lord, you know that I love
you." Jesus said to him, "Feed my lambs." He then said
to him a second time, "Simon, son of John, do you love
me?" He answered him, "Yes, Lord, you know that I
love you." He said to him, "Tend my sheep." He said to
him the third time, "Simon, son of John, do you love me?"
Peter was distressed that Jesus had said to him a third
time, "Do you love me?" and he said to him, "Lord, you
know everything; you know that I love you." Jesus said
to him, "Feed my sheep. Amen, amen, I say to you, when
you were younger, you used to dress yourself and go
where you wanted; but when you grow old, you will
stretch out your hands, and someone else will dress you
and lead you where you do not want to go." He said this
signifying by what kind of death he would glorify God.
And when he had said this, he said to him, "Follow
me."—The Gospel of the Lord. ℟. **Praise to you, Lord
Jesus Christ.** → No. 15, p. 18

PRAYER OVER THE OFFERINGS   [Rejoice in Salvation]

We bring offerings to your altar, O Lord,
as we glory in the solemn feast
of the blessed Apostles Peter and Paul,
so that the more we doubt our own merits,
the more we may rejoice that we are to be saved
by your loving kindness.
Through Christ our Lord.
R/. **Amen.**   → Pref. P 63, p. 445

COMMUNION ANT. Cf. Jn 21:15, 17   [Peter's Love for Jesus]

**Simon, Son of John, do you love me more than these?
Lord, you know everything; you know that I love you.** ↓

PRAYER AFTER COMMUNION   [Apostles' Teaching]

By this heavenly Sacrament, O Lord, we pray,
strengthen your faithful,
whom you have enlightened with the teaching of the
    Apostles.
Through Christ our Lord.
R/. **Amen.**   → No. 30, p. 77

Optional Solemn Blessings, p. 97, and Prayers over the People, p. 105

AT THE MASS DURING THE DAY

ENTRANCE ANT.   [Friends of God]

**These are the ones who, living in the flesh, planted the
Church with their blood; they drank the chalice of the
Lord and became the friends of God.**   → No. 2, p. 10

COLLECT   [Follow Apostles' Teaching]

O God, who on the Solemnity of the Apostles Peter and
    Paul,
give us the noble and holy joy of this day,
grant, we pray, that your Church
may in all things follow the teaching

of those through whom she received
the beginnings of right religion.
Through our Lord Jesus Christ, your Son,
who lives and reigns with you in the unity of the Holy
    Spirit,
God, for ever and ever. ℟. **Amen.** ↓

FIRST READING Acts 12:1-11   [A Miraculous Escape]

The apostles are not stopped by accusations and imprisonment. They continue their witnessing to the Good News of
Jesus Christ. The Lord works with them and through them,
and often saves them from death. This text relates one such
incident.

A reading from the Acts of the Apostles

IN those days, King Herod laid hands upon some
members of the Church to harm them. He had
James, the brother of John, killed by the sword, and
when he saw that this was pleasing to the Jews he proceeded to arrest Peter also.—It was the feast of Unleavened Bread.—He had him taken into custody and
put in prison under the guard of four squads of four
soldiers each. He intended to bring him before the people after Passover. Peter thus was being kept in prison,
but prayer by the Church was fervently being made to
God on his behalf.

On the very night before Herod was to bring him to
trial, Peter, secured by double chains, was sleeping
between two soldiers, while outside the door guards kept
watch on the prison. Suddenly the angel of the Lord
stood by him and a light shone in the cell. He tapped
Peter on the side and awakened him, saying, "Get up
quickly." The chains fell from his wrists. The angel said
to him, "Put on your belt and your sandals." He did so.
Then he said to him, "Put on your cloak and follow me."
So he followed him out, not realizing that what was happening through the angel was real; he thought he was

seeing a vision. They passed the first guard, then the second, and came to the iron gate leading out to the city, which opened for them by itself. They emerged and made their way down an alley, and suddenly the angel left him. Then Peter recovered his senses and said, "Now I know for certain that the Lord sent his angel and rescued me from the hand of Herod and from all that the Jewish people had been expecting."—The word of the Lord. ℟. **Thanks be to God.** ↓

RESPONSORIAL PSALM Ps 34   [The Lord's Protection]

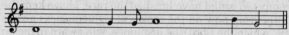

℟. The angel of the Lord will rescue those who fear him.

I will bless the LORD at all times;
  his praise shall be ever in my mouth.
Let my soul glory in the LORD;
  the lowly will hear me and be glad.

℟. **The angel of the Lord will rescue those who fear him.**

Glorify the LORD with me,
  let us together extol his name.
I sought the LORD, and he answered me
  and delivered me from all my fears.

℟. **The angel of the Lord will rescue those who fear him.**

Look to him that you may be radiant with joy,
  and your faces may not blush with shame.
When the afflicted man called out, the LORD heard,
  and from all his distress he saved him.

℟. **The angel of the Lord will rescue those who fear him.**

The angel of the LORD encamps
  around those who fear him, and delivers them.
Taste and see how good the LORD is;
  blessed the man who takes refuge in him.

℟. **The angel of the Lord will rescue those who fear him.** ↓

SECOND READING 2 Tm 4:6-8, 17-18   [A Merited Crown]

The apostles had to rely totally on God to guide them and grant faith to those who heard their preaching. Their human weakness made God's power more obvious.

A reading from the second Letter of Saint Paul to Timothy

I, PAUL, am already being poured out like a libation, and the time of my departure is at hand. I have competed well; I have finished the race; I have kept the faith. From now on the crown of righteousness awaits me, which the Lord, the just judge, will award to me on that day, and not only to me, but to all who have longed for his appearance.

The Lord stood by me and gave me strength, so that through me the proclamation might be completed and all the Gentiles might hear it. And I was rescued from the lion's mouth. The Lord will rescue me from every evil threat and will bring me safe to his heavenly Kingdom. To him be glory forever and ever. Amen.— The word of the Lord. ℟. **Thanks be to God.** ↓

ALLELUIA Mt 16:18   [The First Pope]

℟. **Alleluia, alleluia.**
You are Peter and upon this rock I will build my Church, and the gates of the netherworld shall not prevail against it.

℟. **Alleluia, alleluia.** ↓

GOSPEL Mt 16:13-19   [Peter the Rock]

To the Jews, a change of name meant a change of the very person and of that person's life. Jesus changes the name of Simon to Peter, which means "rock." He would be the human rock of firmness that would protect the word of God and would guide the whole Church.

℣. The Lord be with you. ℟. **And with your spirit.**
✠ A reading from the holy Gospel according to
Matthew. ℟. **Glory to you, O Lord.**

W HEN Jesus went into the region of Caesarea
Philippi he asked his disciples, "Who do people say
that the Son of Man is?" They replied, "Some say John the
Baptist, others Elijah, still others Jeremiah or one of the
prophets." He said to them, "But who do you say that I
am?" Simon Peter said in reply, "You are the Christ, the
Son of the living God." Jesus said to him in reply, "Blessed
are you, Simon son of Jonah. For flesh and blood has not
revealed this to you, but my heavenly Father. And so I say
to you, you are Peter, and upon this rock I will build my
Church, and the gates of the netherworld shall not prevail against it. I will give you the keys to the Kingdom of
heaven. Whatever you bind on earth shall be bound in
heaven; and whatever you loose on earth shall be loosed
in heaven." —The Gospel of the Lord. ℟. **Praise to you,
Lord Jesus Christ.**   → No. 15, p. 18

PRAYER OVER THE OFFERINGS   [United in Prayer]

May the prayer of the Apostles, O Lord,
accompany the sacrificial gift
that we present to your name for consecration,
and may their intercession make us devoted to you
in celebration of the sacrifice.
Through Christ our Lord. ℟. **Amen.** ↓

PREFACE (P 63)   [Two Great Apostles]

℣. The Lord be with you. ℟. **And with your spirit.**
℣. Lift up your hearts. ℟. **We lift them up to the Lord.**
℣. Let us give thanks to the Lord our God. ℟. **It is right
and just.**

It is truly right and just, our duty and our salvation,
always and everywhere to give you thanks,
Lord, holy Father, almighty and eternal God.

For by your providence
the blessed Apostles Peter and Paul bring us joy:
Peter, foremost in confessing the faith,
Paul, its outstanding preacher,
Peter, who established the early Church from the
    remnant of Israel,
Paul, master and teacher of the Gentiles that you call.

And so, each in a different way
gathered together the one family of Christ;
and revered together throughout the world,
they share one Martyr's crown.

And therefore, with all the Angels and Saints,
we praise you, as without end we acclaim:

→ No. 23, p. 23

COMMUNION ANT. Cf. Mt 16:16, 18   [Head of the Church]
**Peter said to Jesus: You are the Christ, the Son of the
living God. And Jesus replied: You are Peter, and upon
this rock I will build my Church.** ↓

PRAYER AFTER COMMUNION   [Renew the Church]
Grant us, O Lord,
who have been renewed by this Sacrament,
so to live in the Church,
that, persevering in the breaking of the Bread
and in the teaching of the Apostles,
we may be one heart and one soul,
made steadfast in your love.
Through Christ our Lord.
℟. **Amen.**   → No. 30, p. 77

Optional Solemn Blessings, p. 97, and Prayers over the People, p. 105

"The harvest is abundant but the laborers are few."

JULY 6

14th SUNDAY IN ORDINARY TIME

ENTRANCE ANT. Cf. Ps 48 (47):10-11 **[God's Love and Justice]**
Your merciful love, O God, we have received in the midst of your temple. Your praise, O God, like your name, reaches the ends of the earth; your right hand is filled with saving justice. → No. 2, p. 10

COLLECT [Holy Joy]
O God, who in the abasement of your Son
have raised up a fallen world,
fill your faithful with holy joy,
for on those you have rescued from slavery to sin
you bestow eternal gladness.
Through our Lord Jesus Christ, your Son,
who lives and reigns with you in the unity of the Holy
    Spirit,
God, for ever and ever. ℟. **Amen.** ↓

FIRST READING Is 66:10-14c   [God's Goodness]

We may apply this reading to the Church. The Church is Jerusalem, a loving, protecting mother, who receives the blessing of God.

A reading from the Book of the Prophet Isaiah

T HUS says the LORD:
    Rejoice with Jerusalem and be glad because of her,
        all you who love her;
exult, exult with her,
        all you who were mourning over her!
Oh, that you may suck fully
        of the milk of her comfort,
that you may nurse with delight
        at her abundant breasts!
        For thus says the LORD:
Lo, I will spread prosperity over Jerusalem like a river,
        and the wealth of the nations like an overflowing
            torrent.
As nurslings, you shall be carried in her arms,
        and fondled in her lap;
as a mother comforts her child,
        so will I comfort you;
        in Jerusalem you shall find your comfort.

When you see this, your heart shall rejoice
        and your bodies flourish like the grass;
the LORD's power shall be known to his servants.
The word of the Lord. ℟. **Thanks be to God.** ↓

RESPONSORIAL PSALM Ps 66   [Praise of God]

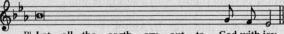

℟. Let all the earth cry out to God with joy.

Shout joyfully to God, all the earth,
   sing praise to the glory of his name;
   proclaim his glorious praise.
Say to God, "How tremendous are your deeds!"

℟. **Let all the earth cry out to God with joy.**

"Let all on earth worship and sing praise to you,
   sing praise to your name!"
Come and see the works of God,
   his tremendous deeds among the children of Adam.

℟. **Let all the earth cry out to God with joy.**

He has changed the sea into dry land;
   through the river they passed on foot;
   therefore let us rejoice in him.
He rules by his might forever.

℟. **Let all the earth cry out to God with joy.**

Hear now, all you who fear God,
   while I declare what he has done for me.
Blessed be God who refused me not
   my prayer or his kindness!

℟. **Let all the earth cry out to God with joy.** ↓

SECOND READING Gal 6:14-18   [Boasting in the Lord]
   **Through the Cross of Christ we are created anew. This is
   all that really matters.**

A reading from the Letter of Saint Paul to the Galatians

BROTHERS and sisters: May I never boast except in
the cross of our Lord Jesus Christ, through which
the world has been crucified to me, and I to the world.
For neither does circumcision mean anything, nor
does uncircumcision, but only a new creation. Peace
and mercy be to all who follow this rule and to the
Israel of God.
   From now on, let no one make troubles for me; for I
bear the marks of Jesus on my body.

The grace of our Lord Jesus Christ be with your spirit, brothers and sisters. Amen.—The word of the Lord. ℟. **Thanks be to God.** ↓

ALLELUIA Col 3:15a, 16a   [Peace of Christ]

℟. **Alleluia, alleluia.**
Let the peace of Christ control your hearts;
let the word of Christ dwell in you richly.
℟. **Alleluia, alleluia.** ↓

GOSPEL Lk 10:1-12, 17-20 or 10:1-9 [Spreading the Good News]

Even though our good works may be fruitful, we rejoice not in them but in our perseverance in grace.

[If the "Shorter Form" is used, the indented text in brackets is omitted.]

℣. The Lord be with you. ℟. **And with your spirit.**
✚ A reading from the holy Gospel according to Luke.
℟. **Glory to you, O Lord.**

AT that time the Lord appointed seventy-two others whom he sent ahead of him in pairs to every town and place he intended to visit. He said to them, "The harvest is abundant but the laborers are few; so ask the master of the harvest to send out laborers for his harvest. Go on your way; behold, I am sending you like lambs among wolves. Carry no money bag, no sack, no sandals; and greet no one along the way. Into whatever house you enter, first say, 'Peace to this household.' If a peaceful person lives there, your peace will rest on him; but if not, it will return to you. Stay in the same house and eat and drink what is offered to you, for the laborer deserves his payment. Do not move about from one house to another. Whatever town you enter and they welcome you, eat what is set before you, cure the sick in it and say to them, 'The kingdom of God is at hand for you.'

[Whatever town you enter and they do not receive you, go out into the streets and say, 'The dust of your town that clings to our feet, even that we shake off against you.' Yet know this: the kingdom of God is at hand. I tell you, it will be more tolerable for Sodom on that day than for that town."

The seventy-two returned rejoicing, and said, "Lord, even the demons are subject to us because of your name." Jesus said, "I have observed Satan fall like lightning from the sky. Behold, I have given you the power to 'tread upon serpents' and scorpions and upon the full force of the enemy and nothing will harm you. Nevertheless, do not rejoice because the spirits are subject to you, but rejoice because your names are written in heaven."]

The Gospel of the Lord. ℟. **Praise to you, Lord Jesus Christ.**   → No. 15, p. 18

PRAYER OVER THE OFFERINGS   [Purify Us]

May this oblation dedicated to your name
purify us, O Lord,
and day by day bring our conduct
closer to the life of heaven.
Through Christ our Lord.
℟. **Amen.**   → No. 21, p. 22 (Pref. P 29-36)

COMMUNION ANT. Ps 34 (33):9   [The Lord's Goodness]

Taste and see that the Lord is good; blessed the man who seeks refuge in him. ↓

OR Mt 11:28   [God Refreshes]

Come to me, all who labor and are burdened, and I will refresh you, says the Lord. ↓

PRAYER AFTER COMMUNION   [Salvation and Praise]

Grant, we pray, O Lord,
that, having been replenished by such great gifts,

we may gain the prize of salvation
and never cease to praise you.
Through Christ our Lord.
℟. **Amen.**   → No. 30, p. 77

Optional Solemn Blessings, p. 97, and Prayers over the People, p. 105

*"He approached the victim, poured oil and wine
over his wounds and bandaged them."*

JULY 13
15th SUNDAY IN ORDINARY TIME

ENTRANCE ANT. Cf. Ps 17 (16):15   [God's Face]
**As for me, in justice I shall behold your face; I shall be
filled with the vision of your glory.**   → No. 2, p. 10

COLLECT   [Right Path]
O God, who show the light of your truth
to those who go astray,
so that they may return to the right path,
give all who for the faith they profess
are accounted Christians
the grace to reject whatever is contrary to the name of
   Christ

and to strive after all that does it honor.
Through our Lord Jesus Christ, your Son,
who lives and reigns with you in the unity of the Holy
  Spirit,
God, for ever and ever. ℟. **Amen.** ↓

FIRST READING Dt 30:10-14   [Obeying the Law]

**We heed the word of the Lord by living his command-
ments. His word is not foreign to us.**

A reading from the Book of Deuteronomy

MOSES said to the people:"If only you would heed
the voice of the LORD, your God, and keep his
commandments and statutes that are written in this
book of the law, when you return to the LORD, your
God, with all your heart and all your soul.

"For this command that I enjoin on you today is not
too mysterious and remote for you. It is not up in the
sky, that you should say, 'Who will go up in the sky to
get it for us and tell us of it, that we may carry it out?'
Nor is it across the sea, that you should say, 'Who will
cross the sea to get it for us and tell us of it, that we
may carry it out?' No, it is something very near to you,
already in your mouths and in your hearts; you have
only to carry it out."—The word of the Lord. ℟. **Thanks
be to God.** ↓

RESPONSORIAL PSALM Ps 69   [The Lord's Salvation]

℟. **Turn to the Lord in your need, and you will live.**

I pray to you, O LORD,
  for the time of your favor, O God!
In your great kindness answer me
  with your constant help.
Answer me, O LORD, for bounteous is your kindness:
  in your great mercy turn toward me.

℟. **Turn to the Lord in your need, and you will live.**

I am afflicted and in pain;
  let your saving help, O God, protect me.
I will praise the name of God in song,
  and I will glorify him with thanksgiving.

℟. **Turn to the Lord in your need, and you will live.**

"See, you lowly ones, and be glad;
  you who seek God, may your hearts revive!
For the LORD hears the poor,
  and his own who are in bonds he spurns not."

℟. **Turn to the Lord in your need, and you will live.**

For God will save Zion
  and rebuild the cities of Judah.
The descendants of his servants shall inherit it,
  and those who love his name shall inhabit it.

℟. **Turn to the Lord in your need, and you will live.** ↓

OR

RESPONSORIAL PSALM Ps 19   [Word of Life]

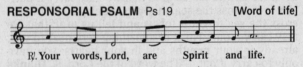

℟. Your words, Lord, are Spirit and life.

The law of the LORD is perfect,
  refreshing the soul;
the decree of the LORD is trustworthy,
  giving wisdom to the simple.

℟. **Your words, Lord, are Spirit and life.**

The precepts of the LORD are right,
  rejoicing the heart;
the command of the LORD is clear,
  enlightening the eye.

℟. **Your words, Lord, are Spirit and life.**

The fear of the LORD is pure,
  enduring forever;

the ordinances of the L<small>ORD</small> are true,
  all of them just.

℟. **Your words, Lord, are Spirit and life.**

They are more precious than gold,
  than a heap of purest gold;
sweeter also than syrup
  or honey from the comb.

℟. **Your words, Lord, are Spirit and life.** ↓

SECOND READING Col 1:15-20   [The Primacy of Christ]
  The glory of Christ is proclaimed for all to know.

A reading from the Letter of Saint Paul to the Colossians

CHRIST Jesus is the image of the invisible God,
  the firstborn of all creation.
For in him were created all things in heaven and on
    earth,
  the visible and the invisible,
    whether thrones or dominions or principalities or
      powers;
    all things were created through him and for him.
He is before all things,
  and in him all things hold together.
He is the head of the body, the church.
He is the beginning, the firstborn from the dead,
  that in all things he himself might be preeminent.
For in him all the fullness was pleased to dwell,
  and through him to reconcile all things for him,
  making peace by the blood of his cross
  through him, whether those on earth or those in
    heaven.

The word of the Lord. ℟. **Thanks be to God.** ↓

ALLELUIA Cf. Jn 6:63c, 68c   [Spirit and Life]
℟. **Alleluia, alleluia.**
Your words, Lord, are Spirit and life;

you have the words of everlasting life.

℟. **Alleluia, alleluia.** ↓

GOSPEL Lk 10:25-37   **[The Good Samaritan]**

> A man is mugged. Who cares? How do we love others as
> we love ourselves?

℣. The Lord be with you. ℟. **And with your spirit.**

✜ A reading from the holy Gospel according to Luke.

℟. **Glory to you, O Lord.**

THERE was a scholar of the law who stood up to test
Jesus and said, "Teacher, what must I do to inherit
eternal life?" Jesus said to him, "What is written in the
law? How do you read it?" He said in reply, "*You shall
love the Lord, your God, with all your heart, with all your
being, with all your strength, and with all your mind, and
your neighbor as yourself.*" He replied to him, "You have
answered correctly; do this and you will live."

But because he wished to justify himself, he said to
Jesus, "And who is my neighbor?" Jesus replied, "A man
fell victim to robbers as he went down from Jerusalem
to Jericho. They stripped and beat him and went off
leaving him half-dead. A priest happened to be going
down that road, but when he saw him, he passed by on
the opposite side. Likewise a Levite came to the place,
and when he saw him, he passed by on the opposite
side. But a Samaritan traveler who came upon him
was moved with compassion at the sight. He
approached the victim, poured oil and wine over his
wounds and bandaged them. Then he lifted him up on
his own animal, took him to an inn, and cared for him.
The next day he took out two silver coins and gave
them to the innkeeper with the instruction, 'Take care
of him. If you spend more than what I have given you,
I shall repay you on my way back.' Which of these
three, in your opinion, was neighbor to the robbers'
victim?" He answered, "The one who treated him with

mercy." Jesus said to him, "Go and do likewise."—The Gospel of the Lord. ℟. **Praise to you, Lord Jesus Christ.**   ➙ No. 15, p. 18

PRAYER OVER THE OFFERINGS   [Greater Holiness]

Look upon the offerings of the Church, O Lord,
as she makes her prayer to you,
and grant that, when consumed by those who believe,
they may bring ever greater holiness.
Through Christ our Lord.
℟. **Amen.**   ➙ No. 21, p. 22 (Pref. P 29-36)

COMMUNION ANT. Cf. Ps 84 (83):4-5   [The Lord's House]

The sparrow finds a home, and the swallow a nest for her young: by your altars, O Lord of hosts, my King and my God. Blessed are they who dwell in your house, for ever singing your praise. ↓

OR Jn 6:57   [Remain in Jesus]

Whoever eats my flesh and drinks my blood remains in me and I in him, says the Lord. ↓

PRAYER AFTER COMMUNION   [Saving Effects]

Having consumed these gifts, we pray, O Lord,
that, by our participation in this mystery,
its saving effects upon us may grow.
Through Christ our Lord.
℟. **Amen.**   ➙ No. 30, p. 77

Optional Solemn Blessings, p. 97, and Prayers over the People, p. 105

*"Mary has chosen the better part and
it will not be taken from her."*

JULY 20

16th SUNDAY IN ORDINARY TIME

ENTRANCE ANT. Ps 54 (53):6, 8   [God Our Help]

See, I have God for my help. The Lord sustains my soul.
I will sacrifice to you with willing heart, and praise your
name, O Lord, for it is good.   → No. 2, p. 10

COLLECT   [Keeping God's Commands]

Show favor, O Lord, to your servants
and mercifully increase the gifts of your grace,
that, made fervent in hope, faith and charity,
they may be ever watchful in keeping your commands.
Through our Lord Jesus Christ, your Son,
who lives and reigns with you in the unity of the Holy
    Spirit,
God, for ever and ever. ℟. **Amen.** ↓

FIRST READING Gn 18:1-10a   [Hospitality]

Abraham extends hospitality and the Lord reveals that his
promise to Abraham will be fulfilled.

A reading from the Book of Genesis

THE LORD appeared to Abraham by the terebinth of Mamre, as he sat in the entrance of his tent, while the day was growing hot. Looking up, Abraham saw three men standing nearby. When he saw them, he ran from the entrance of the tent to greet them; and bowing to the ground, he said: "Sir, if I may ask you this favor, please do not go on past your servant. Let some water be brought, that you may bathe your feet, and then rest yourselves under the tree. Now that you have come this close to your servant, let me bring you a little food, that you may refresh yourselves; and afterward you may go on your way." The men replied, "Very well, do as you have said."

Abraham hastened into the tent and told Sarah, "Quick, three measures of fine flour! Knead it and make rolls." He ran to the herd, picked out a tender, choice steer, and gave it to a servant, who quickly prepared it. Then Abraham got some curds and milk, as well as the steer that had been prepared, and set these before the three men; and he waited on them under the tree while they ate.

They asked Abraham, "Where is your wife Sarah?" He replied, "There in the tent." One of them said, "I will surely return to you about this time next year, and Sarah will then have a son."—The word of the Lord. ℟. **Thanks be to God.** ↓

RESPONSORIAL PSALM Ps 15   [The Just Man]

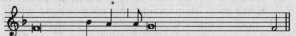

℟. He who does just - tice   will live in the presence of the Lord.

One who walks blamelessly and does justice;
    who thinks the truth in his heart
    and slanders not with his tongue.

℞. **He who does justice will live in the presence of the Lord.**

Who harms not his fellow man,
  nor takes up a reproach against his neighbor;
by whom the reprobate is despised,
  while he honors those who fear the LORD.

℞. **He who does justice will live in the presence of the Lord.**

Who lends not his money at usury
  and accepts no bribe against the innocent.
One who does these things
  shall never be disturbed.

℞. **He who does justice will live in the presence of the Lord.** ↓

SECOND READING Col 1:24-28   [The Mystery of Christ]

   The word of God in its fullness is then revealed in the mystery of Christ.

A reading from the Letter of Saint Paul to the Colossians

BROTHERS and sisters: Now I rejoice in my sufferings for your sake, and in my flesh I am filling up what is lacking in the afflictions of Christ on behalf of his body, which is the church, of which I am a minister in accordance with God's stewardship given to me to bring to completion for you the word of God, the mystery hidden from ages and from generations past. But now it has been manifested to his holy ones, to whom God chose to make known the riches of the glory of this mystery among the Gentiles; it is Christ in you, the hope for glory. It is he whom we proclaim, admonishing everyone and teaching everyone with all wisdom, that we may present everyone perfect in Christ.—The word of the Lord. ℞. **Thanks be to God.** ↓

ALLELUIA Cf. Lk 8:15   [Perseverance]

℟. **Alleluia, alleluia.**

Blessed are they who have kept the word with a
    generous heart

and yield a harvest through perseverance.

℟. **Alleluia, alleluia.** ↓

GOSPEL Lk 10:38-42   [Martha and Mary]

   Strive for a sense of proportion—maintain a balance in all
   things.

℣. The Lord be with you. ℟. **And with your spirit.**

✣ A reading from the holy Gospel according to Luke.

℟. **Glory to you, O Lord.**

JESUS entered a village where a woman whose
    name was Martha welcomed him. She had a sister
named Mary who sat beside the Lord at his feet listening to him speak. Martha, burdened with much serving, came to him and said, "Lord, do you not care that
my sister has left me by myself to do the serving? Tell
her to help me." The Lord said to her in reply, "Martha,
Martha, you are anxious and worried about many
things. There is need of only one thing. Mary has chosen the better part and it will not be taken from her."—
The Gospel of the Lord. ℟. **Praise to you, Lord Jesus
Christ.**   ➙ No. 15, p. 18

PRAYER OVER THE OFFERINGS   [Saving Offerings]

O God, who in the one perfect sacrifice
brought to completion varied offerings of the law,
accept, we pray, this sacrifice from your faithful
    servants
and make it holy, as you blessed the gifts of Abel,
so that what each has offered to the honor of your
    majesty
may benefit the salvation of all.

Through Christ our Lord.

℟. **Amen.**   ➙ No. 21, p. 22 (Pref. P 29-36)

COMMUNION ANT. Ps 111 (110):4-5   [Jesus Gives]

The Lord, the gracious, the merciful, has made a memorial of his wonders; he gives food to those who fear him. ↓

OR Rv 3:20   [Jesus Knocks]

Behold, I stand at the door and knock, says the Lord. If anyone hears my voice and opens the door to me, I will enter his house and dine with him, and he with me. ↓

PRAYER AFTER COMMUNION   [New Life]

Graciously be present to your people, we pray, O Lord, and lead those you have imbued with heavenly mysteries
to pass from former ways to newness of life.

Through Christ our Lord.

℟. **Amen.**   ➙ No. 30, p. 77

Optional Solemn Blessings, p. 97, and Prayers over the People, p. 105

"Lord, teach us to pray just as John taught his disciples."

JULY 27

17th SUNDAY IN ORDINARY TIME

ENTRANCE ANT. Cf. Ps 68 (67):6-7, 36 **[God Our Strength]**

God is in his holy place, God who unites those who
dwell in his house; he himself gives might and
strength to his people.   → No. 2, p. 10

COLLECT   **[Enduring Things]**

O God, protector of those who hope in you,
without whom nothing has firm foundation, nothing is
    holy,
bestow in abundance your mercy upon us
and grant that, with you as our ruler and guide,
we may use the good things that pass
in such a way as to hold fast even now
to those that ever endure.
Through our Lord Jesus Christ, your Son,
who lives and reigns with you in the unity of the Holy
    Spirit,
God, for ever and ever. ℟. **Amen.** ↓

FIRST READING Gn 18:20-32   **[Praying with Perseverance]**
   The Lord is just and merciful.

A reading from the Book of Genesis

IN those days, the LORD said: "The outcry against
Sodom and Gomorrah is so great, and their sin so
grave, that I must go down and see whether or not
their actions fully correspond to the cry against them
that comes to me. I mean to find out."

While Abraham's visitors walked on farther toward
Sodom, the LORD remained standing before Abraham.
Then Abraham drew nearer and said: "Will you sweep
away the innocent with the guilty? Suppose there were
fifty innocent people in the city; would you wipe out the
place, rather than spare it for the sake of the fifty innocent people within it? Far be it from you to do such a
thing, to make the innocent die with the guilty so that
the innocent and the guilty would be treated alike!
Should not the judge of all the world act with justice?"
The LORD replied, "If I find fifty innocent people in the
city of Sodom, I will spare the whole place for their
sake." Abraham spoke up again: "See how I am presuming to speak to my Lord, though I am but dust and
ashes! What if there are five less than fifty innocent
people? Will you destroy the whole city because of those
five?" He answered, "I will not destroy it, if I find forty-
five there." But Abraham persisted, saying, "What if only
forty are found there?" He replied, "I will forbear doing it
for the sake of the forty." Then Abraham said, "Let not
my Lord grow impatient if I go on. What if only thirty are
found there?" He replied, "I will forbear doing it if I can
find but thirty there." Still Abraham went on, "Since I
have thus dared to speak to my Lord, what if there are
no more than twenty?" The LORD answered, "I will not
destroy it, for the sake of the twenty." But he still persisted: "Please, let not my Lord grow angry if I speak up this
last time. What if there are at least ten there?" He replied,

"For the sake of those ten, I will not destroy it."—The word of the Lord. ℟. **Thanks be to God.** ↓

RESPONSORIAL PSALM Ps 138   [The Lord's Help]

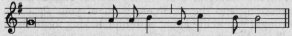

℟. Lord, on the day I called for help, you an - swered me.

I will give thanks to you, O LORD, with all my heart,
  for you have heard the words of my mouth;
  in the presence of the angels I will sing your praise;
I will worship at your holy temple
  and give thanks to your name.

℟. **Lord, on the day I called for help, you answered me.**

Because of your kindness and your truth;
  for you have made great above all things
  your name and your promise.
When I called you answered me;
  you built up strength within me.

℟. **Lord, on the day I called for help, you answered me.**

The LORD is exalted, yet the lowly he sees,
  and the proud he knows from afar.
Though I walk amid distress, you preserve me;
  against the anger of my enemies you raise your
    hand.

℟. **Lord, on the day I called for help, you answered me.**

Your right hand saves me.
  The LORD will complete what he has done for me;
your kindness, O LORD, endures forever;
  forsake not the work of your hands.

℟. **Lord, on the day I called for help, you answered me.** ↓

SECOND READING Col 2:12-14   [New Life from God]
The merciful Lord cancels our debt, pardons all our sins.
A reading from the Letter of Saint Paul
to the Colossians

BROTHERS and sisters: You were buried with him in baptism, in which you were also raised with him through faith in the power of God, who raised him from the dead. And even when you were dead in transgressions and the uncircumcision of your flesh, he brought you to life along with him, having forgiven us all our transgressions; obliterating the bond against us, with its legal claims, which was opposed to us, he also removed it from our midst, nailing it to the cross.—The word of the Lord. ℟. **Thanks be to God.** ↓

ALLELUIA Rom 8:15bc   [Children of God]

℟. **Alleluia, alleluia.**
You have received a Spirit of adoption,
through which we cry, Abba, Father.
℟. **Alleluia, alleluia.** ↓

GOSPEL Lk 11:1-13   [The Lord's Prayer]
   In the Lord's Prayer Jesus urges us to persevere in prayer
   and trust in the goodness of our loving Father.

℣. The Lord be with you. ℟. **And with your spirit.**
✛ A reading from the holy Gospel according to Luke.
℟. **Glory to you, O Lord.**

JESUS was praying in a certain place, and when he had finished, one of his disciples said to him, "Lord, teach us to pray just as John taught his disciples." He said to them, "When you pray, say:

   Father, hallowed be your name,
      your kingdom come.
      Give us each day our daily bread
      and forgive us our sins
      for we ourselves forgive everyone in debt to us,
      and do not subject us to the final test."

And he said to them, "Suppose one of you has a friend to whom he goes at midnight and says, 'Friend, lend me three loaves of bread, for a friend of mine has arrived at my house from a journey and I have nothing to offer him,' and he says in reply from within, 'Do not bother me; the door has already been locked and my children and I are already in bed. I cannot get up to give you anything.' I tell you, if he does not get up to give the visitor the loaves because of their friendship, he will get up to give him whatever he needs because of his persistence.

"And I tell you, ask and you will receive; seek and you will find; knock and the door will be opened to you. For everyone who asks, receives; and the one who seeks, finds; and to the one who knocks, the door will be opened. What father among you would hand his son a snake when he asks for a fish? Or hand him a scorpion when he asks for an egg? If you then, who are wicked, know how to give good gifts to your children, how much more will the Father in heaven give the Holy Spirit to those who ask him?"—The Gospel of the Lord. ℟. **Praise to you, Lord Jesus Christ.**   ➜ No. 15, p. 18

PRAYER OVER THE OFFERINGS   [Sanctifying Mysteries]

Accept, O Lord, we pray, the offerings
which we bring from the abundance of your gifts,
that through the powerful working of your grace
these most sacred mysteries may sanctify our present
    way of life
and lead us to eternal gladness.
Through Christ our Lord.
℟. **Amen.**   ➜ No. 21, p. 22 (Pref. P 29-36)

COMMUNION ANT. Ps 103 (102):2   [Bless the Lord]
Bless the Lord, O my soul, and never forget all his benefits. ↓

OR Mt 5:7-8   [Blessed the Clean of Heart]

**Blessed are the merciful, for they shall receive mercy.
Blessed are the clean of heart, for they shall see God.** ↓

PRAYER AFTER COMMUNION   [Memorial of Christ]

We have consumed, O Lord, this divine Sacrament,
the perpetual memorial of the Passion of your Son;
grant, we pray, that this gift,
which he himself gave us with love beyond all telling,
may profit us for salvation.
Through Christ our Lord.
℟. **Amen.**   → No. 30, p. 77

Optional Solemn Blessings, p. 97, and Prayers over the People, p. 105

*"There was a rich man whose land produced
a bountiful harvest."*

AUGUST 3

18th SUNDAY IN ORDINARY TIME

ENTRANCE ANT. Ps 70 (69):2, 6   [God's Help]

O God, come to my assistance; O Lord, make haste to
help me! You are my rescuer, my help; O Lord, do not
delay.   → No. 2, p. 10

COLLECT   [God's Unceasing Kindness]

Draw near to your servants, O Lord,
and answer their prayers with unceasing kindness,
that, for those who glory in you as their Creator and
    guide,
you may restore what you have created
and keep safe what you have restored.
Through our Lord Jesus Christ, your Son,
who lives and reigns with you in the unity of the Holy
    Spirit,
God, for ever and ever. ℟. **Amen.** ↓

FIRST READING Eccl 1:2; 2:21-23   [The Folly of Vanity]
    Without our faith all our strivings lead to nothing.

A reading from the Book of Ecclesiastes

VANITY of vanities, says Qoheleth,
    vanity of vanities! All things are vanity!
Here is one who has labored with wisdom and
knowledge and skill, and yet to another who has not
labored over it, he must leave property. This also is
vanity and a great misfortune. For what profit comes
to man from all the toil and anxiety of heart with
which he has labored under the sun? All his days sorrow and grief are his occupation; even at night his
mind is not at rest. This also is vanity.—The word of the
Lord. ℟. **Thanks be to God.** ↓

RESPONSORIAL PSALM Ps 90   [Worship the Lord]

℟. **If today you hear his voice, harden not your hearts.**

You turn man back to dust,
    saying, "Return, O children of men."
For a thousand years in your sight
    are as yesterday, now that it is past,
    or as a watch of the night.

℟. **If today you hear his voice, harden not your hearts.**

You make an end of them in their sleep;
  the next morning they are like the changing grass,
which at dawn springs up anew,
  but by evening wilts and fades.

℟. **If today you hear his voice, harden not your hearts.**

Teach us to number our days aright,
  that we may gain wisdom of heart.
Return, O LORD! How long?
  Have pity on your servants!

℟. **If today you hear his voice, harden not your hearts.**

Fill us at daybreak with your kindness,
  that we may shout for joy and gladness all our days.
And may the gracious care of the LORD our God be
    ours;
  prosper the work of our hands for us!
  Prosper the work of our hands!

℟. **If today you hear his voice, harden not your hearts.** ↓

SECOND READING Col 3:1-5, 9-11   [Christ Our Life]

A life worthy of the Lord consists of selflessness, gentleness, patience, and bearing love for one another.

A reading from the Letter of Saint Paul to the Colossians

BROTHERS and sisters: If you were raised with Christ, seek what is above, where Christ is seated at the right hand of God. Think of what is above, not of what is on earth. For you have died, and your life is hidden with Christ in God. When Christ your life appears, then you too will appear with him in glory.

Put to death, then, the parts of you that are earthly: immorality, impurity, passion, evil desire, and the greed that is idolatry. Stop lying to one another, since you have taken off the old self with its practices and have put on the new self, which is being renewed, for knowledge, in the image of its creator. Here there is not Greek and Jew, circumcision and uncircumcision, barbarian, Scythian, slave, free; but Christ is all and in all.—The word of the Lord. ℟. **Thanks be to God.** ↓

ALLELUIA Mt 5:3   [Heirs of Heaven]
℟. **Alleluia, alleluia.**
Blessed are the poor in spirit,
for theirs is the kingdom of heaven.
℟. **Alleluia, alleluia.** ↓

GOSPEL Lk 12:13-21   [True Wealth in God]
How foolish and vain are those who put all their trust in their own devices.

℣. The Lord be with you. ℟. **And with your spirit.**
✠ A reading from the holy Gospel according to Luke.
℟. **Glory to you, O Lord.**

SOMEONE in the crowd said to Jesus, "Teacher, tell my brother to share the inheritance with me." He replied to him, "Friend, who appointed me as your judge and arbitrator?" Then he said to the crowd, "Take care to guard against all greed, for though one may be rich, one's life does not consist of possessions."

Then he told them a parable. "There was a rich man whose land produced a bountiful harvest. He asked himself, 'What shall I do, for I do not have space to store my harvest?' And he said, 'This is what I shall do: I shall tear down my barns and build larger ones. There I shall store all my grain and other goods and I shall say to myself, "Now as for you, you have so many good things stored up for many years, rest, eat, drink, be merry!"' But God

said to him, 'You fool, this night your life will be demanded of you; and the things you have prepared, to whom
will they belong?' Thus will it be for all who store up
treasure for themselves but are not rich in what matters
to God."—The Gospel of the Lord. ℟. **Praise to you, Lord
Jesus Christ.**   ➔ No. 15, p. 18

PRAYER OVER THE OFFERINGS   [Spiritual Sacrifice]

Graciously sanctify these gifts, O Lord, we pray,
and, accepting the oblation of this spiritual sacrifice,
make of us an eternal offering to you.
Through Christ our Lord.
℟. **Amen.**   ➔ No. 21, p. 22 (Pref. P 29-36)

COMMUNION ANT. Wis 16:20   [Bread from Heaven]
**You have given us, O Lord, bread from heaven, endowed
with all delights and sweetness in every taste.** ↓

OR Jn 6:35   [Bread of Life]
**I am the bread of life, says the Lord; whoever comes
to me will not hunger and whoever believes in me will
not thirst.** ↓

PRAYER AFTER COMMUNION   [Heavenly Gifts]

Accompany with constant protection, O Lord,
those you renew with these heavenly gifts
and, in your never-failing care for them,
make them worthy of eternal redemption.
Through Christ our Lord.
℟. **Amen.**   ➔ No. 30, p. 77

Optional Solemn Blessings, p. 97, and Prayers over the People, p. 105

"Gird your loins and light your lamps."

AUGUST 10

19th SUNDAY IN ORDINARY TIME

ENTRANCE ANT. Cf. Ps 74 (73):20, 19, 22, 23

[Arise, O God]

Look to your covenant, O Lord, and forget not the life of your poor ones for ever. Arise, O God, and defend your cause, and forget not the cries of those who seek you.
➡ No. 2, p. 10

COLLECT [Spirit of Adoption]

Almighty ever-living God,
whom, taught by the Holy Spirit,
we dare to call our Father,
bring, we pray, to perfection in our hearts
the spirit of adoption as your sons and daughters,
that we may merit to enter into the inheritance
which you have promised.
Through our Lord Jesus Christ, your Son,
who lives and reigns with you in the unity of the Holy
   Spirit,
God, for ever and ever. ℟. **Amen.** ↓

499

FIRST READING Wis 18:6-9   [Salvation of the Just]

The first Passover is recalled, when the faithful people of
God prayed behind closed doors, and the Angel of Death
struck at the firstborn of Egypt.

A reading from the Book of Wisdom

THE night of the passover was known beforehand
to our fathers,
   that, with sure knowledge of the oaths in which
      they put their faith,
   they might have courage.
Your people awaited the salvation of the just
   and the destruction of their foes.
For when you punished our adversaries,
   in this you glorified us whom you had summoned.
For in secret the holy children of the good were
      offering sacrifice
   and putting into effect with one accord the divine
      institution.
The word of the Lord. ℟. **Thanks be to God.** ↓

RESPONSORIAL PSALM Ps 33   [Refuge in God]

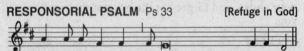

℟. Bles - sed the peo - ple   the Lord has chosen to be his own.

Exult, you just, in the LORD;
   praise from the upright is fitting.
Blessed the nation whose God is the LORD,
   the people he has chosen for his own inheritance.

℟. **Blessed the people the Lord has chosen to be his
own.**

See, the eyes of the LORD are upon those who fear him,
   upon those who hope for his kindness,
to deliver them from death
   and preserve them in spite of famine.

℟. **Blessed the people the Lord has chosen to be his own.**

Our soul waits for the LORD,
who is our help and our shield.
May your kindness, O LORD, be upon us
who have put our hope in you.

℟. **Blessed the people the Lord has chosen to be his own.** ↓

SECOND READING Heb 11:1-2, 8-19 or 11:1-2, 8-12   [Faith]

Abraham, our father in faith, relies on the confident assurance of what he hopes for. May we take courage from his example.

[If the "Shorter Form" is used, the indented text in brackets is omitted.]

A reading from the Letter to the Hebrews

BROTHERS and sisters: Faith is the realization of what is hoped for and evidence of things not seen. Because of it the ancients were well attested.

By faith Abraham obeyed when he was called to go out to a place that he was to receive as an inheritance; he went out, not knowing where he was to go. By faith he sojourned in the promised land as in a foreign country, dwelling in tents with Isaac and Jacob, heirs of the same promise; for he was looking forward to the city with foundations, whose architect and maker is God. By faith he received power to generate, even though he was past the normal age—and Sarah herself was sterile—for he thought that the one who had made the promise was trustworthy. So it was that there came forth from one man, himself as good as dead, descendants as numerous as the stars in the sky and as countless as the sands on the seashore.

[All these died in faith. They did not receive what had been promised but saw it and greeted it from afar and acknowledged themselves to be strangers and aliens on earth, for those who speak thus show that they are seeking a homeland. If they had been thinking of the land from which they had come, they would have had opportunity to return. But now they desire a better homeland, a heavenly one. Therefore, God is not ashamed to be called their God, for he has prepared a city for them.

By faith Abraham, when put to the test, offered up Isaac, and he who had received the promises was ready to offer his only son, of whom it was said, "Through Isaac descendants shall bear your name." He reasoned that God was able to raise even from the dead, and he received Isaac back as a symbol.]

The word of the Lord. ℞. **Thanks be to God.** ↓

ALLELUIA Mt 24:42a, 44   [Be Ready]

℞. **Alleluia, alleluia.**
Stay awake and be ready!
For you do not know on what day your Lord will come.
℞. **Alleluia, alleluia.** ↓

GOSPEL Lk 12:32-48 or 12:35-40   [Awaiting the Lord]

As the faithful people of God, we must act in accordance with our faith. We must be constant.

[If the "Shorter Form" is used, the indented text in brackets is omitted.]

℣. The Lord be with you. ℞. **And with your spirit.**
✙ A reading from the holy Gospel according to Luke.
℞. **Glory to you, O Lord.**

JESUS said to his disciples:
["Do not be afraid any longer, little flock, for your Father is pleased to give you the kingdom. Sell your belongings and give alms. Provide money

bags for yourselves that do not wear out, an inexhaustible treasure in heaven that no thief can reach nor moth destroy. For where your treasure is, there also will your heart be.]

"Gird your loins and light your lamps and be like servants who await their master's return from a wedding, ready to open immediately when he comes and knocks. Blessed are those servants whom the master finds vigilant on his arrival. Amen, I say to you, he will gird himself, have them recline at table, and proceed to wait on them. And should he come in the second or third watch and find them prepared in this way, blessed are those servants. Be sure of this: if the master of the house had known the hour when the thief was coming, he would not have let his house be broken into. You also must be prepared, for at an hour you do not expect, the Son of Man will come."

[Then Peter said, "Lord, is this parable meant for us or for everyone?" And the Lord replied, "Who, then, is the faithful and prudent steward whom the master will put in charge of his servants to distribute the food allowance at the proper time? Blessed is that servant whom his master on arrival finds doing so. Truly, I say to you, the master will put the servant in charge of all his property. But if that servant says to himself, 'My master is delayed in coming,' and begins to beat the menservants and the maidservants, to eat and drink and get drunk, then that servant's master will come on an unexpected day and at an unknown hour and will punish the servant severely and assign him a place with the unfaithful. That servant who knew his master's will but did not make preparations nor act in accord with his will shall be beaten severely; and the servant who was ignorant of his master's will but acted in a way deserving of a severe beating shall be beaten only lightly. Much will be required of the person entrusted with much, and still more will be demanded of the person entrusted with more."]

The Gospel of the Lord. ℟. **Praise to you, Lord Jesus Christ.**   ➜ No. 15, p. 18

PRAYER OVER THE OFFERINGS   [Mystery of Salvation]

Be pleased, O Lord, to accept the offerings of your Church,
for in your mercy you have given them to be offered
and by your power you transform them
into the mystery of our salvation.
Through Christ our Lord.
℟. **Amen.**   ➜ No. 21, p. 22 (Pref. P 29-36)

COMMUNION ANT. Ps 147 (146):12, 14   [Glorify the Lord]

O Jerusalem, glorify the Lord, who gives you your fill of finest wheat. ↓

OR Cf. Jn 6:51   [The Flesh of Jesus]

The bread that I will give, says the Lord, is my flesh for the life of the world. ↓

PRAYER AFTER COMMUNION [Confirm Us in God's Truth]

May the communion in your Sacrament
that we have consumed, save us, O Lord,
and confirm us in the light of your truth.
Through Christ our Lord.
℟. **Amen.**   ➜ No. 30, p. 77

Optional Solemn Blessings, p. 97, and Prayers over the People, p. 105

"Alleluia. Mary is taken up to heaven."

AUGUST 15

THE ASSUMPTION OF
THE BLESSED VIRGIN MARY

Solemnity

AT THE VIGIL MASS (August 14)

ENTRANCE ANT. [Mary Exalted]

Glorious things are spoken of you, O Mary, who today were exalted above the choirs of Angels into eternal triumph with Christ. → No. 2, p. 10

COLLECT [Crowned with Glory]

O God, who, looking on the lowliness of the Blessed
    Virgin Mary,
raised her to this grace,
that your Only Begotten Son was born of her
    according to the flesh
and that she was crowned this day with surpassing
    glory,
grant through her prayers,
that, saved by the mystery of your redemption,
we may merit to be exalted by you on high.

Through our Lord Jesus Christ, your Son,
who lives and reigns with you in the unity of the Holy
　Spirit,
God, for ever and ever. ℟. **Amen.** ↓

FIRST READING 1 Chr 15:3-4, 15-16; 16:1-2

[Procession of Glory]

Under David's direction the Israelites brought the ark of
the Lord to the tent prepared for it. They showed great
respect for it. They offered holocausts and peace offerings.
This becomes a figure of Mary who bore the Son of God.

A reading from the first Book of Chronicles

D AVID assembled all Israel in Jerusalem to bring the
ark of the LORD to the place which he had prepared
for it. David also called together the sons of Aaron and
the Levites.

The Levites bore the ark of God on their shoulders
with poles, as Moses had ordained according to the word
of the LORD.

David commanded the chiefs of the Levites to appoint
their kinsmen as chanters, to play on musical instruments, harps, lyres, and cymbals, to make a loud sound
of rejoicing.

They brought in the ark of God and set it within the
tent which David had pitched for it. Then they offered up
burnt offerings and peace offerings to God. When David
had finished offering up the burnt offerings and peace
offerings, he blessed the people in the name of the
LORD.—The word of the Lord. ℟. **Thanks be to God.** ↓

RESPONSORIAL PSALM Ps 132　　　[Mary, Ark of God]

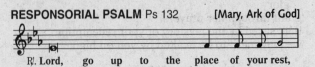

℟. Lord,　go　up　to　the　place　of　your rest,

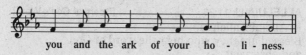

you and the ark of your ho - li - ness.

Behold, we heard of it in Ephrathah;
   we found it in the fields of Jaar.
Let us enter into his dwelling,
   let us worship at his footstool.—℟.

May your priests be clothed with justice;
   let your faithful ones shout merrily for joy.
For the sake of David your servant,
   reject not the plea of your anointed.—℟.

For the LORD has chosen Zion;
   he prefers her for his dwelling.
"Zion is my resting place forever;
   in her will I dwell, for I prefer her."—℟. ↓

SECOND READING 1 Cor 15:54b-57   [Victory over Death]
   **Paul reminds the Corinthians that in life after death there
   is victory. Through his love for us, God has given victory
   over sin and death in Jesus, his Son.**

A reading from the first Letter of Saint Paul
to the Corinthians

BROTHERS and sisters: When that which is mortal
clothes itself with immortality, then the word that
is written shall come about:
   Death is swallowed up in victory.
   Where, O death, is your victory?
   Where, O death, is your sting?
The sting of death is sin, and the power of sin is the
law. But thanks be to God who gives us the victory
through our Lord Jesus Christ.—The word of the Lord.
℟. **Thanks be to God.** ↓

ALLELUIA Lk 11:28   [Doers of God's Word]

℟. **Alleluia, alleluia.**
Blessed are they who hear the word of God
and observe it.
℟. **Alleluia, alleluia.** ↓

GOSPEL Lk 11:27-28   [Keeping God's Word]

Mary's relationship as the mother of Jesus is unique in all of
history. But Jesus reminds us that those who keep his word
are most pleasing to God. In this Mary has set an example.

℣. The Lord be with you. ℟. **And with your spirit.**
✛ A reading from the holy Gospel according to Luke.
℟. **Glory to you, O Lord.**

WHILE Jesus was speaking, a woman from the crowd
called out and said to him, "Blessed is the womb
that carried you and the breasts at which you nursed." He
replied, "Rather, blessed are those who hear the word of
God and observe it."—The Gospel of the Lord. ℟. **Praise
to you, Lord Jesus Christ.**   ➔ No. 15, p. 18

PRAYER OVER THE OFFERINGS   [Sacrifice of Praise]

Receive, we pray, O Lord,
the sacrifice of conciliation and praise,
which we celebrate on the Assumption of the holy
    Mother of God,
that it may lead us to your pardon
and confirm us in perpetual thanksgiving.
Through Christ our Lord. ℟. **Amen.**

➔ Pref. P 59, p. 513

COMMUNION ANT. Cf. Lk 11:27   [Mary Carried Christ]

**Blessed is the womb of the Virgin Mary, which bore
the Son of the eternal Father.** ↓

PRAYER AFTER COMMUNION   [Beseech God's Mercy]

Having partaken of this heavenly table,
we beseech your mercy, Lord our God,

that we, who honor the Assumption of the Mother of
    God,
may be freed from every threat of harm.
Through Christ our Lord.
R̸. **Amen.**   → No. 30, p. 77

Optional Solemn Blessings, p. 97, and Prayers over the People, p. 105

AT THE MASS DURING THE DAY

ENTRANCE ANT. Cf. Rev 12:1   [Mary's Glory]
**A great sign appeared in heaven: a woman clothed
with the sun, and the moon beneath her feet, and on
her head a crown of twelve stars.**   → No. 2, p. 10

OR   [Joy in Heaven]
**Let us all rejoice in the Lord, as we celebrate the feast
day in honor of the Virgin Mary, at whose Assumption
the Angels rejoice and praise the Son of God.**
                                                    → No. 2, p. 10

COLLECT   [Sharing Mary's Glory]
Almighty ever-living God,
who assumed the Immaculate Virgin Mary, the Mother
    of your Son,
body and soul into heavenly glory,
grant, we pray,
that, always attentive to the things that are above,
we may merit to be sharers of her glory.
Through our Lord Jesus Christ, your Son,
who lives and reigns with you in the unity of the Holy
    Spirit,
God, for ever and ever. R̸. **Amen.** ↓

FIRST READING Rv 11:19a; 12:1-6a, 10ab   [Mary, the Ark]

The appearance of the Ark in this time of retribution indicates that God is now accessible—no longer hidden, but
present in the midst of his people. Filled with hatred, the
devil spares no pains to destroy Christ and his Church. The
dragon seeks to destroy the celestial woman and her Son.
Its hatred is futile.

A reading from the Book of Revelation

G OD'S temple in heaven was opened, and the ark of
his covenant could be seen in the temple.
A great sign appeared in the sky, a woman clothed
with the sun, with the moon beneath her feet, and on
her head a crown of twelve stars. She was with child
and wailed aloud in pain as she labored to give birth.
Then another sign appeared in the sky; it was a huge
red dragon, with seven heads and ten horns, and on its
heads were seven diadems. Its tail swept away a third
of the stars in the sky and hurled them down to the
earth. Then the dragon stood before the woman about
to give birth, to devour her child when she gave birth.
She gave birth to a son, a male child, destined to rule all
the nations with an iron rod. Her child was caught up
to God and his throne. The woman herself fled into the
desert where she had a place prepared by God.
Then I heard a loud voice in heaven say:
"Now have salvation and power come,
   and the Kingdom of our God
   and the authority of his Anointed One."
The word of the Lord. ℟. **Thanks be to God.** ↓

RESPONSORIAL PSALM Ps 45   [Mary the Queen]

℟. **The queen stands at your right hand, ar-rayed in gold.**

The queen takes her place at your right hand in gold
of Ophir.—R̸.

Hear, O daughter, and see; turn your ear,
    forget your people and your father's house.—R̸.

So shall the king desire your beauty;
    for he is your lord.—R̸.

They are borne in with gladness and joy;
    they enter the palace of the king.—R̸. ↓

SECOND READING 1 Cor 15:20-27   [Christ the King]

> The offering of the firstfruits was the symbol of the dedication
> of the entire harvest to God. So the Resurrection of Christ
> involves the resurrection of all who are in him. Since his glo-
> rious Resurrection, Christ reigns in glory; he is the Lord.

A reading from the first Letter of Saint Paul
to the Corinthians

BROTHERS and sisters: Christ has been raised from
the dead, the firstfruits of those who have fallen
asleep. For since death came through man, the resurrection of the dead came also through man. For just as in
Adam all die, so too in Christ shall all be brought to life,
but each one in proper order: Christ the firstfruits; then,
at his coming, those who belong to Christ; then comes the
end, when he hands over the Kingdom to his God and
Father, when he has destroyed every sovereignty and
every authority and power. For he must reign until he has
put all his enemies under his feet. The last enemy to be
destroyed is death, for "he subjected everything under his
feet."—The word of the Lord. R̸. **Thanks be to God.** ↓

ALLELUIA   [Mary in Heaven]
R̸. **Alleluia, alleluia.**
Mary is taken up to heaven;
a chorus of angels exults.
R̸. **Alleluia, alleluia.** ↓

GOSPEL Lk 1:39-56   [Blessed among Women]

Mary visits her kinswoman, Elizabeth. Mary's song of
thanksgiving, often called the "Magnificat," has been put
together from many Old Testament phrases.

℣. The Lord be with you. ℟. **And with your spirit.**
✝ A reading from the holy Gospel according to Luke.
℟. **Glory to you, O Lord.**

MARY set out and traveled to the hill country in
haste to a town of Judah, where she entered the
house of Zechariah and greeted Elizabeth. When
Elizabeth heard Mary's greeting, the infant leaped in
her womb, and Elizabeth, filled with the Holy Spirit,
cried out in a loud voice and said, "Blessed are you
among women, and blessed is the fruit of your womb.
And how does this happen to me, that the mother of my
Lord should come to me? For at the moment the sound
of your greeting reached my ears, the infant in my
womb leaped for joy. Blessed are you who believed that
what was spoken to you by the Lord would be fulfilled."

And Mary said:
"My soul proclaims the greatness of the Lord;
     my spirit rejoices in God my Savior
     for he has looked with favor upon his lowly servant.
From this day all generations will call me blessed:
     the Almighty has done great things for me,
     and holy is his Name.
He has mercy on those who fear him
     in every generation.
He has shown the strength of his arm,
     and has scattered the proud in their conceit.
He has cast down the mighty from their thrones,
     and has lifted up the lowly.
He has filled the hungry with good things,
     and the rich he has sent away empty.

He has come to the help of his servant Israel
    for he has remembered his promise of mercy,
    the promise he made to our fathers,
    to Abraham and his children forever."

Mary remained with her about three months and
then returned to her home.—The Gospel of the Lord.
℟. **Praise to you, Lord Jesus Christ.** → No. 15, p. 18

PRAYER OVER THE OFFERINGS   **[Longing for God]**

May this oblation, our tribute of homage,
rise up to you, O Lord,
and, through the intercession of the most Blessed
    Virgin Mary,
whom you assumed into heaven,
may our hearts, aflame with the fire of love,
constantly long for you.
Through Christ our Lord.
℟. **Amen.** ↓

PREFACE (P 59)   **[Assumption—Sign of Hope]**

℣. The Lord be with you. ℟. **And with your spirit.**
℣. Lift up your hearts. ℟. **We lift them up to the Lord.**
℣. Let us give thanks to the Lord our God. ℟. **It is right
and just.**

It is truly right and just, our duty and our salvation,
always and everywhere to give you thanks,
Lord, holy Father, almighty and eternal God,
through Christ our Lord.

For today the Virgin Mother of God
was assumed into heaven
as the beginning and image
of your Church's coming to perfection
and a sign of sure hope and comfort to your pilgrim
    people;
rightly you would not allow her
to see the corruption of the tomb

since from her own body she marvelously brought forth
your incarnate Son, the Author of all life.

And so, in company with the choirs of Angels,
we praise you, and with joy we proclaim:

→ No. 23, p. 23

COMMUNION ANT. Lk 1:48-49   [Blessed Is Mary]

**All generations will call me blessed, for he who is
mighty has done great things for me.** ↓

PRAYER AFTER COMMUNION   [Mary's Intercession]

Having received the Sacrament of salvation,
we ask you to grant, O Lord,
that, through the intercession of the Blessed Virgin
  Mary,
whom you assumed into heaven,
we may be brought to the glory of the resurrection.
Through Christ our Lord.
℟. **Amen.**   → No. 30, p. 77

Optional Solemn Blessings, p. 97, and Prayers over the People, p. 105

"I have come to set the earth on fire."

AUGUST 17

20th SUNDAY IN ORDINARY TIME

ENTRANCE ANT. Ps 84 (83):10-11   [God Our Shield]
Turn your eyes, O God, our shield; and look on the face of your anointed one; one day within your courts is better than a thousand elsewhere.   ➜ No. 2, p. 10

COLLECT   [Attaining God's Promises]
O God, who have prepared for those who love you good things which no eye can see,
fill our hearts, we pray, with the warmth of your love,
so that, loving you in all things and above all things,
we may attain your promises,
which surpass every human desire.
Through our Lord Jesus Christ, your Son,
who lives and reigns with you in the unity of the Holy
   Spirit,
God, for ever and ever. ℟. **Amen.** ↓

FIRST READING Jer 38:4-6, 8-10 [Imprisonment of Jeremiah]

In a symbolic way the prophet's experience is a resurrection. He is buried in the cistern and later drawn up from it.

A reading from the Book of the Prophet Jeremiah

IN those days, the princes said to the king: "Jeremiah ought to be put to death; he is demoralizing the soldiers who are left in this city, and all the people, by speaking such things to them; he is not interested in the welfare of our people, but in their ruin." King Zedekiah answered: "He is in your power"; for the king could do nothing with them. And so they took Jeremiah and threw him into the cistern of Prince Malchiah, which was in the quarters of the guard, letting him down with ropes. There was no water in the cistern, only mud, and Jeremiah sank into the mud.

Ebed-melech, a court official, went there from the palace and said to him: "My lord king, these men have been at fault in all they have done to the prophet Jeremiah, casting him into the cistern. He will die of famine on the spot, for there is no more food in the city." Then the king ordered Ebed-melech the Cushite to take three men along with him, and draw the prophet Jeremiah out of the cistern before he should die.—The word of the Lord. ℟. **Thanks be to God.** ↓

RESPONSORIAL PSALM Ps 40   [The Lord Our Help]

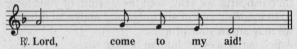

℟. Lord, come to my aid!

I have waited, waited for the LORD,
    and he stooped toward me.
℟. **Lord, come to my aid!**
The LORD heard my cry.
He drew me out of the pit of destruction,
    out of the mud of the swamp;

he set my feet upon a crag;
    he made firm my steps.

℟. **Lord, come to my aid!**

And he put a new song into my mouth,
    a hymn to our God.
Many shall look on in awe
    and trust in the LORD.

℟. **Lord, come to my aid!**

Though I am afflicted and poor,
    yet the LORD thinks of me.
You are my help and my deliverer;
    O my God, hold not back!

℟. **Lord, come to my aid!** ↓

SECOND READING Heb 12:1-4   [Perseverance]

**Take courage from the example of Christ. Do not lose sight
of the eternal reward.**

A reading from the Letter to the Hebrews

BROTHERS and sisters: Since we are surrounded by
so great a cloud of witnesses, let us rid ourselves of
every burden and sin that clings to us and persevere in
running the race that lies before us while keeping our
eyes fixed on Jesus, the leader and perfecter of faith. For
the sake of the joy that lay before him he endured the
cross, despising its shame, and has taken his seat at the
right of the throne of God. Consider how he endured
such opposition from sinners, in order that you may not
grow weary and lose heart. In your struggle against sin
you have not yet resisted to the point of shedding
blood.—The word of the Lord. ℟. **Thanks be to God.** ↓

ALLELUIA Jn 10:27   [Christ's Sheep]

℟. **Alleluia, alleluia.**

My sheep hear my voice, says the Lord;

I know them, and they follow me.
℟. **Alleluia, alleluia.** ↓

GOSPEL Lk 12:49-53   [A Divided Household]

> Many cannot find peace because they do not accept Christ.
> To them his coming is the cause of division.

℣. The Lord be with you. ℟. **And with your spirit.**
✝ A reading from the holy Gospel according to Luke.
℟. **Glory to you, O Lord.**

JESUS said to his disciples: "I have come to set the
earth on fire, and how I wish it were already blazing! There is a baptism with which I must be baptized,
and how great is my anguish until it is accomplished!
Do you think that I have come to establish peace on
the earth? No, I tell you, but rather division. From now
on a household of five will be divided, three against
two and two against three; a father will be divided
against his son and a son against his father, a mother
against her daughter and a daughter against her mother, a mother-in-law against her daughter-in-law and a
daughter-in-law against her mother-in-law."—The
Gospel of the Lord. ℟. **Praise to you, Lord Jesus
Christ.**   → No. 15, p. 18

PRAYER OVER THE OFFERINGS   [Glorious Exchange]

Receive our oblation, O Lord,
by which is brought about a glorious exchange,
that, by offering what you have given,
we may merit to receive your very self.
Through Christ our Lord.
℟. **Amen.**   → No. 21, p. 22 (Pref. P 29-36)

COMMUNION ANT. Ps 130 (129):7   [Plentiful Redemption]
**With the Lord there is mercy; in him is plentiful
redemption.** ↓

OR Jn 6:51   [Eternal Life]

**I am the living bread that came down from heaven,
says the Lord. Whoever eats of this bread will live for
ever.** ↓

PRAYER AFTER COMMUNION   [Coheirs in Heaven]

Made partakers of Christ through these Sacraments,
we humbly implore your mercy, Lord,
that, conformed to his image on earth,
we may merit also to be his coheirs in heaven.
Who lives and reigns for ever and ever.
℟. **Amen.**   → No. 30, p. 77

Optional Solemn Blessings, p. 97, and Prayers over the People, p. 105

"Strive to enter through the narrow gate."

AUGUST 24

21st SUNDAY IN ORDINARY TIME

ENTRANCE ANT. Cf. Ps 86 (85):1-3   [Save Us]

Turn your ear, O Lord, and answer me; save the servant who trusts in you, my God. Have mercy on me, O Lord, for I cry to you all the day long. → No. 2, p. 10

COLLECT   [One in Mind and Heart]

O God, who cause the minds of the faithful
to unite in a single purpose,
grant your people to love what you command
and to desire what you promise,
that, amid the uncertainties of this world,
our hearts may be fixed on that place
where true gladness is found.
Through our Lord Jesus Christ, your Son,
who lives and reigns with you in the unity of the Holy
   Spirit,
God, for ever and ever.
℟. **Amen.** ↓

FIRST READING Is 66:18-21   [Salvation Offered to All]

Salvation is offered to all and will embrace all, even the alien, some of whom will receive the sacred duty to minister the Holy Mysteries.

A reading from the Book of the Prophet Isaiah

THUS says the LORD: I know their works and their thoughts, and I come to gather nations of every language; they shall come and see my glory. I will set a sign among them; from them I will send fugitives to the nations: to Tarshish, Put and Lud, Mosoch, Tubal and Javan, to the distant coastlands that have never heard of my fame, or seen my glory; and they shall proclaim my glory among the nations. They shall bring all your brothers and sisters from all the nations as an offering to the LORD, on horses and in chariots, in carts, upon mules and dromedaries, to Jerusalem, my holy mountain, says the LORD, just as the Israelites bring their offering to the house of the LORD in clean vessels. Some of these I will take as priests and Levites, says the LORD.—The word of the Lord. ℟. **Thanks be to God.** ↓

RESPONSORIAL PSALM Ps 117   [God's Kindness]

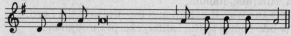

℟. Go out to all the world and tell the Good News.
Or: ℟. Alleluia.

Praise the LORD, all you nations;
    glorify him, all you peoples!
℟. **Go out to all the world and tell the Good News.**
Or: ℟. **Alleluia.**
For steadfast is his kindness toward us,
    and the fidelity of the LORD endures forever.

℟. **Go out to all the world and tell the Good News.** ↓
Or: ℟. **Alleluia.** ↓

SECOND READING Heb 12:5-7, 11-13   [Discipline]
Look beyond trials and tribulations, remain steadfast in
faith, and rely on the goodness and love of God.

A reading from the Letter to the Hebrews

BROTHERS and sisters, You have forgotten the
exhortation addressed to you as children: "My son,
do not disdain the discipline of the Lord or lose heart
when reproved by him; for whom the Lord loves, he
disciplines; he scourges every son he acknowledges."
Endure your trials as "discipline"; God treats you as
sons. For what "son" is there whom his father does not
discipline? At the time, all discipline seems a cause not
for joy but for pain, yet later it brings the peaceful fruit
of righteousness to those who are trained by it.

So strengthen your drooping hands and your weak
knees. Make straight paths for your feet, that what is
lame may not be disjointed but healed.—The word of
the Lord. ℟. **Thanks be to God.** ↓

ALLELUIA Jn 14:6   [Through Christ]
℟. **Alleluia, alleluia.**
I am the way, the truth and the life, says the Lord;
no one comes to the Father, except through me.
℟. **Alleluia, alleluia.** ↓

GOSPEL Lk 13:22-30   [Saved Through Repentance]
The kingdom of God will extend to people from all over,
and some who have rejected the Word will find themselves as outcasts.

℣. The Lord be with you. ℟. **And with your spirit.**
✚ A reading from the holy Gospel according to Luke.
℟. **Glory to you, O Lord.**

JESUS passed through towns and villages, teaching as he went and making his way to Jerusalem. Someone asked him, "Lord, will only a few people be saved?" He answered them, "Strive to enter through the narrow gate, for many, I tell you, will attempt to enter but will not be strong enough. After the master of the house has arisen and locked the door, then will you stand outside knocking and saying, 'Lord, open the door for us.' He will say to you in reply, 'I do not know where you are from.' And you will say, 'We ate and drank in your company and you taught in our streets.' Then he will say to you, 'I do not know where you are from. Depart from me, all you evildoers!' And there will be wailing and grinding of teeth when you see Abraham, Isaac, and Jacob and all the prophets in the kingdom of God and you yourselves cast out. And people will come from the east and the west and from the north and the south and will recline at table in the kingdom of God. For behold, some are last who will be first, and some are first who will be last."—The Gospel of the Lord. ℟. **Praise to you, Lord Jesus Christ.**

↪ No. 15, p. 18

PRAYER OVER THE OFFERINGS   [Unity and Peace]

O Lord, who gained for yourself a people by adoption
through the one sacrifice offered once for all,
bestow graciously on us, we pray,
the gifts of unity and peace in your Church.
Through Christ our Lord.
℟. **Amen.**   → No. 21, p. 22 (Pref. P 29-36)

COMMUNION ANT. Cf. Ps 104 (103):13-15
                                   [Sacred Bread and Wine]

The earth is replete with the fruits of your work, O Lord; you bring forth bread from the earth and wine to cheer the heart. ↓

OR Cf. Jn 6:54 [Eternal Life]

Whoever eats my flesh and drinks my blood has eternal life, says the Lord, and I will raise him up on the last day. ↓

PRAYER AFTER COMMUNION [Pleasing God]

Complete within us, O Lord, we pray,
the healing work of your mercy
and graciously perfect and sustain us,
so that in all things we may please you.
Through Christ our Lord.
℟. **Amen.** → No. 30, p. 77

Optional Solemn Blessings, p. 97, and Prayers over the People, p. 105

"Everyone who exalts himself will be humbled. . . ."

AUGUST 31

22nd SUNDAY IN ORDINARY TIME

ENTRANCE ANT. Cf. Ps 86 (85):3, 5 [Call Upon God]
Have mercy on me, O Lord, for I cry to you all the day long. O Lord, you are good and forgiving, full of mercy to all who call to you. → No. 2, p. 10

COLLECT   [God's Watchful Care]

God of might, giver of every good gift,
put into our hearts the love of your name,
so that, by deepening our sense of reverence,
you may nurture in us what is good
and, by your watchful care,
keep safe what you have nurtured.
Through our Lord Jesus Christ, your Son,
who lives and reigns with you in the unity of the Holy
    Spirit,
God, for ever and ever. ℟. **Amen.** ↓

FIRST READING Sir 3:17-18, 20, 28-29   [Humility]

Know your own limitations. Live within your own capabil-
ities.

A reading from the Book of Sirach

MY child, conduct your affairs with humility,
    and you will be loved more than a giver of gifts.
Humble yourself the more, the greater you are,
    and you will find favor with God.
What is too sublime for you, seek not,
    into things beyond your strength search not.
The mind of a sage appreciates proverbs,
    and an attentive ear is the wise man's joy.
Water quenches a flaming fire,
    and alms atone for sins.
The word of the Lord. ℟. **Thanks be to God.** ↓

RESPONSORIAL PSALM Ps 68   [Defender of the Poor]

℟. God, in your good-ness, you have made a home for the poor.

The just rejoice and exult before God;
    they are glad and rejoice.
Sing to God, chant praise to his name;
    whose name is the LORD.

℟. **God, in your goodness, you have made a home for the poor.**

The father of orphans and the defender of widows
   is God in his holy dwelling.
God gives a home to the forsaken;
   he leads forth prisoners to prosperity.

℟. **God, in your goodness, you have made a home for the poor.**

A bountiful rain you showered down, O God, upon
      your inheritance;
   you restored the land when it languished;
your flock settled in it;
   in your goodness, O God, you provided it for the
      needy.

℟. **God, in your goodness, you have made a home for the poor.** ↓

SECOND READING Heb 12:18-19, 22-24a
                         [The Heavenly Jerusalem]

We are drawn to God because of his love and his gift of
faith. We are not driven to him out of fear.

A reading from the Letter to the Hebrews

Brothers and sisters: You have not approached
that which could be touched and a blazing fire and
gloomy darkness and storm and a trumpet blast and a
voice speaking words such that those who heard
begged that no message be further addressed to them.
No, you have approached Mount Zion and the city of
the living God, the heavenly Jerusalem, and countless
angels in festal gathering, and the assembly of the
firstborn enrolled in heaven, and God the judge of all,
and the spirits of the just made perfect, and Jesus, the
mediator of a new covenant, and the sprinkled blood
that speaks more eloquently than that of Abel.—The
word of the Lord. ℟. **Thanks be to God.** ↓

ALLELUIA Mt 11:29ab   [Christ's Yoke]

℟. **Alleluia, alleluia.**
Take my yoke upon you, says the Lord,
and learn from me, for I am meek and humble of heart.
℟. **Alleluia, alleluia.** ↓

GOSPEL Lk 14:1, 7-14   [The Reward of Humility]

> Act in true humility. Do not be frustrated by trying to just
> create an "image" for yourself.

℣. The Lord be with you. ℟. **And with your spirit.**
✠ A reading from the holy Gospel according to Luke.
℟. **Glory to you, O Lord.**

O N a sabbath Jesus went to dine at the home of one
of the leading Pharisees, and the people there
were observing him carefully.
   He told a parable to those who had been invited,
noticing how they were choosing the places of honor
at the table. "When you are invited by someone to a
wedding banquet, do not recline at table in the place of
honor. A more distinguished guest than you may have
been invited by him, and the host who invited both of
you may approach you and say, 'Give your place to this
man,' and then you would proceed with embarrass-
ment to take the lowest place. Rather, when you are
invited, go and take the lowest place so that when the
host comes to you he may say, 'My friend, move up to
a higher position.' Then you will enjoy the esteem of
your companions at the table. For everyone who exalts
himself will be humbled, but the one who humbles
himself will be exalted." Then he said to the host who
invited him, "When you hold a lunch or a dinner, do not
invite your friends or your brothers or your relatives
or your wealthy neighbors, in case they may invite you
back and you have repayment. Rather, when you hold

a banquet, invite the poor, the crippled, the lame, the blind; blessed indeed will you be because of their inability to repay you. For you will be repaid at the resurrection of the righteous."—The Gospel of the Lord.
℟. **Praise to you, Lord Jesus Christ.** ➜ No. 15, p. 18

PRAYER OVER THE OFFERINGS [Blessing of Salvation]

May this sacred offering, O Lord,
confer on us always the blessing of salvation,
that what it celebrates in mystery
it may accomplish in power.
Through Christ our Lord.
℟. **Amen.** ➜ No. 21, p. 22 (Pref. P 29-36)

COMMUNION ANT. Ps 31 (30):20 [God's Goodness]

How great is the goodness, Lord, that you keep for those who fear you. ↓

OR Mt 5:9-10 [Blessed the Peacemakers]

Blessed are the peacemakers, for they shall be called children of God. Blessed are they who are persecuted for the sake of righteousness, for theirs is the Kingdom of Heaven. ↓

PRAYER AFTER COMMUNION [Serving God in Neighbor]

Renewed by this bread from the heavenly table,
we beseech you, Lord,
that, being the food of charity,
it may confirm our hearts
and stir us to serve you in our neighbor.
Through Christ our Lord.
℟. **Amen.** ➜ No. 30, p. 77

Optional Solemn Blessings, p. 97, and Prayers over the People, p. 105

"Whoever does not carry his own cross and come after me cannot be my disciple."

SEPTEMBER 7

23rd SUNDAY IN ORDINARY TIME

ENTRANCE ANT. Ps 119 (118):137, 124   [Plea for Mercy]

You are just, O Lord, and your judgment is right; treat your servant in accord with your merciful love.

➔ No. 2, p. 10

COLLECT   [Christian Freedom]

O God, by whom we are redeemed and receive adoption,
look graciously upon your beloved sons and daughters,
that those who believe in Christ
may receive true freedom
and an everlasting inheritance.
Through our Lord Jesus Christ, your Son,
who lives and reigns with you in the unity of the Holy
  Spirit,
God, for ever and ever. ℟. **Amen.** ↓

FIRST READING Wis 9:13-18b   [God's Counsel]

  Our human knowledge (science) alone cannot reach the
  heights attained by faith.

A reading from the Book of Wisdom

WHO can know God's counsel,
 or who can conceive what the LORD intends?
For the deliberations of mortals are timid,
 and unsure are our plans.
For the corruptible body burdens the soul
 and the earthen shelter weighs down the mind
  that has many concerns.
And scarce do we guess the things on earth,
 and what is within our grasp we find with difficulty;
 but when things are in heaven, who can search
  them out?
Or who ever knew your counsel, except you had
 given wisdom
and sent your holy spirit from on high?
And thus were the paths of those on earth made
 straight.
The word of the Lord. ℟. **Thanks be to God.** ↓

RESPONSORIAL PSALM Ps 90   [The Lord Our Refuge]

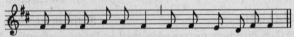

℟. In ev - ery age, O Lord, you have been our ref-uge.

You turn man back to dust,
 saying,"Return, O children of men."
For a thousand years in your sight,
 are as yesterday, now that it is past,
 or as a watch of the night.

℟. **In every age, O Lord, you have been our refuge.**

You make an end of them in their sleep;
 the next morning they are like the changing grass,
which at dawn springs up anew,
 but by evening wilts and fades.

℟. **In every age, O Lord, you have been our refuge.**

Teach us to number our days aright,
   that we may gain wisdom of heart.
Return, O LORD! How long?
   Have pity on your servants!

℟. **In every age, O Lord, you have been our refuge.**

Fill us at daybreak with your kindness,
   that we may shout for joy and gladness all our days.
And may the gracious care of the LORD our God be ours;
   prosper the work of our hands for us!
   Prosper the work of our hands!

℟. **In every age, O Lord, you have been our refuge.** ↓

SECOND READING Phlm 9-10, 12-17   [Brothers in Christ]
   Paul has converted a runaway slave, and he asks the slave's master to forgive the man.

A reading from the Letter of Saint Paul to Philemon

I, PAUL, an old man, and now also a prisoner for Christ Jesus, urge you on behalf of my child Onesimus, whose father I have become in my imprisonment; I am sending him, that is, my own heart, back to you. I should have liked to retain him for myself, so that he might serve me on your behalf in my imprisonment for the gospel, but I did not want to do anything without your consent, so that the good you do might not be forced but voluntary. Perhaps this is why he was away from you for a while, that you might have him back forever, no longer as a slave but more than a slave, a brother, beloved especially to me, but even more so to you, as a man and in the Lord. So if you regard me as a partner, welcome him as you would me.—The word of the Lord. ℟. **Thanks be to God.** ↓

ALLELUIA Ps 119:135   [Teach Us]
℟. **Alleluia, alleluia.**
Let your face shine upon your servant;

and teach me your laws.
℟. **Alleluia, alleluia.** ↓

GOSPEL Lk 14:25-33   [Following Christ]
> We are all careful to estimate the cost of worldly ventures.
> We also must be willing to sacrifice whatever is necessary
> to preserve our faith.

℣. The Lord be with you. ℟. **And with your spirit.**
✛ A reading from the holy Gospel according to Luke.
℟. **Glory to you, O Lord.**

GREAT crowds were traveling with Jesus, and he
turned and addressed them, "If anyone comes to me
without hating his father and mother, wife and children,
brothers and sisters, and even his own life, he cannot be
my disciple. Whoever does not carry his own cross and
come after me cannot be my disciple. Which of you wishing to construct a tower does not first sit down and calcu-
late the cost to see if there is enough for its completion?
Otherwise, after laying the foundation and finding himself unable to finish the work the onlookers should laugh
at him and say, 'This one began to build but did not have
the resources to finish.' Or what king marching into battle would not first sit down and decide whether with ten
thousand troops he can successfully oppose another king
advancing upon him with twenty thousand troops? But if
not, while he is still far away, he will send a delegation to
ask for peace terms. In the same way, anyone of you who
does not renounce all his possessions cannot be my disciple."—The Gospel of the Lord. ℟. **Praise to you, Lord
Jesus Christ.**   ➜ No. 15, p. 18

PRAYER OVER THE OFFERINGS [True Prayer and Peace]
O God, who give us the gift of true prayer and of peace,
graciously grant that, through this offering,
we may do fitting homage to your divine majesty
and, by partaking of the sacred mystery,

we may be faithfully united in mind and heart.
Through Christ our Lord.
℟. **Amen.**   → No. 21, p. 22 (Pref. P 29-36)

COMMUNION ANT. Cf. Ps 42 (41):2-3   [Yearning for God]
**Like the deer that yearns for running streams, so my
soul is yearning for you, my God; my soul is thirsting
for God, the living God.** ↓

OR Jn 8:12   [The Light of Life]
**I am the light of the world, says the Lord; whoever fol-
lows me will not walk in darkness, but will have the
light of life.** ↓

PRAYER AFTER COMMUNION   [Word and Sacrament]
Grant that your faithful, O Lord,
whom you nourish and endow with life
through the food of your Word and heavenly
   Sacrament,
may so benefit from your beloved Son's great gifts
that we may merit an eternal share in his life.
Who lives and reigns for ever and ever.
℟. **Amen.**   → No. 30, p. 77

Optional Solemn Blessings, p. 97, and Prayers over the People, p. 105

"God so loved the world that he gave his only Son."

SEPTEMBER 14

THE EXALTATION OF THE HOLY CROSS

Feast

ENTRANCE ANT. Cf. Gal 6:14   [Glory in the Cross]

We should glory in the Cross of our Lord Jesus Christ,
in whom is our salvation, life and resurrection, through
whom we are saved and delivered.   → No. 2, p. 10

COLLECT   [Grace of Redemption]

O God, who willed that your Only Begotten Son
should undergo the Cross to save the human race,
grant, we pray,
that we, who have known his mystery on earth,
may merit the grace of his redemption in heaven.
Through our Lord Jesus Christ, your Son,
who lives and reigns with you in the unity of the Holy
    Spirit,
God, for ever and ever. ℟. **Amen.** ↓

FIRST READING Nm 21:4b-9   [The Bronze Serpent]

    The bronze serpent raised on high is a healing force for all
    the afflicted who look upon it.

A reading from the Book of Numbers

W ITH their patience worn out by the journey, the people complained against God and Moses, "Why have you brought us up from Egypt to die in this desert, where there is no food or water? We are disgusted with this wretched food!"

In punishment the Lord sent among the people saraph serpents, which bit the people so that many of them died. Then the people came to Moses and said, "We have sinned in complaining against the Lord and you. Pray the Lord to take the serpents from us." So Moses prayed for the people, and the Lord said to Moses, "Make a saraph and mount it on a pole, and if any who have been bitten look at it, they will live." Moses accordingly made a bronze serpent and mounted it on a pole, and whenever anyone who had been bitten by a serpent looked at the bronze serpent, he lived.—The word of the Lord. ℟. **Thanks be to God.** ↓

RESPONSORIAL PSALM Ps 78   [Remember God's Works]

℟. Do not for - get   the works of   the Lord!

Hearken, my people, to my teaching;
  incline your ears to the words of my mouth.
I will open my mouth in a parable,
  I will utter mysteries from of old.

℟. **Do not forget the works of the Lord!**

While he slew them they sought him
  and inquired after God again,
Remembering that God was their rock
  and the Most High God, their redeemer.

℟. **Do not forget the works of the Lord!**

But they flattered him with their mouths
  and lied to him with their tongues,

Though their hearts were not steadfast toward him,
  nor were they faithful to his covenant.

℟. **Do not forget the works of the Lord!**

Yet he, being merciful, forgave their sin
  and destroyed them not;
Often he turned back his anger
  and let none of his wrath be roused.

℟. **Do not forget the works of the Lord!** ↓

SECOND READING Phil 2:6-11 [Christ Humbled Himself]
  **Jesus' death on the cross began his rise to exaltation:
  Jesus Christ is Lord!**

A reading from the letter of Saint Paul to the Philippians

B ROTHERS and sisters:
  Christ Jesus, though he was in the form of God,
    did not regard equality with God
      something to be grasped.
  Rather, he emptied himself,
    taking the form of a slave,
    coming in human likeness;
    and found human in appearance,
    he humbled himself,
    becoming obedient to the point of death,
      even death on a cross.
  Because of this, God greatly exalted him
    and bestowed on him the name
    which is above every name,
    that at the name of Jesus
    every knee should bend,
    of those in heaven and on earth and under the earth,
    and every tongue confess that
    Jesus Christ is Lord,
    to the glory of God the Father.
The word of the Lord. ℟. **Thanks be to God.** ↓

ALLELUIA   [Power of the Cross]

℟. **Alleluia, alleluia.**
We adore you, O Christ, and we bless you,
because by your Cross you have redeemed the world.
℟. **Alleluia, alleluia.** ↓

GOSPEL Jn 3:13-17   [Lifted Up on the Cross]

Moses' lifting up the serpent in the desert had the salutary
effect of healing. The lifting up of the Son of Man on the
cross had the saving effect of redemption.

℣. The Lord be with you. ℟. **And with your spirit.**
✝ A reading from the holy Gospel according to John.
℟. **Glory to you, O Lord.**

JESUS said to Nicodemus: "No one has gone up to
heaven except the one who has come down from
heaven, the Son of Man. And just as Moses lifted up
the serpent in the desert, so must the Son of Man be
lifted up, so that everyone who believes in him may
have eternal life."

For God so loved the world that he gave his only
Son, so that he who believes in him might not perish
but might have eternal life. For God did not send his
Son into the world to condemn the world, but that the
world might be saved through him.—The Gospel of the
Lord. ℟. **Praise to you, Lord Jesus Christ.**

→ No. 15, p. 18

PRAYER OVER THE OFFERINGS   [Forgiveness]

May this oblation, O Lord,
which on the altar of the Cross
canceled the offense of the whole world,
cleanse us, we pray, of all our sins.
Through Christ our Lord.
℟. **Amen.** ↓

PREFACE (P 46) [Saved through the Cross]

℣. The Lord be with you. ℟. **And with your spirit.**
℣. Lift up your hearts. ℟. **We lift them up to the Lord.** ℣. Let us give thanks to the Lord our God. ℟. **It is right and just.**

It is truly right and just, our duty and our salvation,
always and everywhere to give you thanks,
Lord, holy Father, almighty and eternal God.

For you placed the salvation of the human race
on the wood of the Cross,
so that, where death arose,
life might again spring forth
and the evil one, who conquered on a tree,
might likewise on a tree be conquered,
through Christ our Lord.

Through him the Angels praise your majesty,
Dominions adore and Powers tremble before you.
Heaven and the Virtues of heaven and the blessed
    Seraphim
worship together with exultation.

May our voices, we pray, join with theirs
in humble praise, as we acclaim: → No. 23, p. 23

COMMUNION ANT. Jn 12:32 [Union with Christ]

**When I am lifted up from the earth, I will draw every-
one to myself, says the Lord. ↓**

PRAYER AFTER COMMUNION [Holy Banquet]

Having been nourished by your holy banquet,
we beseech you, Lord Jesus Christ,
to bring those you have redeemed
by the wood of your life-giving Cross
to the glory of the resurrection.
Who live and reign for ever and ever.
℟. **Amen.**   → No. 30, p. 77

Optional Solemn Blessings, p. 97, and Prayers over the People, p. 105

"Prepare a full account of your stewardship. . . ."

SEPTEMBER 21

25th SUNDAY IN ORDINARY TIME

ENTRANCE ANT. [Salvation of People]
I am the salvation of the people, says the Lord. Should they cry to me in any distress, I will hear them, and I will be their Lord for ever. ➜ No. 2, p. 10

COLLECT [Attaining Eternal Life]
O God, who founded all the commands of your sacred
  Law
upon love of you and of our neighbor,
grant that, by keeping your precepts,
we may merit to attain eternal life.
Through our Lord Jesus Christ, your Son,
who lives and reigns with you in the unity of the Holy
  Spirit,
God, for ever and ever. ℟. **Amen.** ↓

FIRST READING Am 8:4-7   [The Just Are Persecuted]

The Lord will punish those who cheat and oppress the poor. There is no place for the gouger, the con artist, the greedy.

A reading from the Book of the Prophet Amos

HEAR this, you who trample upon the needy
and destroy the poor of the land!
"When will the new moon be over," you ask,
    "that we may sell our grain,
    and the sabbath, that we may display the wheat?
We will diminish the ephah,
    add to the shekel,
    and fix our scales for cheating!
We will buy the lowly for silver,
    and the poor for a pair of sandals;
    even the refuse of the wheat we will sell!"
The LORD has sworn by the pride of Jacob:
    Never will I forget a thing they have done!
The word of the Lord. ℟. **Thanks be to God.** ↓

RESPONSORIAL PSALM Ps 113   [Praise the Lord]

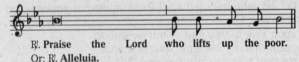

℟. **Praise   the   Lord   who   lifts   up   the   poor.**
Or: ℟. **Alleluia.**

Praise, you servants of the LORD,
    praise the name of the LORD.
Blessed be the name of the LORD
    both now and forever.
℟. **Praise the Lord who lifts up the poor.**
Or: ℟. **Alleluia.**

High above all nations is the LORD;
    above the heavens is his glory.

Who is like the LORD, our God, who is enthroned on high
and looks upon the heavens and the earth below?

℟. **Praise the Lord who lifts up the poor.**
Or: ℟. **Alleluia.**

He raises up the lowly from the dust;
from the dunghill he lifts up the poor
to seat them with princes,
with the princes of his own people.

℟. **Praise the Lord who lifts up the poor.** ↓
Or: ℟. **Alleluia.** ↓

SECOND READING 1 Tm 2:1-8   [Christ Our Mediator]

**We should pray with a pure heart and blameless hands.
Our Penitential Act in the liturgy must be sincere if our
prayers are to meet this demand.**

A reading from the first Letter of Saint Paul to Timothy

BELOVED: First of all, I ask that supplications,
prayers, petitions, and thanksgivings be offered for
everyone, for kings and for all in authority, that we
may lead a quiet and tranquil life in all devotion and
dignity. This is good and pleasing to God our savior,
who wills everyone to be saved and to come to knowledge of the truth.

For there is one God.

There is also one mediator between God and men,
the man Christ Jesus,
who gave himself as ransom for all.

This was the testimony at the proper time. For this I
was appointed preacher and apostle—I am speaking
the truth, I am not lying—, teacher of the Gentiles in
faith and truth.

It is my wish, then, that in every place the men should
pray, lifting up holy hands, without anger or argument.—The word of the Lord. ℟. **Thanks be to God.** ↓

ALLELUIA Cf. 2 Cor 8:9   [Poor But Rich]

℟. **Alleluia, alleluia.**

Though our Lord Jesus Christ was rich, he became poor,

so that by his poverty you might become rich.

℟. **Alleluia, alleluia.** ↓

GOSPEL Lk 16:1-13 or 16:10-13   [The Wily Manager]

If we are shrewd in an evil way, we may be admired by other evil people for our cleverness. But we cannot win in the long run. We cannot divide ourselves between God and worldly gain.

[If the "Shorter Form" is used, the indented text in brackets is omitted.]

℣. The Lord be with you. ℟. **And with your spirit.**

✤ A reading from the holy Gospel according to Luke.

℟. **Glory to you, O Lord.**

JESUS said to his disciples,
  ["A rich man had a steward who was reported to him for squandering his property. He summoned him and said, 'What is this I hear about you? Prepare a full account of your stewardship, because you can no longer be my steward.' The steward said to himself, 'What shall I do, now that my master is taking the position of steward away from me? I am not strong enough to dig and I am ashamed to beg. I know what I shall do so that, when I am removed from the stewardship, they may welcome me into their homes.' He called in his master's debtors one by one. To the first he said, 'How much do you owe my master?' He replied, 'One hundred measures of olive oil.' He said to him, 'Here is your promissory note. Sit down and quickly write one for fifty.' Then to another the steward said, 'And you, how much do

you owe?' He replied, 'One hundred kors of wheat.'
The steward said to him, 'Here is your promissory
note; write one for eighty.' And the master commended that dishonest steward for acting pru-
dently.

"For the children of this world are more prudent
in dealing with their own generation than are the
children of light. I tell you, make friends for yourselves with dishonest wealth, so that when it fails,
you will be welcomed into eternal dwellings.]
The person who is trustworthy in very small matters is
also trustworthy in great ones; and the person who is
dishonest in very small matters is also dishonest in
great ones. If, therefore, you are not trustworthy with
dishonest wealth, who will trust you with true wealth?
If you are not trustworthy with what belongs to another, who will give you what is yours? No servant can
serve two masters. He will either hate one and love the
other, or be devoted to one and despise the other. You
cannot serve both God and mammon."—The Gospel of
the Lord. ℟. **Praise to you, Lord Jesus Christ.**

➔ No. 15, p. 18

PRAYER OVER THE OFFERINGS   [Devotion and Faith]

Receive with favor, O Lord, we pray,
the offerings of your people,
that what they profess with devotion and faith
may be theirs through these heavenly mysteries.
Through Christ our Lord.
℟. **Amen.**   ➔ No. 21, p. 22 (Pref. P 29-36)

COMMUNION ANT. Ps 119 (118):4-5
[Keeping God's Statutes]
**You have laid down your precepts to be carefully kept;
may my ways be firm in keeping your statutes.** ↓

OR Jn 10:14 [The Good Shepherd]

I am the Good Shepherd, says the Lord; I know my sheep, and mine know me. ↓

PRAYER AFTER COMMUNION [Possessing Redemption]

Graciously raise up, O Lord,
those you renew with this Sacrament,
that we may come to possess your redemption
both in mystery and in the manner of our life.
Through Christ our Lord.
℟. **Amen.** → No. 30, p. 77

Optional Solemn Blessings, p. 97, and Prayers over the People, p. 105

"From the netherworld [he] . . . saw Abraham far off and Lazarus at his side."

SEPTEMBER 28

26th SUNDAY IN ORDINARY TIME

ENTRANCE ANT. Dn 3:31, 29, 30, 43, 42   [God's Mercy]

All that you have done to us, O Lord, you have done with true judgment, for we have sinned against you and not obeyed your commandments. But give glory to your name and deal with us according to the bounty of your mercy.   → No. 2, p. 10

COLLECT   [God's Pardon]

O God, who manifest your almighty power
above all by pardoning and showing mercy,
bestow, we pray, your grace abundantly upon us
and make those hastening to attain your promises
heirs to the treasures of heaven.
Through our Lord Jesus Christ, your Son,
who lives and reigns with you in the unity of the Holy
   Spirit,
God, for ever and ever. ℟. **Amen.** ↓

FIRST READING Am 6:1a, 4-7   [Lack of Compassion]

    There is no security in wealth. Those who seek only plea-
sure will not find peace and happiness.

A reading from the Book of the Prophet Amos

T HUS says the LORD the God of hosts:
   Woe to the complacent in Zion!
Lying upon beds of ivory,
   stretched comfortably on their couches,
they eat lambs taken from the flock,
   and calves from the stall!
Improvising to the music of the harp,
   like David, they devise their own accompaniment.
They drink wine from bowls
   and anoint themselves with the best oils;
   yet they are not made ill by the collapse of Joseph!
Therefore, now they shall be the first to go into exile,
   and their wanton revelry shall be done away with.
The word of the Lord. ℟. **Thanks be to God.** ↓

RESPONSORIAL PSALM Ps 146   [Praise the Lord]

℟. **Praise**   the   Lord,   my   soul!
Or: ℟. **Alleluia.**

Blessed is he who keeps faith forever,
   secures justice for the oppressed,
   gives food to the hungry.
The LORD sets captives free.

℟. **Praise the Lord, my soul!**
Or: ℟. **Alleluia.**

The LORD gives sight to the blind;
   the LORD raises up those who were bowed down.
The LORD loves the just;
   the LORD protects strangers.

℟. **Praise the Lord, my soul!**

Or: ℟. **Alleluia.**

The fatherless and the widow he sustains,
   but the way of the wicked he thwarts.
The LORD shall reign forever;
   your God, O Zion, through all generations. Alleluia.

℟. **Praise the Lord, my soul!** ↓

Or: ℟. **Alleluia.** ↓

SECOND READING 1 Tm 6:11-16   [A Virtuous Life]
   **In faith is salvation. Be positive and steadfast; hold firm
   for the Lord Jesus will come again.**

A reading from the first Letter of Saint Paul to Timothy

BUT you, man of God, pursue righteousness, devotion,
faith, love, patience, and gentleness. Compete well
for the faith. Lay hold of eternal life, to which you were
called when you made the noble confession in the presence of many witnesses. I charge you before God, who
gives life to all things, and before Christ Jesus, who gave
testimony under Pontius Pilate for the noble confession,
to keep the commandment without stain or reproach
until the appearance of our Lord Jesus Christ that the
blessed and only ruler will make manifest at the proper
time, the King of kings and Lord of lords, who alone has
immortality, who dwells in unapproachable light, and
whom no human being has seen or can see. To him be
honor and eternal power. Amen.—The word of the Lord.
℟. **Thanks be to God.** ↓

ALLELUIA Cf. 2 Cor 8:9   [Rich in Christ]
℟. **Alleluia, alleluia.**
Though our Lord Jesus Christ was rich, he became
   poor,
so that by his poverty you might become rich.
℟. **Alleluia, alleluia.** ↓

GOSPEL Lk 16:19-31   [Eternal Consolation]

Even the richest person cannot buy salvation. This comes from being faithful to the Word of God.

℣. The Lord be with you. ℟. **And with your spirit.**
✝ A reading from the holy Gospel according to Luke.
℟. **Glory to you, O Lord.**

JESUS said to the Pharisees: "There was a rich man who dressed in purple garments and fine linen and dined sumptuously each day. And lying at his door was a poor man named Lazarus, covered with sores, who would gladly have eaten his fill of the scraps that fell from the rich man's table. Dogs even used to come and lick his sores. When the poor man died, he was carried away by angels to the bosom of Abraham. The rich man also died and was buried, and from the netherworld, where he was in torment, he raised his eyes and saw Abraham far off and Lazarus at his side. And he cried out, 'Father Abraham, have pity on me. Send Lazarus to dip the tip of his finger in water and cool my tongue, for I am suffering torment in these flames.' Abraham replied, 'My child, remember that you received what was good during your lifetime while Lazarus likewise received what was bad; but now he is comforted here, whereas you are tormented. Moreover, between us and you a great chasm is established to prevent anyone from crossing who might wish to go from our side to yours or from your side to ours.' He said, 'Then I beg you, father, send him to my father's house, for I have five brothers, so that he may warn them, lest they too come to this place of torment.' But Abraham replied, 'They have Moses and the prophets. Let them listen to them.' He said, 'Oh no, father Abraham, but if someone from the dead goes to them, they will repent.' Then Abraham said, 'If they will not listen to Moses and the prophets, neither will they be

persuaded if someone should rise from the dead.' "—
The Gospel of the Lord. ℟. **Praise to you, Lord Jesus
Christ.**
→ No. 15, p. 18

PRAYER OVER THE OFFERINGS   [Offering as a Blessing]

Grant us, O merciful God,
that this our offering may find acceptance with you
and that through it the wellspring of all blessing
may be laid open before us.
Through Christ our Lord.
℟. **Amen.**
→ No. 21, p. 22 (Pref. P 29-36)

COMMUNION ANT. Cf. Ps 119 (118):49-50 [Words of Hope]

**Remember your word to your servant, O Lord, by
which you have given me hope. This is my comfort
when I am brought low. ↓**

OR 1 Jn 3:16
[Offering of Self]

**By this we came to know the love of God: that Christ
laid down his life for us; so we ought to lay down our
lives for one another. ↓**

PRAYER AFTER COMMUNION   [Coheirs with Christ]

May this heavenly mystery, O Lord,
restore us in mind and body,
that we may be coheirs in glory with Christ,
to whose suffering we are united
whenever we proclaim his Death.
Who lives and reigns for ever and ever.
℟. **Amen.**
→ No. 30, p. 77

Optional Solemn Blessings, p. 97, and Prayers over the People, p. 105

"If you have faith the size of a mustard seed, you would say to this mulberry tree, 'Be uprooted. . . .' "

OCTOBER 5

27th SUNDAY IN ORDINARY TIME

ENTRANCE ANT. Cf. Est 4:17   [Lord of All]

Within your will, O Lord, all things are established, and there is none that can resist your will. For you have made all things, the heaven and the earth, and all that is held within the circle of heaven; you are the Lord of all. → No. 2, p. 10

COLLECT   [Mercy and Pardon]

Almighty ever-living God,
who in the abundance of your kindness
surpass the merits and the desires of those who
    entreat you,
pour out your mercy upon us
to pardon what conscience dreads
and to give what prayer does not dare to ask.
Through our Lord Jesus Christ, your Son,
who lives and reigns with you in the unity of the Holy
    Spirit,
God, for ever and ever. ℟. **Amen.** ↓

FIRST READING Hb 1:2-3; 2:2-4   [Reward of the Just]

We might become discouraged. But let us take heart; in his own time the Lord will save us.

A reading from the Book of the Prophet Habakkuk

Hᴏᴡ long, O Lᴏʀᴅ? I cry for help
    but you do not listen!
I cry out to you, "Violence!"
    but you do not intervene.
Why do you let me see ruin;
    why must I look at misery?
Destruction and violence are before me;
    there is strife, and clamorous discord.
Then the Lᴏʀᴅ answered me and said:
    Write down the vision clearly upon the tablets,
    so that one can read it readily.
For the vision still has its time,
    presses on to fulfillment, and will not disappoint;
if it delays, wait for it,
    it will surely come, it will not be late.
The rash one has no integrity;
    but the just one, because of his faith, shall live.
The word of the Lord. ℞. **Thanks be to God.** ↓

RESPONSORIAL PSALM Ps 95   [Worship the Lord]

℞. **If today you hear his voice, harden not your hearts.**

Come, let us sing joyfully to the Lᴏʀᴅ;
    let us acclaim the Rock of our salvation.
Let us come into his presence with thanksgiving;
    let us joyfully sing psalms to him.
℞. **If today you hear his voice, harden not your hearts.**
Come, let us bow down in worship;
    let us kneel before the Lᴏʀᴅ who made us.

For he is our God,
  and we are the people he shepherds, the flock he
    guides.

℟. **If today you hear his voice, harden not your
hearts.**

Oh, that today you would hear his voice:
  "Harden not your hearts as at Meribah,
  as in the day of Massah in the desert,
where your fathers tempted me;
  they tested me though they had seen my works."

℟. **If today you hear his voice, harden not your
hearts.** ↓

SECOND READING   2 Tm 1:6-8, 13-14   [Gift of the Spirit]

**Be firm in faith despite all adversity. The Holy Spirit dwells
in us—he is the spirit of strength.**

A reading from the second Letter of Saint Paul
to Timothy

BELOVED: I remind you to stir into flame the gift of
God that you have through the imposition of my
hands. For God did not give us a spirit of cowardice but
rather of power and love and self-control. So do not be
ashamed of your testimony to our Lord, nor of me, a
prisoner for his sake; but bear your share of hardship
for the gospel with the strength that comes from God.

Take as your norm the sound words that you heard
from me, in the faith and love that are in Christ Jesus.
Guard this rich trust with the help of the Holy Spirit
that dwells within us.—The word of the Lord.

℟. **Thanks be to God.** ↓

ALLELUIA   1 Pt 1:25   [Eternal Word]

℟. **Alleluia, alleluia.**
The word of the Lord remains for ever.
This is the word that has been proclaimed to you.

℟. **Alleluia, alleluia.** ↓

GOSPEL Lk 17:5-10   [The Power of Faith]

Our faith is to be lived. We cannot be satisfied with merely doing no more than our duty. We must strive to excel.

℣. The Lord be with you. ℟. **And with your spirit.**

✛ A reading from the holy Gospel according to Luke.

℟. **Glory to you, O Lord.**

THE apostles said to the Lord, "Increase our faith." The Lord replied, "If you have faith the size of a mustard seed, you would say to this mulberry tree, 'Be uprooted and planted in the sea,' and it would obey you.

"Who among you would say to your servant who has just come in from plowing or tending sheep in the field, 'Come here immediately and take your place at table'? Would he not rather say to him, 'Prepare something for me to eat. Put on your apron and wait on me while I eat and drink. You may eat and drink when I am finished'? Is he grateful to that servant because he did what was commanded? So should it be with you. When you have done all you have been commanded, say, 'We are unprofitable servants; we have done what we were obliged to do.' "—The Gospel of the Lord. ℟. **Praise to you, Lord Jesus Christ.**   ➔ No. 15, p. 18

PRAYER OVER THE OFFERINGS   [Sanctifying Work]

Accept, O Lord, we pray,
the sacrifices instituted by your commands
and, through the sacred mysteries,
which we celebrate with dutiful service,
graciously complete the sanctifying work
by which you are pleased to redeem us.
Through Christ our Lord.
℟. **Amen.**   ➔ No. 21, p. 22 (Pref. P 29-36)

COMMUNION ANT. Lam 3:25   [Hope in the Lord]

The Lord is good to those who hope in him, to the soul that seeks him. ↓

OR Cf. 1 Cor 10:17   [One Bread, One Body]
**Though many, we are one bread, one body, for we all
partake of the one Bread and one Chalice.** ↓

PRAYER AFTER COMMUNION   [Nourished by Sacrament]
Grant us, almighty God,
that we may be refreshed and nourished
by the Sacrament which we have received,
so as to be transformed into what we consume.
Through Christ our Lord.
℟. **Amen.**   → No. 30, p. 77

Optional Solemn Blessings, p. 97, and Prayers over the People, p. 105

"Stand up and go; your faith has saved you."

OCTOBER 12
28th SUNDAY IN ORDINARY TIME

ENTRANCE ANT. Ps 130 (129):3-4   [A Forgiving God]
If you, O Lord, should mark iniquities, Lord, who
could stand? But with you is found forgiveness, O God
of Israel.   → No. 2, p. 10

COLLECT   [Good Works]

May your grace, O Lord, we pray,
at all times go before us and follow after
and make us always determined
to carry out good works.
Through our Lord Jesus Christ, your Son,
who lives and reigns with you in the unity of the Holy
    Spirit,
God, for ever and ever. ℟. **Amen.** ↓

FIRST READING 2 Kgs 5:14-17   [Gratitude to God]
**The healing power of God comes to a man who does not
belong to the chosen people, and he proclaims his faith in
the Lord.**

A reading from the second Book of Kings

N AAMAN went down and plunged into the Jordan
    seven times at the word of Elisha, the man of God.
His flesh became again like the flesh of a little child,
and he was clean of his leprosy.

Naaman returned with his whole retinue to the man of
God. On his arrival he stood before Elisha and said,
"Now I know that there is no God in all the earth, except
in Israel. Please accept a gift from your servant."

Elisha replied, "As the LORD lives whom I serve, I will
not take it"; and despite Naaman's urging, he still
refused. Naaman said: "If you will not accept, please let
me, your servant, have two mule-loads of earth, for I
will no longer offer holocaust or sacrifice to any other
god except to the LORD."—The word of the Lord.
℟. **Thanks be to God.** ↓

RESPONSORIAL PSALM Ps 98   [Wondrous Deeds]

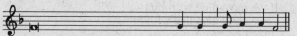

℟. **The Lord has revealed to the na-tions his   sav-ing pow'r.**

Sing to the LORD a new song,
  for he has done wondrous deeds;
his right hand has won victory for him,
  his holy arm.

℟. **The Lord has revealed to the nations his saving power.**

The LORD has made his salvation known:
  in the sight of the nations he has revealed his justice.
He has remembered his kindness and his faithfulness
  toward the house of Israel.

℟. **The Lord has revealed to the nations his saving power.**

All the ends of the earth have seen
  the salvation by our God.
Sing joyfully to the LORD, all you lands:
  break into song; sing praise.

℟. **The Lord has revealed to the nations his saving power.** ↓

SECOND READING 2 Tm 2:8-13   [Life in Christ]

In Christ we have died. Through Christ we are to rise, and with him we shall reign.

A reading from the second Letter of Saint Paul
to Timothy

BELOVED: Remember Jesus Christ, raised from the dead, a descendant of David: such is my gospel, for which I am suffering, even to the point of chains, like a criminal. But the word of God is not chained. Therefore, I bear with everything for the sake of those who are chosen, so that they too may obtain the salvation that is in Christ Jesus, together with eternal glory. This saying is trustworthy:
  If we have died with him
    we shall also live with him;
  if we persevere
    we shall also reign with him.

But if we deny him
 he will deny us.
If we are unfaithful
 he remains faithful,
  for he cannot deny himself.
The word of the Lord. ℟. **Thanks be to God.** ↓

ALLELUIA 1 Thes 5:18   [Give Thanks]
℟. **Alleluia, alleluia.**
In all circumstances, give thanks,
for this is the will of God for you in Christ Jesus.
℟. **Alleluia, alleluia.** ↓

GOSPEL Lk 17:11-19   [Salvation Through Faith]
**The healing power of God comes through Christ, even to
a man who does not belong to the chosen people. This
man's faith prompts his thankfulness.**

℣. The Lord be with you. ℟. **And with your spirit.**
✛ A reading from the holy Gospel according to Luke.
℟. **Glory to you, O Lord.**

AS Jesus continued his journey to Jerusalem, he
traveled through Samaria and Galilee. As he was
entering a village, ten lepers met him. They stood at a
distance from him and raised their voices, saying,
"Jesus, Master! Have pity on us!" And when he saw
them, he said, "Go show yourselves to the priests." As
they were going they were cleansed. And one of them,
realizing he had been healed, returned, glorifying God
in a loud voice; and he fell at the feet of Jesus and
thanked him. He was a Samaritan. Jesus said in reply,
"Ten were cleansed, were they not? Where are the
other nine? Has none but this foreigner returned to
give thanks to God?" Then he said to him, "Stand up
and go; your faith has saved you."—The Gospel of the
Lord. ℟. **Praise to you, Lord Jesus Christ.**

→ No. 15, p. 18

PRAYER OVER THE OFFERINGS   [Devotedness]

Accept, O Lord, the prayers of your faithful
with the sacrificial offerings,
that, through these acts of devotedness,
we may pass over to the glory of heaven.
Through Christ our Lord.
℟. **Amen.**   → No. 21, p. 22 (Pref. P 29-36)

COMMUNION ANT. Cf. Ps 34 (33):11   [God's Providence]

**The rich suffer want and go hungry, but those who
seek the Lord lack no blessing. ↓**

OR 1 Jn 3:2   [Vision of God]

**When the Lord appears, we shall be like him, for we
shall see him as he is. ↓**

PRAYER AFTER COMMUNION   [Christ's Divine Nature]

We entreat your majesty most humbly, O Lord,
that, as you feed us with the nourishment
which comes from the most holy Body and Blood of
    your Son,
so you may make us sharers of his divine nature.
Who lives and reigns for ever and ever.
℟. **Amen.**   → No. 30, p. 77

Optional Solemn Blessings, p. 97, and Prayers over the People, p. 105

*God will "secure the rights of his chosen ones
who call out to him day and night."*

OCTOBER 19
29th SUNDAY IN ORDINARY TIME

ENTRANCE ANT. Cf. Ps 17 (16):6, 8   [Refuge in God]
To you I call; for you will surely heed me, O God; turn
your ear to me; hear my words. Guard me as the apple
of your eye; in the shadow of your wings protect me.

    → No. 2, p. 10

COLLECT   [Sincerity of Heart]
Almighty ever-living God,
grant that we may always conform our will to yours
and serve your majesty in sincerity of heart.
Through our Lord Jesus Christ, your Son,
who lives and reigns with you in the unity of the Holy
  Spirit,
God, for ever and ever. ℟. **Amen.** ↓

FIRST READING Ex 17:8-13   [God Our Warrior]
    Moses prays without ceasing, not losing heart despite
physical fatigue.

A reading from the Book of Exodus

IN those days, Amalek came and waged war against
Israel. Moses, therefore, said to Joshua, "Pick out
certain men, and tomorrow go out and engage Amalek
in battle. I will be standing on top of the hill with the
staff of God in my hand." So Joshua did as Moses told
him: he engaged Amalek in battle after Moses had
climbed to the top of the hill with Aaron and Hur. As
long as Moses kept his hands raised up, Israel had the
better of the fight, but when he let his hands rest,
Amalek had the better of the fight. Moses' hands, however, grew tired; so they put a rock in place for him to
sit on. Meanwhile Aaron and Hur supported his hands,
one on one side and one on the other, so that his hands
remained steady till sunset. And Joshua mowed down
Amalek and his people with the edge of the sword.—
The word of the Lord. ℞. **Thanks be to God.** ↓

RESPONSORIAL PSALM Ps 121   [God Our Guardian]

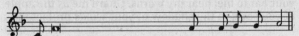

℞. Our help is from the Lord, who made heav'n and earth.

I lift up my eyes toward the mountains;
  whence shall help come to me?
My help is from the LORD,
  who made heaven and earth.

℞. **Our help is from the Lord, who made heaven and
  earth.**

May he not suffer your foot to slip;
  may he slumber not who guards you:
indeed he neither slumbers nor sleeps,
  the guardian of Israel.

℞. **Our help is from the Lord, who made heaven and
  earth.**

The LORD is your guardian; the LORD is your shade;
   he is beside you at your right hand.
The sun shall not harm you by day,
   nor the moon by night.

℞. **Our help is from the Lord, who made heaven and earth.**

The LORD will guard you from all evil;
   he will guard your life.
The LORD will guard your coming and your going,
   both now and forever.

℞. **Our help is from the Lord, who made heaven and earth.** ↓

SECOND READING 2 Tm 3:14—4:2 [Inspiration of Scripture]

   The Bible is the source of teaching, the safe guide for the man of God in every good work.

A reading from the second Letter of Saint Paul
to Timothy

BELOVED: Remain faithful to what you have learned and believed, because you know from whom you learned it, and that from infancy you have known the sacred Scriptures, which are capable of giving you wisdom for salvation through faith in Christ Jesus. All Scripture is inspired by God and is useful for teaching, for refutation, for correction, and for training in righteousness, so that one who belongs to God may be competent, equipped for every good work.

   I charge you in the presence of God and of Christ Jesus, who will judge the living and the dead, and by his appearing and his kingly power: proclaim the word; be persistent whether it is convenient or inconvenient; convince, reprimand, encourage through all patience and teaching.—The word of the Lord.
℞. **Thanks be to God.** ↓

ALLELUIA Heb 4:12   [Living Word]

℞. **Alleluia, alleluia.**
The word of God is living and effective,
discerning reflections and thoughts of the heart.
℞. **Alleluia, alleluia.** ↓

GOSPEL Lk 18:1-8   [The Justice of God]

Jesus urges us to pray without ceasing and to have faith in
the goodness of God.

℣. The Lord be with you. ℞. **And with your spirit.**
✠ A reading from the holy Gospel according to Luke.
℞. **Glory to you, O Lord.**

JESUS told his disciples a parable about the necessity for them to pray always without becoming weary. He said, "There was a judge in a certain town who neither feared God nor respected any human being. And a widow in that town used to come to him and say, 'Render a just decision for me against my adversary.' For a long time the judge was unwilling, but eventually he thought, 'While it is true that I neither fear God nor respect any human being, because this widow keeps bothering me I shall deliver a just decision for her lest she finally come and strike me.' " The Lord said, "Pay attention to what the dishonest judge says. Will not God then secure the rights of his chosen ones who call out to him day and night? Will he be slow to answer them? I tell you, he will see to it that justice is done for them speedily. But when the Son of Man comes, will he find faith on earth?"—The Gospel of the Lord. ℞. **Praise to you, Lord Jesus Christ.**

→ No. 15, p. 18

PRAYER OVER THE OFFERINGS   [Respect Gifts]

Grant us, Lord, we pray,
a sincere respect for your gifts,

that, through the purifying action of your grace,
we may be cleansed by the very mysteries we serve.
Through Christ our Lord.
℞. **Amen.**   ➔   No. 21, p. 22 (Pref. P 29-36)

COMMUNION ANT. Cf. Ps 33 (32):18-19 [Divine Protection]
**Behold, the eyes of the Lord are on those who fear
him, who hope in his merciful love, to rescue their
souls from death, to keep them alive in famine. ↓**

OR Mk 10:45   [Christ Our Ransom]
**The Son of Man has come to give his life as a ransom
for many. ↓**

PRAYER AFTER COMMUNION   [Eternal Gifts]
Grant, O Lord, we pray,
that, benefiting from participation in heavenly things,
we may be helped by what you give in this present age
and prepared for the gifts that are eternal.
Through Christ our Lord.
℞. **Amen.**   ➔   No. 30, p. 77

Optional Solemn Blessings, p. 97, and Prayers over the People, p. 105

"O God, I thank you that I am not like the rest of humanity."

OCTOBER 26

30th SUNDAY IN ORDINARY TIME

ENTRANCE ANT. Cf. Ps 105 (104):3-4   [Seek the Lord]

Let the hearts that seek the Lord rejoice; turn to the Lord and his strength; constantly seek his face.

→ No. 2, p. 10

COLLECT   [Increase Virtues]

Almighty ever-living God,
increase our faith, hope and charity,
and make us love what you command,
so that we may merit what you promise.
Through our Lord Jesus Christ, your Son,
who lives and reigns with you in the unity of the Holy
   Spirit,
God, for ever and ever. ℟. **Amen.** ↓

FIRST READING Sir 35:12-14, 16-18   [A God of Justice]

No one is unimportant in the sight of God. If we serve God
willingly he will receive our prayers.

A reading from the Book of Sirach

THE LORD is a God of justice,
who knows no favorites.
Though not unduly partial toward the weak,
yet he hears the cry of the oppressed.
The Lord is not deaf to the wail of the orphan,
nor to the widow when she pours out her complaint.
He who serves God willingly is heard;
his petition reaches the heavens.
The prayer of the lowly pierces the clouds;
it does not rest till it reaches its goal,
nor will it withdraw till the Most High responds,
judges justly and affirms the right,
and the Lord will not delay.
The word of the Lord. ℟. **Thanks be to God.** ↓

RESPONSORIAL PSALM Ps 34   [Refuge in the Lord]

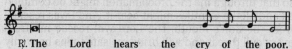

℟. The   Lord   hears   the   cry of   the poor.

I will bless the LORD at all times;
his praise shall be ever in my mouth.
Let my soul glory in the LORD;
the lowly will hear me and be glad.

℟. **The Lord hears the cry of the poor.**

The LORD confronts the evildoers,
to destroy remembrance of them from the earth.
When the just cry out, the LORD hears them,
and from all their distress he rescues them.

℟. **The Lord hears the cry of the poor.**

The LORD is close to the brokenhearted;
and those who are crushed in spirit he saves.
The LORD redeems the lives of his servants;
no one incurs guilt who takes refuge in him.

℟. **The Lord hears the cry of the poor.** ↓

SECOND READING 2 Tm 4:6-8, 16-18 [A Merited Crown]

Paul sees time running out and his life drawing to a close. He is comforted by faith in God's just judgment.

A reading from the second Letter of Saint Paul to Timothy

BELOVED: I am already being poured out like a libation, and the time of my departure is at hand. I have competed well; I have finished the race; I have kept the faith. From now on the crown of righteousness awaits me, which the Lord, the just judge, will award to me on that day, and not only to me, but to all who have longed for his appearance.

At my first defense no one appeared on my behalf, but everyone deserted me. May it not be held against them! But the Lord stood by me and gave me strength, so that through me the proclamation might be completed and all the Gentiles might hear it. And I was rescued from the lion's mouth. The Lord will rescue me from every evil threat and will bring me safe to his heavenly kingdom. To him be glory forever and ever. Amen.— The word of the Lord. ℟. **Thanks be to God.** ↓

ALLELUIA 2 Cor 5:19   [Reconciliation in Christ]

℟. **Alleluia, alleluia.**
God was reconciling the world to himself in Christ, and entrusting to us the message of salvation.
℟. **Alleluia, alleluia.** ↓

GOSPEL Lk 18:9-14   [Humility]

Pride brings no true reward but only projects an "image." In humility true values are seen.

℣. The Lord be with you. ℟. **And with your spirit.**
✛ A reading from the holy Gospel according to Luke.
℟. **Glory to you, O Lord.**

JESUS addressed this parable to those who were convinced of their own righteousness and despised everyone else. "Two people went up to the temple area to pray; one was a Pharisee and the other was a tax collector. The Pharisee took up his position and spoke this prayer to himself, 'O God, I thank you that I am not like the rest of humanity—greedy, dishonest, adulterous—or even like this tax collector. I fast twice a week, and I pay tithes on my whole income.' But the tax collector stood off at a distance and would not even raise his eyes to heaven but beat his breast and prayed, 'O God, be merciful to me a sinner.' I tell you, the latter went home justified, not the former; for whoever exalts himself will be humbled, and the one who humbles himself will be exalted."—The Gospel of the Lord.

℟. **Praise to you, Lord Jesus Christ.**   → No. 15, p. 18

PRAYER OVER THE OFFERINGS   [Glorifying God]

Look, we pray, O Lord,
on the offerings we make to your majesty,
that whatever is done by us in your service
may be directed above all to your glory.
Through Christ our Lord.

℟. **Amen.**   → No. 21, p. 22 (Pref. P 29-36)

COMMUNION ANT. Cf. Ps 20 (19):6   [Saving Help]

We will ring out our joy at your saving help and exult in the name of our God. ↓

OR Eph 5:2   [Christ's Offering for Us]

Christ loved us and gave himself up for us, as a fragrant offering to God. ↓

PRAYER AFTER COMMUNION   [Celebrate in Signs]

May your Sacraments, O Lord, we pray,
perfect in us what lies within them,
that what we now celebrate in signs
we may one day possess in truth.
Through Christ our Lord.

℟. **Amen.**   → No. 30, p. 77

Optional Solemn Blessings, p. 97, and Prayers over the People, p. 105

"Blessed are the clean of heart, for they will see God."

NOVEMBER 1

ALL SAINTS

Solemnity

ENTRANCE ANT. [Honoring All the Saints]

Let us all rejoice in the Lord, as we celebrate the feast day in honor of all the Saints, at whose festival the Angels rejoice and praise the Son of God. ➜ No. 2, p. 10

COLLECT [Reconciliation]

Almighty ever-living God,
by whose gift we venerate in one celebration
the merits of all the Saints,
bestow on us, we pray,
through the prayers of so many intercessors,
an abundance of the reconciliation with you
for which we earnestly long.
Through our Lord Jesus Christ, your Son,
who lives and reigns with you in the unity of the Holy
    Spirit,
God, for ever and ever. ℟. **Amen.** ↓

FIRST READING Rv 7:2-4, 9-14   [A Huge Crowd of Saints]

The elect give thanks to God and the Lamb who saved them. The whole court of heaven joins the acclamation of the Saints.

A reading from the Book of Revelation

I, JOHN, saw another angel come up from the East, holding the seal of the living God. He cried out in a loud voice to the four angels who were given power to damage the land and the sea, "Do not damage the land or the sea or the trees until we put the seal on the foreheads of the servants of our God." I heard the number of those who had been marked with the seal, one hundred and forty-four thousand marked from every tribe of the children of Israel.

After this I had a vision of a great multitude, which no one could count, from every nation, race, people, and tongue. They stood before the throne and before the Lamb, wearing white robes and holding palm branches in their hands. They cried out in a loud voice:

"Salvation comes from our God, who is seated on the
    throne,
    and from the Lamb."

All the angels stood around the throne and around the elders and the four living creatures. They prostrated themselves before the throne, worshiped God, and exclaimed:

"Amen. Blessing and glory, wisdom and thanks-
    giving,
    honor, power, and might
    be to our God forever and ever. Amen."

Then one of the elders spoke up and said to me, "Who are these wearing white robes, and where did they come from?" I said to him, "My lord, you are the one who knows." He said to me, "These are the ones who have survived the time of great distress; they have washed their robes and made them white in the Blood of the Lamb."—The word of the Lord. ℟. **Thanks be to God.** ↓

RESPONSORIAL PSALM Ps 24   [Longing To See God]

℟. **Lord, this is the peo-ple that longs to see your face.**

The LORD's are the earth and its fullness;
    the world and those who dwell in it.
For he founded it upon the seas
    and established it upon the rivers.

℟. **Lord, this is the people that longs to see your face.**

Who can ascend the mountain of the LORD?
    or who may stand in his holy place?
One whose hands are sinless, whose heart is clean,
    who desires not what is vain.

℟. **Lord, this is the people that longs to see your face.**

He shall receive a blessing from the LORD,
    a reward from God his savior.
Such is the race that seeks for him,
    that seeks the face of the God of Jacob.

℟. **Lord, this is the people that longs to see your face.** ↓

SECOND READING 1 Jn 3:1-3   [We Shall See God]

God's gift of love has been the gift of His only Son as Savior of the world. It is this gift that has made it possible for us to be called the children of God.

A reading from the first Letter of Saint John

BELOVED: See what love the Father has bestowed on us that we may be called the children of God. Yet so we are. The reason the world does not know us is that it did not know him. Beloved, we are God's children now;

what we shall be has not yet been revealed. We do
know that when it is revealed we shall be like him, for
we shall see him as he is. Everyone who has this hope
based on him makes himself pure, as he is pure.—The
word of the Lord. ℟. **Thanks be to God.** ↓

ALLELUIA Mt 11:28   [Rest in Christ]
℟. **Alleluia, alleluia.**
Come to me, all you who labor and are burdened,
and I will give you rest, says the Lord.
℟. **Alleluia, alleluia.** ↓

GOSPEL Mt 5:1-12a   [The Beatitudes]
> Jesus is meant to be the new Moses proclaiming the new
> revelation on a new Mount Sinai. This is the proclamation of
> the reign, or the "Good News." Blessings are pronounced on
> those who do not share the values of the world.

℣. The Lord be with you. ℟. **And with your spirit.**
✛ A reading from the holy Gospel according to
Matthew. ℟. **Glory to you, O Lord.**

WHEN Jesus saw the crowds, he went up the
mountain, and after he had sat down, his disci-
ples came to him. He began to teach them, saying:
  "Blessed are the poor in spirit,
     for theirs is the Kingdom of heaven.
  Blessed are they who mourn,
     for they will be comforted.
  Blessed are the meek,
     for they will inherit the land.
  Blessed are they who hunger and thirst for
        righteousness,
     for they will be satisfied.
  Blessed are the merciful,
     for they will be shown mercy.

Blessed are the clean of heart,
    for they will see God.
Blessed are the peacemakers,
    for they will be called children of God.
Blessed are they who are persecuted for the sake of
        righteousness,
    for theirs is the Kingdom of heaven.
Blessed are you when they insult you and persecute
you and utter every kind of evil against you falsely
because of me. Rejoice and be glad, for your reward
will be great in heaven."—The Gospel of the Lord.
℟. **Praise to you, Lord Jesus Christ.** → No. 15, p. 18

PRAYER OVER THE OFFERINGS
[The Saints' Concern for Us]

May these offerings we bring in honor of all the Saints
be pleasing to you, O Lord,
and grant that, just as we believe the Saints
to be already assured of immortality,
so we may experience their concern for our salvation.
Through Christ our Lord. ℟. **Amen.** ↓

PREFACE (P 71)   [Strength and Example]

℣. The Lord be with you. ℟. **And with your spirit.**
℣. Lift up your hearts. ℟. **We lift them up to the Lord.**
℣. Let us give thanks to the Lord our God. ℟. **It is right
and just.**

It is truly right and just, our duty and our salvation,
always and everywhere to give you thanks,
Lord, holy Father, almighty and eternal God.

For today by your gift we celebrate the festival of your
    city,
the heavenly Jerusalem, our mother,
where the great array of our brothers and sisters
already gives you eternal praise.

Towards her, we eagerly hasten
  as pilgrims advancing by faith,
rejoicing in the glory bestowed upon those exalted
  members of the Church
through whom you give us, in our frailty, both strength
  and good example.

And so, we glorify you with the multitude of Saints
  and Angels,
as with one voice of praise we acclaim: ➔ No. 23, p. 23

COMMUNION ANT. Mt 5:8-10 [The Saints: Children of God]
**Blessed are the clean of heart, for they shall see God.
Blessed are the peacemakers, for they shall be called
children of God. Blessed are they who are persecuted
for the sake of righteousness, for theirs is the
Kingdom of Heaven.** ↓

PRAYER AFTER COMMUNION   [Heavenly Homeland]

As we adore you, O God, who alone are holy
and wonderful in all your Saints,
we implore your grace,
so that, coming to perfect holiness in the fullness of
  your love,
we may pass from this pilgrim table
to the banquet of our heavenly homeland.
Through Christ our Lord.
℟. **Amen.**   ➔ No. 30, p. 77

Optional Solemn Blessings, p. 97, and Prayers over the People, p. 105

"Give them eternal rest, O Lord. . . ."

NOVEMBER 2

THE COMMEMORATION OF
ALL THE FAITHFUL DEPARTED
(ALL SOULS' DAY)

Even when November 2 falls on a Sunday, the Mass cele-
brated is that of the Commemoration of All the Faithful
Departed.

1

ENTRANCE ANT. Cf. 1 Thes 4:14; 1 Cor 15:22   [Life in Christ]
Just as Jesus died and has risen again, so through
Jesus God will bring with him those who have fallen
asleep; and as in Adam all die, so also in Christ will all
be brought to life.   → No. 2, p. 10

COLLECT   [For All the Departed]
Listen kindly to our prayers, O Lord,
and, as our faith in your Son,
raised from the dead, is deepened,
so may our hope of resurrection for your departed
    servants

also find new strength.
Through our Lord Jesus Christ, your Son,
who lives and reigns with you in the unity of the Holy
    Spirit,
God, for ever and ever. ℟. **Amen.** ↓

*The readings found in Masses 2 and 3 may also be used, as
well as those listed on p. 588.*

FIRST READING   Wis 3:1-9   [In God's Care]

This is one of the clearest texts of the Old Testament about
God's future vindication of the just. It is not as clear as
later New Testament texts, but it does emphatically proclaim existence after death and our vision of God.

A reading from the Book of Wisdom

THE souls of the just are in the hand of God,
    and no torment shall touch them.
They seemed, in the view of the foolish, to be dead;
    and their passing away was thought an affliction
    and their going forth from us, utter destruction.
But they are in peace.
For if before men, indeed, they be punished,
    yet is their hope full of immortality;
chastised a little, they shall be greatly blessed,
    because God tried them
    and found them worthy of himself.
As gold in the furnace, he proved them,
    and as sacrificial offerings he took them to himself.
In the time of their visitation they shall shine,
    and shall dart about as sparks through stubble;
they shall judge nations and rule over peoples,
    and the LORD shall be their King forever.
Those who trust in him shall understand truth,
    and the faithful shall abide with him in love:
because grace and mercy are with his holy ones,
    and his care is with his elect.
The word of the Lord. ℟. **Thanks be to God.** ↓

RESPONSORIAL PSALM Ps 23   [Fearing No Evil]

℟. The Lord is my shep - herd; there is noth-ing   I shall want.

Or: ℟. Though I walk in the valley of darkness, I fear no evil, for
  you are with me.

The LORD is my shepherd; I shall not want.
  In verdant pastures he gives me repose;
beside restful waters he leads me;
  he refreshes my soul.

℟. **The Lord is my shepherd; there is nothing I shall
  want.**

Or: ℟. **Though I walk in the valley of darkness, I fear
  no evil, for you are with me.**

He guides me in right paths
  for his name's sake.
Even though I walk in the dark valley
  I fear no evil; for you are at my side
with your rod and your staff
  that give me courage.

℟. **The Lord is my shepherd; there is nothing I shall
  want.**

Or: ℟. **Though I walk in the valley of darkness, I fear
  no evil, for you are with me.**

You spread the table before me
  in the sight of my foes;
you anoint my head with oil;
  my cup overflows.

℟. **The Lord is my shepherd; there is nothing I shall
  want.**

Or: ℟. **Though I walk in the valley of darkness, I fear
  no evil, for you are with me.**

Only goodness and kindness follow me
  all the days of my life;
and I shall dwell in the house of the LORD
  for years to come.

℟. **The Lord is my shepherd; there is nothing I shall want.** ↓

Or: ℟. **Though I walk in the valley of darkness, I fear no evil, for you are with me.** ↓

SECOND READING 1 Cor 15:51-57

[O Death, Where Is Your Victory?]

St. Paul tells us that our risen body will be a body so changed by the power of God as to be immortal. Christ died for sin which is the cause of our death; he rose from the dead to be the cause of our resurrection.

A reading from the first Letter of Saint Paul
to the Corinthians

BROTHERS and sisters: Behold, I tell you a mystery. We shall not all fall asleep, but we will all be changed, in an instant, in the blink of an eye, at the last trumpet. For the trumpet will sound, the dead will be raised incorruptible, and we shall be changed. For that which is corruptible must clothe itself with incorruptibility, and that which is mortal must clothe itself with immortality. And when this which is corruptible clothes itself with incorruptibility and this which is mortal clothes itself with immortality, then the word that is written shall come about:

Death is swallowed up in victory.
Where, O death, is your victory?
Where, O death, is your sting?

The sting of death is sin, and the power of sin is the law. But thanks be to God who gives us the victory through our Lord Jesus Christ.—The word of the Lord.
℟. **Thanks be to God.** ↓

ALLELUIA Mt 25:34   [Inherit the Kingdom]

℟. **Alleluia, alleluia.**
Come, you who are blessed by my Father;
inherit the kingdom prepared for you
from the foundation of the world.
℟. **Alleluia, alleluia.** ↓

GOSPEL Jn 6:37-40   [Eternal Life for Believers]

Jesus here indicates that God wills to save all people. Everyone who approaches the Son and believes in him will be raised up on the last day to the glory of eternal life.

℣. The Lord be with you. ℟. **And with your spirit.**
✣ A reading from the holy Gospel according to John.
℟. **Glory to you, O Lord.**

JESUS said to the crowds: "Everything that the Father gives me will come to me, and I will not reject anyone who comes to me, because I came down from heaven not to do my own will but the will of the one who sent me. And this is the will of the one who sent me, that I should not lose anything of what he gave me, but that I should raise it on the last day. For this is the will of my Father, that everyone who sees the Son and believes in him may have eternal life, and I shall raise him up on the last day."—The Gospel of the Lord. ℟. **Praise to you, Lord Jesus Christ.**   → No. 15, p. 18

PRAYER OVER THE OFFERINGS [United in Christ's Love]

Look favorably on our offerings, O Lord,
so that your departed servants
may be taken up into glory with your Son,
in whose great mystery of love we are all united.
Who lives and reigns for ever and ever.
℟. **Amen.**   → No. 21, p. 22 (Pref. P 77-81)

COMMUNION ANT. Cf. Jn 11:25-26

[The Resurrection and the Life]

I am the Resurrection and the Life, says the Lord. Whoever believes in me, even though he dies, will live, and everyone who lives and believes in me will not die for ever. ↓

PRAYER AFTER COMMUNION   [Light and Peace]

Grant we pray, O Lord, that your departed servants, for whom we have celebrated this paschal Sacrament, may pass over to a dwelling place of light and peace. Through Christ our Lord.

℟. **Amen.**   → No. 30, p. 77

The Solemn Blessing formula on p. 105 may be used.

ALL SOULS' DAY
2

ENTRANCE ANT. Cf. 4 Esdr 2:34-35   [Eternal Rest]

Eternal rest grant unto them, O Lord, and let perpetual light shine upon them.   → No. 2, p. 10

COLLECT   [Eternal Happiness]

O God, glory of the faithful and life of the just,
by the Death and Resurrection of whose Son
we have been redeemed,
look mercifully on your departed servants,
that, just as they professed the mystery of our
    resurrection,
so they may merit to receive the joys of eternal
    happiness.
Through our Lord Jesus Christ, your Son,
who lives and reigns with you in the unity of the Holy
    Spirit,
God, for ever and ever. ℟. **Amen.** ↓

*The readings found in Masses 1 and 3 may also be used, as
well as those listed on p. 588.*

FIRST READING Wis 4:7-15   [The Just Are with God]

In contrast to the illusions of worldly wisdom, the "hope" of
those who have known and believed in God is "full of immortality." After being tried by God they will reap their reward.

A reading from the Book of Wisdom

T HE just man, though he die early,
    shall be at rest.
For the age that is honorable comes not with the
        passing of time,
    nor can it be measured in terms of years.
Rather, understanding is the hoary crown for men,
    and an unsullied life, the attainment of old age.
He who pleased God was loved;
    he who lived among sinners was transported—
snatched away, lest wickedness pervert his mind
    or deceit beguile his soul;
for the witchery of paltry things obscures what is right
    and the whirl of desire transforms the innocent
        mind.
Having become perfect in a short while,
    he reached the fullness of a long career;
    for his soul was pleasing to the LORD,
    therefore he sped him out of the midst of wicked-
        ness.
But the people saw and did not understand,
    nor did they take this into account.
The word of the Lord. ℞. **Thanks be to God.** ↓

RESPONSORIAL PSALM Ps 25   [Preserve My Life]

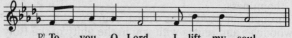

℞. To you, O Lord, I lift my soul.
Or: ℞. **No one who waits for you, O Lord, will ever be
    put to shame.**

Remember that your compassion, O LORD,
   and your love are from of old.
In your kindness remember me,
   because of your goodness, O LORD.

℟. **To you, O Lord, I lift my soul.**

Or: ℟. **No one who waits for you, O Lord, will ever be
   put to shame.**

Relieve the troubles of my heart,
   and bring me out of my distress.
Put an end to my affliction and my suffering;
   and take away all my sins.

℟. **To you, O Lord, I lift my soul.**

Or: ℟. **No one who waits for you, O Lord, will ever be
   put to shame.**

Preserve my life, and rescue me;
   let me not be put to shame, for I take refuge in you.
Let integrity and uprightness preserve me,
   because I wait for you, O LORD.

℟. **To you, O Lord, I lift my soul.** ↓

Or: ℟. **No one who waits for you, O Lord, will ever be
   put to shame.** ↓

SECOND READING Phil 3:20-21   [Citizenship in Heaven]

**While toiling for the building up of this earth, Christians
know that their ultimate citizenship is in heaven. Salvation
does not lie in the body but in Christ, who at his second
coming will transform the body of all his faithful to be like
his glorious body.**

A reading from the Letter of Saint Paul
to the Philippians

BROTHERS and sisters: Our citizenship is in heaven,
and from it we also await a savior, the Lord Jesus
Christ. He will change our lowly body to conform with
his glorified Body by the power that enables him also to

bring all things into subjection to himself.—The word of
the Lord. ℟. **Thanks be to God.** ↓

ALLELUIA Jn 11:25a, 26   [No Death for Believers]

℟. **Alleluia, alleluia.**
I am the resurrection and the life, says the Lord;
whoever believes in me will never die.
℟. **Alleluia, alleluia.** ↓

GOSPEL Jn 11:17-27   [Rising with Christ]

Amid the human continuous quest for immortality, there is
only one who can impart it to us: Jesus, "the resurrection
and the life." And this immortality will be coupled with a
joy without end.

℣. The Lord be with you. ℟. **And with your spirit.**
✢ A reading from the holy Gospel according to John.
℟. **Glory to you, O Lord.**

WHEN Jesus arrived in Bethany, he found that
Lazarus had already been in the tomb for four
days. Now Bethany was near Jerusalem, only about two
miles away. Many of the Jews had come to Martha and
Mary to comfort them about their brother. When Martha
heard that Jesus was coming, she went to meet him; but
Mary sat at home. Martha said to Jesus, "Lord, if you had
been here, my brother would not have died. But even
now I know that whatever you ask of God, God will give
you." Jesus said to her, "Your brother will rise." Martha
said to him, "I know he will rise, in the resurrection on
the last day." Jesus told her, "I am the resurrection and the
life; he who believes in me, even if he dies, will live, and
he who lives and believes in me will never die. Do you
believe this?" She said to him, "Yes, Lord. I have come to
believe that you are the Christ, the Son of God, the one
who is coming into the world."—The Gospel of the Lord.
℟. **Praise to you, Lord Jesus Christ.**   → No. 15, p. 18

PRAYER OVER THE OFFERINGS   [Merciful Forgiveness]

Almighty and merciful God,
by means of these sacrificial offerings
wash away, we pray, in the Blood of Christ,
the sins of your departed servants,
for you purify unceasingly by your merciful
   forgiveness
those you once cleansed in the waters of Baptism.
Through Christ our Lord.
℞. **Amen.**   → No. 21, p. 22 (Pref. P 77-81)

COMMUNION ANT. Cf. 4 Esdr 2:35, 34   [Perpetual Light]

**Let perpetual light shine upon them, O Lord, with
your Saints for ever, for you are merciful.** ↓

PRAYER AFTER COMMUNION   [For Departed Servants]

Having received the Sacrament of your Only Begotten
   Son,
who was sacrificed for us and rose in glory,
we humbly implore you, O Lord,
for your departed servants,
that, cleansed by the paschal mysteries,
they may glory in the gift of the resurrection to come.
Through Christ our Lord.
℞. **Amen.**   → No. 30, p. 77

The Solemn Blessing formula on p. 105 may be used.

ALL SOULS' DAY
3

ENTRANCE ANT. Cf. Rom 8:11 [New Life through the Spirit]
**God, who raised Jesus from the dead, will give life
also to your mortal bodies, through his Spirit that
dwells in you.**   → No. 2, p. 10

COLLECT   [Mortality Overcome]

O God, who willed that your Only Begotten Son,
having conquered death,
should pass over into the realm of heaven,
grant, we pray, to your departed servants
that, with the mortality of this life overcome,
they may gaze eternally on you,
their Creator and Redeemer.
Through our Lord Jesus Christ, your Son,
who lives and reigns with you in the unity of the Holy
   Spirit,
God, for ever and ever. ℟. **Amen.** ↓

*The readings found in Masses 1 and 2 may also be used, as
well as those listed on p. 588.*

FIRST READING Is 25:6-9   [Death Has Been Destroyed]

This is the earliest statement of the doctrine that prayers
and sacrifices for the dead are beneficial. It is a holy and
pious thought to think of the dead.

A reading from the Book of the Prophet Isaiah

O N this mountain the LORD of hosts
   will provide for all peoples.
On this mountain he will destroy
   the veil that veils all peoples,
the web that is woven over all nations;
   he will destroy death forever.
The Lord GOD will wipe away
   the tears from all faces;

the reproach of his people he will remove
   from the whole earth; for the LORD has spoken.
   On that day it will be said:
"Behold our God, to whom we looked to save us!
   This is the LORD for whom we looked;
   let us rejoice and be glad that he has saved us!"
The word of the Lord. ℟. **Thanks be to God.** ↓

RESPONSORIAL PSALM Ps 27   [Union with God]

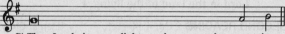

℟. The Lord is my light and my sal - va - tion.

Or: ℟. I believe that I shall see the good things of the Lord
         in the land of the living.

The LORD is my light and my salvation;
   whom should I fear?
The LORD is my life's refuge;
   of whom should I be afraid?

℟. **The Lord is my light and my salvation.**

Or: ℟. **I believe that I shall see the good things of the
         Lord in the land of the living.**

One thing I ask of the LORD;
   this I seek:
to dwell in the house of the LORD
   all the days of my life,
that I may gaze on the loveliness of the LORD
   and contemplate his temple.

℟. **The Lord is my light and my salvation.**

Or: ℟. **I believe that I shall see the good things of the
         Lord in the land of the living.**

Hear, O LORD, the sound of my call;
   have pity on me and answer me.
Your presence, O LORD, I seek!
   Hide not your face from me.

℟. **The Lord is my light and my salvation.**

Or: ℞. **I believe that I shall see the good things of the
    Lord in the land of the living.**

I believe that I shall see the bounty of the LORD
  in the land of the living.
Wait for the LORD with courage;
  be stouthearted and wait for the LORD!

℞. **The Lord is my light and my salvation.** ↓

Or: ℞. **I believe that I shall see the good things of the
    Lord in the land of the living.** ↓

SECOND READING 2 Cor 4:14—5:1   [Eternal Glory]

In addition to faith in Jesus there is also need of good
works. These will accompany the doers after death to their
advantage. Happy are the dead who die thus in the Lord.

A reading from the second Letter of Saint Paul
to the Corinthians

Brothers and sisters: We know that the One who
raised the Lord Jesus will raise us also with Jesus
and place us with you in his presence. Everything indeed
is for you, so that the grace bestowed in abundance on
more and more people may cause the thanksgiving to
overflow for the glory of God. Therefore, we are not discouraged; rather, although our outer self is wasting
away, our inner self is being renewed day by day. For this
momentary light affliction is producing for us an eternal
weight of glory beyond all comparison, as we look not to
what is seen but to what is unseen; for what is seen is
transitory, but what is unseen is eternal. For we know
that if our earthly dwelling, a tent, should be destroyed,
we have a building from God, a dwelling not made with
hands, eternal in heaven.—The word of the Lord.
℞. **Thanks be to God.** ↓

ALLELUIA Cf. Jn 3:16   [Faith unto Life]
℞. **Alleluia, alleluia.**
God so loved the world that he gave us his only Son

that everyone who sees the Son and believes in him
may have eternal life.
℟. **Alleluia, alleluia.** ↓

GOSPEL Jn 14:1-6   [A Place for Us]

> Jesus is our way, truth and life who has preceded us to our
> Father's heavenly house in order to prepare a place also for
> us. If we trust in him we will safely reach our home at our
> journey's end.

℣. The Lord be with you. ℟. **And with your spirit.**
✝ A reading from the holy Gospel according to John.
℟. **Glory to you, O Lord.**

JESUS said to his disciples: "Do not let your hearts be
troubled. You have faith in God; have faith also in me.
In my Father's house there are many dwelling places. If
there were not, would I have told you that I am going to
prepare a place for you? And if I go and prepare a place
for you, I will come back again and take you to myself,
so that where I am you also may be. Where I am going
you know the way." Thomas said to him, "Master, we do
not know where you are going; how can we know the
way?" Jesus said to him, "I am the way and the truth and
the life. No one comes to the Father except through
me."—The Gospel of the Lord. ℟. **Praise to you, Lord
Jesus Christ.**   → No. 15, p. 18

PRAYER OVER THE OFFERINGS   [Eternal Life]

Receive, Lord, in your kindness,
the sacrificial offering we make
for all your servants who sleep in Christ,
that, set free from the bonds of death
by this singular sacrifice,
they may merit eternal life.
Through Christ our Lord.
℟. **Amen.**   → No. 21, p. 22 (Pref. P 77-81)

COMMUNION ANT. Cf. Phil 3:20-21   [Copies of Christ's Body]

We await a savior, the Lord Jesus Christ, who will change our mortal bodies, to conform with his glorified body. ↓

PRAYER AFTER COMMUNION   [Mercy and Joy]

Through these sacrificial gifts
which we have received, O Lord,
bestow on your departed servants your great mercy
and, to those you have endowed with the grace of
    Baptism,
grant also the fullness of eternal joy.
Through Christ our Lord.
℟. **Amen.**   → No. 30, p. 77

The Solemn Blessing formula on p. 105 may be used.

———————————

OTHER POSSIBLE READINGS

Second Reading: Rom 5:5-11; Rom 5:17-21; Rom 6:3-9; Rom 8:14-23; Rom 8:31b-35, 37-39; Rom 14:7-9, 10c-12; 1 Cor 15:20-28; 2 Cor 5:1, 6-10; 1 Thes 4:13-18; 2 Tm 2:8-13.

Gospel: Mt 5:1-12a; Mt 11:25-30; Mt 25:31-46; Lk 7:11-17; Lk 23:44-46, 50, 52-53; 24:1-6a; Lk 24:13-16, 28-35; Jn 5:24-29; Jn 6:51-58; Jn 11:32-45.

The Readings and Responsorial Psalms given in the Masses for the Dead may also be used.

"Stop making my Father's house a marketplace."

NOVEMBER 9

THE DEDICATION OF THE LATERAN BASILICA

Feast

ENTRANCE ANT. Cf. Rev 21: 2   [A New Jerusalem]

I saw the holy city, a new Jerusalem, coming down out of heaven from God, prepared like a bride adorned for her husband.   → No. 2, p. 10

OR Cf. Rev 21:3   [God's Dwelling]

Behold God's dwelling with the human race. He will dwell with them and they will be his people, and God himself with them will be their God.   → No. 2, p. 10

COLLECT   [Eternal Dwelling]

O God, who from living and chosen stones
prepare an eternal dwelling for your majesty,
increase in your Church the spirit of grace you have
   bestowed,

so that by new growth your faithful people
may build up the heavenly Jerusalem.
Through our Lord Jesus Christ, your Son,
who lives and reigns with you in the unity of the Holy
   Spirit,
God, for ever and ever. R⁣. **Amen.** ↓

OR   [God's Church the Bride]

O God, who were pleased to call your Church the Bride,
grant that the people that serves your name
may revere you, love you and follow you,
and may be led by you
to attain your promises in heaven.
Through our Lord Jesus Christ, your Son,
who lives and reigns with you in the unity of the Holy
   Spirit,
God, for ever and ever. R⁣. **Amen.** ↓

FIRST READING Ez 47:1-2, 8-9, 12   [Life-Giving Temple]

This text is a figure of the life that flows from the new temple
(which signifies our churches and the Body of Christ) and
from the new worship brought by Christ. It will overflow the
earth, producing trees, herbs, and fruits that will become the
food and medicine of human beings. Water is a sign and
promise of life.

A reading from the Book of the Prophet Ezekiel

THE angel brought me back to the entrance of the
   temple, and I saw water flowing out from beneath the
threshold of the temple toward the east, for the facade of
the temple was toward the east; the water flowed down
from the southern side of the temple, south of the altar.
He led me outside by the north gate, and around to the
outer gate facing the east, where I saw water trickling
from the southern side. He said to me, "This water flows
into the eastern district down upon the Arabah, and
empties into the sea, the salt waters, which it makes

fresh. Wherever the river flows, every sort of living creature that can multiply shall live, and there shall be abundant fish, for wherever this water comes the sea shall be
made fresh. Along both banks of the river, fruit trees of
every kind shall grow; their leaves shall not fade, nor
their fruit fail. Every month they shall bear fresh fruit,
for they shall be watered by the flow from the sanctuary.
Their fruit shall serve for food, and their leaves for medicine."—The word of the Lord. ℟. **Thanks be to God.** ↓

RESPONSORIAL PSALM Ps 46   [God in Its Midst]

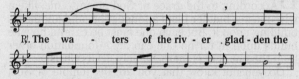

℟. The wa - ters of the riv - er . glad - den the

ci - ty of God, the ho-ly dwel-ling of the Most High!

God is our refuge and our strength,
    an ever-present help in distress.
Therefore we fear not, though the earth be shaken
    and mountains plunge into the depths of the sea.
℟. **The waters of the river gladden the city of God,**
    the holy dwelling of the Most High!

There is a stream whose runlets gladden the city of
        God,
    the holy dwelling of the Most High.
God is in its midst; it shall not be disturbed;
    God will help it at the break of dawn.
℟. **The waters of the river gladden the city of God,**
    the holy dwelling of the Most High!

The LORD of hosts is with us;
    our stronghold is the God of Jacob.
Come! behold the deeds of the LORD,
    the astounding things he has wrought on earth.

℟. **The waters of the river gladden the city of God,
the holy dwelling of the Most High!** ↓

SECOND READING 1 Cor 3:9c-11, 16-17   [God's Building]

Paul elaborates on the temple figure, of which your parish
church is a sign. God's people can only be a solid building,
in which the Spirit of God dwells, if it is built on the solid
foundation that is Christ.

A reading from the first letter of Saint Paul
to the Corinthians

BROTHERS and sisters: You are God's building.
According to the grace of God given to me, like a
wise master builder I laid a foundation, and another is
building upon it. But each one must be careful how he
builds upon it, for no one can lay a foundation other
than the one that is there, namely, Jesus Christ.

Do you not know that you are the temple of God,
and that the Spirit of God dwells in you? If anyone
destroys God's temple, God will destroy that person;
for the temple of God, which you are, is holy.—The
word of the Lord. ℟. **Thanks be to God.** ↓

ALLELUIA 2 Chr 7:16   [Consecrated House]

℟. **Alleluia, alleluia.**

I have chosen and consecrated this house, says the
Lord,

that my name may be there forever.

℟. **Alleluia, alleluia.** ↓

GOSPEL Jn 2:13-22   [Jesus: Living Temple]

John wants to teach that Jesus put an end to the old way
of worship (in the temple), and inaugurated a new worship, "in Spirit and truth." This transition was accomplished by Jesus' death and resurrection.

℣. The Lord be with you. ℟. **And with your spirit.**

✛ A reading from the holy Gospel according to John.

℟. **Glory to you, O Lord.**

SINCE the Passover of the Jews was near, Jesus went up to Jerusalem. He found in the temple area those who sold oxen, sheep, and doves, as well as the money-changers seated there. He made a whip out of cords and drove them all out of the temple area, with the sheep and oxen, and spilled the coins of the money-changers and overturned their tables, and to those who sold doves he said, "Take these out of here, and stop making my Father's house a marketplace." His disciples recalled the words of Scripture, *Zeal for your house will consume me.* At this the Jews answered and said to him, "What sign can you show us for doing this?" Jesus answered and said to them, "Destroy this temple and in three days I will raise it up." The Jews said, "This temple has been under construction for forty-six years, and you will raise it up in three days?" But he was speaking about the temple of his Body. Therefore, when he was raised from the dead, his disciples remembered that he had said this, and they came to believe the Scripture and the word Jesus had spoken.—The Gospel of the Lord. ℟. **Praise to you, Lord Jesus Christ.**   → No. 15, p. 18

PRAYER OVER THE OFFERINGS   [Answered Prayers]

Accept, we pray, O Lord, the offering made here,
and grant that by it those who seek your favor
may receive in this place
the power of the Sacraments
and the answer to their prayers.
Through Christ our Lord.
℟. **Amen.** ↓

PREFACE (P 53)   [A House of Prayer]

℣. The Lord be with you. ℟. **And with your spirit.**
℣. Lift up your hearts. ℟. **We lift them up to the Lord.**

℣. Let us give thanks to the Lord our God. ℟. **It is right and just.**

It is truly right and just, our duty and our salvation,
always and everywhere to give you thanks,
Lord, holy Father, almighty and eternal God.

For in your benevolence you are pleased
to dwell in this house of prayer
in order to perfect us as the temple of the Holy Spirit,
supported by the perpetual help of your grace
and resplendent with the glory of a life acceptable to
    you.

Year by year you sanctify the Church, the Bride of
    Christ,
foreshadowed in visible buildings,
so that, rejoicing as the mother of countless children,
she may be given her place in your heavenly glory.

And so, with all the Angels and Saints,
we praise you, as without end we acclaim:

→ No. 23, p. 23

COMMUNION ANT. Cf. 1 Pt 2:5   [A Spiritual House]
**Be built up like living stones, into a spiritual house, a
holy priesthood.** ↓

PRAYER AFTER COMMUNION   [Temple of God's Grace]

O God, who chose to foreshadow for us
the heavenly Jerusalem
through the sign of your Church on earth,
grant, we pray,
that, by our partaking of this Sacrament,
we may be made the temple of your grace
and may enter the dwelling place of your glory.
Through Christ our Lord.
℟. **Amen.**   → No. 30, p. 77

Optional Solemn Blessings, p. 97, and Prayers over the People, p. 105

"The days will come when there will not be left a stone upon another stone that will not be thrown down."

NOVEMBER 16

33rd SUNDAY IN ORDINARY TIME

ENTRANCE ANT. Jer 29:11, 12, 14   [God Hears Us]
The Lord said: I think thoughts of peace and not of affliction. You will call upon me, and I will answer you, and I will lead back your captives from every place.
→ No. 2, p. 10

COLLECT   [Glad Devotion]
Grant us, we pray, O Lord our God,
the constant gladness of being devoted to you,
for it is full and lasting happiness
to serve with constancy
the author of all that is good.
Through our Lord Jesus Christ, your Son,
who lives and reigns with you in the unity of the Holy
     Spirit,
God, for ever and ever.
℟. **Amen.** ↓

FIRST READING Mal 3:19-20a   [The Sun of Justice]

The time of judgment is coming. For the faithful it will be a day of glory.

A reading from the Book of the Prophet Malachi

L O, the day is coming, blazing like an oven,
　when all the proud and all evildoers will be stubble,
and the day that is coming will set them on fire,
　　leaving them neither root nor branch,
　　says the LORD of hosts.
But for you who fear my name, there will arise
　　the sun of justice with its healing rays.
The word of the Lord. ℟. **Thanks be to God.** ↓

RESPONSORIAL PSALM Ps 98   [Rule with Justice]

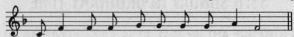

℟. **The Lord comes to   rule the earth with   jus - tice.**

Sing praise to the LORD with the harp,
　with the harp and melodious song.
With trumpets and the sound of the horn
　sing joyfully before the King, the LORD.

℟. **The Lord comes to rule the earth with justice.**

Let the sea and what fills it resound,
　the world and those who dwell in it;
let the rivers clap their hands,
　the mountains shout with them for joy.

℟. **The Lord comes to rule the earth with justice.**

Before the LORD, for he comes,
　for he comes to rule the earth;
he will rule the world with justice
　and the peoples with equity.

℟. **The Lord comes to rule the earth with justice.** ↓

SECOND READING 2 Thes 3:7-12   [Models for Imitation]

We all must work together and cooperate with one another. No one can sit back and enjoy the fruits of another's labor.

A reading from the second Letter of Saint Paul
to the Thessalonians

BROTHERS and sisters: You know how one must imitate us. For we did not act in a disorderly way among you, nor did we eat food received free from anyone. On the contrary, in toil and drudgery, night and day we worked, so as not to burden any of you. Not that we do not have the right. Rather, we wanted to present ourselves as a model for you, so that you might imitate us. In fact, when we were with you, we instructed you that if anyone was unwilling to work, neither should that one eat. We hear that some are conducting themselves among you in a disorderly way, by not keeping busy but minding the business of others. Such people we instruct and urge in the Lord Jesus Christ to work quietly and to eat their own food.—The word of the Lord. ℟. **Thanks be to God.** ↓

ALLELUIA Lk 21:28   [Redemption]

℟. **Alleluia, alleluia.**
Stand erect and raise your heads
because your redemption is at hand.
℟. **Alleluia, alleluia.** ↓

GOSPEL Lk 21:5-19   [Salvation in Christ]

Nothing in this world will last forever, and we can be sure of trials and tribulations. But if we put our trust and hope in Christ, we will find life.

℣. The Lord be with you. ℟. **And with your spirit.**
✛ A reading from the holy Gospel according to Luke.
℟. **Glory to you, O Lord.**

W HILE some people were speaking about how the
temple was adorned with costly stones and
votive offerings, Jesus said, "All that you see here—the
days will come when there will not be left a stone upon
another stone that will not be thrown down."

Then they asked him, "Teacher, when will this happen? And what sign will there be when all these things
are about to happen?" He answered, "See that you not
be deceived, for many will come in my name, saying, 'I
am he,' and 'The time has come.' Do not follow them!
When you hear of wars and insurrections, do not be
terrified; for such things must happen first, but it will
not immediately be the end." Then he said to them,
"Nation will rise against nation, and kingdom against
kingdom. There will be powerful earthquakes,
famines, and plagues from place to place; and awesome sights and mighty signs will come from the sky.

"Before all this happens, however, they will seize
and persecute you, they will hand you over to the synagogues and to prisons, and they will have you led
before kings and governors because of my name. It
will lead to your giving testimony. Remember, you are
not to prepare your defense beforehand, for I myself
shall give you a wisdom in speaking that all your
adversaries will be powerless to resist or refute. You
will even be handed over by parents, brothers, relatives, and friends, and they will put some of you to
death. You will be hated by all because of my name, but
not a hair on your head will be destroyed. By your perseverance you will secure your lives."—The Gospel of
the Lord. ℟. **Praise to you, Lord Jesus Christ.**

→ No. 15, p. 18

PRAYER OVER THE OFFERINGS   [Everlasting Happiness]

Grant, O Lord, we pray,
that what we offer in the sight of your majesty

may obtain for us the grace of being devoted to you
and gain us the prize of everlasting happiness.
Through Christ our Lord.

℟. **Amen.**   ➔ No. 21, p. 22 (Pref. P 29-36)

COMMUNION ANT. Ps 73 (72):28   [Hope in God]

**To be near God is my happiness, to place my hope in
God the Lord.** ↓

OR Mk 11:23-24   [Believing Prayer]

**Amen, I say to you: Whatever you ask in prayer,
believe that you will receive, and it shall be given to
you, says the Lord.** ↓

PRAYER AFTER COMMUNION   [Growth in Charity]

We have partaken of the gifts of this sacred mystery,
humbly imploring, O Lord,
that what your Son commanded us to do
in memory of him
may bring us growth in charity.
Through Christ our Lord.

℟. **Amen.**   ➔ No. 30, p. 77

Optional Solemn Blessings, p. 97, and Prayers over the People, p. 105

"The Lord will reign for ever."

NOVEMBER 23

Last Sunday in Ordinary Time

OUR LORD JESUS CHRIST, KING OF THE UNIVERSE

Solemnity

ENTRANCE ANT. Rv 5:12; 1:6   [Christ's Glory]

How worthy is the Lamb who was slain, to receive power and divinity, and wisdom and strength and honor. To him belong glory and power for ever and ever. → No. 2, p. 10

COLLECT   [King of the Universe]

Almighty ever-living God,
whose will is to restore all things
in your beloved Son, the King of the universe,
grant, we pray,
that the whole creation, set free from slavery,
may render your majesty service
and ceaselessly proclaim your praise.
Through our Lord Jesus Christ, your Son,

who lives and reigns with you in the unity of the Holy
   Spirit,
God, for ever and ever. ℟. **Amen.** ↓

FIRST READING 2 Sm 5:1-3   [Shepherd My People]
   **David is anointed to be king in fulfillment of the promise
   of the Lord.**

   A reading from the second Book of Samuel

IN those days, all the tribes of Israel came to David in
Hebron and said: "Here we are, your bone and your
flesh. In days past, when Saul was our king, it was you
who led the Israelites out and brought them back. And
the LORD said to you, 'You shall shepherd my people
Israel and shall be commander of Israel.' " When all
the elders of Israel came to David in Hebron, King
David made an agreement with them there before the
LORD, and they anointed him king of Israel.—The word
of the Lord. ℟. **Thanks be to God.** ↓

RESPONSORIAL PSALM Ps 122   [The House of the Lord]

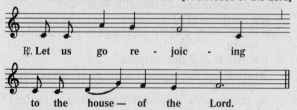

℟. Let us   go re - joic - ing

to the house — of the Lord.

I rejoiced because they said to me,
   "We will go up to the house of the LORD."
And now we have set foot
   within your gates, O Jerusalem.

℟. **Let us go rejoicing to the house of the Lord.**

Jerusalem, built as a city
   with compact unity.

To it the tribes go up,
   the tribes of the LORD.

℟. **Let us go rejoicing to the house of the Lord.**

According to the decree for Israel,
   to give thanks to the name of the LORD.
In it are set up judgment seats,
   seats for the house of David.

℟. **Let us go rejoicing to the house of the Lord.** ↓

SECOND READING   Col 1:12-20   [Primacy of Christ]
   **We belong to the Kingdom of God through his Son who
   has dominion over all creation.**

A reading from the Letter of Saint Paul to the Colossians

BROTHERS and sisters: Let us give thanks to the
Father, who has made you fit to share in the inheritance of the holy ones in light. He delivered us from
the power of darkness and transferred us to the king-
dom of his beloved Son, in whom we have redemption,
the forgiveness of sins.
   He is the image of the invisible God,
      the firstborn of all creation.
   For in him were created all things in heaven and on
         earth,
      the visible and the invisible,
      whether thrones or dominions or principalities or
            powers;
      all things were created through him and for him.
   He is before all things,
      and in him all things hold together.
   He is the head of the body, the church.
   He is the beginning, the firstborn from the dead,
      that in all things he himself might be preeminent.
   For in him all the fullness was pleased to dwell,
      and through him to reconcile all things for him,
      making peace by the blood of his cross

through him, whether those on earth or those in heaven.

The word of the Lord. ℟. **Thanks be to God.** ↓

ALLELUIA Mk 11:9, 10   [Son of David]

℟. **Alleluia, alleluia.**

Blessed is he who comes in the name of the Lord!

Blessed is the kingdom of our father David that is to come!

℟. **Alleluia, alleluia.** ↓

GOSPEL Lk 23:35-43   [The Crucifixion]

The son of David, King of the Jews, the crucified Savior, reigns—he is King of paradise.

℣. The Lord be with you. ℟. **And with your spirit.**

✚ A reading from the holy Gospel according to Luke.

℟. **Glory to you, O Lord.**

THE rulers sneered at Jesus and said, "He saved others, let him save himself if he is the chosen one, the Christ of God." Even the soldiers jeered at him. As they approached to offer him wine they called out, "If you are King of the Jews, save yourself." Above him there was an inscription that read, "This is the King of the Jews."

Now one of the criminals hanging there reviled Jesus, saying, "Are you not the Christ? Save yourself and us." The other, however, rebuking him, said in reply, "Have you no fear of God, for you are subject to the same condemnation? And indeed, we have been condemned justly, for the sentence we received corresponds to our crimes, but this man has done nothing criminal." Then he said, "Jesus, remember me when you come into your kingdom." He replied to him, "Amen, I say to you, today you will be with me in Paradise."—The Gospel of the Lord. ℟. **Praise to you, Lord Jesus Christ.**   → No. 15, p. 18

PRAYER OVER THE OFFERINGS   [Unity and Peace]

As we offer you, O Lord, the sacrifice
by which the human race is reconciled to you,
we humbly pray
that your Son himself may bestow on all nations
the gifts of unity and peace.
Through Christ our Lord.
℟. **Amen.** ↓

PREFACE (P 51)   [Marks of Christ's Kingdom]

℣. The Lord be with you. ℟. **And with your spirit.**
℣. Lift up your hearts. ℟. **We lift them up to the Lord.**
℣. Let us give thanks to the Lord our God. ℟. **It is right and just.**

It is truly right and just, our duty and our salvation,
always and everywhere to give you thanks,
Lord, holy Father, almighty and eternal God.

For you anointed your Only Begotten Son,
our Lord Jesus Christ, with the oil of gladness
as eternal Priest and King of all creation,
so that, by offering himself on the altar of the Cross
as a spotless sacrifice to bring us peace,
he might accomplish the mysteries of human
    redemption
and, making all created things subject to his rule,
he might present to the immensity of your majesty
an eternal and universal kingdom,
a kingdom of truth and life,
a kingdom of holiness and grace,
a kingdom of justice, love and peace.

And so, with Angels and Archangels,
with Thrones and Dominions,
and with all the hosts and Powers of heaven,
we sing the hymn of your glory,
as without end we acclaim: ➔ No. 23, p. 23

COMMUNION ANT. Ps 29 (28):10-11   [Blessing of Peace]

The Lord sits as King for ever. The Lord will bless his people with peace.↓

PRAYER AFTER COMMUNION   [Christ's Heavenly Kingdom]

Having received the food of immortality,
we ask, O Lord,
that, glorying in obedience
to the commands of Christ, the King of the universe,
we may live with him eternally in his heavenly
   Kingdom.
Who lives and reigns for ever and ever.
℟. **Amen.**   ➜ No. 30, p. 77

Optional Solemn Blessings, p. 97, and Prayers over the People, p. 105

Saint Joseph

HYMNAL

1 ## Praise My Soul, the King of Heaven

F. Lyte   John Goss

1. Praise my soul, the King of hea - ven; To his feet thy
2. Praise him for his grace and fa - vor; To his children
3. Fa-ther-like he tends and spares us; Well our feeble
4. An-gels help us to a - dore him; You be-hold him

1. tri-bute bring; Ran-somed, healed, re-stored, for-giv-en
2. in dis - tress; Praise him still the same as ev - er
3. frame he knows; In his hand he gen - tly bears us,
4. face to face; Sun and moon, bow down be-fore him,

1. Ev - er more his prais - es sing: Al - le - lu - ia!
2. Slow to chide, and swift to bless: Al - le - lu - ia!
3. Re-cues us from all our foes: Al - le - lu - ia!
4. Dwell-ers all in time and space. Al - le - lu - ia!

1. Al - le - lu - ia! Praise the ev - er - last - ing King.
2. Al - le - lu - ia! Glo - rious in his faith - ful - ness.
3. Al - le - lu - ia! Wide - ly yet his mer - cy flows.
4. Al - le - lu - ia! Praise with us the God of grace.

Praise to the Lord

1. Praise to the Lord,
   The almighty, the King of creation;
   O my soul, praise him,
   For he is our health and salvation;
   Hear the great throng,
   Joyous with praises and song,
   Sounding in glad adoration.

2. Praise to the Lord,
   Who doth prosper thy way and defend thee;
   Surely his goodness
   And mercy shall ever attend thee;
   Ponder anew
   What the almighty can do,
   Who with his love doth befriend thee.

3. Praise to the Lord,
   O let all that is in me adore him!
   All that hath breath join
   In our praises now to adore him!
   Let the "Amen"
   Sung by all people again
   Sound as we worship before him. Amen.

3 Eye Has Not Seen

Tune: Marty Haugen, b. 1950

Text: 1 Corinthians 2:9-10;
Marty Haugen, b. 1950

Refrain

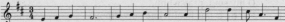

Eye has not seen, ear has not heard what God has read-y for

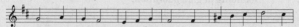

those who love him; Spir-it of love, come, give us the mind of

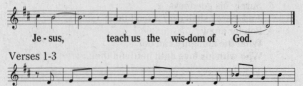

Je - sus, teach us the wis-dom of God.

Verses 1-3

1. When pain and sor-row weigh us down, be near to us, O
2. Our lives are but a sin-gle breath, we flow-er and we
3. To those who see with eyes of faith, the Lord is ev - er

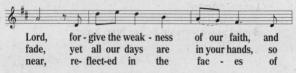

Lord, for - give the weak - ness of our faith, and
fade, yet all our days are in your hands, so
near, re- flect-ed in the fac - es of

D.C.

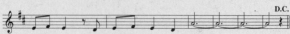

bear us up with-in your peace-ful word.
we re-turn in love what love has made.
all the poor and low-ly of the world.

Verse 4

4. We sing a mys-t'ry from the past in halls where saints have

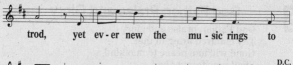

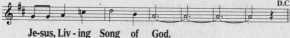

trod,　yet ev-er new　the　mu-sic rings　to

Je-sus, Liv-ing Song　of　God.

Praise God from Whom All Blessings Flow 4

1. Praise God, from whom all blessings flow;
   Praise him, all creatures here below;
   Praise him above, ye heav'nly host:
   Praise Father, Son, and Holy Ghost.

2. All people that on earth do dwell,
   Sing to the Lord with cheerful voice;
   Him serve with mirth, his praise forth tell,
   Come ye before him and rejoice.

3. Know that the Lord is God indeed;
   Without our aid he did us make;
   We are his flock, he doth us feed,
   And for his sheep he doth us take.

4. O enter then his gates with praise,
   Approach with joy his courts unto;
   Praise, laud, and bless his name always,
   For it is seemly so to do. Amen.

Faith of Our Fathers 5

1. Faith of our fathers! living still,
   In spite of dungeon, fire, and sword;
   O how our hearts beat high with joy,
   Whene'er we hear that glorious word!

   Refrain: Faith of our fathers holy faith,
   　　　　　　We will be true to thee till death.

2. Faith of our fathers! We will love
   Both friend and foe in all our strife,
   And preach thee too, as love knows how,
   By kindly words and virtuous life.

3. Faith of our fathers! Mary's prayers
   Shall keep our country close to thee;
   And through the truth that comes from God,
   O we shall prosper and be free.

609

6   God Father, Praise and Glory

1. God Father, praise and glory
   Thy children bring to thee.
   Good will and peace to mankind
   Shall now forever be.

Refrain: O most Holy Trinity,
               Undivided Unity; Holy God,
               Mighty God, God immortal be adored.

2. And thou, Lord Coeternal.
   God's sole begotten Son;
   O Jesus, King anointed,
   Who hast redemption won.—*Refrain*

3. O Holy Ghost, Creator.
   Thou gift of God most high;
   Life, love and sacred Unction
   Our weakness thou supply.—*Refrain*

7   Praise the Lord of Heaven

Praise the Lord of Heaven,
Praise Him in the height.
Praise Him all ye angels,
Praise Him stars and light;
Praise Him skies and waters
    which above the skies
When His word commanded,
Mighty did arise,

Praise Him man and maiden,
Princes and all kings,
Praise Him hills and mountains,
All created things;
Heav'n and earth He fashioned
    mighty oceans raised;
This day and forever
His name shall be praised.

8   Holy, Holy, Holy

1. Holy, holy, holy! Lord God almighty.
   Early in the morning our song shall rise to thee:
   Holy, holy, holy! Merciful and mighty,
   God in three persons, blessed Trinity.

2. Holy, holy, holy! Lord God almighty.
   All thy works shall praise thy name in earth and sky
       and sea;
   Holy, holy, holy! Merciful and mighty,
   God in three persons, blessed Trinity.

3. Holy, holy, holy! All thy saints adore thee,
   Praising thee in glory, with thee to ever be;
   Cherubim and Seraphim, falling down before thee,
   Which wert and art and evermore shall be.

610

Now Thank We All Our God

9

1. Now thank we all our God,
   With heart and hands and voices,
   Who wondrous things hath done,
   In whom the world rejoices;
   Who from our mother's arms
   Hath blessed us on our way
   With countless gifts of love,
   And still is ours today.

2. All praise and thanks to God,
   The Father now be given,
   The Son, and him who reigns
   With them in highest heaven,
   The one eternal God
   Whom earth and heav'n adore;
   For thus it was, is now,
   And shall be ever more.

The Church's One Foundation

10

1

The Church's one foundation
Is Jesus Christ her Lord.
She is his new creation,
By water and the Word;
From heav'n he came and sought her,
To be his holy bride;
With his own blood he bought her,
And for her life he died.

2

Elect from ev'ry nation,
Yet one o'er all the earth.
Her charter of salvation,
One Lord, one faith, one birth;
One holy Name she blesses,
Partakes one holy food;
And to one hope she presses,
With ev'ry grace endued.

3

Mid toil and tribulation,
And tumult of her war.
She waits the consummation
Of peace for evermore;
Till with the vision glorious
Her loving eyes are blest,
And the great Church victorious
Shall be the Church at rest.

11 We Praise Thee, O God, Our Redeemer

Ps 26:12
Tr. Julia B. Cady

E. Kremser

1. We praise Thee, O God, our Re-deem-er, Cre - a - tor, In grate-ful de-vo - tion our trib - ute we bring; We lay it be -fore Thee, we kneel and a-dore Thee, We bless Thy ho - ly name, glad prais - es we sing.

2. We wor - ship Thee, God of our fa - thers, we bless Thee; Thro' trou - ble and tem - pest our Guide hast Thou been; When per - ils o'er - take us, es - cape Thou wilt make us, And with Thy help, O Lord, our bat - tles we win.

3. With voic - es u - nit - ed our prais - es we of - fer, To Thee, great Je - ho - vah, glad an - thems we raise. Thy strong arm will guide us, our God is be - side us, To Thee, our great Re-deem - er for - ev - er be praise. A - men.

Crown Him with Many Crowns

12

1. Crown him with many crowns,
   The Lamb upon his throne;
   Hark how the heav'nly anthem drowns
   All music but its own;

   Awake my soul, and sing
   Of him who died for thee,
   And hail him as thy matchless King
   Through all eternity.

2. Crown him of lords the Lord,
   Who over all doth reign,
   Who once on earth, the incarnate Word,
   For ransomed sinners slain.

   Now lives in realms of light,
   Where saints with angels sing
   Their songs before him day and night,
   Their God, Redeemer, King.

O Perfect Love

13

1. O perfect Love, all human thought transcending.
   Lowly we kneel in prayer before thy throne,
   That theirs may be the love that knows no ending,
   Whom thou for evermore dost join in one.

2. O perfect Life, be thou their full assurance
   Of tender charity and steadfast faith,
   Of patient hope, and quiet, brave endurance,
   With child-like trust that fears not pain nor death.

On Jordan's Bank

14

1. On Jordan's bank the Baptist's cry
   Announces that the Lord is nigh,
   Awake and hearken, for he brings
   Glad tidings of the King of Kings.

2. Then cleansed be ev'ry breast from sin;
   Make straight the way of God within,
   Oh, let us all our hearts prepare
   For Christ to come and enter there.

Gather Us In

Tune: GATHER US IN, Irreg.,
Marty Haugen, b. 1950

Text: Marty Haugen, b. 1950

1. Here in this place   new light is stream-ing,
2. We are the young—our   lives are a mys-t'ry,
3. Here we will take   the   wine and the wa - ter,
4. Not in the dark   of   build-ings con - fin -ing,

Now is the dark - ness   van-ished a - way,
We are the old— who   yearn for your face,
Here we will take the   bread of new birth,
Not in some heav - en,   light-years a -way,   But

See in this space our   fears and our dream-ings,
We have been sung through-out all of his - t'ry,
Here you shall call   your   sons and your daugh-ters,
here in this place   the   new light is shin-ing,

Brought here to you in   the light of this day.
Called to be light to   the whole hu-man race.
Call us a - new to   be salt for the earth.
Now is the King-dom,   now is the day.

Gath - er us in— the lost and for - sak - en,
Gath - er us in— the rich and the haugh-ty,
Give us to drink the wine of com - pas-sion,
Gath - er us in and hold us for ev - er,

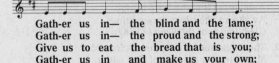

Gath-er us in— the blind and the lame;
Gath-er us in— the proud and the strong;
Give us to eat the bread that is you;
Gath-er us in and make us your own;

Call to us now, and we shall a-wak-en,
Give us a heart so meek and so low-ly,
Nour-ish us well, and teach us to fash-ion
Gath-er us in— all peo-ples to-geth-er,

We shall a-rise at the sound of our name.
Give us the cour-age to en-ter the song.
Lives that are ho-ly and hearts that are true.
Fire of love in our flesh and our bone.

Confitemini Domino / Come and Fill

Tune: Jacques Berthier, 1923-1994

Text: Psalm 137,
Give thanks to the Lord for he is good;
Taizé Community, 1982

Ostinato Refrain

Con - fi - te - mi - ni Do - mi - no
Come and fill our hearts with your peace.

quo - ni - am bo-nus. Con - fi - te - mi - ni
You a - lone, O Lord, are ho - ly. Come and fill our hearts

Do - mi - no, Al - le - lu - ia!
with your peace, Al - le - lu - ia!

17   O Come, O Come, Emmanuel

John M. Neal, Tr.   Melody adapted by T. Helmore

O come, O come, Emmanuel,
And ransom captive Israel,
That mourns in lowly exile here,
Until the Son of God appear.

> *Refrain:*   Rejoice! Rejoice! O Israel,
> To thee shall come Emmanuel.

18   Come, Thou Long Expected Jesus

1. Come, thou long expected Jesus,
   Born to set thy people free;
   From our sins and fears release us,
   Let us find our rest in thee.

2. Israel's strength and consolation,
   Hope of all the earth thou art;
   Dear desire of every nation,
   Joy of every longing heart.

3. Born thy people to deliver,
   Born a child and yet a king.
   Born to reign in us for ever,
   Now thy gracious kingdom bring.

19   O Come Little Children

O come little children, O come one and all
Draw near to the crib here in Bethlehem's stall
And see what a bright ray of heaven's delight,
Our Father has sent on this thrice holy night.

He lies there, O children, on hay and straw,
Dear Mary and Joseph regard HIm with awe,
The shepherds, adoring, how humbly in pray'r
Angelical choirs with song rend the air.

O children bend low and adore Him today,
O lift up your hands like the shepherds, and pray
Sing joyfully children, with hearts full of love
In jubilant song join the angels above.

616

O Come, All Ye Faithful

20

1. O come, all ye faithful, joyful and triumphant,
   O come ye, O come ye to Bethlehem;
   Come and behold Him born, the King of angels.

   Refrain:
   O come, let us adore Him,
   O come, let us adore Him,
   O come, let us adore Him, Christ the Lord.

2. Sing choirs of angels, Sing in exultation.
   Sing all ye citizens of Heav'n above;
   Glory to God, Glory to the highest.—*Refrain*

3. Yea, Lord, we greet thee, born this happy morning,
   Jesus to thee be all glory giv'n;
   Word of the Father, now in flesh appearing.—*Refrain*

The First Noel

21

1. The first Noel the angel did say,
   Was to certain poor shepherds in fields as they lay;
   In fields where they lay keeping their sheep
   On a cold winter's night that was so deep.

   Refrain:
   Noel, Noel, Noel, Noel,
   Born is the King of Israel.

2. They looked up and saw a star,
   Shining in the east, beyond them far,
   And to the earth it gave great light,
   And so it continued both day and night.—*Refrain*

3. This star drew nigh to the northwest,
   O'er Bethlehem it took its rest,
   And there it did stop and stay,
   Right over the place where Jesus lay.—*Refrain*

4. Then entered in those wise men three,
   Full reverently upon their knee,
   And offered there, in his presence,
   Their gold and myrrh and frankincense.—*Refrain*

22

A Child Is Born in Bethlehem
Three Magi Kings

Carlton

1. A Child is born in Beth-le-hem, al-
2. Though found with-in a man-ger poor, al-
3. O let us sing in one ac-cord, al-
1. Three Ma-gi Kings came from a-far, al-
2. Their pre-cious gifts to Him they bring, al-

1. le-lu-ia; O come, re-joice Je-ru-
2. le-lu-ia; His King-dom shall for-e'er
3. le-lu-ia; And bless, for-ev-er Christ
1. le-lu-ia; Led by a light, the Christ-
2. le-lu-ia; An of-f'ring to the In-

1. sa-lem, al-le-lu-ia, al-le-lu-ia.
2. en-dure, al-le-lu-ia, al-le-lu-ia.
3. the Lord, al-le-lu-ia, al-le-lu-ia.
1. mas star, al-le-lu-ia, al-le-lu-ia.
2. fant King, al-le-lu-ia, al-le-lu-ia.

Responsory: All

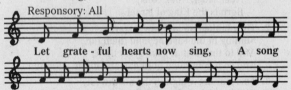

Let grate-ful hearts now sing, A song
of joy and ho-ly praise to Christ the new-born King.

Silent Night

23

Silent night, holy night!
All is calm, all is bright.
'Round yon Virgin Mother and Child,
Holy Infant so tender and mild:
Sleep in heavenly peace,
Sleep in heavenly peace.

Silent night, holy night!
Shepherds quake at the sight!
Glories stream from heaven afar,
Heav'nly hosts sing Alleluia:
Christ, the Savior is born,
Christ, the Savior is born!

3. Silent night, holy night!
   Son of God, love's pure light.
   Radiant beams from thy holy face,
   With the dawn of redeeming grace,
   Jesus, Lord, at thy birth,
   Jesus, Lord, at thy birth.

Hark! The Herald Angels Sing

24

1. Hark! The herald angels sing.
   "Glory to the new-born King.
   Peace on earth, and mercy mild
   God and sinners reconciled."
   Joyful all ye nations rise,
   Join the triumph of the skies.
   With th' angelic host proclaim,
   "Christ is born in Bethlehem."

   Refrain:
   Hark! The herald angels sing,
   "Glory to the new-born King."

2. Christ, by highest heaven adored,
   Christ, the everlasting Lord.
   Late in time behold Him come,
   Off-spring of a virgin's womb.
   Veiled in flesh, the God-head see;
   Hail th' incarnate Deity!
   Pleased as Man with men to appear,
   Jesus, our Immanuel here!—*Refrain*

O Sing a Joyous Carol

25

1. O sing a joyous carol
Unto the Holy Child,
And praise with gladsome
     voices
His mother undefiled.
Our gladsome voices greeting
Shall hail our Infant King;
And our sweet Lady listens
When joyful voices sing.

2. Who is there meekly lying
In yonder stable poor?
Dear children, it is Jesus;
He bids you now adore.
Who is there kneeling by him
In virgin beauty fair?
It is our Mother Mary,
She bids you all draw near.

Good Christian Men Rejoice

Tr. John Mason Neale

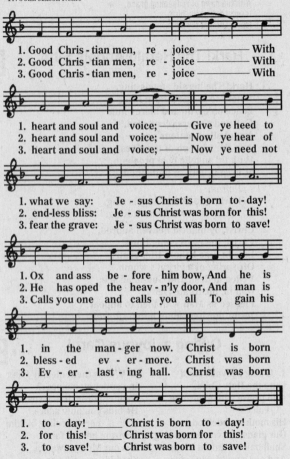

1. Good Chris-tian men, re - joice ———— With
2. Good Chris-tian men, re - joice ———— With
3. Good Chris-tian men, re - joice ———— With

1. heart and soul and voice; ——— Give ye heed to
2. heart and soul and voice; ——— Now ye hear of
3. heart and soul and voice; ——— Now ye need not

1. what we say: Je - sus Christ is born to-day!
2. end-less bliss: Je - sus Christ was born for this!
3. fear the grave: Je - sus Christ was born to save!

1. Ox and ass be - fore him bow, And he is
2. He has oped the heav-n'ly door, And man is
3. Calls you one and calls you all To gain his

1. in the man-ger now. Christ is born
2. bless - ed ev - er - more. Christ was born
3. Ev - er - last - ing hall. Christ was born

1. to - day! ——— Christ is born to - day!
2. for this! ——— Christ was born for this!
3. to save! ——— Christ was born to save!

Angels We Have Heard on High

1. Angels we have heard on high,
   Sweetly singing o'er the plains,
   And the mountains in reply
   Echoing their joyous strains.

   Refrain: Gloria in excelsis Deo. (Repeat)

2. Shepherds, why this jubilee,
   Why your rapturous song prolong?
   What the gladsome tidings be
   Which inspire your heav'nly song?—*Refrain*

3. Come to Bethlehem and see
   Him whose birth the angels sing;
   Come, adore on bended knee
   Christ the Lord, the new-born King.—*Refrain*

Away in a Manger

28

1. Away in a manger, no crib for his bed,
   The little Lord Jesus laid down his sweet head.
   The stars in the bright sky looked down where he lay,
   The little Lord Jesus asleep on the hay.

2. The cattle are lowing, the baby awakes,
   But little Lord Jesus no crying he makes.
   I love thee, Lord Jesus! Look down from the sky,
   And stay by my side until morning is nigh.

3. Be near me Lord Jesus, I ask thee to stay
   Close by me forever, and love me I pray.
   Bless all the dear children in thy tender care,
   And fit us for heaven to live with thee there.

O Little Town of Bethlehem

O little town of Bethlehem,
How still we see thee lie!
Above the deep and dreamless sleep
The silent stars go by;
Yet in the dark streets shineth
The everlasting Light;
The hopes and fears of all the years
Are met in thee tonight.

For Christ is born of Mary,
And gathered all above,
While mortals sleep, the angels keep
Their watch of wondering love.
O morning stars, together
Proclaim the holy birth!
And praising sing to God the King
And peace to men on earth.

O holy Child of Bethlehem!
Descend on us we pray;
Cast out our sin, and enter in,
Be born in us today.
We hear the Christmas angels,
The great glad tidings tell;
O come to us, abide with us,
Our Lord Emmanuel.

30 What Child Is This?

What child is this, who laid to rest,
On Mary's lap is sleeping?
Whom angels greet with anthems sweet,
While shepherds watch are keeping?

Refrain:
This, this is Christ the King,
Whom shepherds guard and angels sing;
Haste, haste to bring him laud,
The Babe, the Son of Mary.

Why lies he in such mean estate
Where ox and ass are feeding?
Good Christian fear, for sinners here
The silent Word is pleading.—*Refrain*

So bring him incense, gold, and myrrh,
Come peasant, king to own him,
The King of kings salvation brings,
Let loving hearts enthrone him.—*Refrain*

We Three Kings

1. We three kings of Orient are
   Bearing gifts we traverse afar,
   Field and fountain, moor and mountain,
   Following yonder star.

   Refrain:
   O Star of wonder, Star of night,
   Star with royal beauty bright,
   Westward leading, still proceeding,
   Guide us to thy perfect light.

2. Born a king on Bethlehem's plain,
   Gold I bring to crown Him again,
   King forever, ceasing never,
   Over us all to reign.—*Refrain*

3. Frankincense to offer have I
   Incense owns a Deity high,
   Prayer and praising, all men raising,
   Worship Him, God most High.—*Refrain*

4. Myrrh is mine, its bitter perfume
   Breathes a life of gathering gloom:
   Sorrowing, sighing, bleeding, dying,
   Sealed in the stone-cold tomb.—*Refrain*

5. Glorious now behold Him arise,
   King and God and Sacrifice,
   Alleluia, Alleluia,
   Earth to the heavens replies.—*Refrain*

Holy God, We Praise Thy Name

32

1. Holy God, we praise Thy Name!
   Lord of all, we bow before Thee!
   All on earth Thy sceptre claim,
   All in heaven above adore Thee.
   Infinite Thy vast domain,
   Everlasting is Thy reign. *Repeat last two lines*

2. Hark! the loud celestial hymn,
   Angel choirs above are raising;
   Cherubim and seraphim,
   In unceasing chorus praising,
   Fill the heavens with sweet accord;
   Holy, holy, holy Lord! *Repeat last two lines*

33 Lord, Who throughout These 40 Days

1. Lord, who throughout these forty days
   For us did fast and pray,
   Teach us with you to mourn our sins,
   And close by you to stay.

2. And through these days of penitence,
   And through your Passiontide,
   Yea, evermore, in life and death,
   Jesus! with us abide.

3. Abide with us, that so, this life
   Of suff'ring over past,
   An Easter of unending joy
   We may attain at last. Amen.

34 When I Behold the Wondrous Cross

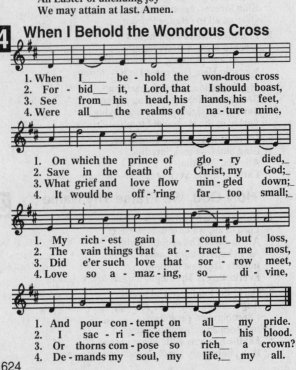

1. When I____ be - hold the won-drous cross
2. For - bid__ it, Lord, that I should boast,
3. See from__ his head, his hands, his feet,
4. Were all____ the realms of na - ture mine,

1. On which the prince of glo - ry died,_
2. Save in the death of Christ, my God;_
3. What grief and love flow min - gled down;_
4. It would be off - 'ring far__ too small;_

1. My rich - est gain I count_ but loss,
2. The vain things that at - tract__ me most,
3. Did e'er such love that sor - row meet,
4. Love so a - maz - ing, so____ di - vine,

1. And pour con - tempt on all__ my pride.
2. I sac - ri - fice them to__ his blood.
3. Or thorns com - pose so rich__ a crown?
4. De - mands my soul, my life,__ my all.

624

Jesus, Remember Me

35

Tune: Jacques Berthier, 1923-1994

Text: Luke 23:42
Taizé Community, 1981

Ostinato Refrain

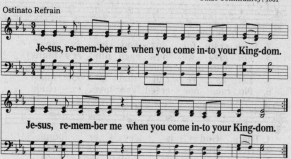

Je-sus, re-mem-ber me when you come in-to your King-dom.

Je-sus, re-mem-ber me when you come in-to your King-dom.

O Sacred Head Surrounded

36

1. O sacred Head surrounded
   By crown of piercing thorn!
   O bleeding Head, so wounded,
   Reviled, and put to scorn!
   Death's pallid hue comes ov'r you,
   The glow of life decays,
   Yet angel hosts adore you,
   And tremble as they gaze.

2. I see your strength and vigor
   All fading in the strife,
   And death with cruel rigor,
   Bereaving you of life.
   O agony and dying!
   O love to sinners free!
   Jesus, all grace supplying,
   O turn your face on me.

37   Where Charity and Love Prevail

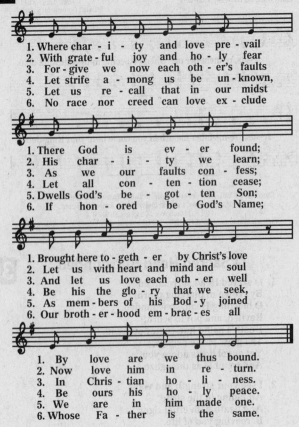

1. Where char - i - ty and love pre - vail
2. With grate - ful joy and ho - ly fear
3. For - give we now each oth - er's faults
4. Let strife a - mong us be un - known,
5. Let us re - call that in our midst
6. No race nor creed can love ex - clude

1. There God is ev - er found;
2. His char - i - ty we learn;
3. As we our faults con - fess;
4. Let all con - ten - tion cease;
5. Dwells God's be - got - ten Son;
6. If hon - ored be God's Name;

1. Brought here to - geth - er by Christ's love
2. Let us with heart and mind and soul
3. And let us love each oth - er well
4. Be his the glo - ry that we seek,
5. As mem - bers of his Bod - y joined
6. Our broth - er - hood em - brac - es all

1. By love are we thus bound.
2. Now love him in re - turn.
3. In Chris - tian ho - li - ness.
4. Be ours his ho - ly peace.
5. We are in him made one.
6. Whose Fa - ther is the same.

626

O Faithful Cross

38

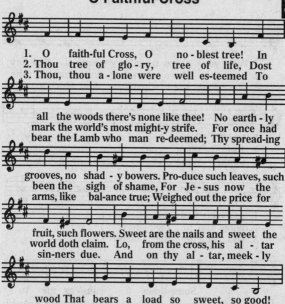

1. O faith-ful Cross, O no - blest tree! In all the woods there's none like thee! No earth - ly grooves, no shad - y bowers. Pro-duce such leaves, such fruit, such flowers. Sweet are the nails and sweet the wood That bears a load so sweet, so good!

2. Thou tree of glo - ry, tree of life, Dost mark the world's most might-y strife. For once had been the sigh of shame, For Je - sus now the world doth claim. Lo, from the cross, his al - tar throne, He gent - ly draws and rules his own.

3. Thou, thou a - lone were well es-teemed To bear the Lamb who man re-deemed; Thy spread-ing arms, like bal-ance true; Weighed out the price for sin-ners due. And on thy al - tar, meek - ly laid, The Lamb of God a - tone-ment made.

O God, Our Help in Ages Past

39

I. Watts

1.
O God, our help in ages past,
Our hope for years to come,
Our shelter from the stormy blast,
And our eternal home.

2.
Under the shadow of Thy throne,
Thy saints have dwelt secure.
Sufficient is Thine arm alone,
And our defense is sure.

3.
A thousand ages in Thy sight,
Are like an evening gone;
Short as the watch that ends the night,
Before the rising sun.

4.
O God, our help in ages past,
Our hope for years to come,
Be Thou our guide while troubles last,
And our eternal home.

627

Were You There

1. Were you there when they cru-ci-fied my
2. Were you there when they nailed him to the
3. Were you there when they laid him in the

1. Lord? Were you there when they
2. tree? Were you there when they
3. tomb? Were you there when they

1. cru-ci-fied my Lord? } Oh_____
2. nailed him to the tree? }
3. laid him in the tomb? }

Some-times it caus-es me to

trem-ble, trem-ble, trem-ble. { 1. Were you
2. Were you
3. Were you

1. there when they cru-ci-fied my Lord?
2. there when they nailed him to the tree?
3. there when they laid him in the tomb?

At the Cross Her Station Keeping

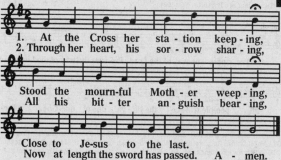

1. At the Cross her sta-tion keep-ing,
2. Through her heart, his sor-row shar-ing,

Stood the mourn-ful Moth-er weep-ing,
All his bit-ter an-guish bear-ing,

Close to Je-sus to the last.
Now at length the sword has passed. A - men.

3. Oh, how sad and sore distressed
Was that Mother highly blessed
Of the sole begotten One!

4. Christ above in torment hangs,
She beneath beholds the pangs
Of her dying, glorious Son.

5. Is there one who would not weep
'Whelmed in miseries so deep
Christ's dear Mother to behold?

6. Can the human heart refrain
From partaking in her pain,
In that mother's pain untold?

7. Bruised, derided, cursed, defiled,
She beheld her tender Child,
All with bloody scourges rent.

8. For the sins of His own nation
Saw Him hang in desolation
Till His spirit forth He sent.

9. O sweet Mother! fount of love,
Touch my spirit from above,
Make my heart with yours accord.

10. Make me feel as you have felt.
Make my soul to glow and melt
With the love of Christ, my Lord.

11. Holy Mother, pierce me through,
In my heart each wound renew
Of my Savior crucified.

12. Let me share with you His pain,
Who for all our sins was slain,
Who for me in torments died.

13. Let me mingle tears with you
Mourning Him Who mourned for me,
All the days that I may live.

14. By the Cross with you to stay,
There with you to weep and pray,
Is all I ask of you to give.

15. Virgin of all virgins blest!
Listen to my fond request.
Let me share your grief divine.

16. Let me, to my latest breath
In my body bear the death
Of that dying Son of yours.

17. Wounded with His every wound,
Steep my soul till it has swooned
In His very blood away.

18. Be to me, O Virgin, nigh,
Lest in flames I burn and die,
In His awful judgment day.

19. Christ, when You shall call me hence
Be Your Mother my defense.
Be Your Cross my victory.

20. While my body here decays,
May my soul Your goodness praise
Safe in heaven eternally.
Amen. Alleluia.

42 Prepare the Way of the Lord

Tune: Jacques Berthier, 1923-1994

Text: Luke 3:4, 6;
Taizé Community

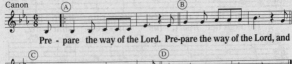

Pre - pare the way of the Lord. Pre-pare the way of the Lord, and

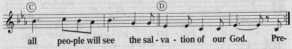

all peo-ple will see the sal - va - tion of our God. Pre-

43 Jesus Christ Is Risen Today

1. Jesus Christ is ris'n today, alleluia!
   Our triumphant holy day, alleluia!
   Who did once upon the cross, alleluia!
   Suffer to redeem our loss, alleluia!

2. Hymns of praise then let us sing, alleluia!
   Unto Christ our heav'nly King, alleluia!
   Who endured the cross and grave, alleluia!
   Sinners to redeem and save, alleluia!

3. Sing we to our God above, alleluia!
   Praise eternal as his love, alleluia!
   Praise him, all ye heav'nly host, alleluia!
   Father, Son and Holy Ghost, alleluia!

44 At the Lamb's High Feast We Sing

1. At the Lamb's high feast we sing
   Praise to our victor'ous King,
   Who has washed us in the tide
   Flowing from his pierced side;
   Praise we him whose love divine
   Gives the guests his Blood for wine,
   Gives his Body for the feast,
   Love the Victim, Love the Priest.

2. When the Paschal blood is poured,
   Death's dark Angel sheathes his sword;
   Israel's hosts triumphant go
   Through the wave that drowns the foe.

Christ, the Lamb whose Blood was shed,
Paschal victim, Paschal bread;
With sincerity and love
Eat we Manna from above.

Christ the Lord Is Risen Today

Tr. Jane E. Leeson, 1807-1882

Traditional

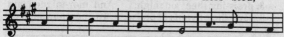

1. Christ, the Lord is risn' to-day,
2. Christ, the Vic-tim un-de-filed,
3. Christ, Who once for sin-ners bled,

Chris-tians, haste your vows to pay; Of-fer ye your
Man to God hath re-con-ciled; When in strange and
Now the first born of the dead, Thron'd in end-less

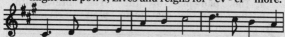

prais-es meet At the Pas-chal Vic-tim's feet.
aw-ful strife Met to-geth-er death and life;
might and pow'r, Lives and reigns for-ev-er more.

For the sheep the Lamb hath bled; Sin-less in the
Chris-tians on this hap-py day Haste with joy your
Hail, e-ter-nal Hope on high! Hail, Thou King of

sin-ner's stead; Christ, the Lord, is ris'n on high,
vows to pay. Christ, the Lord, is ris'n on high,
Vic-to-ry! Hail, Thou Prince of Life a-dored!

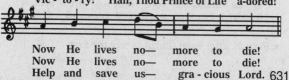

Now He lives no— more to die!
Now He lives no— more to die!
Help and save us— gra-cious Lord. 631

All Glory, Laud, and Honor

Tr. John Mason Neale, 1851

Melchior Teschner, pub. 1615

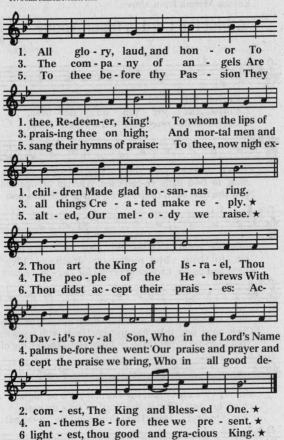

1. All glo-ry, laud, and hon-or To
3. The com-pa-ny of an-gels Are
5. To thee be-fore thy Pas-sion They

1. thee, Re-deem-er, King! To whom the lips of
3. prais-ing thee on high; And mor-tal men and
5. sang their hymns of praise: To thee, now nigh ex-

1. chil-dren Made glad ho-san-nas ring.
3. all things Cre-a-ted make re-ply. ★
5. alt-ed, Our mel-o-dy we raise. ★

2. Thou art the King of Is-ra-el, Thou
4. The peo-ple of the He-brews With
6. Thou didst ac-cept their prais-es: Ac-

2. Dav-id's roy-al Son, Who in the Lord's Name
4. palms be-fore thee went: Our praise and prayer and
6 cept the praise we bring, Who in all good de-

2. com-est, The King and Bless-ed One. ★
4. an-thems Be-fore thee we pre-sent. ★
6 light-est, thou good and gra-cious King. ★

★ *Refrain:* after each stanza except the first.

The Strife Is O'er

Alleluia! Alleluia! Alleluia!

1. The strife is o'er, the battle done!
   The victory of life is won!
   The song of triumph has begun! Alleluia!

2. The powers of death have done their worst,
   But Christ their legions has dispersed;
   Let shouts of holy joy outburst! Alleluia!

3. The three sad days are quickly sped,
   He rises glor'ous from the dead;
   All glory to our risen Head! Alleluia!

4. He closed the yawning gates of hell;
   The bars from heaven's high portals fell;
   Let hymns of praise His triumph tell! Alleluia!

O Sons and Daughters, Let Us Sing!

48

Alleluia! Alleluia! Alleluia!

1. O sons and daughters, let us sing!
   The King of heav'n, the glorious King,
   Today is ris'n and triumphing. Alleluia!

2. On Easter morn, at break of day,
   The faithful women went their way
   To seek the tomb where Jesus lay. Alleluia!

3. An angel clad in white they see,
   Who sat and spoke unto the three,
   "Your Lord doth go to Galilee." Alleluia!

4. On this most holy day of days,
   To you our hearts and voice we raise,
   In laud and jubilee and praise. Alleluia!

5. Glory to Father and to Son,
   Who has for us the vict'ry won
   And Holy Ghost; blest Three in One. Alleluia!

49 Psalm 23: Shepherd Me, O God

Music: Marty Haugen   Text: Psalm 23; Marty Haugen

Refrain

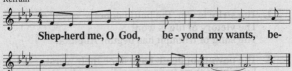

Shep-herd me, O God, be-yond my wants, be-yond my fears, from death in-to life.

Verses

1. God is my shepherd, so nothing shall I want,
   I rest in the meadows of faithfulness and love,
   I walk by the quiet waters of peace.

2. Gently you raise me and heal my weary soul,
   you lead me by pathways of righteousness and truth,
   my spirit shall sing the music of your name.

3. Though I should wander the valley of death,
   I fear no evil, for you are at my side, your rod and your staff,
   my comfort and my hope.

4. Surely your kindness and mercy follow me all the days
   of my life;
   I will dwell in the house of my God for evermore.

50 Eat This Bread

Tune: Jacques Berthier, 1923-1994 Text: John 6; adapt. by Robert J. Batastini, b. 1942
and the Taizé Community

Refrain

Eat this bread, drink this cup, come to him and nev-er be hun-gry.

Eat this bread, drink this cup, trust in him and you will not thirst.

Taste and See

51

Tune: James E. Moore, Jr., b. 1951

Text: Psalm 34;
James E. Moore, Jr., b. 1951

Refrain

Taste and see, taste and see the good-ness of the
Lord. O taste and see, taste and see the
good - ness of the Lord, of the Lord.

Verses

1. I will bless the Lord at all times.
2. Glo - ri - fy the Lord with me,
3. Wor-ship the Lord, all you peo-ple.

Praise shall al-ways be on my lips;
To-geth-er let us all praise God's name.
You'll want for noth-ing if you ask.

my soul shall glo-ry in the Lord
I called the Lord who an - swered me;
Taste and see that the Lord is good;

D.C.

for God has been so good to me.
from all my tou-bles I was set free.
in God we need put all our trust.

52 I Am the Bread of Life

Tune: BREAD OF LIFE, Irreg with refrain;
Suzanne Toolan, SM, b. 1927.

Text: John 6;
Suzanne Toolan, SM, b. 1927

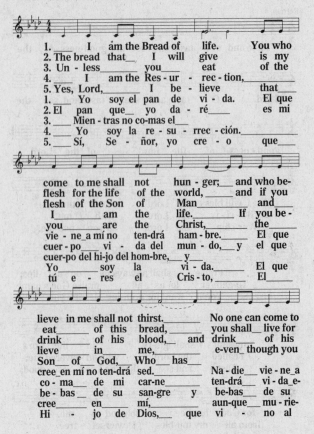

1. ___ I am the Bread of life. You who come to me shall not hun - ger;___ and who be-lieve in me shall not thirst._____ No one can come to
2. The bread that___ I will give is my flesh for the life of the world,_____ and if you eat_____ of this bread,_____ you shall__ live for
3. Un - less_____ you eat of the flesh of the Son of Man_____ and___ drink_____ of his blood,__ and drink____ of his
4. ___ I am the Res - ur - rec - tion,_____ I am the life._____ If you be-lieve _____ in me,_____ e - ven_ though you
5. Yes, Lord,_____ I be - lieve that___ you_____ are the Christ,_____ the_____ Son of God,__ Who___ has__

1. ___ Yo soy el pan de vi - da. El que vie - ne a mí no ten-drá ham - bre._____ El que cree en mí no ten-drá sed._____ Na - die vie - ne a
2. El pan que__ yo da - ré____ es mi cuer - po__ vi - da del mun - do,__ y el que co - ma__ de mi car - ne_____ ten-drá__ vi - da e-
3. Mien - tras no co-mas el__ cuer-po del hi-jo del hom-bre,__ y be - bas__ de su san-gre y be-bas__ de su
4. ___ Yo soy la re - su - rrec - ción._____ Yo_____ soy la vi - da._____ El que cree_____ en_____ mí,_____ aun-que__ mu - rie-
5. ___ Sí, Se - ñor, yo cre - o que___ tú e - res el Cris - to,_____ El___ Hi - jo de Dios,___ que vi - no al

me unless the__ Fa - ther beck-ons.
ev - er,_____ you shall__live for ev - er.
blood,_____ you shall not have life with - in you.
die,_____ you shall__live for ev - er.
come in - to_____ the_____ world.__
mí_____ mien - tras el Pa - dre lla - me.
ter - na, _____ ten - drá__ vi - da e - ter - na.
san - gre, no ten - drá__ vi - da en ti.
ra,_____ ten - drá vi - da e - ter - na.
mun - do_____ pa - ra sal - var - nos.

And I will raise you up, and I will
Yo le re - su - ci - ta - ré, Yo lo re -

raise you up, and I will raise you
su - ci - ta - ré, Yo lo re - su - ci - ta -

up on the last day.
ré el di - a de_El.

O Lord, I Am Not Worthy 53

1. O Lord, I am not worthy,
   That thou should come to me,
   But speak the word of comfort
   My spirit healed shall be.

2. And humbly I'll receive thee,
   The bridegroom of my soul,
   No more by sin to grieve thee
   Or fly thy sweet control.

3. O Sacrament most holy,
   O Sacrament divine,
   All praise and all thanksgiving
   Be every moment thine.

The Summons

Tune: KELVINGROVE, 7 6 7 6 777 6;
Scottish traditional; arr. by John L. Bell, b. 1949

Text: John L. Bell, b. 1949;

1. Will you come and fol - low me If I but call your name? Will you go where you don't know And nev - er be the same? Will you let my love be shown, Will you let my name be known, Will you let my life be grown In you and you in me?

2. Will you leave your - self be - hind If I but call your name? Will you care for cruel and kind And nev - er be the same? Will you risk the hos - tile stare Should your life at-tract or scare? Will you let me an - swer prayer In you and you in me?

3. Will you let the blind - ed see If I but call your name? Will you set the pris - 'ners free And nev - er be the same? Will you kiss the lep - er clean, And do such as this un - seen, And ad - mit to what I mean In you and you in me?

4. Will you love the 'you' you hide If I but call your name? Will you quell the fear in - side And nev - er be the same? Will you use the faith you've found To re - shape the world a - round, Through my sight and touch and sound In you and you in me?

We Walk by Faith

Tune: SHANTI, CM;
Marty Haugen, b. 1950

Text: Henry Alford, 1810-1871, alt.

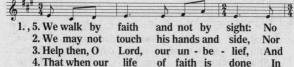

1., 5. We walk by faith and not by sight: No
2. We may not touch his hands and side, Nor
3. Help then, O Lord, our un-be-lief, And
4. That when our life of faith is done In

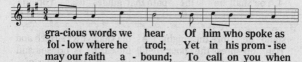

gra-cious words we hear Of him who spoke as
fol-low where he trod; Yet in his prom-ise
may our faith a-bound; To call on you when
realms of clear-er light We may be-hold you

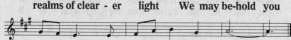

none e'er spoke, But we be-lieve him near.
we re-joice, And cry "My Lord and God!"
you are near, And seek where you are found:
as you are In full and end-less sight.

Amazing Grace

56

1. Amazing grace! how sweet the sound
   That saved a wretch like me!
   I once was lost, but now am found,
   Was blind, but now I see.

2. 'Twas grace that taught my heart to fear,
   And grace my fears relieved;
   How precious did that grace appear
   The hour I first believed!

3. Through many dangers, toils, and snares,
   I have already come;
   'Tis grace hath brought me safe thus far,
   And grace will lead me home.

4. The Lord has promised good to me,
   His word my hope secures;
   He will my shield and portion be,
   As long as life endures.

57 God of Day and God of Darkness

Tune: BEACH SPRING, 8 7 8 7 D;
The Sacred Harp, 1844;
harm. by Marty Haugen, b. 1950

Text: Marty Haugen, b. 1950;

1. God of day and God of dark - ness, Now we
2. Still the na - tions curse the dark - ness, Still the
3. Show us Christ in one an - oth - er, Make us
4. You shall be the path that guides us, You the

stand be - fore the night; As the shad - ows stretch and
rich op - press the poor; Still the earth is bruised and
ser - vants strong and true; Give us all your love of
light that in us burns; Shin-ing deep with - in all

deep - en, Come and make our dark-ness bright. All cre-
brok - en By the ones who still want more. Come and
jus - tice So we do what you would do. Let us
peo - ple, Yours the love that we must learn, For our

a - tion still is groan-ing For the dawn-ing of your
wake us from our sleep-ing, So our hearts can - not ig -
call all peo-ple ho - ly, Let us pledge our lives a -
hearts shall wan-der rest-less 'Til they safe to you re -

might, When the Sun of peace and jus - tice
nore all your peo - ple lost and bro - ken,
new, Make us one with all the low - ly,
turn; Find - ing you in one an - oth - er,

Fills the earth with ra-diant light.
All your chil - dren at our door.
Let us all be one in you.
We shall all your face dis - cern.

Sing My Tongue the Savior's Glory

1. Sing my tongue, the Savior's glory,
   Of his flesh the mystr'y sing;
   Of the Blood all price exceeding,
   Shed by our immortal King,
   Destined for the world's redemption,
   From a noble womb to spring.

2. Of a pure and spotless Virgin
   Born for us on earth below,
   He, as Man, with man conversing,
   Stayed, the seeds of truth to sow;
   Then he closed in solemn order
   Wondrously his life of woe.

3. On the night of that Last Supper,
   Seated with his chosen band,
   He the Paschal victim eating,
   First fulfills the Law's command;
   Then as food to his Apostles
   Gives himself with his own hand.

4. Word made flesh the bread of nature
   By his word to Flesh he turns;
   Wine into his blood he changes
   What though sense no change discerns?
   Only be the heart in earnest,
   Faith her lesson quickly learns.

   (Tantum ergo)

5. Down in adoration falling
   Lo! the sacred Host we hail,
   Lo! o'er ancient forms departing,
   Newer rites of grace prevail;
   Faith for all defects supplying,
   Where the feeble senses fail.

6. To the Everlasting Father,
   And the Son who reigns on high,
   With the Holy Ghost proceeding
   Forth from each eternally
   Be salvation, honor, blessing,
   Might, and endless majesty. Amen.

Immaculate Mary

59

1. Immaculate Mary, thy praises we sing,
   Who reignest in splendor with Jesus, our King.

   Refrain:
   Ave, ave, ave, Maria! Ave, ave, Maria!

2. In heaven, the blessed thy glory proclaim,
   On earth, we thy children invoke thy fair name.
   —*Refrain*

3. Thy name is our power, thy virtues our light,
   Thy love is our comfort, thy pleading our might.
   —*Refrain*

4. We pray for our mother, the Church upon earth,
   And bless, dearest Lady, the land of our birth.
   —*Refrain*

Hail, Holy Queen Enthroned Above

60

1. Hail, holy Queen enthroned above, O Maria!
   Hail, Mother of mercy and of love, O Maria!

   Refrain:
   Triumph, ail ye cherubim,
   Sing with us, ye seraphim,
   Heav'n and earth resound the hymn.
   Salve; salve, salve Regina.

2. Our life, our sweetness here below, O Maria!
   Our hope in sorrow and in woe, O Maria!
   —*Refrain*

3. To thee we cry, poor sons of Eve, O Maria!
   To thee we sigh, we mourn, we grieve, O Maria!
   —*Refrain*

4. Turn, then, most gracious Advocate, O Maria!
   Toward us thine eyes compassionate, O Maria!
   —*Refrain*

5. When this our exile's time is o'er, O Maria!
   Show us thy Son for evermore, O Maria!
   —*Refrain*

For All the Saints

William W. How
Moderately, in unison

R. Vaughan Williams, 1872-1958

61

1. For all the saints,
   who from their labors
   rest,
   Who Thee by faith
   before the world con-
   fessed,
   Thy Name, O Jesus, be
   for ever blest.
   Alleluia, alleluia!

2. O blest communion!
   fellowship divine!
   We feebly struggle,
   they in glory shine;
   Yet all are one in Thee,
   for all are Thine.
   Alleluia, alleluia!

3. From earth's wide
   bounds,
   from ocean's farthest
   coast,
   Through gates of pearl
   streams
   in the countless host,
   Singing to Father, Son
   and Holy Ghost.
   Alleluia, alleluia!

America

62

1.
My country, 'tis of thee,
Sweet land of liberty,
Of thee I sing;
Land where my fathers died,
Land of the pilgrim's pride
From ev'ry mountainside
Let freedom ring.

2.
My native country, thee,
Land of the noble free,
Thy name I love;
I love thy rocks and rills,
Thy woods and templed hills;
My heart with rapture thrills
Like that above.

America the Beautiful

63

1. O beautiful for spacious skies,
   For amber wave of grain,
   For purple mountain majesties
   Above the fruited plain.
   America! America! God shed his grace on thee.
   And crown thy good with brotherhood
   From sea to shining sea.

2. O beautiful for pilgrim feet
   Whose stern impassioned stress
   A thoroughfare for freedom beat
   Across the wilderness.
   America! America! God mend thy ev'ry flaw,
   Confirm thy soul in self control,
   Thy liberty in law.

HYMN INDEX

No.	Page
22 - A Child Is Born	618
46 - All Glory, Laud, and Honor	632
56 - Amazing Grace	639
62 - America	643
63 - America the Beautiful	643
27 - Angels We Have Heard	621
41 - At the Cross Her Station Keeping	629
44 - At the Lamb's High Feast	630
28 - Away in a Manger	621
45 - Christ the Lord Is Risen Today	631
18 - Come, Thou Long Expected Jesus	616
16 - Confitemini Domino / Come and Fill	615
12 - Crown Him with Many Crowns	613
50 - Eat This Bread	634
3 - Eye Has Not Seen	608
5 - Faith of Our Fathers	609
61 - For All the Saints	643
15 - Gather Us In	614
6 - God Father, Praise and Glory	610
57 - God of Day and God of Darkness	640
26 - Good Christian Men	620
60 - Hail, Holy Queen	642
24 - Hark! The Herald Angels Sing	619
32 - Holy God, We Praise Thy Name	623
8 - Holy, Holy, Holy	610
52 - I Am the Bread of Life	636
59 - Immaculate Mary	642
43 - Jesus Christ Is Risen Today	630
35 - Jesus, Remember Me	625
33 - Lord, Who throughout These 40 Days	624
9 - Now Thank We All Our God	611
20 - O Come, All Ye Faithful	617
19 - O Come Little Children	616
17 - O Come, O Come, Emmanuel	616
38 - O Faithful Cross	627
39 - O God, Our Help in Ages Past	627
29 - O Little Town of Bethlehem	621
53 - O Lord, I Am Not Worthy	637
14 - On Jordan's Bank	613
13 - O Perfect Love	613
36 - O Sacred Head Surrounded	625
25 - O Sing a Joyous Carol	619
48 - O Sons and Daughters	633
4 - Praise God from Whom All Blessings Flow	609
1 - Praise My Soul	606
7 - Praise the Lord of Heaven	610
2 - Praise to the Lord	607
42 - Prepare the Way of the Lord	630

No.	Page
49 - Shepherd Me, O God	634
23 - Silent Night	618
58 - Sing My Tongue	641
51 - Taste and See	635
10 - The Church's One Foundation	611
21 - The First Noel	617
47 - The Strife Is O'er	633
54 - The Summons	638

No.	Page
11 - We Praise Thee, O God, Our Redeemer	612
40 - Were You There	628
31 - We Three Kings	623
55 - We Walk by Faith	639
30 - What Child Is This?	622
34 - When I Behold the Wondrous Cross	624
37 - Where Charity and Love Prevail	626

TREASURY OF PRAYERS

PRAYERS BEFORE HOLY COMMUNION

Act of Faith

Lord Jesus Christ, I firmly believe that you are present in this Blessed Sacrament as true God and true Man, with your Body and Blood, Soul and Divinity. My Redeemer and my Judge, I adore your Divine Majesty together with the angels and saints. I believe, O Lord; increase my faith.

Act of Hope

Good Jesus, in you alone I place all my hope. You are my salvation and my strength, the Source of all good. Through your mercy, through your Passion and Death, I hope to obtain the pardon of my sins, the grace of final perseverance and a happy eternity.

Act of Love

Jesus, my God, I love you with my whole heart and above all things, because you are the one supreme Good and an infinitely perfect Being. You have given your life for me, a poor sinner, and in your mercy you have even offered yourself as food for my soul. My God, I love you. Inflame my heart so that I may love you more.

Act of Contrition

O my Savior, I am truly sorry for having offended you because you are infinitely good and sin displeases you. I detest all the sins of my life and I desire to atone for them. Through the merits of your Precious Blood, wash from my soul all stain of sin, so that, cleansed in body and soul, I may worthily approach the Most Holy Sacrament of the Altar.

PRAYERS AFTER HOLY COMMUNION

Act of Faith

Jesus, I firmly believe that you are present within me as God and Man, to enrich my soul with graces and to fill my heart with the happiness of the blessed. I believe that you are Christ, the Son of the living God!

Act of Adoration

With deepest humility, I adore you, my Lord and God; you have made my soul your dwelling place. I adore you as my Creator from whose hands I came and with whom I am to be happy forever.

Act of Love

Dear Jesus, I love you with my whole heart, my whole soul, and with all my strength. May the love of your own Sacred Heart fill my soul and purify it so that I may die to the world for love of you, as you died on the Cross for love of me. My God, you are all mine; grant that I may be all yours in time and in eternity.

Act of Thanksgiving

From the depths of my heart I thank you, dear Lord, for your infinite kindness in coming to me. How good you are to me! With your most holy Mother and all the angels, I praise your mercy and generosity toward me, a poor sinner. I thank you for nourishing my soul with your Sacred Body and Precious Blood. I will try to show my gratitude to you in the Sacrament of your love, by obedience to your holy commandments, by fidelity to my duties, by kindness to my neighbor and by an earnest endeavor to become more like you in my daily conduct.

Prayer to Mary

O Jesus living in Mary, come and live in your servants, in the spirit of your holiness, in the fullness of your power, in the perfection of your ways, in the truth of your mysteries. Reign in us over all adverse powers by your Holy Spirit, and for the glory of the Father. Amen.

Anima Christi

Soul of Christ, sanctify me.
Body of Christ, save me.
Blood of Christ, inebriate me.
Water from the side of Christ, wash me.
Passion of Christ, strengthen me.
O good Jesus, hear me.
Within your wounds hide me.
Separated from you let me never be.
From the malignant enemy, defend me.
At the hour of death, call me.
And close to you bid me.
That with your saints I may be
Praising you, forever and ever. Amen.

Partial indulgence

THE SCRIPTURAL WAY OF THE CROSS

The Way of the Cross is a devotion in which we accompany, in spirit, our Blessed Lord in his sorrowful journey to Calvary, and devoutly meditate on his suffering and death.

A *plenary indulgence* is granted the Christian faithful who devoutly make the Stations of the Cross.

1. Jesus Is Condemned to Death—God so loved the world that he gave his only-begotten Son to save it (Jn 3:16).

2. Jesus Bears His Cross—If anyone wishes to come after me, let him deny himself, and take up his cross daily (Lk 9:23).

3. Jesus Falls the First Time—The Lord laid upon him the guilt of us all (Is 53:6).

4. Jesus Meets His Mother—Come, all you who pass by the way, look and see whether there is any suffering like my suffering (Lam 1:13).

5. Jesus Is Helped by Simon—As long as you did it for one of these, the least of my brethren, you did it for me (Mt 25:40).

6. Veronica Wipes the Face of Jesus—He who sees me, sees also the Father (Jn 14:9).

7. Jesus Falls a Second Time—Come to me, all you who labor, and are burdened, and I will give you rest (Mt 11:28).

8. Jesus Speaks to the Women—Daughters of Jerusalem, do not weep for me, but weep for yourselves and for your children (Lk 23:2).

9. Jesus Falls a Third Time—Everyone who exalts himself shall be humbled, and he who humbles himself shall be exalted (Lk 14:11).

10. Jesus Is Stripped of His Garments—Every one of you who does not renounce all that he possesses cannot be my disciple (Lk 14:33).

11. Jesus Is Nailed to the Cross—I have come down from heaven, not to do my own will, but the will of him who sent me (Jn 6:38).

12. Jesus Dies on the Cross—He humbled himself, becoming obedient to death, even to death on a cross. Therefore God has exalted him (Phil 2:8-9).

13. Jesus Is Taken Down from the Cross—Did not the Christ have to suffer those things before entering into his glory? (Lk 24:26).

14. Jesus Is Placed in the Tomb—Unless the grain of wheat falls into the ground and dies, it remains alone. But if it dies, it brings forth much fruit (Jn 12:24-25).

STATIONS
of the
CROSS

1. Jesus Is Condemned to Death

O Jesus, help me to appreciate Your sanctifying grace more and more.

2. Jesus Bears His Cross

O Jesus, You chose to die for me. Help me to love You always with all my heart.

3. Jesus Falls the First Time

O Jesus, make me strong to conquer my wicked passions, and to rise quickly from sin.

4. Jesus Meets His Mother

O Jesus, grant me a tender love for Your Mother, who offered You for love of me.

STATIONS
of the
CROSS

5. Jesus Is Helped by Simon

O Jesus, like Simon lead me ever closer to You through my daily crosses and trials.

6. Jesus and Veronica

O Jesus, imprint Your image on my heart that I may be faithful to You all my life.

7. Jesus Falls a Second Time

O Jesus, I repent for having offended You. Grant me forgiveness of all my sins.

8. Jesus Speaks to the Women

O Jesus, grant me tears of compassion for Your sufferings and of sorrow for my sins.

STATIONS
of the
CROSS

9. Jesus Falls a Third Time

O Jesus, let me never yield to despair. Let me come to You in hardship and spiritual distress.

10. He Is Stripped of His Garments

O Jesus, let me sacrifice all my attachments rather than imperil the divine life of my soul.

11. Jesus Is Nailed to the Cross

O Jesus, strengthen my faith and increase my love for You. Help me to accept my crosses.

12. Jesus Dies on the Cross

O Jesus, I thank You for making me a child of God. Help me to forgive others.

STATIONS
of the
CROSS

13. Jesus Is Taken Down from the Cross

O Jesus, through the intercession of Your holy Mother, let me be pleasing to You.

14. Jesus Is Laid in the Tomb

O Jesus, strengthen my will to live for You on earth and bring me to eternal bliss in heaven.

Prayer after the Stations

JESUS, You became an example of humility, obedience and patience, and preceded me on the way of life bearing Your Cross. Grant that, inflamed with Your love, I may cheerfully take upon myself the sweet yoke of Your Gospel together with the mortification of the Cross and follow You as a true disciple so that I may be united with You in heaven. Amen.

THE HOLY ROSARY

PRAYER BEFORE THE ROSARY

QUEEN of the Holy Rosary, you have deigned to come to Fatima to reveal to the three shepherd children the treasures of grace hidden in the Rosary. Inspire my heart with a sincere love of this devotion, in order that by meditating on the Mysteries of our Redemption which are recalled in it, I may be enriched with its fruits and obtain peace for the world, the conversion of sinners and of Russia, and the favor which I ask of you in this Rosary. *(Here mention your request.)* I ask it for the greater glory of God, for your own honor, and for the good of souls, especially for my own. Amen.

The Five Joyful Mysteries

1. The Annunciation
For the love of humility.

2. The Visitation
For charity toward my neighbor.

4. The Presentation
For the virtue of obedience.

3. The Nativity
For the spirit of poverty.

5. Finding in the Temple
For the virtue of piety.

The Five

Luminous

Mysteries *

Said on Thursdays [except during Lent].

* Added to the Mysteries of the Rosary by Pope John Paul II in his Apostolic Letter of October 16, 2002, entitled *The Rosary of the Virgin Mary.*

3. Proclamation of the Kingdom
For seeking God's forgiveness.

1. The Baptism of Jesus
For living my Baptismal Promises.

4. The Transfiguration
Becoming a New Person in Christ.

2. The Wedding at Cana
For doing whatever Jesus says.

5. Institution of the Eucharist
For active participation at Mass.

1. Agony in the Garden
For true contrition.

The Five

Sorrowful

Mysteries

Said on Tuesdays and Fridays throughout the year, and every day from Ash Wednesday until Easter.

2. Scourging at the Pillar
For the virtue of purity.

4. Carrying of the Cross
For the virtue of patience.

3. Crowning with Thorns
For moral courage.

5. The Crucifixion
For final perseverance.

The Five Glorious Mysteries

Said on Wednesdays [except during Lent], and the Sundays from Easter to Advent.

3. Descent of the Holy Spirit
For love of God.

1. The Resurrection
For the virtue of faith.

4. Assumption of the BVM
For devotion to Mary.

2. The Ascension
For the virtue of hope.

5. Crowning of the BVM
For eternal happiness.

THE HAIL! HOLY QUEEN

HAIL! Holy Queen, Mother of Mercy, our life, our sweetness, and our hope. To you do we cry, poor banished children of Eve. To you do we send up our sighs, mourning and weeping in this valley of tears. Turn then, O most gracious advocate, your eyes of mercy toward us; and after this, our exile, show unto us the blessed fruit of your womb, Jesus. O clement! O loving! O sweet Virgin Mary!

℣. Pray for us, O Holy Mother of God. ℟. That we may be made worthy of the promises of Christ.

PRAYER AFTER THE ROSARY

O GOD, Whose Only Begotten Son, by His Life, Death, and Resurrection, has purchased for us the rewards of eternal life; grant, we beseech You, that, meditating upon these Mysteries of the Most Holy Rosary of the Blessed Virgin Mary, we may imitate what they contain and obtain what they promise, through the same Christ our Lord. Amen.

℣. May the Divine assistance remain always with us. ℟. Amen.

℣. And may the souls of the faithful departed, through the mercy of God, rest in peace. ℟. Amen.

The Litany of Loreto

Lord, have mercy.
Christ, have mercy.
Lord, have mercy.
Christ, hear us.
Christ, graciously hear us.
God, the Father of heaven,
have mercy on us.
God, the Son, Redeemer of the world,
have mercy on us.
God, the Holy Spirit,
have mercy on us.
Holy Trinity, one God,
have mercy on us.
Holy Mary, *pray for us.**
Holy Mother of God,
Holy Virgin of virgins,
Mother of Christ,
Mother of the Church,
Mother of mercy,
Mother of Divine grace,
Mother of hope,
Mother most pure,
Mother most chaste,
Mother inviolate,
Mother undefiled,
Mother most amiable,
Mother most admirable,
Mother of good counsel,
Mother of our Creator,
Mother of our Savior,
Virgin most prudent,
Virgin most venerable,
Virgin most renowned,
Virgin most powerful,
Virgin most merciful,
Virgin most faithful,
Mirror of justice,
Seat of wisdom,
Cause of our joy,
Spiritual vessel,
Vessel of honor,
Singular vessel of devotion,
Mystical rose,
Tower of David,
Tower of ivory,
House of gold,
Ark of the covenant,
Gate of heaven,
Morning star,
Health of the sick,
Refuge of sinners,
Solace of migrants,
Comforter of the afflicted,
Help of Christians,
Queen of angels,
Queen of patriarchs,
Queen of prophets,

* *Pray for us* is repeated after each invocation.

Queen of apostles,
Queen of martyrs,
Queen of confessors,
Queen of virgins,
Queen of all saints,
Queen conceived without original sin,
Queen assumed into heaven,
Queen of the most holy Rosary,
Queen of families,
Queen of peace,
Lamb of God, You take away the sins of the world; *spare us, O Lord!*

Lamb of God, You take away the sins of the world; *graciously hear us, O Lord!*
Lamb of God, You take away the sins of the world; *have mercy on us.*

℣. Pray for us, O holy Mother of God.

℟. *That we may be made worthy of the promises of Christ.*

Let us pray.
Grant, we beg You, O Lord God,
that we Your servants
may enjoy lasting health of mind and body,
and by the glorious intercession
of the Blessed Mary, ever Virgin,
be delivered from present sorrow
and enter into the joy of eternal happiness.
Through Christ our Lord.
℟. *Amen.*

ESSENTIAL CATHOLIC PRAYERS

Spiritual Communion Prayer

My Jesus, I believe that You are present in the most Blessed Sacrament. I love You above all things, and I desire to receive You into my soul. Since I cannot now receive You sacramentally, come at least spiritually into my heart. I embrace You as if You were already there and unite myself wholly to You. Never permit me to be separated from You. Amen.

Prayer to the Holy Spirit

Come, Holy Spirit, fill the hearts of Your faithful and kindle in them the fire of Your love.

℣. Send forth Your Spirit, and they shall be created.

℟. **And You shall renew the face of the earth.**

Let us pray. O God, Who did instruct the hearts of the faithful by the light of the Holy Spirit: grant that, by the gift of the same Spirit, we may be always truly wise, and ever rejoice in His consolation. Through Christ our Lord. Amen.

The Angelus

℣. The Angel of the Lord declared unto Mary.

℟. **And she conceived of the Holy Spirit.**

Hail Mary, etc.

℣. Behold the handmaid of the Lord.

℟. **Be it done unto me according to Your word.**

Hail Mary, etc.

℣. And the Word was made flesh.

℟. **And dwelt among us.**

Hail Mary, etc.

℣. Pray for us, O holy Mother of God.

℟. **That we may be made worthy of the promises of Christ.**

Let us pray. Pour forth, we beseech You, O Lord, Your grace into our hearts, that we to whom the Incarnation of Christ, Your Son, was made known by the message of an angel, may by His Passion and Cross be brought to the glory of His Resurrection, through the same Christ our Lord. Amen.

The Memorare

Remember, O most gracious Virgin Mary,
that never was it known
that anyone who fled to your protection,
implored your help, or sought your intercession
was left unaided.
Inspired by this confidence,
I fly unto you, O Virgin of virgins, my Mother;
to you do I come,
before you I stand, sinful and sorrowful.
O Mother of the Word Incarnate,
despise not my petitions,
but in your mercy hear and answer me. Amen.

Partial indulgence

MAJOR PRACTICES

GUIDELINES FOR THE RECEPTION
OF COMMUNION

For Catholics

As Catholics, we fully participate in the celebration of the Eucharist when we receive Holy Communion. We are encouraged to receive Communion devoutly and frequently. In order to be properly disposed to receive Communion, participants should not be conscious of grave sin and normally should have fasted for one hour. A person who is conscious of grave sin is not to receive the Body and Blood of the Lord without prior sacramental confession except for a grave reason where there is no opportunity for confession. In this case, the person is to be mindful of the obligation to make an act of perfect contrition, including the intention of confessing as soon as possible (*Code of Canon Law, canon 916*). A frequent reception of the Sacrament of Penance is encouraged for all.

For Fellow Christians

We welcome our fellow Christians to this celebration of the Eucharist as our brothers and sisters. We pray that our common baptism and the action of the Holy Spirit in this Eucharist will draw us closer to one another and begin to dispel the sad divisions that separate us. We pray that these will lessen and finally disappear, in keeping with Christ's prayer for us "that they may all be one" (John 17:21).

Because Catholics believe that the celebration of the Eucharist is a sign of the reality of the oneness of faith, life, and worship, members of those churches with whom we are not yet fully united are ordinarily not admitted to Holy Communion. Eucharistic sharing in exceptional circumstances by other Christians requires permission according to the directives of the diocesan bishop and the provisions of canon law (*canon 844 § 4*). Members of the Orthodox Churches, the Assyrian Church of the East, and the Polish National Catholic Church are urged to respect the discipline of their own Churches. According to Roman Catholic discipline, the Code of Canon Law does not object to the reception of Communion by Christians of these Churches (*canon 844 § 3*).

For Those Not Receiving Holy Communion

All who are not receiving Holy Communion are encouraged to express in their hearts a prayerful desire for unity with the Lord Jesus and with one another.

For Non-Christians

We also welcome to this celebration those who do not share our faith in Jesus Christ. While we cannot admit them to Holy Communion, we ask them to offer their prayers for the peace and the unity of the human family.

THE ORDER OF PENANCE
(Extracted from The Order of Penance*)*

THE ORDER FOR RECONCILING INDIVIDUAL PENITENTS

Texts for the Penitent

The penitent should prepare for the celebration of the Sacrament by prayer, reading of Sacred Scripture, and silent reflection. The penitent should think over and should regret all sins since the last celebration of the Sacrament.

THE RECEPTION OF THE PENITENT

When the penitent comes to confess his (her) sins, the Priest welcomes him (her) with kindness and greets him (her) with friendly words.

Both penitent and, if appropriate, the Priest make the Sign of the Cross, saying:

In the name of the Father, and of the Son, and of the Holy Spirit. Amen.

The Priest invites the penitent to have trust in God and the penitent replies:

Amen.

THE READING OF THE WORD OF GOD

The Priest may read a text of Sacred Scripture that announces God's mercy and calls people to conversion.

THE CONFESSION OF SINS AND THE ACCEPTANCE OF SATISFACTION

The penitent tells the Priest when he (she) last celebrated the Sacrament and then confesses his (her) sins, asking appropriate questions, if necessary. The penitent then listens to any advice the Priest may give and accepts the satisfaction (or "penance") from the Priest.

THE PRAYER OF THE PENITENT AND THE ABSOLUTION

The Priest then invites the penitent to express his (her) contrition, which the penitent may do in these or similar words:

O my God,
I am sorry and repent with all my heart
for all the wrong I have done

and for the good I have failed to do,
because by sinning I have offended you,
who are all good and worthy to be loved above all things.
I firmly resolve, with the help of your grace,
to do penance,
to sin no more,
and to avoid the occasions of sin.
Through the merits of the Passion of our Savior Jesus Christ,
Lord, have mercy.

Or:

> Remember, Lord, the compassion and mercy
> you showed long ago.
> Do not recall my sins and failings.
> In your mercy remember me, Lord,
> because of your goodness.

> (Psalm 25 [24]:6-7)

Or:

> Wash me, O Lord, from my iniquity
> and cleanse me from my sin.
> I acknowledge my offense;
> my sin is before me always.

> (Psalm 51 [50]:4-5)

Or:

> Father, I have sinned against you
> and I am not worthy to be called your son.
> Be merciful to me, a sinner.

> (Luke 15:18; 18:13)

Or:

> O God, most merciful Father,
> like the Prodigal Son, I turn to you and say:
> I have sinned against you;
> I am no longer worthy to be called your child.

> O Jesus Christ, Savior of the world,
> like the thief to whom you opened
> the gates of paradise, I beg you:
> Lord, remember me in your Kingdom.

> O Holy Spirit, fount of love,
> with trust I call upon you:
> Purify me;
> make me walk as a child of the light.

Or:

> Lord Jesus,
> who opened the eyes of the blind, healed the sick,
> forgave the sinful woman,
> and, after his denial, confirmed Peter in your love,
> hear my plea:
> forgive all my sins,
> renew me in your love,
> and grant that I may live in perfect communion
> with my brothers and sisters
> and so proclaim your salvation to all.

Or:

> Lord Jesus,
> who chose to be called the friend of sinners,
> through the mystery of your Death and Resurrection,
> free me from my sins.
> May your peace grow strong in me,
> that I may bear the fruits of charity, justice, and truth.

Or:

> Lord Jesus Christ, Lamb of God,
> who take away the sin of the world,
> through the grace of the Holy Spirit
> be pleased to reconcile me with your Father;
> cleanse me in your Blood from every fault
> and make me fully alive to the praise of your glory.

Or:

> Have mercy on me, O God,
> according to your merciful love;
> turn your face from my sins
> and blot out all my guilt;
> create a pure heart in me, O God,
> renew an upright spirit deep within me.

Or:

> Lord Jesus, Son of God,
> have mercy on me, a sinner.

Or:

> O my God,
> I am heartily sorry for having offended you,
> and I detest all my sins
>   because of your just punishments,
> but most of all because they offend you, my God,
> who are all good and deserving of all my love.

**I firmly resolve, with the help of your grace,
to sin no more
and to avoid the near occasions of sin.
Amen.**

The Priest extends his hands (or at least extends his right hand) and says:

God, the Father of mercies,
through the Death and Resurrection of his Son
has reconciled the world to himself
and poured out the Holy Spirit for the forgiveness of sins;
through the ministry of the Church
may God grant you pardon and peace.
AND I ABSOLVE YOU FROM YOUR SINS,
IN THE NAME OF THE FATHER, AND OF THE SON, ✠
AND OF THE HOLY SPIRIT.

The penitent replies:

Amen.

THE PROCLAMATION OF PRAISE OF GOD AND THE DISMISSAL OF THE PENITENT

After the absolution:

Priest: Give thanks to the Lord for he is good.
Penitent: For his mercy endures for ever.

Then the Priest dismisses the penitent:

Priest: The Lord has forgiven your sins.
          Go in peace.

The Priest may use these or other words of dismissal.

FORM FOR THE EXAMINATION OF CONSCIENCE

1. This form is proposed for the examination of conscience, to be completed and adapted according to local usages and the needs of different individuals.

2. When an examination of conscience is made before the Sacrament of Penance, it is appropriate that each should ask himself (herself) the following questions before all others:

1. Do I come to the Sacrament of Penance with a sincere desire for purification, conversion, renewal of life, and deeper friendship with God, or do I consider it rather as a burden to be undertaken as seldom as possible?

2. Did I forget, or deliberately fail to mention, any grave sins in previous confessions?

3. Have I performed the penance imposed on me? Have I made reparation for injuries committed? Have I put into practice the purpose of amendment of life, according to the Gospel?

3. In the light of the word of God, each individual should examine his (her) life.

I. The Lord says: "You shall love the Lord your God with all your heart" (Mt 22:37).

1. Is my heart directed to God, so that I truly love him above all things by the faithful keeping of his commandments, as a son loves his father, or am I more concerned with worldly matters? Do I have a right intention in what I do?

2. Do I have firm faith in God, who has spoken to us through his Son? Have I adhered firmly to the teaching of the Church? Have I taken care to be instructed in the Christian faith, listening to the word of God, participating in catechesis, avoiding things harmful to the faith? Have I always professed my faith in God and the Church boldly, without fear? Have I been willing to be known as a Christian in my private and public life?

3. Have I said my morning and evening prayers, or not? Is my prayer a true conversation with God, in mind and heart, or merely an exterior observance? Have I offered to God my difficulties, my joys, and my sorrows? Do I turn to him in temptations?

4. Do I have reverence and love for God's name, or have I offended God by blasphemy, by swearing falsely, or by taking his name in vain? Have I been irreverent to the Blessed Virgin Mary or to the Saints?

5. Do I keep the Lord's Day and the feasts of the Church by actively, reverently, and attentively participating in public worship, especially the Mass? Have I obeyed the precept of annual confession and Communion at Easter?

6. Do I perhaps have other gods, that is to say, things for which I care more, or in which I trust more than God, such as money, superstitions, spirit-worship, or other occult practices?

II. The Lord says: "This is my commandment, that you love one another as I have loved you" (Jn 15:12).

1. Do I have a genuine love for my neighbor, or do I misuse them for my own ends, or do to them what I do not wish to be done to me by others? Have I given grave scandal to them by my words and actions?

2. Consider whether, within your family, you have contributed to the good and joy of others through patience and genuine love, whether as children you have been obedient to your parents, showing them honor and offering them help in their spiritual and material needs; or whether, as parents, you have been careful to bring your children up in the Christian faith, helping them by good example and parental discipline; or as spouses, you have been faithful to one another in your hearts and in your dealings with others?

3. Do I share my goods with others who are poorer than myself? As far as I can, do I defend the oppressed, comfort the sorrowful, help those in need, or have I despised my neighbor, especially the poor, the frail, the old, strangers, and people of a different race?

4. Am I mindful, in my life, of the mission I received at my Confirmation? Have I taken part in the apostolic and charitable works of the Church and in the life of the parish? Have I helped to meet the needs of the Church and prayed for them, e.g., for the unity of the Church, for the evangelization of peoples, for peace and justice, etc.?

5. Am I concerned for the good and prosperity of the human community in which I live, or do I spend my life caring only for myself? Do I take part, to the best of my ability, in promoting justice, morality, concord, and charity in human society? Have I done my civic duty? Have I paid my taxes?

6. In my work or profession am I just, industrious, honest, offering my services to society out of love? Have I given a fair wage to my employees and those who serve me? Have I kept my promises and contracts?

7. Have I obeyed the lawful authorities and shown them due respect?

8. If I am in a position of responsibility or authority, do I use it for my own benefit or for the good of others, in a spirit of service?

9. Have I been truthful and faithful, or have I done harm to others by lies, calumny, detraction, rash judgment, or breaking confidentiality?

10. Have I violated the life, physical health, reputation or honor, or goods of others? Have I caused them any loss? Have I advised or procured an abortion? Have I fostered hatred towards others? Have I cut myself off from others through quarrels, enmity, insults, or anger? Have I, through culpable selfishness, neglected to bear witness to the innocence of my neighbor?

11. Have I stolen things that do not belong to me? Have I unjustly and inordinately desired them or damaged them? Have I made restitution of stolen goods and reparation for damage?

12. If I have suffered injuries, have I been ready, for the love of Christ, to grant peace and forgiveness, or do I harbor hatred and the desire for revenge?

III. Christ the Lord says:"Whoever has my commandments and observes them is the one who loves me"(Jn 14:21).

1. What is the fundamental motivating force of my life? Am I inspired by the hope of eternal life? Have I tried to grow in the spiritual life by prayer, by listening to and meditating on the word of God, by partaking in the Sacraments, by self-denial? Have I tried to control my vices, my evil passions and inclinations, such as envy or the love of food and drink? Have I, motivated by pride and boastfulness, exalted myself in the sight of God and had contempt for others, considering myself better than them? Have I imposed my will on others, not respecting the liberty and rights of others?

2. What use have I made of my time, of my powers, of the gifts which I have received from God like the talents of the Gospel? Do I use these things to make myself more perfect day by day? Have I been lazy and slothful?

3. Have I borne the sorrows and difficulties of life patiently? To what extent have I disciplined myself so as to "make up those things which are lacking in the Passion of Christ"? Have I kept the law of fasting and abstinence?

4. Have I preserved my senses and my whole body in purity and chastity as a temple of the Holy Spirit destined for resurrection and glory and as a sign of the love which the faithful God has for his people, as is clearly manifest in the Sacrament of Matrimony? Have I debased my flesh by fornication, impurity, unworthy words and thoughts, or disordered desires or actions? Have I indulged my appetites? Have I indulged in readings, conversations, or watched things contrary to Christian and human decency? Have I incited others to sin by my own indecency? Have I kept the moral law in married life?

5. Have I acted contrary to my conscience through fear or hypocrisy?

6. Have I always tried to act truly in the freedom of the children of God, according to the law of the Spirit, or am I the slave of any passion?